STATE OF THE
WORLD
1984

Other Norton/Worldwatch Books

Lester R. Brown / *The Twenty-Ninth Day:
Accommodating Human Needs and Numbers to the
Earth's Resources*

Lester R. Brown / *Building a Sustainable Society*

Lester R. Brown, Christopher Flavin, and Colin
Norman / *Running on Empty: The Future of the
Automobile in an Oil-Short World*

Daniel Deudney and Christopher Flavin / *Renewable
Energy: The Power to Choose*

Erik P. Eckholm / *Losing Ground: Environmental
Stress and World Food Prospects*

Erik P. Eckholm / *The Picture of Health:
Environmental Sources of Disease*

Denis Hayes / *Rays of Hope: The Transition to a
Post-Petroleum World*

Kathleen Newland / *The Sisterhood of Man*

Colin Norman / *The God That Limps: Science and
Technology in the Eighties*

Bruce Stokes / *Helping Ourselves: Local Solutions to
Global Problems*

STATE OF THE WORLD
1984

A Worldwatch Institute Report on Progress Toward a Sustainable Society

PROJECT DIRECTOR
Lester R. Brown

PROJECT ASSISTANT
Edward Wolf

EDITOR
Linda Starke

SENIOR RESEARCHERS
Lester R. Brown
William U. Chandler
Christopher Flavin
Sandra Postel

W·W·NORTON & COMPANY
NEW YORK   LONDON

Copyright © 1984 by Worldwatch Institute
ALL RIGHTS RESERVED
Published simultaneously in Canada by Stoddart Publishing
PRINTED IN THE UNITED STATES OF AMERICA

The text of this book is composed in Baskerville, with
display type set in Caslon. Composition and
manufacturing by The Haddon Craftsmen, Inc.

FIRST EDITION

Library of Congress Cataloging in Publication Data
Brown, Lester Russell, 1934–
    State of the World—1984.

    Includes index.
    Contents: Overview / by Lester R. Brown—Stabilizing
population / by Lester R. Brown—Reducing dependence on
oil / by Lester R. Brown—[etc.]
    1. Economic history—1971–   —Addresses, essays,
lectures.   2. Economic policy—Addresses, essays, lectures.   I. Title.
HC59.B766 1984   338.9   83–25123

ISBN 0-393-01835-0

ISBN 0-393-30176-1 PBK.

W. W. Norton & Company, Inc., 500 Fifth Avenue, New York, N. Y. 10110
W. W. Norton & Company Ltd., 37 Great Russell Street, London WC1B 3NU

1 2 3 4 5 6 7 8 9 0

Contents

List of Tables and Figures

LIST OF FIGURES

Chapter 5. Protecting Forests

Chapter 6. Recycling Materials

Chapter 7. Reassessing the Economics of Nuclear Power

Chapter 8. Developing Renewable Energy

Chapter 9. Reconsidering the Automobile's Future

Chapter 10. Securing Food Supplies

Acknowledgments

The idea of a progress report first surfaced in a discussion with Larry Rockefeller, a trustee of the Rockefeller Brothers Fund, as we were casting about for projects that could "make a difference." As we considered this particular possibility, it became more and more appealing, consistent with the interests of the Fund and a logical outgrowth of the Institute's research program.

Obtaining funding for new projects these days is never easy but in this case the task was simplified by the willingness of Rockefeller Brothers Fund President William Dietel, who was instrumental in the Institute's establishment several years ago, to lead the fundraising effort. This relieved me of the duties that so often absorb a project director's time during the start-up period, enabling me to concentrate on producing this first annual edition of the report. Early commitments from the Rockefeller Brothers Fund, the Winthrop Rockefeller Trust, and David Rockefeller, meant the project could be launched even while the fundraising effort continued.

In addition to specific project funding, the report draws on ongoing Institute research that is supported by several foundations, including the Geraldine R. Dodge, George W. Gund, William and Flora Hewlett, W. Alton Jones, Edna McConnell Clark, Andrew W. Mellon, and Edward John Noble Foundations, and the United Nations Fund for Population Activities.

The personal interest of several key people in the project facilitated its launching. Prominent among these were Orville Freeman and Andrew Rice, chairman and vice chairman respectively of the Worldwatch Board of Directors, who enthusiastically supported the *State of the World—1984* from the beginning. Besides William Dietel, two other foundation representatives, Scott McVay of the Dodge Foundation and Anne Firth Murray of the Hewlett Foundation, strongly endorsed the concept of such a report. And finally, the personal interest of George Brockway, board chairman of W.W. Norton, facilitated speedy publication.

Edward Wolf worked closely with me as project assistant from the time the project was launched until the manuscript went to the publisher. Ted helped with research, served as a testing ground for new ideas, and reviewed early chapter drafts. His many skills and commitment to the project made it immeasurably easier for me. Authors and readers alike are indebted to Linda Starke, who was for many years editor of the Worldwatch Papers, for bringing her exceptional editorial skills to bear on the project. As production coordinator, Linda also worried about such things as design, layout, and proofreading.

Dozens of outside reviewers have helped us strengthen individual chapters and refine our overall objective. Gerald O. Barney and Erik Eckholm reviewed the entire manuscript at short notice, and the final copy owes much to their comments. The following people reviewed individual chapters or generously shared their knowledge and expertise: Norman Berg, C. Fred Bergsten, Leon Bouvier, Ken Cook, Richard Curry, Herschel Cutler, Derrel DePasse, Harold Dregne, J. Rodney Edwards, Martin Enowitz, Scott Fenn, Gail Finsterbush, Kathleen Gray, Tom Gray, Holly L. Gwin, Maureen Hinkle, Howard Hjort, Robert Johnson, Charles Komanoff, George Ledec, Amory Lovins, Paul Maycock, Sandie Nelson, Philip Patterson, Andrew Rice, Ross Pumfrey, Richard Rosen, R. Neil Sampson, Alfredo Sfeir-Younis, and Edward Sullivan.

None of our debts is greater than that to the Worldwatch Institute staff, whose dedication and efficiency did much to smooth the rough spots on the road to production. Linda Doherty and Susan Hill handled the bulk of the typing and wrestled cheerfully with the countless idiosyncracies of a new word processing system. Marianne Hunter pitched in to ease the sudden crunch of last-minute typing and helped proofread the manuscript at a critical stage. Brian Brown and Jodi Johnson joined us just when extra hands were needed and kept the office functioning normally. John Foggle assisted the research for the nuclear energy chapter and helped draft some early sections of the renewable energy chapter, while Paige Tolbert laid the groundwork for the geothermal section before the report was even begun. From New York, Milena P. Roos used her intimate knowledge of the United Nations system to gather research documents, some of them unpublished, for several chapters.

The administrative skills of Blondeen Gravely, Felix Gorrell, and Marge Hubbard helped maintain an exceptionally stable work environment for the research staff. David Macgregor managed to maintain the flow of Worldwatch Papers despite all the extra activity associated with the report's completion.

We extend special thanks to visitors to the Institute, among them Gary Hirshberg of the New Alchemy Institute; Amory and Hunter Lovins of the Rocky Mountain Institute; Helena Norberg-Hodge of the Ladakh Project; and B.B. Vohra, Director of the Ministry of Environment in India. In relating their experiences they conveyed an enthusiasm and commitment, which assured us not only that change is possible, but that it is already well under way.

Lester R. Browm

Foreword

This is the Worldwatch Institute's first State of the World report. The intent is not merely to describe how things are, but to indicate whether they are getting better or worse. The yardstick by which we measure progress is sustainability—the extent to which our economic and social systems are successfully adjusting to changes in the underlying natural resource base.

The primary focus in *State of the World —1984* is on the interplay between the changing resource base and the economic system. Recent concern with this relationship was heightened by publication of *The Limits to Growth* in 1972 and dramatically underlined the following year by the OPEC oil price hike. The return of famine during the early seventies after nearly a quarter-century's absence raised questions about long-term food security. These and other issues led the U.S. Government to undertake a study of global resource issues facing the country as it approaches the twenty-first century, which culminated in *The Global 2000 Report to the President*, published in 1980.

In an effort to regularly monitor changing conditions worldwide, a number of organizations now issue annual reports. The International Monetary Fund, for example, publishes a *World Economic Outlook*. The World Bank produces the *World Development Report*, an annual review of economic conditions in developing countries. Several U.N. agencies compile yearly reports in their special areas of responsibility, such as UNICEF'S *State of the World's Children.* The United Nations Environment Programme publishes a state of the environment report. The Food and Agriculture Organization has been publishing for many years a *State of Food and Agriculture* and the U.N. Fund for Population Activities issues an annual report on population.

At the national level, some governments—Japan and Israel, for example—issue annual "state of the environment" reports. In the United States, the Conservation Foundation last year put out *State of the Environment—1982* in an effort to supplement the diminishing efforts of the U.S. Council on Environmental Quality. Half-a-world away this was paralleled by *The State of India's Environment —1982*, prepared by the Centre for Science and Environment in New Delhi. Within the U.S. Government, the Department of Energy issues an *International Energy Annual* and the Department of Agriculture maintains a steady flow of reports on the world food situation.

Worldwatch's contribution to this growing dialogue is an attempt to analyze not only the major developments and trends in these specific areas but also the way they relate to each other. The canvas on which this report is sketched is necessarily broad. Its purpose is not to replace any of the more detailed reports, but rather to supplement them and perhaps even to enhance their usefulness by integrating their findings in a broader analysis. We try to determine, for example, how the depletion of oil reserves affects the global economy, both directly and indirectly. How will the shift from oil to renewable energy alter global economic structures? How does population growth affect soil erosion and what effect will erosion have on food production? Will population growth eventually be slowed by falling birth rates or by rising death rates? These questions may not yet be at the top of national political agendas, but we believe they are issues that will shape the human prospect.

The *State of the World—1984* tries to measure progress toward sustainability and determine why some countries are doing better on a given front than others. Is progress due to the play of market forces, tax incentives, public education, government regulation, the emergence of a new technology, or intelligent leadership? We try to convey what is working and why. We see the report as a vehicle for quickly disseminating news of innovative initiatives—whether it be Sweden's national plan to use reverse vending machines to recycle aluminum beverage containers, Thailand's innovative family planning incentives, or California's policies to spur a massive breakthrough in wind electrical generation.

The *State of the World* will not cover the same topics each year but rather will deal with the shifting constellation of issues that relate to sustainability. This year, for example, we have analyzed worldwide soil erosion; next year we may focus on the conversion of cropland to nonfarm uses. This year we have a detailed analysis of deforestation and the various tree planting efforts that are under way. We may focus next on the condition of the world's grasslands, a major source of protein in the human diet. This year's chapter on renewable energy examines wind power, firewood, geothermal energy, and photovoltaics. In the 1985 report, we anticipate covering hydropower, solar collectors, alcohol fuels, and methane generation from biological wastes.

In general, this first assessment shows that existing priorities in the use of both fiscal and natural resources are not compatible with the long-term sustainability of society. A resumption of the broad-based improvements in the human condition that characterized the third quarter of this century will require a shift in development strategies and a reordering of priorities. A major purpose of this report is to provide a sense of that needed reordering and of new ways to evaluate improvements in the human prospect.

We have tried to design a report that will be useful to policymakers. For example, in analyzing energy trends we have sought to help national energy planners who are faced with difficult choices. The chapter on nuclear power economics is the most comprehensive international compilation currently available on the costs of nuclear power. Unfortunately, few energy planners have had access to these international cost data. The chapter that charts the reduced dependence on oil worldwide enables national energy officials to compare their progress with that in other countries.

One by-product of global assessments of this sort is the identification of basic information gaps. Our effort to analyze topsoil loss from erosion indicates that few countries have systematically gathered data on soil formation and loss on their croplands. Although soil is a basic resource, most countries lack the data needed for its intelligent management.

The analysis underlying the report is integrated, or what is sometimes described as interdisciplinary. We have consciously chosen not to consider issues exclusively in biological, economic, political, or other disciplinary frameworks. Rather, we attempt to examine issues in all their complexity, much as policymakers must consider them. Anyone who has attempted to combine ecologic and economic analysis understands the difficulties inherent in interdisciplinary research. Even the starting assumptions of the two disciplines conflict. Where ecologists see specialization as a risk, economists are inclined to see it as a virtue. Ecologists see the world in terms of cycles, such as hydrological and carbon cycles; economists are more likely to see it in terms of continuous exponential growth. Ecologists seek a yield that can be sustained over the long term; economists are more interested in maximizing short-term profits.

Given these differing frames of reference, the stumbling blocks in integrated research are obvious. Confining research on an issue to a particular discipline is obviously much more comfortable. Ecologists can wrap themselves in the principles of ecology and economists have their economic theories, but interdisciplinary researchers lack such a security blanket. They can selectively draw on theory from various disciplines, but when the theories do not mesh they must rely on judgment and occasionally even on intuition.

The tone of this report is not intended to be optimistic or pessimistic. Neither unfounded optimism nor undue pessimism provide a solid foundation for policymaking. Only realism will do.

* * *

With this project, Worldwatch is responding further to a strong worldwide demand for policy-oriented interdisciplinary research, a demand that is reflected in sales of the 67 studies—57 Worldwatch Papers and 10 books—that the Institute has published during its first several years. For the first six Worldwatch books, where arrangements for foreign language editions have been largely completed, 74 publishing contracts have been signed in some 24 languages. For several Worldwatch Papers the number of copies in print in all languages combined has passed the hundred thousand mark.

Sales of Worldwatch Papers and book royalties have helped put the Institute, a nonprofit research organization, in the unusual position of earning a large share of its financial support. Indeed, these earnings and the interest on earnings saved, which now account for nearly half of the Institute's budget, have provided some of the funding for this project.

The launching of this global assessment represents a natural evolution of the Institute's ongoing research program on energy, environment, food, population, and other global issues. In undertaking this progress report, the Institute has relied on its existing information-gathering networks, including publication exchanges with some 70 other research institutes around the world, and an extensive international network of contacts in agriculture, business, demography, economics, energy, environment, and science. The Institute has also taken advantage of its location in Washington, D.C., to tap the information sources of the U.S. Government, World Bank, International Monetary Fund, local universities, and other research organizations.

Since this is our first *State of the World,* we welcome suggestions on how to make succeeding editions more useful. Comments and queries may be directed either to me or to the authors of individual chapters.

Lester R. Brown
Worldwatch Institute
1776 Massachusetts Avenue, N.W.
Washington, D.C. 20036

December 1983

STATE OF THE
WORLD
1984

1

Overview

Lester R. Brown

The news headlines of the eighties describe the worst worldwide economic crisis in half a century. In many countries incomes are falling. Record budget deficits plague national and local governments on every continent. The external debts of several countries in the Third World and Eastern Europe verge on the unmanageable. Corporate bankruptcies in major industrial countries are more numerous than at any time since the Great Depression. Unemployment ratchets upward in both industrial and developing countries. More countries are threatened with famine than at any time in the modern era.

The belated U.S. economic recovery in 1983 notwithstanding, the world economy is in the worst crisis since the Great Depression. There are, however, major differences between the thirties and the eighties. The crisis of the thirties was almost entirely the product of economic mismanagement during the twenties, of ill-conceived economic policies that fueled an economic boom until it went out of control. On both sides of the Atlantic the boom psychology led to

financial speculation that eventually culminated in the Great Depression. Once under way, the Depression seemed to feed on itself as international trade declined and countries turned inward, adopting protectionist policies that further reduced trade.

Although the economic crisis of the eighties is exacerbated by economic mismanagement, its roots lie in the depletion of resources, both nonrenewable and renewable. During the fifties and sixties the world economy steadily boosted its use of oil, a finite resource, putting it on a path that by definition was not sustainable over the long run. The depletion of oil reserves, and its effect on world oil prices, is the most immediate threat to world economic stability, but the depletion of soil resources by erosion may be the most serious long-term threat. The unprecedented doubling of world food supplies over the last generation was achieved in part by adopting agricultural practices that led to excessive soil erosion, erosion that is draining the land of its productivity. After a point agriculture can no longer be sustained and the land is abandoned.

Sustainability is an ecologic concept with economic implications. It recog-

Units of measurement are usually metric unless common usage dictates otherwise.

nizes that economic growth and human well-being depend on the natural resource base that supports all living systems. Technology has greatly expanded the earth's human carrying capacity, most obviously with advances in agriculture. But while the human ingenuity embodied in advancing technology can raise the natural limits on human economic activity, it cannot entirely remove them. A sustainable society is one that shapes its economic and social systems so that natural resources and life-support systems are maintained. Today we study the archaeological sites of earlier civilizations that failed to do so, depleting their soils, mismanaging their irrigation systems, or otherwise embarking on an unsustainable development path.

Humanity's newly acquired capacity to self-destruct with nuclear weapons has added another dimension to the concept of sustainability. Recent research by U.S. and Soviet scientists on the climatic and biological consequences of nuclear war indicates that a successful preemptive nuclear strike by either superpower would lead to a "nuclear winter," the end of civilization and quite possibly the end of human life on earth. Against the backdrop of this new potential for self-destruction, achieving sustainability presents unprecedented political and moral challenges.[1]

Nuclear weapons are not the only explosive force threatening civilization. As populations have multiplied, their demands have begun to exceed the sustainable yield of the economy's biological support systems. In country after country these thresholds have been crossed, leading to consumption of the basic resources themselves. Deforestation is reducing firewood and lumber supplies, driving up the cost of cooking fuel in Third World villages and the cost of housing everywhere. Overfishing and overgrazing have become commonplace as human claims on these major protein-producing biological systems have spiraled.

Today's economic headlines describe a world that is finding it difficult to live within its means. Eager to maximize output today, we are borrowing from tomorrow. Our economic problems are of our own making, the product of shortsighted economic policies designed to promote expansion at any cost, of agricultural policies designed to boost food output at the expense of soils, and of failed or nonexistent population policies.

In our preoccupation with monthly economic indicators we have lost touch with the environmental resource base on which the economy rests. We keep detailed data on the stock of plant and equipment while virtually ignoring the condition of soils, the health of forests, and the level of water tables. Only when environmental deterioration or resource depletion translates into economic decline do we seem to notice it.

GOOD NEWS, BAD NEWS

Over the past generation the world has yielded to an excessive dependence on oil, moved from farming soils to mining them, and begun to consume the economy's biological support systems. In short, the world economy has moved onto a development path that is unsustainable. Although at least some political leaders and their economic advisors are vaguely aware of this, the effort to return to a sustainable development path is not yet well defined. Most national governments, lacking a clearly defined sustainable development strategy, are attempting to "muddle through." As a result, successes are infrequent, often outnumbered by failures.

The essential components of a sustainable development strategy are straightforward. They include stabilizing population, reducing dependence on oil, developing renewable energy resources, conserving soil, protecting the earth's biological support systems, and recycling materials. The good news is that in each case at least a few countries are making some impressive progress, providing a model for others. The bad news is that in only one area, reducing dependence on oil, is the worldwide performance close to adequate.

After several years of trying to reduce dependence on oil, the world finally turned the corner in 1979. Since then, progress has been broadly based, exceeding expectations. Oftentimes historical turning points are tied to a specific event. With oil, the turning point came in 1979, when OPEC oil prices rose sharply for the second time in six years. After peaking in 1979 at 23.8 billion barrels, world oil consumption has fallen sharply in each of the four years since, declining some 14 percent.[2]

After three decades of rising oil use, it was clear by the early seventies that the world's growing dependence on a dwindling resource, though convenient, was not sustainable. Throughout this period oil use per unit of output was rising. Between 1950 and 1973 the oil used per $1,000 worth of gross world product (GWP) climbed from 1.33 barrels to 2.27 barrels, increasing the oil intensity of economic output by 71 percent. (See Table 1-1.) During the seventies the oil used per unit of GWP reached a plateau, but after the second oil price rise of the seventies it began a steady decline, falling from 2.15 barrels per $1,000 of product in 1979 to 1.74 barrels in 1983, a drop of 19 percent. In this critical area the world was not only headed in the right direction, but making impressive gains.

Following the 1973 oil price hike energy planners generally assumed that

Table 1-1. Oil Intensity of World Economic Output, 1950–83 (in 1980 dollars)

Year	Oil Used Per $1,000 of Output
	(barrels)
1950	1.33
1955	1.46
1960	1.67
1965	1.90
1970	2.17
1971	2.21
1972	2.23
1973	2.27
1974	2.13
1975	2.05
1976	2.15
1977	2.16
1978	2.14
1979	2.15
1980	2.05
1981	1.93
1982	1.86
1983	1.74

SOURCES: American Petroleum Institute; Herbert R. Block, *The Planetary Product in 1980* (Washington, D.C.: U.S. Department of State, 1981); and Worldwatch Institute estimates.

the development of nuclear power would surge forward, beginning to fill the void that would be left by oil. But this was not to be. In 1970 the Organisation for Economic Co-operation and Development (OECD) projected that its members—the Western industrial countries plus Japan—would have 563,000 megawatts of nuclear generating capacity by 1985. A 1978 OECD projection foresaw a 1985 generating capacity of just 214,-000 megawatts, just over one-third the earlier figure. A 1983 Worldwatch projection shows a further reduction to 183,000 megawatts, largely because of the cancellation of partially completed plants. In the United States, where the industry has been plagued by nightmarish cost overruns, no new reactors have been ordered since 1976 and some 87 reactor orders have been canceled. Barring any more new starts, U.S. nuclear power may peak in the early nineties. The country that led the world into the age of nuclear power may well lead it out.[3]

With nuclear power failing the market test and with serious environmental and meteorological consequences associated with the expanded use of coal, the world is turning to renewable energy resources. Although the development of renewable energy has not received the governmental support it deserves, some individual countries have made spectacular gains. In the United States, where forests are widely underharvested or not harvested at all, firewood now supplies twice as much delivered energy as nuclear power. Public attention focuses on the soaring residential use of firewood, which has tripled since 1973, yet it is exceeded by industry's use of wood and wood waste as a fuel.[4]

The country that led the world into the age of nuclear power may well lead it out.

A dramatic breakthrough in wind electrical generation is also occurring in the United States, in California. By the end of 1983 an estimated 4,600 wind turbines were installed in wind farms, 95 percent of them built during the preceding 24 months. Their collective generating capacity totals some 300 megawatts of electricity, enough to satisfy the residential electrical needs of some 120,000 Californians.[5]

Other renewable energy success stories are scattered around the globe.

Worldwide, over five million homes now heat water with rooftop solar collectors. As oil prices climbed during the seventies, energy-deficit Third World countries, aided by international development agencies, turned to hydropower development with renewed vigor. Both industrial and developing countries demonstrated an interest in mini-hydro development, a resource largely ignored during the era of cheap oil. And in Brazil nearly one-fourth of all automotive fuel used in 1983 came from agriculturally based fuels, principally alcohol distilled from sugarcane.[6]

If living standards are to be maintained and improved as energy becomes more expensive, the systematic recycling of materials will have to replace the throwaway economy. Some countries already understand this. For example, the Netherlands and Japan now lead the world in paper recycling, reusing nearly half the paper they consume. In the United States, nine states have passed legislation requiring returnable deposits on beverage containers, making it likely that over 90 percent of these containers will be returned for recycling and reuse. Worldwide recycling of aluminum has increased from 17 percent in 1970 to 28 percent in 1981. More important, recycling of this energy-intensive metal appears to be poised for sharp gains in the years ahead.[7]

On the population front, the news has been mixed. After peaking shortly before 1970 at about 1.9 percent per year, world population growth has slowed to 1.7 percent in the early eighties. Unfortunately this decade-long ebbing of the growth rate has not been sufficient to reduce the actual number added. The annual increase, which was roughly 70 million per year in 1970, has now edged up to 79 million. (See Table 1-2.) Until the rate of world population growth slows markedly, improving the human condition will be difficult.

**Table 1-2. World Population Growth,
1970 and 1983**

Year	Population	Annual Rate of Growth	Annual Increase
	(billion)	(percent)	(million)
1970	3.68	1.9	70
1983	4.66	1.7	79

SOURCE: Population Reference Bureau, *World Population Data Sheet* (Washington, D.C.: annual).

At the national level, however, some countries have performed admirably. Twelve countries in Europe have brought population growth to a halt. More importantly, China, home to 22 percent of the world's people, has reduced its population growth to just over 1 percent per year, comparable to that in some industrial countries. In a near desperate effort to break the momentum of its population growth, China has shifted from birth planning and the adoption of birth quotas at the commune or production-team level to the national goal of a one-child family.[8]

Elsewhere in the Third World, progress has been uneven. India, the other population giant, appears to be getting its family planning program back on track after several years of neglect, but valuable time has been lost. Without decisive action, India's population of 715 million is projected to grow by another billion people—as many as China now has—before stabilizing.[9]

The lack of movement toward sustainability in several other key areas is also of great concern. Efforts to protect the world's forests are not faring well. Each year they shrink by an area roughly the size of Hungary. In the great majority of Third World countries deforestation is a serious matter—one with long-term economic and ecologic consequences. One notable exception to this generalization is South Korea, which has successfully reforested its once denuded mountains and hills, planting in trees an area two-thirds that in rice, the country's food staple. Although national successes are rare, there are scores of promising local initiatives, such as in the Indian state of Gujarat, that must be multiplied many times if future firewood needs are to be assured.[10]

Soil erosion, as mentioned, has now reached epidemic proportions. But no major country, industrial or developing, has responded effectively to this threat to sustainable agriculture. As pressures on the land have intensified over the past generation, erosion has increased until close to half the world's cropland is losing topsoil at a debilitating rate.[11] In the United States, the crop surpluses of the early eighties, which are sometimes cited as a sign of a healthy agriculture, are partly the product of mining soils.

With food security, what little good news there is has been overshadowed by the bad. During the early eighties, world food reserves increased, climbing to their highest level in a decade. Unfortunately, reserves accumulated for the wrong reason—the lack of progress in raising the purchasing power and per capita food consumption of the world's poor. Since 1973, little progress has been made in raising food consumption per person for the world as a whole.[12] While North American agricultural output surged ahead during the late seventies and early eighties, that in Africa and the Soviet Union lagged. In Africa falling per capita food production has, since 1970, slowly but steadily dragged that continent into a crisis. Perhaps even more disturbing, the forces leading to this deterioration in Africa—rapid population growth, soil erosion, and underinvestment in agriculture—may well lead to a decline in per capita food production in other regions as well, such as northeastern Brazil, the Andean countries, Central America, the Indian subcontinent, and the Middle East.

The widely disparate regional performances in food production are mirrored in the shift in world grain trade patterns. More and more countries have become importers, increasing their dependence on the North American breadbasket. In 1982, the United States controlled 55 percent of world grain exports; Saudi Arabia, by comparison, controlled 32 percent of world oil exports.[13] This overwhelming reliance on one region for food leaves the world vulnerable to North American climatic variability and politically inspired export embargoes.

The value of arms imports into the Third World has now climbed above that of grain imports.

If the scientific and financial resources needed to put the world economy on a sustainable footing in all these areas are to be mobilized, they may have to come at the expense of the military sector. But during the years since 1979, a period distinguished by a lack of economic progress, the militarization of the world economy has accelerated, almost as though mounting economic stresses were causing political leaders to try to offset these insecurities by spending more on weapons. Between 1979 and 1983, global military expenditures climbed from $554 billion to $663 billion (1980 dollars), an increase of one-fifth, and pushed global military expenditures to $145 per person.[14]

Not only do many of the world's scientists devote their skills to developing new weapons, but political leaders appear to devote more and more of their time to military matters. And, disappointingly, the value of arms imports into the Third World has now climbed above that of grain imports.[15] As a result, many Third World populations,

though poorer and hungrier, are better armed.

On another key front—the threat of nuclear annihilation—there was serious regression. Hard-line posturing by the two superpowers raised concern over nuclear war to a new high. Many of the estimated 50,000 nuclear weapons, both strategic and tactical, are poised for launch at the push of a button.[16] If ever unleashed, this destructive power would bring civilization as we know it to an end. The one encouraging development on this front has been the rising level of public awareness, particularly in Europe and the United States. Public interest groups, religious organizations, professional associations, and business groups have joined hands in an effort to reduce the potential for nuclear annihilation. On balance, perhaps the key gain during the early eighties has been this growing understanding of the many threats to the sustainability of civilization. By this indicator, at least, we are gaining.

THE CHANGING ECONOMIC PROSPECT

For most of humanity the century's third quarter was a period of unprecedented prosperity. World output of goods and services expanded 5 percent annually, tripling in less than a generation. Rapid growth had become commonplace, built into the aspirations of consumers, the earnings projections of corporations, and the revenue expectations of governments. Few stopped to calculate that even a 4 percent rate of economic growth, if continued, would lead to a fiftyfold expansion in a century. And even fewer considered the pressures this would put on the earth's resources, both renewable and nonrenewable.

Cheap energy, specifically cheap oil, quite literally fueled this record economic expansion. At less than $2 a barrel, oil was so cheap that now, from the perspective of the late twentieth century, it appears to have been almost a free good. It was not only inexpensive, but it was versatile and easily transported. It could be used equally well as a fuel for generating electricity or powering machinery or as a chemical feedstock.

Cheap oil pushed back many of the traditional resource constraints on growth. In its various forms it was substituted for scarcer resources. Fertilizer was substituted for cropland, kerosene for firewood, synthetic fibers for natural ones, and, as tractors replaced draft animals, gasoline and diesel fuel for forage and grain. Cheap oil had become a safety valve, alleviating pressure on less abundant resources. But as the price of oil began to climb, substitution became more costly and the safety valve began to close.

The transition to costly oil has affected world economic performance both directly and indirectly. Capital requirements in the energy sector, especially for the development of new energy sources, have soared, draining capital from other sectors. Rising real energy costs have led to higher wage demands and general inflation. And realization that the age of

energy abundance is ending has dampened the outlook for investors and consumers alike. (See Table 1-3.)

Among the sectors most affected by the changing oil situation is the oil industry itself, a major part of the world economy. As demand for oil dropped because of high prices, world economic activity has been reduced by downturns in oil production, transport, and refining. After increasing by well over 7 percent per year from 1950 to 1973, oil production dropped to 2 percent per year between 1973 and 1979. After the second oil price hike of the seventies it began to decline, falling some 5 percent per year for the next four years.

Rising oil prices have also slowed the growth in world grain production. (Other factors slowing the growth in food output include soil erosion, water shortages, and diminishing returns on fertilizer use.) Although attention has focused on the effects of higher oil prices on food production, the effect of escalating oil prices on the world economy has also weakened the growth in demand for food. After increasing by 3.1 percent per year from 1950 to 1973, world grain production has averaged less than 2 percent per year ever since.

Industries that are even more directly tied to oil have been hit still harder by the changing oil outlook. Of these none

Table 1-3. Basic World Economic Indicators at Three Oil Price Levels, 1950–83 (in 1980 dollars)

Period	Oil Price Per Barrel	Annual Growth			
		Oil Production	Grain Production	Automobile Production	Gross World Product
	(dollars)	(percent)			
1950–73	2	7.6	3.1	5.8	5.0
1973–79	12	2.0	1.9	1.1	3.5
1979–83	31	− 5.2	1.0[1]	− 3.0	1.7

[1]Severe drought in North America and Africa and a record idling of cropland under U.S. farm programs reduced the 1983 harvest well below trend.

SOURCES: Based on data from American Petroleum Institute, U.S. Department of Agriculture, Motor Vehicle Manufacturers Association, and U.S. Department of State.

has suffered more than automobile production, the world's largest manufacturing industry. Between 1950 and 1973 world auto production expanded by 5.8 percent per year. With oil averaging $12 a barrel between 1973 and 1979, the growth in auto output slowed markedly, to just over 1 percent per year. When the world oil price was pushed over $30 in 1979, the slowdown in production growth became a decline, with output falling from 31 million automobiles in 1979 to an estimated 27 million in 1983. Although this four-year slide is obviously not a trend to be projected to the end of the century, it does suggest that the automobile's future is clouded.

The effect of higher oil prices on automobile sales is both direct and indirect. Most immediately, higher fuel prices discourage automobile ownership. But to the extent that the changing oil situation translates into slower economic growth, growth in the number of potential buyers also slows. Although it is analytically difficult to separate these two effects, they are combining to alter the automobile's future.

A decline in the demand for automobiles ripples through the world economy, depressing demand in basic supply industries such as steel, rubber, and glass. Companies producing auto parts and machine tools are also adversely affected. Downturns in these basic industries have contributed to the economic growth slowdown in the leading industrial societies.

Given the emerging constraints on growth, particularly in such basic sectors as food and energy, the world will have great difficulty resuming the rapid economic growth of the 1950–73 period. High-technology industries such as microelectronics and biotechnology can expand dramatically, helping to improve the efficiency of energy use and boost agricultural production, but their growth cannot begin to offset the slower

growth or decline in the basic sectors. Economic growth in the next several years, and quite possibly throughout the rest of this century, is more likely to be slow than rapid, more likely to average 2 percent per year than the 4–5 percent that characterized the century's third quarter.

Assessing future economic prospects is complicated by the difficulty of separating the effects on growth of the changing resource situation, evidenced for example by the 1979 oil price hike, and the cyclical behavior of the world economy. In short, is the slow growth of the 1979–83 period merely a cyclical downturn, as some economists argue, or is it the early stage of a transition to a future when economic growth will be much slower? The analysis underlying this report, which assesses the effects of a broad range of resource constraints on world economic growth, indicates it is the latter.

THE SHRINKING RESOURCE BASE

Of all the resources that are being depleted, losses of oil and topsoil pose the greatest threats to economic progress and stability. With reserves of both being steadily depleted, the world is facing major economic adjustments that, at a minimum, will extend over several decades.

Oil reserves are commonly measured at two levels, those that are proven and the larger, less precise category of those that are ultimately recoverable. Proven reserves have been physically verified and can be extracted profitably at current prices, relying largely on natural pressure in the oil-bearing structures.

Ultimately recoverable reserves include not only an estimate of any additional oil likely to be discovered, but also any reserves that can be extracted using the more expensive secondary and tertiary recovery techniques, which rely on the use of pressure and solvents. Extracting all the estimated 2.1 trillion barrels of ultimately recoverable oil would require prices well above current levels.[17]

By the late seventies annual world oil consumption was just under 23 billion barrels per year, nearly 3 percent of proven reserves of 670 billion barrels. It was this wholesale depletion of reserves that helped convert the world oil economy from a buyer's to a seller's market almost overnight. At the 1983 oil production level of 18 billion barrels, proven reserves of oil would last 37 years. (See Table 1-4.) Applying this same rate to the ultimately recoverable reserves would stretch production out to 114 years, obviously a preferable time span.

As the demand for food has climbed with each passing year, the world has begun to mine its soils, converting them into a nonrenewable resource. Even in an agriculturally sophisticated country like the United States, the loss of soil through erosion exceeds new soil formation on over one-third of the cropland.[18] Assuming there is still on average seven inches of topsoil on the world's cropland, there are some 3.5 trillion tons of topsoil that can be used to produce food. If erosion on cropland exceeds new soil formation by 23 billion tons per year (the rate that is calculated in Chapter 4), topsoil reserves will disappear in about 150 years, only a few decades after the exhaustion of ultimately recoverable reserves of oil.

There are, however, important differences in the ways these two basic resources are being depleted. For example, it is reasonable to expect that essentially all the world's oil reserves will one day be depleted, but this is unlikely to occur with topsoil because not all the world's cropland is subject to excessive erosion under normal agricultural use. Yet much of the world's topsoil will be lost if steps are not taken to protect it.

A second contrast in the depletion of these two basic resources is that the world is far more aware of oil depletion and its consequences. Governments everywhere have responded to the growing scarcity of oil but such is not the case for soil. With only occasional exceptions, agricultural and population policies have not taken soil depletion into account. In part, the contrasting awareness of oil and soil depletion is the understandable product of differing levels of information. The world oil crisis received a great deal of attention largely because oil is a widely traded commod-

Table 1-4. World Depletion of Oil and Topsoil, 1983

Resource	1983	Annual Rate of Depletion	Time To Deplete
	(billion barrels)		(years)
Proven Reserves of Oil	670	18	37
Ultimately Recoverable Reserves of Oil	2,100	18	114
	(billion tons)		
Reserves of Topsoil on Cropland	3,500	23	152

SOURCES: American Petroleum Institute; World Energy Conference, *Survey of Energy Resources 1980* (London: 1980); topsoil reserves are Worldwatch Institute estimates (see Chapter 4).

ity, with most countries being importers. With soil, however, the crisis is a quiet one. Estimates are regularly made for oil reserves, adjusting annually both for depletion through production and new discoveries. Such a procedure does not exist for world soil reserves. Indeed, not until topsoil has largely disappeared and food shortages or even famine have developed does this loss become apparent.

The depletion of oil reserves will make the remaining soil even more valuable.

The effect of price on the depletion of the two resources also varies. Higher prices for oil raise the amount that can be ultimately recovered, but higher prices for food may simply lead to more-intensive land use and faster topsoil loss. And the depletion of oil reserves will make the substitution of energy for cropland more difficult, rendering the remaining soil even more valuable.

Beyond these key resources of oil and soil, a daunting range of renewable support systems are deteriorating under mounting pressures. As a result of overcutting and clearing for farming and grazing, the world's forests are shrinking by nearly 1 percent per year. Each year the forested area of the tropics, where most deforestation occurs, is reduced by 11.3 million hectares, and each year the demand for forest products increases.[19] Distribution is a key factor. Although there is an abundance of fuelwood in Siberia, it might as well be on the moon as far as Ethiopian villagers are concerned because the cost of transporting firewood long distances is prohibitive.

A newly recognized threat to the world's forests, particularly those in the northern tier of industrial countries, is acid rain. Poland, Czechoslovakia, East and West Germany, and the United States are the countries most obviously affected. One-third of West Germany's forests show signs of damage, and some 500,000 hectares of forests in Czechoslovakia are dead or deteriorating. In North America there are also signs that trees are dying and that forest productivity is declining as a result of growing soil acidity. One of the disturbing characteristics of this forest dieback is that by the time the problem becomes evident it may be too late to save the trees.[20]

In many areas grasslands are disappearing under the weight of excessive numbers of cattle, sheep, and goats. In the United States the Council on Environmental Quality reported that one-third of U.S. rangeland (excluding Alaska) was in fair condition and one-third in poor.[21] Long evident in the Middle East and North Africa, the excessive pressures are spreading to Africa south of the Sahara, to the Indian subcontinent, and to China, Australia, and Mexico. Desertification, the word that describes the conversion of productive ranchland into desert, has become part of the international lexicon.

Between 1950 and 1976 the world's grasslands sustained a doubling of beef output, but since then there has been no growth at all. With overgrazing now commonplace, the world's herders, farmers, and ranchers are no longer able to expand their herds apace with world population. The result has been a steady decline in the world's per capita beef consumption since 1976 and stagnation in this subsector of the world agricultural economy.[22]

Fisheries, too, are under excessive pressure. The world fish catch, which had tripled between 1950 and 1970, has increased little since then. Its annual rate of increase fell from nearly 6 percent in 1950–70 to less than 1 percent. The catch from some of the leading fisheries in the North Atlantic peaked in the late sixties and early seventies and is now only a fraction of what it was 15 years ago. Even recently exploited fisheries, such as those in the Gulf of Thailand, have reached their limits and begun to decline in the face of the growing world demand for protein.[23]

In the eyes of some scientists, the loss of genetic diversity as plant and animal species disappear is the principal threat to a sustainable society. At the broadest level this consists of the loss of many species of plants and animals as habitats are destroyed. Clearing tropical forests, with their richness of flora and fauna, can eliminate countless uncatalogued species that have yet to be evaluated for their potential commercial value. Once again, mounting economic demands are leading directly to a resource deterioration that adversely affects the economic prospect, in this case by reducing the potential for new discoveries and for commercial innovations based on those discoveries.[24]

ENERGY-RELATED STRUCTURAL ADJUSTMENTS

Aside from its adverse effect on economic growth, the severalfold increase in the price of oil during the seventies contributed to a massive redistribution of wealth from oil-importing countries to those that export petroleum. A few industrial countries—the United Kingdom, Norway, and the Soviet Union—have benefited from higher oil prices. But it has been the members of the Organization of Petroleum Exporting Countries (OPEC) and Mexico, all of which were preindustrial societies, that gained most from the dramatic shift in the terms of trade between oil and other products.

The dimensions of this shift are perhaps best illustrated by the change in the relative prices of grain and oil, both widely traded commodities. Between 1950 and 1973 a bushel of wheat could be traded for a barrel of oil. (See Table 1-5.) Then as the price of oil jumped, the relationship began to shift. By 1977, it took 4.4 bushels of wheat to buy a barrel of oil; in 1982, it took nearly 8. For the United States, which paid much of its mounting oil bill with farm products, this shift in the terms of trade stimulated an enormous expansion of agricultural exports.

Table 1-5. The International Terms of Trade Between Wheat and Oil, 1950–83

Year	World Price		Amount of Wheat To Buy a Barrel of Oil
	Bushel of Wheat	Barrel of Oil	
	(dollars)		(bushels)
1950	1.91	1.71	0.9
1955	1.77	1.93	1.1
1960	1.58	1.50	1.0
1965	1.62	1.33	0.8
1970	1.50	1.30	0.9
1971	1.68	1.65	1.0
1972	1.90	1.90	1.0
1973	3.81	2.70	0.7
1974	4.90	9.76	2.0
1975	4.06	10.72	2.6
1976	3.62	11.51	3.2
1977	2.81	12.40	4.4
1978	3.48	12.70	3.6
1979	4.36	16.97	3.9
1980	4.70	28.67	6.1
1981	4.76	32.50	6.8
1982	4.36	33.47	7.7
1983	4.35	28.50	6.6

SOURCES: International Monetary Fund, *Monthly Financial Statistics 1980 Yearbook* (Washington, D.C.: 1980) and *1983 Yearbook* (Washington, D.C.: 1983).

The same was true for other countries paying for oil with agricultural commodities such as tea, coffee, or sugar. During the early seventies, when a barrel of oil was still priced at $2, it could be purchased with 4 pounds of tea; in 1983, over 30 pounds were required. For coffee, the terms of trade went from 4 pounds in the early seventies to 22 pounds in 1983. With sugar, the most widely exported farm commodity in the Third World, the "sugar price" of a barrel of oil went from just over 30 to nearly 200 pounds during the same period.

In a sense, the terms-of-trade gain for the oil-exporting countries is a desirable result of the rise in price associated with the rapid depletion of an important nonrenewable resource. Unfortunately, the resulting redistribution of wealth was not only from industrial to preindustrial societies but also from preindustrial societies that did not have oil to those that did. By any measurement, the handful of countries that had oil to sell greatly increased their slice of the global economic pie. It was their short-term reward for sharing a nonrenewable resource with the rest of the world.

The OPEC increase in the price of oil launched the transition to alternative energy sources, a shift that is restructuring the global economy. Some sectors are shrinking; others are expanding rapidly. Just as the shift from coal to oil reshaped the economic system during the first three-quarters of this century, the shift from oil to alternatives will bring profound changes in the decades ahead.

One of the industries most immediately affected by the oil downturn was shipping, whose tanker fleets carry the oil to the consuming countries. The introduction of more-efficient supertankers that sparked a shipbuilding boom in the late sixties and seventies also led to enormous growth in tanker tonnage at a time when production of oil was on the brink of turning downward. Although the fall in oil production was abrupt and swift, oil exports fell even faster. Within a few years after being launched, some of the supertankers were in Taiwanese shipyards being cut up for scrap metal. Vast amounts of capital, steel, and energy had been wasted building shipping capacity that would never be used.[25]

Paralleling the decline in oil production was a fall in refining. Excess capacity resulted not only from the fall in output but also from the continued construction of new refineries in oil-exporting countries, which sought to maximize their income by selling less crude oil and more refined products. In 1982 alone, 67 refineries in the United States and 15 in Europe were closed completely; many others operated at less than full capacity.[26]

As mentioned earlier, outside the oil industry itself the greatest adjustments occurred in the automobile industry. Nearly one-third of the 780,000 automobile workers in the United States were unemployed by 1980. Both the number of autos produced and their design were changing. Even as production started to fall, the reins of industry leadership were shifting from the United States to Japan, where higher quality, more-fuel-efficient cars were rolling off the assembly lines. In 1980, for the first time since automobile production began, the United States lost its leadership position to Japan, which produced 7 million cars compared with 6.3 million in the United States.[27]

As world automobile production fell, so did the number of automobile dealers. In the United States, still by far the world's largest automobile market, some 2,500 dealers closed their doors during the two years after the oil price hike of 1979. And service stations also felt the crunch. As gasoline consumption in the United States fell some 13 percent from its peak in the late seventies, the number of service stations needed to handle this gasoline also declined.[28]

Similarly, where water used for irrigation leads to a declining water table or the exhaustion of an underground aquifer, an alternative series of agricultural output data should be developed that would indicate the sustainable output. In the U.S. southern plains, for example, much irrigation comes from the Ogallala aquifer, an essentially nonrechargeable water resource. The increase in output that was associated with the conversion from dryland to irrigated farming in this area is a boost that will last for only a few decades. Indeed, the reconversion to dryland farming has already begun in parts of Colorado, Kansas, and Texas.

In addition to these biological and agronomic deficits, the early eighties has witnessed an enormous increase in debt, both public and private. Underlying the apparent vitality of U.S. agriculture, for example, is a soaring debt burden. Between 1977 and 1983 U.S. farm debt increased from $100 billion to $215 billion. This compares with annual net farm income during the early eighties of some $22 billion per year.[35] The increase in debt is largely the result of farmers borrowing against inflated land values. As land prices soared from the early seventies through 1980, farmers trapped by the cost-price squeeze borrowed more and more money. But as land prices turned downward after 1980 more farmers have been threatened with foreclosure than at any time since the Great Depression.

THE DEBT OVERHANG

Perhaps the principal economic manifestations of our inability to live within our means are soaring national fiscal deficits and foreign debts. In too many countries, national political leaders have failed to adjust population and economic policies to the changing resource situation and instead have engaged in deficit financing to maintain consumption levels. Nowhere is this more evident than in the United States, where the Reagan administration's budget deficits, actual and projected, for 1981 through 1985 will increase the federal debt by an estimated $692 billion, raising it from $914 billion to $1,606 billion. The Reagan deficits will closely approach those of all previous administrations combined. (See Table 1-6.) Over this period every man, woman, and child in the United States will have incurred an average of $2,800 in additional public debt— $11,200 for a family of four.[36] Not only has the United States mortgaged its fu-

Table 1-6. United States: Gross Federal Debt, Total and Per Person, 1950–84

Year	Gross Federal Debt	Annual Increment	Debt Per Person
	(billion dollars)		(dollars)
1950	257		1,691
1960	291		1,616
1970	383		1,875
1971	410	27	1,980
1972	437	27	2,089
1973	468	31	2,216
1974	486	18	2,279
1975	544	58	2,525
1976	632	88	2,904
1977	709	77	3,226
1978	780	71	3,514
1979	834	54	3,712
1980	914	80	4,024
1981	1,004	90	4,378
1982	1,147	143	4,955
1983	1,384	237	5,921
1984	1,606	222	6,827

SOURCES: *Economic Report of the President* and *Statistical Abstract of the United States: 1982–83* (Washington, D.C.: U.S. Government Printing Office, 1983).

ture, but this huge national debt now hangs like a dark cloud over the world economy, sure to push interest rates up in world capital markets for years to come.

Aggravated by the record real interest rates in the United States in late 1982 and 1983, external debt has continued to expand throughout the Third World. Indeed, of all the economic problems facing the world in the mid-eighties, none seems quite so intractable as the management of huge external debts in the Third World and Eastern Europe. By the end of 1983, developing countries owed some $700 billion. The hard currency debt of the East European countries, excluding their ruble debt to the Soviet Union, was $53 billion. Together, these two groups owed three-quarters of a trillion dollars.[37]

Several converging forces contributed to the record debt levels. The 1973 oil price adjustment led to a modest increase in borrowing by many oil-importing countries. For most oil-deficient countries, however, it was not until 1979 that the debt load began its steep climb. Close on the heels of this came high interest rates that sharply boosted the cost of debt servicing. At the same time the prolonged global economic slowdown of 1980–83 reduced the volume of Third World commodity exports and in most cases their prices as well, a combination that sharply reduced export earnings.

The precise contribution of these sources of debt growth varied by individual countries. In some, the depletion of key resources reduced export earnings or raised import needs. For many Third World countries, the loss of topsoil contributed to the rising demand for food imports. Exporters of tropical hardwood, such as the Philippines, Thailand, and Nigeria, are losing this valuable source of foreign exchange as wood harvesting exceeds the sustainable yield of their forests. Indeed, Nigeria has be-

come a net importer of forest products, importing some $221-million worth in 1981.[38] Livestock herds are dwindling in some African countries as grasslands deteriorate, depriving them of a traditional source of export earnings. For these countries, and others such as Peru, with its heavy loss of fish meal exports, the mismanagement of biological systems contributed to a trade deficit. Resource depletion—whether boosting the price of oil imports, increasing the need for food imports, or depriving borrowing countries of raw material exports—figures prominently in the worsening debt situation.

Some oil-exporting countries also found themselves in a financially precarious position. Given the extremely low real interest rates during the high inflation years of 1979 and 1980, borrowing seemed attractive to these apparently credit-worthy governments. What was not foreseen was the extent the demand for petroleum would weaken as a result of both conservation in importing countries and the worldwide slowing of economic growth. The failure to anticipate the drop in exports and oil prices led to serious miscalculations in oil-exporting countries such as Mexico, Nigeria, and Venezuela.

The difficulty of managing these mounting external debts can be seen in the relationship between the cost of debt servicing and exports. Half to two-thirds of all export earnings are now required merely to pay interest on foreign debt in Argentina, Brazil, Chile, Mexico, the Philippines, and Turkey. For the Third World generally, one-fourth of export earnings are claimed for this purpose. In many countries, debt servicing requirements are so large that little foreign exchange remains to import essential commodities such as oil, food, and industrial machinery and parts. (See Table 1-7.)

Because the debt problem threatens the viability of banks in the major indus-

Table 1-7. Interest Payments on External Debt in Relation to Export Earnings of Major Debtor Countries, 1983

Country	Total External Debt	Estimated Export Earnings	Share of Export Earnings to Pay Interest[1]
	(billion dollars)		(percent)
Brazil	93.5	17.5	64
Mexico	86.6	22.2	47
South Korea	40.3	19.4	25
Argentina	38.5	9.2	50
Venezuela	31.5	12.9	29
Indonesia	28.8	16.8	21
Poland	27.0	10.2	31
Turkey	23.6	5.2	54
Philippines	22.7	5.7	47
Yugoslavia	20.0	10.3	23
Chile	18.7	4.1	54
Thailand	13.5	8.4	19
Peru	12.5	3.7	41
Malaysia	11.3	12.4	11
Taiwan	8.5	27.5	4
Ecuador	7.1	2.1	38

[1]Assumes interest rate of 12 percent; total debt service, including principal repayment, is of course much larger.
SOURCES: Morgan Guaranty Trust Company and International Monetary Fund.

trial countries, it has grabbed the attention of leaders in the industrial world as few other Third World economic problems ever have. For example, in many instances outstanding loans by major U.S. banks to debt-burdened Third World countries exceed these banks' capital assets.[39]

If a wave of defaults were to engulf the Third World and some of their loans were to go bad, U.S. banks would face collapse unless rescued by Washington. At a minimum, the inability of debtors to repay the principal will reduce capital available from major banks for new loans in industrial countries.

In the preface to its *World Debt Tables,* published in 1983, the World Bank observes that "the resolution of these difficulties lies in a restoration of economic health to the global economy and a resumption of strong growth in international trade." Other analysts, including those at the International Monetary Fund and the Institute for International Economics, make the same point, indicating that the debtor developing countries and those in Eastern Europe can work their way out from under the debt load with a return to a more traditional rate of growth in the world economy and in world trade.[40]

At issue is whether a rapid rate of global economic growth can be sustained. Since 1979 the world economy has expanded at an average of 1.7 percent per year, exactly the same as population growth. This means that on average there has been no increase in world output per person. Some countries, of course, have registered continuing gains in per capita income, which means that others have experienced declines.

As discussed earlier, the depletion of natural capital, particularly oil, has slowed world economic growth. (See Table 1-8.) When oil was priced at $2 a barrel, the world economy grew at an exceptional 5 percent per year, or roughly 3 percent faster than population, allowing for substantial gains in per capita income. From 1973 to 1979, when the price of oil averaged $12 a barrel, the rate of economic growth dropped to 3.5 percent, roughly double the rate of population growth. But since 1979, when the price of oil has averaged $31 per barrel and when other resource constraints on growth have intensified, the world economy has barely kept pace with population growth.

Given the likely continuation of high oil prices and the growing influence on long-term growth of numerous other inhibitors such as topsoil loss, freshwater scarcity, grassland deterioration, deforestation, and militarization of the world economy, long-term world economic growth may not substantially exceed 2 percent a year. This certainly would not be enough to help Third World countries work their way out of debt. And, given this growth prospect, the economic climate is unlikely to encourage

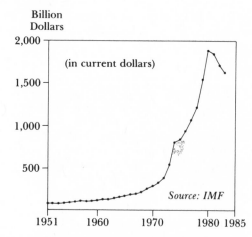

Figure 1-1. World Exports, 1951-83

commercial banks to continually add to the current outstanding debt of the Third World and Eastern Europe.

Nor is future growth in international trade likely to be rapid. According to the International Monetary Fund, the value of world exports peaked at $1,868 billion in 1980 and fell to roughly $1,650 billion in 1983, a decline of nearly 12 percent. (See Figure 1-1.) The General Agreement on Tariffs and Trade, measuring the volume of trade, shows only a negligible decline in trade for this period. But measured by value or volume, there has been no growth in world exports thus far during the eighties.[41]

Several factors are restricting world

Table 1-8. World Economic and Population Growth at Three Oil Price Levels, 1950–83

Period	Oil Price Per Barrel	Annual Growth		
		Gross World Product	Population	Gross World Product Per Person
	(dollars)	(percent)		
1950–73	2	5.0	1.9	3.1
1973–79	12	3.5	1.8	1.7
1979–83	31	1.7	1.7	0.0

SOURCES: Oil price data are from International Monetary Fund; gross world product data are from Herbert R. Block, *The Planetary Product in 1980* (Washington, D.C.: U.S. Department of State, 1981) and Worldwatch Institute estimates; population data are from United Nations and Worldwatch Institute estimates.

trade during the early eighties, such as the economic slowdown and severe import restrictions in debtor countries that are struggling to improve their trade balance. In addition, the slower global economic growth has led many countries to attempt to protect domestic employment and production by adopting protectionist trade measures. But over the long term it is the declining role of oil in the world economy that will constrain growth in trade. Oil, the engine of growth in world trade for a generation, is no longer spurring trade expansion as it once did. The 14 percent fall in world oil consumption since 1979 was exceeded by an even greater decline in oil trade, since importing countries cut consumption more than oil-exporting countries did.[42] Although the declining dependence on oil lowers trade levels, it stems from more-efficient use and the shift to sustainable energy sources, both of which contribute to economic sustainability.

As the curtain slowly descends on the age of oil, investments in more energy-efficient technologies, in other fossil fuels, and in renewable energy resources are expanding. Of these, only the fossil fuels, coal and gas, are traded and they are not as easily or widely transported as oil. As the world shifts to conservation and renewable resources—whether wood, hydropower, wind energy, geothermal energy, or any of the many others—energy production will become more localized. As energy production is such a large sector, the localization of energy production will contribute to the overall localization of economic activity.

In combination, these new influences on world trade suggest it may be unrealistic to expect it to resume the growth that prevailed prior to 1979. If this is true, something more imaginative than the existing "muddle through" approach is needed if the world is to avoid a decade of economic stagnation. Even worse, a continuation of the "muddle through" approach could lead the world into an unmanageable economic crisis. To break out of this mold will require leadership—leadership that will almost certainly have to come from the United States and the International Monetary Fund. Unfortunately, the U.S. Government, with its vast budget deficits, is contributing to the crisis rather than ameliorating it.

Better understanding of the origins of the current economic crisis is the key to formulating workable policies. Fortunately there is a growing awareness that conventional economic policies are no longer working and that many of our economic difficulties are rooted in the depletion of the resource base. This heightened awareness is necessary, though not sufficient, for the formulation of national population and economic policies that will put the world on a sustainable development path, one that will restore a broad-based improvement in the human condition.

2

Stabilizing Population

Lester R. Brown

Progress at halting world population growth has been extraordinarily uneven during the last decade. Some countries have been highly successful, others complete failures. Some have reached zero population growth without trying. At one end of the spectrum are several European countries that have completed the demographic transition and whose population growth has ceased. At the other end are some 34 Third World countries whose populations are expanding at 3 percent or more annually.[1]

Assessing national population policies is complicated by the changing criteria of success. Until recently, progress was defined simply in terms of slowing population growth, so as to widen the margin of economic growth over that of population. During the seventies, however, the inadequacy of this goal became evident. Forests were shrinking, grasslands deteriorating, and soils eroding. Biological thresholds of sustainable yield were crossed in scores of countries. When a biological system is being taxed, even a modest increase in human numbers can be destructive. Failing to halt population growth before such a critical threshold is crossed leads to food shortages, fuel

scarcities, and a declining standard of living.

The relationship between population and economic growth is also changing. When the world economy was expanding at 4 percent or more per year, the average rate of national economic growth was well above that of even the most rapidly expanding population. But the much slower economic growth of the eighties means national rates are beginning to fall below population growth in many of the countries with high birth rates. The failure of these governments to introduce effective population policies is leading to a broad-based decline in living standards. In these circumstances rapid population growth does not merely slow improvements in income, it precludes them.

POPULATION ARITHMETIC

Over the past decade many people concerned about rapid population growth have cited with some relief the gradual decline in the growth rate. Peaking at something like 1.9 percent around 1970, annual growth in world population declined to 1.7 percent in 1983. Although this is encouraging, the rate is not falling fast enough to reduce the number of people added each year. In 1970 world population increased by 70 million; in 1983 the addition was 79 million.[2] By the criterion of sheer numbers, the worldwide effort to get the brakes on population growth is falling short.

There are few areas of public policy in which a lack of understanding of basic arithmetic has hindered effective policy-making as much as it has in population. Few national political leaders seem to understand what an annual population growth of 3 percent, relatively innocuous in the near term, will lead to over a century. Political leaders and economic planners often think of a 3 percent growth rate as simply three times as much as a 1 percent rate. Although this is true for one year, it is not true over the longer term, as the rates compound. A population growing 1 percent annually will not even triple in a century, but one growing 3 percent annually will increase nineteenfold. (See Table 2-1.)

Stopping world population growth requires bringing the number of births and deaths roughly into balance, as they already are in several countries. How far the world has to go in this task can be seen in the data for 1983, when an estimated 131 million births and 52 million deaths yielded the net increase of some 79 million. A clearer idea of the dynamics of this growth can be gained from analyzing the annual additions of various countries. Leading the list is India, where there are now over 15 million more births than deaths each year. (See Table 2-2.) China, which reached the one billion mark in 1981, adds 13.3 million people annually, fewer than India because of its much lower growth rate. Together, these two demographic giants account for over one-third of the earth's new inhabitants each year. The five leading national contributors to world population growth—these two, plus Brazil, Bangladesh, and Nigeria—constitute nearly half the 79 million annual increment.

Many relatively small Third World countries have an astounding number of new citizens to feed, clothe, and shelter each year because their growth rates are so high. Nigeria, for example, has 84 million people, less than one-third as many as the Soviet Union; yet each year there are 2.8 million more Nigerians, compared with 2.2 million more Soviets. In the Western Hemisphere, the U.S. population is four times that of Mexico's but the latter grows by nearly 2 million people a year, whereas the U.S. natural increase is 1.6 million. A similar situation exists in Asia: Burma, with only one-third the population of Japan, adds more people each year.

Table 2-1. Relationship of Population Growth Per Year and Per Century

Population Growth Per Year	Population Growth Per Century
(percent)	(percent)
1	270
2	724
3	1,922

SOURCE: Worldwatch Institute.

COUNTRIES WITH ZERO POPULATION GROWTH

The first country in the modern era to bring births and deaths into equilibrium was East Germany, where population growth came to a halt in 1969. It was closely followed by West Germany, whose population stopped growing in 1972. During the decade since, several

Table 2-2. Principal Sources of World Population Growth, by Country, 1983

Country	Population	Annual Growth Rate	Annual Increase
	(million)	(percent)	(million)
India	730.0	2.1	15.33
China	1,023.3	1.3	13.30
Brazil	131.3	2.3	3.02
Bangladesh	96.5	3.1	2.99
Nigeria	84.2	3.3	2.78
Pakistan	95.7	2.8	2.68
Indonesia	155.6	1.7	2.65
Soviet Union	272.0	0.8	2.18
Mexico	75.7	2.6	1.97
United States	234.2	0.7	1.64

SOURCE: Population Reference Bureau, *1983 World Population Data Sheet* (Washington, D.C.: 1983); China's growth rate is author's estimate based on 1982 census by Chinese Government.

other countries—most recently Italy, Switzerland, and Norway—have joined the ranks of the demographic no-growth countries.

By 1983, there were 12 countries, all in Europe, where births and deaths were in equilibrium.

By 1983 there were 12 countries, all in Europe, where births and deaths were in equilibrium. (See Table 2–3.) For them, in contrast to the rest of the world, a year of zero economic growth does not automatically lead to a decline in living standards. With the exception of East Germany and Hungary, all are in Western Europe. They range from tiny Luxembourg to three of the four largest countries in Western Europe—Italy, the United Kingdom, and West Germany. With the recent addition of Switzerland to the list, Europe's German-speaking population has stabilized. Together, these dozen countries contain some 244 million people. Although this represents only 5.2 percent of the world total, it is

at least a beginning toward the eventual stabilization of world population, a prerequisite of a sustainable society.

Population stabilization was not an explicit national goal in any of these 12 countries. Declines in fertility flowed from economic gains and social improvements. As incomes rose and as employment opportunities for women expanded, couples chose to have fewer children. The improved availability of family planning services and the liberalization of abortion laws gave couples the means to achieve this. Population stabilization in these countries has been the result, therefore, of individual preferences, the product of converging economic, social, and demographic forces.

Several other European countries could reestablish equilibrium between births and deaths in a matter of years. Among these in Western Europe are Finland, France, Greece, the Netherlands, Portugal, and Spain. In Eastern Europe, Bulgaria and Czechoslovakia are soon likely to follow East Germany and Hungary along the path of population stabilization.

Encouraging though it will be when these countries reach population stabil-

Table 2-3. Countries With Zero Population Growth, 1983[1]

Country	Crude Birth Rate	Crude Death Rate	Annual Rate of Increase (+) or Decrease (−)	Population
	(per 1,000 population)		(percent)	(million)
Austria	12	12	0.0	7.6
Belgium	12	11	+0.2	9.9
Denmark	10	11	−0.1	5.1
East Germany	14	14	0.0	16.9
Hungary	13	14	−0.1	10.7
Italy	11	9	+0.2	56.6
Luxembourg	12	11	+0.1	0.4
Norway	12	10	+0.2	4.1
Sweden	11	11	0.0	8.3
Switzerland	11	9	+0.2	6.5
United Kingdom	13	12	+0.1	56.0
West Germany	10	12	−0.2	61.6
Total Population				243.5

[1]Zero population growth is here defined as within a range of plus or minus 0.2 percent change in population size per year.
SOURCE: Worldwatch Institute estimates, based on data in United Nations, *Monthly Bulletin of Statistics,* New York, monthly.

ity, major gains in raising the share of people in the world who live in a similar situation awaits further fertility declines in the three largest industrial countries —Japan, the Soviet Union, and the United States—which now have annual population growth rates of 0.7, 0.8, and 0.7 percent, respectively. The postwar decline in the Soviet crude birth rate leveled off in the early seventies, hovering around 18 since then. The U.S. birth rate, after declining rather steadily from 1957 until the late seventies, picked up slightly during the early eighties. Japan's birth rate, however, has been falling steadily for over a decade and, at 13, is now the lowest of these three.[3]

With the number of young people entering their reproductive years now falling steadily in both the United States and Japan, it is possible to envisage a time in the not-too-distant future when births and deaths will come into balance, as they have in so much of Europe. In both countries this will be hastened by the aging of the population and the consequent increase in death rates. The situation is somewhat less clear for the Soviet Union, which has a highly fertile, rapidly expanding Asian minority. The moderate overall Soviet growth rate embraces both European republics where population growth has ceased and Asian republics where it expands at typical Third World rates. Indeed, some of the Soviet republics in Asia have higher birth rates than some demographically progressive states in India.[4] Overall, nevertheless, barring any unexpected rises in fertility, it is only a matter of time until natural population growth comes to a halt in these three countries, since each has a net reproductive rate well below the replacement rate of 2.1.

RAPID NATIONAL FERTILITY DECLINES

The demographic transition, the shift from high mortality and high fertility to low rates of both, has historically been a slow process. In Western Europe death rates and birth rates fell gradually over a few centuries. In countries now in the early stages of modernization, the start of the transition has been much faster. The precipitous decline in mortality of roughly a generation ago was often compressed into a decade or so and usually occurred before the decline in fertility had begun. This produced record population increases against a backdrop of insufficient, inequitably distributed resources. The result was historically unprecedented growth in human numbers, commonly exceeding 3 percent per year. These rates underline the urgency of completing the last phase of the demographic transition—the decline in fertility—as rapidly as possible. But reducing births is a much more complex undertaking than reducing deaths. Mortality rates can be brought down quickly through public health measures and childhood vaccination programs, whereas the reduction in births requires changes in values that must then translate into changes in reproductive behavior.

As of the mid-eighties hope on this front springs not so much from the broad global trends as from the sharp reduction in fertility in countries that represent a wide cross section of cultures, religions, and political systems. This diversity is evident in the four countries in the Western Hemisphere that have the lowest crude birth rates—Cuba (14), Canada (15), the United States (16), and Barbados (17).[5] It would be hard to find two national cultures more similar than the United States and Canada, so their similar fertility levels are not surprising, but the contrasts between them and the two Caribbean island cultures are striking.

The four developing countries in Asia, on the other hand, that were among the first to lower their birth rates—Hong Kong (17), Singapore (17), Taiwan (23), and South Korea (25)—are rather homogenous in that all are predominantly Sinitic (Chinese-based or -related) cultures.[6] In addition to their common or similar ethnic backgrounds, all four are economically vigorous societies moving rapidly along the path to modernization. And they all have had well-designed family planning programs, with contraceptive services widely available, for at least a decade and a half.

In 1979 China became the first country to launch a one-child family program.

Perhaps the most impressive family planning achievement in the developing world has occurred in China. Family planning was periodically caught up in the ideological crosscurrents of the Chinese communist party from 1949 until the early seventies, but since that time a sustained national effort has been under way to reduce births. By the mid-seventies the Chinese leadership was urging all couples to stop at two children, and in 1979 China became the first country to launch a one-child family program.

By 1980 China had lowered its crude birth rate to 20, an achievement many thought impossible in such a large country still at an early stage of economic development. Although the 1982 census showed a slightly higher birth rate of 21, this does not diminish the success embodied in China's remarkable reduction in fertility from 34 to 20 in only a decade. This precipitous decline closely parallels that in Japan from 1948 to 1958, when the birth rate fell 47 percent, from 34 to 18.[7]

China's family planning program is distinctive in several ways. To begin with, the national leadership has been deeply involved in designing and supporting the program. More than most countries, China has fostered public discussion of the population problem and particularly the effect that continuing growth has on future living standards. As population policy was integrated into overall economic planning, it led in the late seventies to the establishment of birth quotas. The overall plan aimed to ensure that targets for raising living standards were met; couples who had no children were given priority in the quota allocation. Once births were allocated to people at the production-team level, peer pressure played an important role in assuring compliance. To even consider such an ambitious birth control program requires, of course, the ready availability of family planning services, including abortion.

From birth planning it was a relatively small step to the provision of economic incentives to couples who would agree to have only one child. The one-child family campaign was not introduced because China's leaders were enamored with the concept per se, but because the buildup in population pressure left few alternatives. Gaining social acceptance of this concept is not easy in a society where large families are traditional and where there is still a strong preference for sons, particularly in the countryside. This unprecedented policy initiative puts China one step ahead of other Third World countries in trying to halt population growth.

On a smaller scale, neighboring Thailand's reduction of fertility has also been impressive. Its estimated crude birth rate of 26 is not yet as low as China's but it apparently started from a higher level

Table 2-4. Thailand: Share of Married Women Practicing Contraception, 1970–81

Year	Percent
1970	14
1975	37
1979	50
1981	58

SOURCE: *International Family Planning Perspectives*, September 1980 and June 1982.

in 1970. Data on annual birth rates are not available in Thailand, but various fertility surveys taken from 1970 onward have measured contraceptive usage. The proportion of married Thai women of reproductive age who were using contraceptives went from 14 percent in 1970 to nearly 60 percent in 1981, a level approaching that in industrial societies.[8] (See Table 2-4.)

In 1983, Thailand's birth rate was 26 —only one point higher than that of South Korea, which launched its family planning program many years earlier. Indeed, it was roughly the same as the U.S. rate immediately after World War II. Thailand's achievement is all the more laudable because its reproductive revolution has preceded widespread economic development. Central to its success is a public education program that emphasizes both the economic and social advantages of small families and the ready availability of contraceptive services. Its vigorous family planning program is credited with perhaps 80 percent of the national fertility decline since 1970. Behind this imaginative program is Mechai Viravaidya, the innovative and charismatic head of the family planning group.[9]

Analysts of the Thai fertility decline associate the rapid change in reproductive attitudes and behavior with the high degree of social and economic independence of women. The influence of Buddhism, which does not restrict con-

traception and is not particularly pronatalist, may also contribute to the ready
acceptance of family planning. And Buddhism emphasizes individual responsibility, which may have created a social
environment particularly receptive to a
progressive family planning program.

One of the most rapid fertility declines
on record has occurred in Cuba since the
mid-sixties. The country's 1983 crude
birth rate of 14 per 1,000, lower than
that of the United States, is all the more
remarkable because it was not the result
of a concerted national program to
lower fertility and curb population
growth. This recent birth rate decline
should be seen, however, in historical
perspective, since Cuba, along with Uru-
guay and Argentina, experienced a gradual decline in birth rates in the early
decades of the twentieth century. At the
time of the Castro takeover in 1959 the
birth rate was 28, already well below
those of most of Latin America.

One of the early actions of the new
government was to begin enforcing the
rather restrictive abortion law that was
already on the books. This pushed birth
rates up sharply, to over 35 in 1963. (See
Figure 2-1.) In 1964, the interpretation

of the restrictive abortion law was
relaxed and, abetted by widespread social gains for women and broad-based
improvements in health care services,
the birth rate began a precipitous decline that continued for the next 16
years. By 1980 it had fallen to 14. Although the birth rate had been more
than halved, the population growth rate
had been cut by some two-thirds, to less
than 1 percent per year.[10]

After China, the most populous Third
World country to reduce its fertility
sharply is Indonesia. Until the late sixties
Indonesia was a pronatalist country. Its
only population program was one of
transmigration from densely populated
Java to the sparsely populated outer islands. After years of struggling at great
cost to move Javanese to these territories, and discovering that the resettle-
ment flow was a mere trickle compared
with the torrent of births, the Indonesian
Government shifted its attention to family planning.

Indonesia's national family planning
program was launched in 1969. By 1976,
when the World Fertility Survey conducted a study there, fertility had fallen
substantially in some regions—as much
as 12 percent in West Java to 34 percent
in Bali. Indonesia's family planning program has been distinguished by strong
government support and a highly ac-
claimed local approach that goes far beyond the more traditional clinic system.
The direct involvement of the local village leaders as motivators, field workers,
and even contraceptive distributors has
been central to the program's success.
By 1983 Indonesia's birth rate had fallen
to 32 and its population growth rate was
reportedly 1.7 percent per year, well
below the nearly 3 percent that existed
before the program began.[11]

Another Latin American country—
Mexico—is the site of one of the most
recent fertility reductions in a major
Third World country. Prior to 1972 the

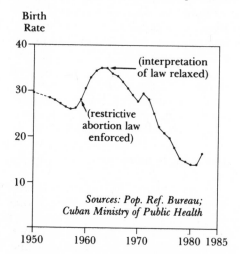

Figure 2-1. Cuba's Crude Birth Rate, 1950-82

official Mexican policy was like Indonesia's—the more people the better. President Echeverria's announcement in 1972 that Mexico would launch a family planning program came as a surprise. At that time Mexico's crude birth rate was 44 and its overall population growth rate was 3.5 percent annually—one of the highest in the world. Within a decade the birth rate dropped to 32. Combined with a death rate of 7, this still resulted in a population growth rate of 2.5 percent, which was far too rapid. And there are remote rural areas where family planning services are not yet available. Nonetheless the progress of a decade indicates that Mexico has at least set the stage for a continuing decline in fertility. The challenge now will be limiting births over the rest of this century among the enormous number of young people entering their reproductive years as a result of the extraordinarily high birth rate before the mid-seventies.[12]

The countries that have achieved rapid national fertility declines represent a wide variety of cultures. The common denominators are a committed leadership and locally designed programs. Experience to date shows a broad popular interest in planning families and a willingness, in some cases an eagerness, to take advantage of services when they become available. Each country desiring to reduce fertility must of course design its own program, one that is responsive to its values, traditions, and needs.

POPULATION VERSUS ECONOMIC GROWTH

Overall, global economic growth during the third quarter of this century was more than double that of population. As

will be noted in Chapter 3, this growth was closely tied to an abundance of cheap oil. With the 1973 oil price hike, economic growth began to slow. With the 1979 increase it slowed further. The following four years the world economy expanded less than 2 percent per year. Although these four years are not in themselves enough to constitute a trend, the less favorable resource conditions that contributed to the slower growth during this time may also lead to slow growth over the long term.

The *Wall Street Journal,* in a survey of European economic analysts at the end of 1982, reported that many expect the prolonged recession of the early eighties to become permanent. In contrast to earlier recessions, when recovery translated into a 4–6 percent growth rate, the *Journal* noted that these analysts saw European recovery from the current recession in terms of a 1–2 percent rate.[13]

For parts of the Third World, prospects are even grimmer. A 1983 assessment of Africa's future by the Economic Commission for Africa reported that "the historical trend scenario is almost a nightmare." It continued: "The potential population explosion would have tremendous repercussions on the region's physical resources such as land. . . . At the national level, the socio-economic conditions would be characterized by a degradation of the very essence of human dignity. The rural population . . . will face an almost disastrous situation of land scarcity whereby whole families would have to subsist on a mere hectare of land." A World Bank analysis of Africa's economic outlook described the Commission's assessment as "graphic but realistic."[14]

Given the emerging constraints on growth, particularly in basic sectors such as food and energy, the world is going to have great difficulty resuming the rapid economic growth of the 1950–73 period. Expanding global economic output even by an average of 2 percent per year may tax the skills of economic policymakers. Countries with rapid population growth may thus face declines in living standards—unless they quickly reduce their birth rates.

Slower economic growth will have an impact everywhere, but the effect will vary widely according to national population growth rates. For West Germany or Belgium, which have attained zero population growth, a 2 percent rate of annual economic growth will still raise incomes 2 percent each year. For countries such as Kenya and Ecuador, whose numbers expand at more than 3 percent per year, a 2 percent economic growth rate will produce steady declines in incomes and living standards.

If an economic growth rate of 2 percent per year becomes the new norm, then nearly half the world's people—those living in countries with annual population growth rates of 2 percent or more—face possible income stagnation or decline. Countries where the threat of falling income is greatest are those whose numbers grow at 3 percent or more per year. These 34 countries, almost all in Africa, the Middle East, and Central America, have a combined population of 394 million.[15]

Within this group, countries with exportable surpluses of oil may be tempted to neglect population policy, with the result that their populations will continue to multiply rapidly, sustained by the imported resources that petroleum buys. Over the long term, however, as oil reserves dwindle and the exportable surplus disappears, they may find themselves with populations that far exceed the carrying capacity of local resources. Countries such as Iran and Nigeria, where oil production and exports have already peaked, illustrate well the risks that oil-producing countries with rapidly expanding populations face over the long term. Situations like these have the

greatest long-term potential for massive human suffering.

Unfortunately, economic growth has already fallen behind population growth in many countries. The World Bank reports that per capita GNP declined in 18 countries from 1970 to 1979. (See Table 2-5.) In a few cases this was caused by disruption of economic activity associated with political conflicts and instability, but in the great majority population growth simply outstripped that of economic output.

Central to the decline in per capita income during the seventies in many of the countries in Africa, a largely rural continent, was the decade-long decline in per capita food production. The growth in

Table 2-5. Countries Experiencing a Decline in Per Capita Income, 1970–79

Country	Population	Annual Rate of Decline
	(million)	(percent)
Angola	6.9	−9.6
Bhutan	1.3	−0.1
Chad	4.4	−2.4
Congo	1.5	−0.2
Ghana	11.3	−3.0
Jamaica	2.2	−3.7
Libya	2.9	−1.6
Madagascar	8.5	−2.5
Mauritania	1.6	−0.7
Mozambique	10.2	−5.3
Nicaragua	2.6	−1.6
Niger	5.2	−1.2
Sierra Leone	3.4	−1.2
Uganda	12.8	−3.5
Upper Volta	5.6	−1.2
Zaire	27.5	−2.6
Zambia	5.6	−1.9
Zimbabwe	7.1	−1.7
Total	120.6	

SOURCE: World Bank, *1981 World Bank Atlas* (Washington, D.C.: 1982).

Africa's food supply compares favorably with that for the world as a whole, but its increase in human numbers is far more rapid. Plagued by the fastest population growth of any continent in history, as well as by widespread soil erosion and desertification, Africa's food production per person has fallen 11 percent since 1970.[16]

Given the prevailing economic conditions of the early eighties, the ranks of the 18 countries with declining per capita GNP are likely to swell dramatically. In a report published in late 1981 the World Bank projected a decline in the average income of 187 million people in 24 low-income countries in sub-Saharan Africa. This is the first time the World Bank has projected a decline in living standards for a major region of the world.[17]

As the growth in the production of material goods and services slows, the distribution issue must be viewed against a new backdrop, one unfamiliar to this generation. With the changing growth prospect, pressure to reformulate economic and social policies with basic human needs in mind will no doubt increase. This task will be far more difficult than it was in the era of rapid economic growth, with its underlying belief that a rising tide raises all ships. As economist Herman Daly has perceptively observed, turning our focus to meeting basic human needs will "make fewer demands on our environmental resources, but much greater demands on our moral resources."[18]

POPULATION/RESOURCE PROJECTIONS

Existing projections of population and resources do not provide a solid foundation for formulating intelligent population policies. U.N. projections show world population continuing to grow until it reaches 11 billion before leveling off a century or so hence.[19] These population figures are the product of two sets of assumptions—one explicit and one implicit. The explicit assumptions are demographic. They include country-by-country assumptions about future fertility levels, sex ratios, life expectancies, and numerous other demographic variables. If these explicit assumptions hold, the projected increases in world population will materialize.

Africa's food production per person has fallen 11 percent since 1970.

But population growth does not occur in a vacuum. Current projections of world population are based on the implicit assumption that the energy, food, and other natural resources required to support human life are going to be as readily available in the future as they have been in the past. They assume that the production of the major biological support systems—fisheries, forests, grasslands, and croplands—that satisfy basic human needs for food, shelter, and clothing will continue to expand along with population. It is perhaps unfortunate that population projections are done by demographers on their own. Projections by an interdisciplinary team of analysts including, for example, agronomists, economists, and ecologists would be more realistic since population growth cannot be divorced from the carrying capacity of local biological systems. Continuing increases in human population on the one hand and the progressive deterioration of life-support systems on the other are not compatible over the long term.

The unreality of current population projections can be seen in the numbers put forth for individual countries. According to the World Bank, which uses slightly lower projections than the U.N. medium-level ones, the growth ahead for some countries can only be described as phenomenal. India is projected to add more than another billion people to its 1983 population of 730 million before stabilizing at 1.84 billion, while neighboring Bangladesh and Pakistan could increase from 96 million each at present to 430 million and 411 million respectively. If these three countries grow as projected, the Indian subcontinent would be home to 2.7 billion people, more than the entire world population in 1950. The 84 million Nigerians of today are projected to increase to 623 million, more people than now live in all of Africa. Mexico would grow from 76 million to 215 million people, roughly the size of the current U.S. population. And the populations of several Central American countries—El Salvador, Guatemala, and Nicaragua—would triple before stabilizing.[20] Clearly, national and global resources would be stretched to the breaking point well before increases of this size materialize.

Many of the economic stresses afflicting the world economy during the mid-eighties have their origins in changing population/resource trends. When world population reached the three billion mark in 1960, the per capita production of almost every major commodity was still increasing. But when world population moved toward four billion, demands began to approach the sustainable yield of many biological support systems: The world harvest of forest products began to fall behind population growth; 20 years of rapid growth in the world fish catch came to an end; and per capita growth in world beef output

halted in 1976. World production of oil, the leading energy resource, peaked in 1979. The growth in world grain production, which had been steadily outdistancing population since mid-century, has barely kept pace with population growth since 1973. In North America food production has continued to outstrip population growth. But in Africa, as mentioned earlier, the reverse is true. Since 1970 per capita food production there has been falling by some 1 percent per year.[21]

Faced with this emerging picture of a new population/resource balance, President Carter was frustrated by the inability of U.S. Government agencies to provide coherent sets of projections in important areas such as energy, water, and food. This lack of global foresight capability led him to launch the Global 2000 study in 1977. Undertaken by the U.S. Council on Environmental Quality and the Department of State in cooperation with 17 specialized government departments and agencies, the study examined, among other things, the consequences of the projected increases in world population.

The Global 2000 study team discovered numerous inconsistencies among government projections and policies. In assembling sector forecasts from the various agencies, overlapping resource claims came to light. The Department of Agriculture, for example, was incorporating in its projections water that the Department of Energy was expecting to use to launch synfuels projects. The risk of such a lack of coherency in planning is that it can lead to resource scarcities, as in the case of water, or to excess capacity, as in the case of electrical generation. In either case resources are wasted.

The *Global 2000 Report,* the end product of this first effort to project global economic, environment, and resource trends, observed in an oft-quoted conclusion that "barring revolutionary advances in technology, life for most people on earth will be more precarious in 2000 than it is now—unless the nations of the world act decisively to alter current trends." Five years have passed since the study went to press. Unfortunately, life is more difficult now for many of the world's people than it was then.[22]

The only other comprehensive attempt to project world trends to the end of the century was undertaken in the mid-seventies by the United Nations. Directed by economist Wassily Leontief, it foresaw a rosy economic future for the world. The weakness of this undertaking was that it was done almost entirely by economists and lacked a solid interdisciplinary foundation. The result was pie-in-the-sky projections and misleading conclusions about where the world was headed. For example, the U.N. study postulated for the remainder of this century an average agricultural growth rate in the developing world of 5.3 percent, a rate with little foundation in either the historical experience of developed countries or in current Third World realities. The authors noted that soil erosion would affect future food production, but because data was sketchy they chose simply to ignore it. If agronomists had been involved in the project they could at least have estimated erosion's impact on future productivity, thus making the projections more realistic and useful.[23]

Concerned with the declines in per capita production of the basic resources that underpin the global economy, several individual countries decided to examine the implications of the Global 2000 study for their own national policies. Countries as varied as Japan, Mexico, and West Germany have expressed interest in the "Global 2000" approach. China, well aware of indigenous resource constraints, is undertaking an ambitious China 2000 study. Japan has organized a Year 2000 Committee to focus on the implications of the changing global resource outlook for the Japanese economy.[24] The United States, unfortunately, has failed to follow through on *Global 2000*. The result has been an international vacuum as the dominant world economy and traditional world leader on such matters sits on the sidelines, failing to provide leadership on this critical complex of issues.

One of the first countries to examine systematically the long-term population/resource balance was China. As part of the post-Mao reassessment, Chinese leaders projected future population size based on the assumption that couples would have only two children. Even under this scenario, given the country's youthful age structure China would add another 300 or 400 million people before population growth ceased. After relating these projections to the availability of land, water, energy, and other basic resources and to the capacity of the economy to provide jobs, the leadership concluded that they had no choice but to press for a one-child family lest they jeopardize their hard-earned gains in living standards.[25]

Elizabeth Croll, China scholar at Oxford University, observes that Beijing had concluded that "unless the population to be fed, housed and clothed is reduced, the goals of any development strategy in China are bound to fail."[26] The principal difference between China and other densely populated developing countries such as Bangladesh, India, Egypt, Nigeria, and Mexico may be that the Chinese have had the courage and the foresight to make these projections and to translate their findings into public policy. If others took a serious look at future population/resource balances, they too might well decide that they should press for a one-child family.

NEW POPULATION INITIATIVES

As world population moves toward five billion, the per capita production of many basic commodities is falling. The effort to raise incomes and living standards is faltering in many countries, particularly where population is growing most rapidly. The fall in global economic growth from over 4 percent annually to 2 percent is dividing the world into two groups: those where economic growth exceeds population growth, and those where it does not. For one group, living standards are rising. For the other they are falling. One group can hope that the future will be better than the present. In the other, hope is turning to despair.

The fall in per capita incomes is occurring, almost without exception, in countries that have given little attention to the human side of the population/resources equation. The attention of political leaders and the allocation of budgetary resources have both focused almost entirely on the supply side, on expanding output. One consequence of this imbalance is that more and more of the growth in output is required to satisfy the increase in population, with little remaining for improvements in per capita consumption.

Where population growth is rapid, changing economic circumstances call for new population policies. Many developing countries are stalled in the middle of the demographic transition discussed earlier. If economic growth remains slow, barely keeping pace with population growth or even falling behind it, then high-fertility developing countries cannot count on economic improvements to reduce births as they did in the industrial countries. Fortunately, recent experience has shown that countries with broad-based but inexpensive health

care systems and well-designed family planning programs that encourage small families can bring fertility down even without the widespread economic gains that characterized the demographic transition in the industrial societies.[27]

Making family planning services universally available is the very first step that all countries should take. Beyond helping to curb population by preventing unwanted births, it makes people aware that they can control their fertility, in effect creating its own demand. And because family planning leads to better spacing of births, it lowers infant mortality, which in turn fosters lower fertility. Although each country represented at the U.N. Conference on World Population in Bucharest in 1974 agreed that access to family planning services was a basic human right, not all governments have followed through. As a result, an estimated one-third of all couples still go to bed unprotected from unplanned pregnancy.[28]

Essential though family planning services are, they are not in themselves sufficient. Data from the World Fertility Survey show the desired family size in many countries is still four or five children. Although this is lower than it was just a few years ago, in some countries having this many children would lead to vast population gains that would steadily reduce living standards.[29] Reducing fertility to the level circumstances call for requires public education programs that inform people about the future relationship between population and resources and about the economic consequences of continuing on the current demographic path. More projections like those done in Beijing are needed. In traditional countries such as China, childbearing decisions are still influenced by a parental desire to be looked after in old age. By emphasizing future population/resource relationships, government officials can shift parents' considerations of childbearing decisions from their own well-being to that of their children.

For most Third World countries, however, the provision of family planning services and public education programs based on projections will not slow population growth quickly enough to avoid a decline in living standards. Governments in these countries will need to reorient economic and social policies to lower fertility further. Traditionally, government policies that affected population growth encouraged large families. In most countries, for example, income tax deductions and maternity leaves are available without restriction. Now some countries are beginning to alter these long-standing policies. For example, South Korea and Pakistan limit income tax deductions to two children. Tanzania, Sri Lanka, and Nepal have gone even further and entirely eliminated tax deductions for dependent children.[30]

Several governments restrict maternity benefits. In the Philippines, they are limited to the first four births; in Ghana, Hong Kong, and Malaysia, to three; and in South Korea, even more stringent, to only two. Tanzania, adapting this general approach to African family planning programs' emphasis on child spacing, provides paid maternity leave to employed women only once every three years.[31]

Some governments use access to education and to public housing or to low-interest loans for the purchase of housing as a carrot to encourage small families. In China, the certificate awarded to couples who pledge to have only one child entitles them to preferred access to schooling for that child. South Korean government employees who stop at two can deduct their educational expenditures from income tax. In Singapore, having no more than two children gives couples preferred access to housing, much of which is government-constructed.[32]

Other countries have designed reward systems to encourage sterilization or the use of contraceptives. India, for example, was the first government to provide small, one-time payments to men and women who were sterilized. In some countries such payments are regarded more as compensation for lost wages and travel costs than as incentives per se. The Indian payments in 1983 ranged from $11–13, for example, roughly two weeks' wages for rural laborers. In Bangladesh, those sterilized receive new clothing—a sari for women and a lungi for men—plus travel-cost reimbursement.[33]

Experience shows that such payments do make sterilization more popular. In a 1983 Worldwatch Paper, Judith Jacobsen noted that "in Sri Lanka, the number of sterilizations performed in government family planning programs increased when payments were first introduced in January 1980. Nine months later, when payments were increased fivefold to match those offered on private estates, sterilization clinics were swamped. The number of sterilizations performed at one clinic increased from 6 to 35 a day after the introduction of the payment and rose to 150 a day after the increase."[34]

Some countries have begun to experiment with community incentives. A community that achieves certain family planning goals, either measured in terms of contraceptive usage or in reduction in births, becomes eligible for a new school, a village well, a community irrigation pump, or even a television set. This approach, being tried in Thailand and Indonesia, has the advantage of mobilizing peer pressure to limit family size.[35]

There is an urgent need for data to be gathered regularly in this vital area, to permit continuing evaluations of progress and reports to the public. The collection and monthly publication of birth rates would help measure progress on this critical front, much as is now the case with employment, inflation, or the balance of payments. It would also contribute to public awareness of the need to reduce family size and halt population growth.

In many countries, reducing the birth rate rapidly enough to avoid a decline in living standards will require a Herculean effort and the constant attention of national political leaders. Administratively, successful implementation of population programs may require that responsibility for them be escalated from a division in the health ministry, where it commonly resides, to a cabinet-level committee that regularly reviews the situation. Unorthodox though this may be, it is the level of attention befitting the gravity of the issue.

Among the Third World countries that have successfully reduced fertility, no two approaches are identical. But all have involved national leaders' commitment to reduce fertility, the widespread availability of family planning services, and a public education program that links population growth to the long-term social interest as well as to benefits for individual families. Several of the more successful countries have often used some combination of economic incentives or disincentives to encourage small families.

Governments will be forced to settle differences between private interests, sometimes better served by larger families, and the public or social interest, which is invariably better served by smaller families. Reconciling these differences can be extraordinarily complex and politically costly. Failure, however, could be catastrophic. The issue is how —not whether—population growth will eventually be slowed. Will it be humanely, through foresight and leadership, or will living standards deteriorate until death rates begin to rise? The latter would certainly reestablish a population equilibrium of sorts, but it would be through high birth and death rates, rather than the low birth and death rates characteristic of countries that have completed the demographic transition.

In an age of slower economic growth, improvements in living standards may depend more on the skills of family planners than on those of economic planners. As the outlines of the new economic era become more visible, population policy seems assured a high place on national political agendas. Too many governments have delayed facing the issue for too long. When they belatedly do so, they may discover, as China has, that circumstances force them to press for a one-child family.

3

Reducing Dependence on Oil

Lester R. Brown

If the 7 percent annual growth in global oil consumption that prevailed from 1950 to 1973 had continued, the world would have increased oil use from 20.4 billion barrels in 1973 to just over 40 billion barrels in 1983. At such a consumption level unprecedented adjustments would be required, adjustments that would place great pressure on the international economic system. But this did not happen, because a group of preindustrial, oil-exporting countries that controlled the lion's share of world oil exports decided in late 1973 that oil was vastly underpriced. To remedy this, they quadrupled its price, sending economic shock waves through the world economy and making OPEC a household word.

The 1973 oil price adjustment checked the runaway consumption trend, but it was the 1979 increase that reversed it. As a result of the two price jolts, world oil consumption in 1983 totaled only 20 billion barrels, not the 40 billion barrels it might have been.[1]

Despite late twentieth century advances in mathematics and widespread access to computers, political leaders and other key economic decision-makers have a dangerously deficient understanding of exponential growth. If the oil consumption trend of the century's third quarter had continued through the fourth, by the year 2000 oil consumption would have reached 127 billion barrels. Proven reserves would have been used up by 1990 and before 2005 all ultimately recoverable reserves would have been exhausted.[2]

By the mid-seventies oil's low cost, mobility, and versatility had made it the fuel of choice everywhere. Countries that did not produce oil imported it. Although it had become the principal energy source powering the world economy, and although the growing worldwide dependence on it was patently unsustainable, few seemed to notice or take heed. In the United States, automobiles were growing larger each year and the number of miles they could travel per gallon was dropping ever lower. Projections of the world auto market through the year 2000 that were done before 1979 showed the industry easily doubling in size, erroneously assuming that the growth in oil consumption could continue indefinitely.[3]

In retrospect, the world may be heavily indebted to OPEC (the Organization of Petroleum Exporting Countries) for having raised the price of oil. It is easy to criticize the group in the short run, especially the failure of cash-surplus countries to assist more vigorously the poorest oil-importing countries. And it would be naive to overlook the self-interest involved in OPEC's move to obtain a better price for the oil of its members and stretch out remaining reserves. But its oil pricing policy is nonetheless socially constructive on the whole. With reserves shrinking, a socially responsible policy would raise prices just fast enough to encourage the conservation and development of alternative energy sources needed to minimize disruption in the transition to the post-petroleum era.

As of 1984, it is hard to argue that the price of oil began rising soon enough to make this smooth transition possible. Prices of petroleum products like gasoline are still controlled or subsidized in too many countries, slowing the adjustments that energy consumers can make. Efforts by governments to partly offset the price rise notwithstanding, OPEC's role in raising oil prices will almost certainly be vindicated over time.

SUCCESS STORIES

Since 1979 world oil consumption has fallen 3.3 billion barrels, a 14 percent drop. (See Table 3-1.) There is a distinct possibility that the 22.9 billion barrels of

Table 3-1. World Oil Consumption, Total and Per Capita, 1950–83

Year	Total	Per Capita
	(billion barrels)	(barrels)
1950	3.9	1.56
1955	5.5	2.01
1960	7.8	2.58
1965	11.4	3.40
1970	16.7	4.54
1971	17.7	4.72
1972	18.7	4.91
1973	20.4	5.26
1974	19.8	5.00
1975	19.3	4.80
1976	21.2	5.16
1977	22.2	5.32
1978	23.0	5.39
1979	23.8	5.48
1980	23.1	5.22
1981	22.1	4.91
1982	21.5	4.70
1983	20.5	4.40

SOURCES: American Petroleum Institute, *Basic Petroleum Data Book* (Washington, D.C.: 1983); "Mid-year Review and Forecast," *Oil and Gas Journal*, July 25, 1983; Worldwatch Institute estimates.

oil produced in 1979 will never again be matched. If so, historians looking back from the twenty-first century will almost certainly see that year as a hinge point in economic history, a year that signaled not only the eventual fading of the age of oil, but the beginning of the post-petroleum age as well.

Given the growth in world population since mid-century, the rise in per capita oil consumption was somewhat less than that of total consumption. Between 1950 and 1979 the average individual's use of oil climbed from 1.56 barrels each year to 5.48 barrels, a gain of nearly fourfold. Since 1979, however, with world oil consumption declining while the number of people continued to increase, the per capita decline has been precipitous. Falling nearly 20 percent in four years, it has affected every facet of human existence from diets to transportation. The substantial adjustments of the last few years will continue for decades to come.

The 14 percent drop in world oil consumption since 1979 is impressive, but some countries have contributed far more to the decline than others. (See Table 3-2.) In fact, a few are still expanding their use of oil. Among the larger economies, the leading Western industrial countries and Japan have been the most successful in reducing their oil dependence. The centrally planned economies have not done as well. The Soviet Union is the only major industrial country that, try as it might, has been unable to reduce oil use.

In retrospect, the world may be heavily indebted to OPEC for having raised the price of oil.

Somewhat surprisingly, the country with the best record in reducing oil consumption is the United Kingdom, the only major Western industrial country that exports oil. U.K. oil use peaked in 1973 at 840 million barrels and turned downward, falling to 606 million barrels in 1982, 28 percent below its high. The

Table 3-2. Petroleum Consumption in Major Countries, 1960–82[1]

Year	United States	United Kingdom	France	West Germany	Japan	Soviet Union	China	India	Brazil	Mexico
				(million barrels)						
1960	3,577	343	204	230	241	869	62	60	99	110
1965	4,201	544	398	588	635	1,318	84	91	120	124
1970	5,366	763	690	887	1,405	1,934	226	134	186	182
1971	5,522	763	748	953	1,526	2,427	288	155	204	190
1972	5,975	818	814	1,007	1,591	2,226	232	154	237	204
1973	6,318	**840**	**883**	1,066	1,851	2,398	409	166	281	223
1974	6,077	781	825	953	1,810	2,559	504	168	303	245
1975	5,957	683	781	916	1,642	2,727	577	182	318	270
1976	6,373	679	832	989	1,741	2,792	613	188	354	292
1977	6,727	686	814	1,037	1,909	2,986	668	201	369	307
1978	**6,880**	675	792	1,113	1,876	3,092	661	225	383	336
1979	6,756	704	872	**1,121**	**2,000**	3,132	**675**	**241**	**431**	329
1980	6,277	632	825	989	1,810	**3,252**	668	235	423	445
1981	5,826	585	725	891	1,680		638		389	485
1982	5,567	606	712	884	1,565					**529**
Fall From Peak (%)	−19	−28	−19	−21	−22		−5	−2		−10

SOURCES: U.S. Department of Energy, Energy Information Administration, *International Petroleum Annual* (Washington, D.C.: various years) and *1981 International Energy Annual* (Washington, D.C.: 1982); 1981–82 data are preliminary estimates by Worldwatch Institute.   [1]Peak year in bold.

other major Western industrial countries have achieved remarkably similar reductions, ranging from 19 percent in the United States and France to 22 percent in Japan. Except for France, where consumption turned downward right after 1973, the peak year was 1978 or 1979.

Among the developing countries trends vary. China, an oil exporter, began reducing oil consumption in 1980; India, an importer, has increased its consumption steadily for the past two decades. Even since the 1973 price increase India's use of petroleum has risen over 40 percent. Although per capita oil use in India is only a small fraction of that in industrial societies, the wisdom of fostering this growing dependence on oil, a dwindling resource, is questionable.[4]

The consumption trends of the two major Latin American countries also contrast. Brazil, which is an oil importer, has reduced its use sharply since 1979. Indeed, from 1979 to 1981 consumption fell 10 percent. Oil-exporting Mexico, meanwhile, consumes more and more petroleum. In 1982 it burned an almost unbelievable 59 percent more oil than in 1979.[5] Even though Mexico exports more oil than it consumes, there are doubts about the wisdom of continuing to raise its dependence on oil given the certain knowledge that its reserves will be largely depleted within this generation.

The 14 percent fall in world oil consumption between 1979 and 1983 was achieved partly by substituting energy from other sources for oil and partly by using all forms of energy more efficiently. The relative contribution of substitution and conservation varies widely by country and by sector. In some cases dramatic falls have been achieved entirely as a result of conservation. In others they are the result of extensive substitution.

THE CONSERVATION CONTRIBUTION

Oil can be conserved in two ways—by using it more efficiently or by not doing certain things that consume oil. Insulation permits a building to be heated (and cooled) more efficiently. Keeping a kitchen list of needed groceries, on the other hand, and thus reducing the frequency of incidental auto trips to the grocery conserves oil by not doing something that uses it. In this case, organized information is substituted for gasoline.

In considering how to conserve oil, the world's transportation system, which depends heavily on petroleum, deserves careful attention. And within the transport sector, it is the automobile that dominates. (The future of the automobile is discussed in greater detail in Chapter 9.) Here it is efficiency that is the key, since, except for the Brazilian alcohol fuel program and the South African coal liquefaction program, there is little immediate practical scope for substituting other fuels for gasoline.

Recognizing this, nearly all industrial societies have established programs and goals to raise the fuel efficiency of automobiles. In 1978, the last year before the second price hike, automobiles coming off U.S. and Canadian assembly lines required half again as much fuel per mile as those being manufactured in France, Japan, Sweden, and West Germany. Standards set after that by the industrial countries with the largest auto fleets were designed to boost efficiency by one-tenth to one-third. With the two countries that were manufacturing the least fuel-efficient cars in 1978, namely the United States and Canada, setting the highest goals, there was a convergence in fuel efficiency standards among countries. (See Table 3-3.) Although the differences among countries will largely

Table 3-3. Fuel Efficiency in New Automobiles in Selected Industrial Countries, 1978 and Targets for 1985

Country	Gasoline Consumption		Projected Reduction in Fuel Use, 1978–85
	1978	1985	
	(kilometer per liter)		(percent)
Australia	8.5	11.8	−28
Canada	7.6	11.6	−34
France	12.2	13.7	−11
Japan	11.6[1]	12.8	− 9
Sweden	10.9[1]	12.0	−10
United Kingdom	10.0	11.0	− 9
United States	7.6	11.6	−34
West Germany	10.4	11.9	−12

[1]Data for 1979.

SOURCE: International Energy Agency, *World Energy Outlook* (Paris: Organisation for Economic Co-operation and Development, 1982).

disappear by 1985, the French and Japanese, whose 1978 cars were already the most fuel-efficient, should still maintain a narrow lead.

In 1973, American automobiles burned roughly half the gasoline consumed by the world fleet. Raising fuel efficiency in the United States is thus a key to reducing world dependence on petroleum. U.S. gasoline use peaked at 113 billion gallons in 1978; after three decades of continuous growth, consumption dropped some 13 percent within five years. Virtually all of this was due to conservation—a combination of improved mileage; changes in driving habits, including reduction of less essential driving and the formation of car pools; and the lowering of speed limits. In per capita terms the trend was even more striking, falling from 515 to 437 gallons between 1978 and 1982.[6] This 15 percent decline in gasoline use in a society thought to have a "love affair with the automobile" was not widely anticipated. And its impact spread far beyond the auto industry (as will be discussed in Chapter 9).

The second area in which conservation has played a major role in reducing the amount of oil used is heating. In the United States, the use of fuel to heat residential and commercial buildings has fallen dramatically, particularly since 1978. (See Figure 3-1.) In 1973 the United States used an average of 2.23 million barrels of oil daily for residential and commercial space heating. By 1982, the figure was 1.27 million barrels, a decline of 43 percent.[7] The bulk of this drop was due to conservation, but there

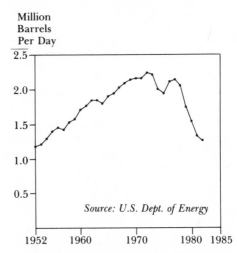

Million Barrels Per Day

Source: U.S. Dept. of Energy

Figure 3-1. U.S. Residential and Commercial Use of Petroleum, 1952-82

has been some substitution of other energy sources, particularly of natural gas and firewood in residential heating. Efficiency gains have largely stemmed from insulation, overall weatherizing, and the more efficient management of heating systems in large buildings.

Impressive though this gain is in the United States, it would have been even larger if the country had adopted stiff energy efficiency building codes like those introduced in France or Sweden during the late seventies. As with automobile efficiency, heating-fuel efficiency also increased in virtually all Western industrial countries.

Some gains in conservation can be made quickly—by reducing speed limits for automobiles, for example, or by turning down thermostats. Others involve the turnover of existing stock of automobiles, airplanes, or buildings, and take much longer. The automobile fleet turns over almost completely every 10–12 years, depending on the country and the durability of the cars. Housing stock changes very slowly, however—over decades or generations. Oftentimes retrofitting provides a way to shortcut this very slow turnover.

In the United States millions of homes switched from heating oil to wood between 1973 and 1983.

A similar situation exists in industry. Some oil efficiency gains can be made quickly by modest adjustments in processes, but others occur over time as equipment is replaced. If the fuel efficiency gains embodied in new equipment are great enough, the replacement of capital stock will accelerate.

Although using substitute, mainly renewable, fuels in developing countries seems the most realistic way to reduce oil use, opportunities for energy conservation may be at least as great as in the industrial world. A 1980 report from Energy/Development International concluded that "conservation, a subject not widely discussed in the context of third world energy policy, appears to be at least as promising as all the renewable technologies taken together in terms of its capacity to replace projected LDC (less developed country) oil demand."[8]

PETROLEUM SUBSTITUTES

While governments everywhere were launching energy conservation programs during the late seventies and early eighties, a combination of governmental mandates and market forces fostered a broad substitution of other fuels for oil. The substitute fuels, varying by country and even by region within countries, include the other fossil fuels (coal and natural gas), numerous renewable sources of energy, and nuclear power. In some sectors, such as electricity generation and heating, the substitution of other energy sources was easy; in others, notably transportation, it was difficult to say the least.

Perhaps the largest single fuel substitution was of coal for oil in the generation of electricity. This was a worldwide shift, driven largely by the wide price gap that opened up between the two fossil fuels as the world oil price climbed. After 1979, the energy-equivalent price of coal was only one-third that of oil. Even with additional expenditures on smokestack scrubbers by utilities, coal—invariably a dirtier fuel—was still far cheaper.[9]

The switch from oil to coal in electrical generation can be illustrated by the changes in the United States. After a steep, decade-long climb, interrupted only briefly after the 1973 oil price hike, U.S. oil consumption by electrical utilities peaked in 1978 at 1.74 million barrels per day. (See Figure 3-2.) By 1982, it had dropped 61 percent—to 680,000 barrels a day. Within four years utilities had cut oil use over a million barrels per day, accounting for roughly one-third of the overall 3 million barrel per day drop in U.S. oil consumption between 1978 and 1982. Since U.S. nuclear electrical generation increased only 2 percent during this period, nearly all the reduction in oil use came from the increased use of coal.[10]

To replace oil-generated electricity, countries have also been turning to hydroelectricity, nuclear power, and various renewable sources (which are discussed in more detail in Chapter 8). As the price of oil has climbed, the Third World has been particularly interested in hydropower as a source of additional electrical power. Strongly supported by the World Bank and other international agencies, the development of hydropower from both large- and small-scale projects has proceeded rapidly since 1973.[11]

The substitution of nuclear power for oil-generated electricity has been concentrated in a few industrial countries, namely those that were heavily dependent on this source of electricity and that had expanded their nuclear electrical generation capacity. Of the major industrial countries, only France and Japan satisfy both criteria. Nuclear electrical generation in West Germany, the United Kingdom, and the United States is expanding slowly and in the Soviet Union there is little substitution of nuclear electricity for oil. Even though the long-term prospect for nuclear power is not promising because of high costs (as discussed in Chapter 7), plants that have been under construction over the last 10–15 years have been coming on stream recently.[12]

A second major area of substitution has been that of wood for heating oil, particularly in residences. This has been most impressive in the United States, where millions of homes switched from heating oil to wood between 1973 and 1983 to take advantage of the lower fuel prices. A national survey in 1981 indicated that 17 million out of 79 million U.S. households relied on wood for part or all of their heating fuel. Of these, 6.5 million relied on wood exclusively. This shift, driven by economic considerations, is expected to continue for the foreseeable future, albeit at a slower pace.[13]

People are relying on wood more in developing countries as well, but for cooking rather than heating. As cities grew and as deforestation progressed in the Third World from the fifties through the seventies, consumers turned to kerosene as a cooking fuel. After the 1979 oil price hike, however, the price of kerosene climbed to over $1.00 a gallon almost everywhere. In Addis Ababa kerosene cost $1.20 in 1981; in Islamabad, $1.05; and in Santiago, $1.29. (See Table 3-4.)

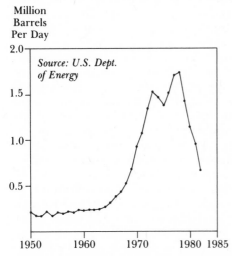

Million
Barrels
Per Day

Source: U.S. Dept. of Energy

Figure 3-2. Petroleum Used by U.S. Electrical Utilities, 1950-82

Table 3-4. Kerosene Prices in Selected Third World Cities, 1981

City	Price Per Gallon
	(dollars)
Mexico City	0.24
New Delhi	0.73
Buenos Aires	0.94
Islamabad	1.05
Bangkok	1.10
Accra	1.20
Addis Ababa	1.20
Nairobi	1.20
Singapore	1.21
Santiago	1.29
Manila	1.49
San Salvador	1.58

SOURCE: U.S. Department of Energy, Energy Information Administration, *1981 International Energy Annual* (Washington, D.C.: 1982).

With these prices, and with annual incomes that frequently average only $200 per person, the cost of kerosene has become prohibitive. The demand for firewood has consequently increased sharply. Where firewood has not been available, consumers have turned to cow dung and crop residues. One unfortunate consequence of this particular substitution for petroleum is that the use of straw, leaves, stems, and roots of agricultural plants for fuel reduces the soil's organic matter content, and hence its productivity.

World substitution of natural gas for oil is concentrated in the industrial sectors of the Soviet Union and in the countries that depend on it for fuel, including particularly Poland, Czechoslovakia, East Germany, and West Germany. Petroleum production is now declining in Romania, once a leading world oil exporter, and apparently leveling off in the Soviet Union, so the pressure to develop oil substitutes is mounting. With the world's largest reserves of natural gas,

the Soviet Union is not only turning to this fuel domestically but is also expanding rapidly its exports to both Eastern and Western Europe. Although the country currently has a rather remarkable balance in its national energy budget—each of the three major fossil fuels supplies roughly one-third of total energy consumption—natural gas is now moving into a dominant position. Recent Soviet efforts to produce more coal as a substitute for oil, a valued source of foreign exchange earnings, have not been very successful.[14]

Within the transportation sector, national successes in developing substitutes for oil-derived fuels have been rare. The numerous coal liquefaction, tar sands, and oil shale projects that were being discussed or launched in the late seventies (see Chapter 9) have largely been canceled, abandoned, or put on hold. There are, however, two notable exceptions to this generalization, as mentioned earlier—Brazil and South Africa.

Brazil, importing some 85 percent of its oil, launched a concerted effort in 1975 to produce alcohol from sugarcane. Using a wide range of government credits and other subsidies, the world's largest producer of sugar has made steady progress. In 1976 the country produced just over 1 million barrels of alcohol for both industrial and fuel uses, scarcely 1 percent of its annual gasoline consumption of 92 million barrels. (See Table 3-5.) By 1983, industrial alcohol production had exceeded 34 million barrels per year, and alcohol for fuel displaced 29 million barrels of oil, accounting for roughly one-fourth of automotive fuel consumption. With a heavy external debt, the pressures to reduce oil imports will continue in Brazil, giving the alcohol fuels program further impetus.[15]

South Africa, mindful of its political vulnerability at the international level,

Table 3-5. Brazil: Alcohol Share of Auto Fuel Consumption, 1970–82

Year	Alcohol	Gasoline	Total	Alcohol Share of Total
	(million barrels)			(percent)
1970	1.1	61.0	62.1	1.8
1971	1.5	66.8	68.3	2.2
1972	2.6	75.2	77.8	3.3
1973	1.8	87.6	89.4	2.0
1974	1.1	90.2	91.3	1.2
1975	1.1	92.0	93.1	1.2
1976	1.1	92.3	93.4	1.2
1977	4.0	88.7	92.7	4.3
1978	9.5	95.3	104.8	9.1
1979	13.9	98.6	112.5	12.4
1980	16.3	88.1	104.4	15.6
1981	19.1	83.3	102.4	18.7
1982	26.2	85.0	111.2	23.6
1983	28.6	—	—	—

SOURCES: 1970–79 from World Energy Industry, *The Energy Decade 1970–80* (Cambridge, Mass.: Ballinger Publishing Co., 1982); 1980–83 from *Journal of Commerce*, April 5, 1983, and Worldwatch Institute estimates.

has made a sustained effort over the last decade or so to increase its production of liquid fuel from coal. Highly successful in this regard, it is now obtaining roughly half its automotive fuel from coal.[16]

THE ROLE OF PRICE

The effect oil price rises have on demand is complicated by the impact of concerns with security of supply in both the immediate future and the long run. For some oil users, the sense of vulnerability during the seventies among those who depended heavily on oil led to a search for substitutes. For others, the dramatic oil price hikes spurred the reduction in oil use.

How fast the demand for a commodity falls as its price rises depends on what economists describe as the price elasticity of demand. This in turn is influenced by the availability of alternatives, including, in the case of oil, the cost of conservation. For petroleum, the tendency of "spot" or short-term prices to rise well above the contract price for oil during times of international shortages indicates the inelasticity of demand in the short run.

The price of oil over the longer term should be seen both in current and real prices—that is, the price after adjustment for inflation. In current terms, the postwar oil price reached a low of $1.28 a barrel in 1969 and a high of $33.47 in 1982. (See Table 3-6.) Yet this greatly overstates the real price change because this was a period of record worldwide inflation.

Using the International Monetary Fund's consumer price index (1975 equals 100) to adjust for inflation reveals a somewhat different trend. In real terms, the postwar price of oil bottomed in 1970 at $2.09 a barrel. It increased in six of the next ten years and reached a high of $16.48 in 1980—almost exactly eight times the price in 1970. Adjusting the price of oil for inflation reveals another interesting, often overlooked trend. Although current oil prices decreased only slightly from 1951 to 1969, the real price of oil fell by some 61 percent, providing an irresistible economic lure to all countries, both industrial and developing.

As a rule, oil-exporting countries have chosen not to raise the domestic price of petroleum products to keep pace with the world oil price. In effect, they are subsidizing their own consumption of oil with income from the much higher export prices. Among the more extreme cases is Venezuela, which had a retail gasoline price in 1981 of 13¢ a gallon.[17] Such a low price could lead to an exag-

Table 3-6. World Price of Petroleum, Current and Constant Dollars, 1951–83

Year	Current[1]	Constant[2]
	(dollars per barrel)	
1951	1.71	5.38
1955	1.93	5.64
1960	1.50	3.71
1965	1.33	2.71
1970	1.30	2.09
1971	1.65	2.50
1972	1.90	2.72
1973	2.70	3.53
1974	9.76	11.06
1975	10.72	10.72
1976	11.51	10.35
1977	12.40	10.01
1978	12.70	9.41
1979	16.97	11.25
1980	28.67	16.48
1981	32.50	16.38
1982	33.47	14.95
1983[3]	29.60	22.22

[1]For Saudi Arabian Crude priced at Ras Tanura. [2]Calculated using IMF index of consumer prices based on 1975 equalling 100.   [3]Preliminary.
SOURCE: International Monetary Fund, *Monthly Financial Statistics* (Washington, D.C.: monthly).

gerated dependence on the automobile, which would be to the country's detriment over the long term.

Within importing countries, the Carter administration's decision to remove controls from U.S. oil prices, announced in April 1979, was certainly the policy change with the greatest effect on world oil consumption. Oil price controls were to be phased out over 30 months, although the Regan administration removed the last of them in February 1981, thus compressing the process into less than two years. This undoubtedly dramatized the price rise, thus further encouraging conservation and substitution.

In Canada, too, the price of oil was below the world market. But in this case it was much more of a political issue, leaving the government reluctant to permit Canadian prices to climb too far. The Canadians have instead adopted a compromise that lets oil prices rise, but not to the world level.[18]

In several countries, the tax on gasoline now exceeds the cost of the fuel itself.

Some governments have used taxes to discourage consumption of petroleum products, particularly gasoline. In several countries, including Argentina, Belgium, the Netherlands, South Korea, and the United Kingdom, the tax on gasoline now exceeds the cost of the fuel itself. According to the latest international compilation, South Korea, where gas costs $4.00 a gallon, and Ghana, at $3.63 a gallon, were among the highest in the world. (See Table 3-7.)

In the Third World, where kerosene consumption often exceeds that of gasoline, governments have attempted to restrain the increase in prices. Because kerosene is the principal cooking fuel and thus a consumer staple for low-income groups, some governments (such as in Sri Lanka) have raised the price of gasoline well above the market price, using the added revenue to subsidize the price of kerosene.[19]

GOVERNMENT REGULATION AND INCENTIVES

Perhaps the easiest way to reduce dependence on oil would be to permit market

Table 3-7. Gasoline Prices in Selected Countries, July 1981

Country	Gasoline Retail Price	Gasoline Tax	Total Retail Price	Countries Where Tax Exceeds Price
	(dollars)			
South Korea	1.77	2.29	4.06	X
Ghana	3.57	0.06	3.63	
Belgium	1.27	1.44	2.71	X
United Kingdom	1.26	1.36	2.62	X
Sweden	1.39	1.22	2.61	
Japan	1.66	0.89[1]	2.55	
Kenya	1.71	0.84	2.55	
Netherlands	1.24	1.25	2.49	X
India	1.46	0.99[2]	2.45	
South Africa	1.26	0.94	2.20	
Ethiopia	1.95	0.23	2.18	
Argentina	0.52	0.77	1.29	X
United States	1.12	0.13	1.25	
Colombia	0.20	0.61	0.81	X
Mexico	0.29	0.15	0.44	
Venezuela	0.12	0.01	0.13	

[1]Plus 3.5 percent value-added tax. [2]Plus 7 percent value-added tax.
SOURCE: U.S. Department of Energy, Energy Information Administration, *1981 International Energy Annual* (Washington, D.C.: 1982).

forces to make the adjustments, but unfortunately markets are imperfect and often shortsighted in behavior. Their shortcomings can frequently be overcome by government regulations or the use of financial or fiscal incentives, such as the taxes described in the previous section. These policy tools can be used both to conserve oil and to encourage the substitution of cheaper, sustainable sources of energy.

Many governmental regulations are designed to increase energy efficiency, making it difficult to single out those aimed specifically at increasing the efficiency of oil use. One area in which the market does not always perform well is in reducing oil use in the residential/commercial sector. Oftentimes builders and potential occupants of buildings, both residential and commercial, have conflicting interests. Builders are interested in minimizing construction costs, since price is an important marketing tool. Occupants, however, are interested in lowering fuel bills. Yet because owners and renters often change frequently, their interest in thermal efficiency is not very strong. Getting governments to establish energy efficiency standards for buildings is thus important.[20]

The northernmost industrial countries have been particularly active in this area. In 1977, for example, Sweden passed a building code requiring a thermal efficiency nearly double the national average of buildings constructed before 1970. Although these new standards are only about 20 percent above the thermal efficiency of homes actually being built in 1977, they are nonetheless playing an important role in increasing the thermal efficiency of the national building stock. Denmark passed a building code in 1979 that also provided for a far more stringent thermal efficiency than the standards voluntarily followed by builders at that time.[21]

Because both residential and commercial buildings are replaced so slowly, societies also have an interest in retrofitting existing structures. Canada's national energy program, adopted in October 1980, includes federal grants of up to $500 to help owners insulate their homes. The government of the United Kingdom provides grants up to £50 for installing home insulation. Another widely used governmental intervention to reduce fuel use is the adoption of maximum building temperatures in winter and minimums in summer. In some cases, such as in France, these temperatures are mandatory in commercial buildings, and government monitors periodically check for compliance. In other countries they are voluntary but widely adhered to; these governments rely on example and exhortation to reduce oil used for space heating.[22]

The market also fails to raise energy efficiency in multifamily apartment buildings where heating and cooking fuel and electricity are bulk-metered for the building as a whole, thus providing little incentive for individual occupants to conserve. One remedy for this, which has been adopted by many governments, is simply to require that apartment units be metered individually.

Energy efficiency standards can be established for household appliances as well as for houses themselves. In an Energy Conservation Law passed in October 1979, Japan set rigorous standards for refrigerators, air conditioners, and lesser appliances.[23] In some cases a combination of regulation and market forces can be effective. Some governments simply require that the energy efficiency of an appliance be clearly stated on a label.

This provides consumers with information needed to minimize energy consumption while responding to market signals.

Sometimes government regulations or incentives are useful when the market does not respond quickly enough, such as in the transportation sector. In addition to the adoption of fuel efficiency standards discussed earlier, most governments of industrial countries have lowered speed limits for automobiles. West Germany, where motorists staunchly resist such limits, is a notable exception.[24]

Governments have also relied on regulations and financial incentives to encourage a switch from oil to less scarce, less costly fuels. Australia, for example, has provided tax concessions to industry for conversion from oil-fired equipment. Canada's 1980 energy program authorized grants to homeowners and businesses to convert from oil-fired heat to alternatives. The Japanese Government provides low-interest loans for the purchase of solar panels to heat water. And the United States provides nonrefundable income tax credits up to $4,000 for homeowners who install solar heating equipment.[25]

Brazil, as noted earlier, has perhaps gone furthest in encouraging the shift from oil to alternative energy sources. In addition to using subsidies to encourage the substitution of alcohol for gasoline as an automotive fuel, the Brazilian Government is also encouraging the chemical industry to switch from petroleum feedstocks to alcohol.[26]

In centrally planned economies, where the market's role is limited, the multiyear development plan itself becomes the central instrument for reducing dependence on oil. For example, in the Soviet Union's eleventh Five-Year Plan (1981–85), reducing dependence on petroleum depends heavily on the substitution of other forms of energy, especially of nuclear power for oil in thermal electrical generating plants. During this period, nuclear power was to provide all the growth in electricity in the European Soviet Union, but its development is lagging badly.[27]

A move to run Soviet industrial boilers on coal is not working well either, largely because coal production has fallen below the plan's target every year since 1976. As a result, Soviet dependence on oil had not declined at all as of 1981. While other industrial countries have moved vigorously away from oil in electrical generation, it still figures prominently in the Soviet Union, accounting for close to one-fifth of the country's total oil use.[28]

The ponderous Soviet planning bureaucracy seems particularly ill equipped to make quick course corrections or to read the changing international scene. Soviet planners placed emphasis on oil-intensive technologies and supply agreements just as Western countries were moving away from oil dependence, making the eventual change to substitute fuels even more abrupt.

Conservation, too, has proved especially difficult in centrally planned economies, though the potential and economic rationale for saving energy appear to be as great as in the West. In contrast to Soviet efforts to phase out oil, which depend on the government's own plan, conserving oil depends on behavioral changes by plant managers and individuals, and these in turn depend upon exhortation, something to which the typical Soviet citizen has become rather inured. Desired changes in this activity may come only with economic liberalization. Czech energy analyst István Dobozi, citing a Soviet source that "with sharply rising production and transport costs for additional output, per energy unit, conservation costs little more than half as much as new supplies," concludes that the major source of conservation in the Eastern bloc is economic reform.[29]

China, on the other hand, is much more adept at adjusting the energy mix quickly. After many years of rapidly rising oil consumption, the government effectively and rather abruptly reversed this trend in 1979 in order to free up oil for export. Oil use is being reduced in China by converting to coal in both electrical generation and in industrial uses.[30]

The experiences of centrally planned and market economies demonstrate the wisdom of relying on the market wherever possible to reduce energy consumption. But one reason market economies, in industrial as well as developing countries, have been much more successful in both conserving oil and switching to alternative sources is that they have been able to effectively combine those market forces with government regulations and incentives.

THE OIL INTENSITY OF ECONOMIC ACTIVITY

With oil consumption declining each year since 1979, the world is far less dependent on oil today than it was during the late seventies. Obviously, as economic output expands and oil consumption declines, the oil intensity of economic activity declines even faster.

Ever since the first oil price hike, energy analysts have focused on changes in this ratio of energy to gross national product (GNP). As the world is running out of oil but not of energy, the oil intensity of economic activity is particularly important. The amount of oil required to produce $1,000 of gross national product has varied widely among countries, from a low of roughly one barrel or less in China and India to a high of five barrels in the United States at the peak of the oil age. (See Table 3-8). Over the past generation the United States has been by far the world's most oil-intensive economy, using easily twice as much oil per $1,000 of GNP as Japan, the Soviet Union, or the United Kingdom.

An abundance of low-cost indigenous oil fostered this U.S. dependence, which the other Western industrial countries and Japan were able to resist because, except for the United Kingdom in recent years, they had to import most of the petroleum they used. Now this too has begun to change. Between 1977 and 1982 the United States reduced its dependence on oil from just under five barrels per $1,000 of gross national product to just under four barrels.

Other major Western industrial countries and Japan have done at least as well as the United States in reducing the oil intensity of their economic output over the last several years. The Soviet Union, however, which has had to rely on economic planning to move toward other energy resources and on exhortation to decrease oil use, has been remarkably unsuccessful. Indeed, the oil intensity of Soviet economic output continued climbing through 1980, the last year for which data are available.

The trends within developing countries are less consistent. India, which relies heavily on coal in its industrial sector, has a relatively low use of oil per $1,000 of GNP. But its oil intensity increased throughout the seventies, reaching a historical peak in 1979. Although followed by a modest downturn in 1980, the Indian performance did not begin to match the decline of one-fifth between

Table 3-8. Oil Intensity of Gross National Product in Major Countries, 1960–82[1]

Year	United States	United Kingdom	France	West Germany	Japan	Soviet Union	China	India	Brazil	Mexico
	(barrels of oil used per $1,000 of GNP)									
1960	4.95	1.82	0.98	0.75	1.11	1.52	0.36	0.38	1.27	2.06
1965	4.60	2.47	1.45	1.50	1.82	1.81	0.38	0.50	1.24	1.67
1970	5.03	3.06	1.93	1.82	2.36	2.05	0.73	0.58	1.33	1.76
1971	5.03	2.98	1.99	1.90	2.45	2.49	0.86	0.66	1.28	1.77
1972	5.11	**3.12**	2.04	1.93	2.35	2.24	0.95	0.67	1.34	1.77
1973	**5.11**	2.97	**2.10**	**1.95**	**2.51**	2.25	1.04	0.69	1.39	1.80
1974	4.94	2.80	1.91	1.73	2.48	2.31	1.23	0.69	1.36	1.87
1975	4.90	2.47	1.80	1.70	2.20	2.42	1.32	0.69	1.35	1.98
1976	4.98	2.37	1.83	1.74	2.22	2.38	1.41	0.70	1.38	2.09
1977	4.98	2.36	1.74	1.78	2.31	2.46	**1.42**	0.70	1.38	2.13
1978	4.88	2.25	1.64	1.84	2.16	2.47	1.26	0.75	1.35	2.18
1979	4.69	2.32	1.75	1.78	2.18	2.48	1.20	**0.83**	**1.42**	1.98
1980	4.36	2.12	1.63	1.54	1.89	**2.54**	1.13	0.78	1.29	**2.48**
1981	4.04									
1982	3.98									

[1]Peak year in bold.
SOURCE: Oil consumption data from U.S. Department of Energy, Energy Information Administration, *1982 Annual Energy Review* (Washington, D.C.: 1983); GNP data (in 1980 dollars) from Herbert R. Block, *The Planetary Product in 1980: A Creative Pause?* (Washington, D.C.: U.S. Department of State, 1981).

1977 and 1980 in the oil intensity of China's gross national product. Ironically India, an oil importer, became more oil-intensive while oil-exporting China was steadily reducing its dependence on petroleum.

Within Latin America the situation was more predictable. Mexico, a leading oil exporter, raised the oil content of its economic output rather steadily, reaching nearly 2.5 barrels per $1,000 of product in 1980—well above all the Western industrial countries except the United States. Brazil, meanwhile, maintained a fairly steady level of about 1.3 barrels during the seventies. A combination of substitution and conservation permitted Brazil to initiate a downturn in the oil content of its economic output in 1980, reducing it by an impressive 9 percent from the preceding year.

For the world as a whole, the oil intensity of economic output increased steadily from 1950 to 1973, going from 1.33 barrels per $1,000 of GNP to 2.27 barrels. (See Figure 3-3.) The two oil price adjustments during the seventies launched what seems certain to be the beginning of a long-term historical de-

cline in the oil intensity of economic activity. Since 1979 the fall has been both steady and substantial, dropping oil use per $1,000 of gross world product to 1.74 barrels.

THE OIL PROSPECT

Future oil consumption will be influenced by constraints on supply as well as demand. Supply-side constraints are both geological and political, while demand considerations involve foreign exchange at the national level and purchasing power at the individual level.

On the supply side, production has peaked and is declining in a number of oil-exporting countries. The big three producers—the United States, the Soviet Union, and Saudi Arabia—illustrate the range of production possibilities. U.S. oil production peaked in 1970 and declined steadily until the late seventies, when there was a modest increase. (See Figure 3-4.) As a result of the frenzy in oil drilling and production associated with the two oil price hikes and the decontrol of oil prices in the United States, production has held steady since 1978 at 8.6 million barrels per day, a million barrels less a day than in 1970.[31] Once this burst of activity associated with rising oil prices has passed, U.S. oil production is expected to resume the decline it started in the seventies.

The big push in Soviet oil development is historically recent, most of it occurring since 1970. The steep growth from 1960 to 1980 reflects the all-out effort by Soviet leaders to develop their oil resource, both as a major internal fuel and also as a source of hard-currency export earnings. Although the Soviets would like to expand production further, the decline in the all-important reserves-to-production ratio that slowed

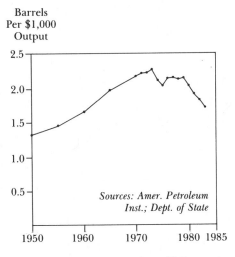

Barrels
Per $1,000
Output

Sources: Amer. Petroleum Inst.; Dept. of State

Figure 3-3. Oil Intensity of World Economic Output, 1950-83

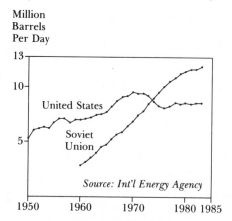

Million
Barrels
Per Day

Figure 3-4. U.S. and Soviet Oil Production, 1950-83

growth in output in the early eighties is likely to lead to a decline in the late eighties and nineties, barring some unexpected major oil field discovery. It is this difficulty in expanding oil output, combined with the failure to increase coal output according to plan, that has led to the Soviet Union's crash program to develop its vast gas reserves.[32]

Of the major oil producers, only Saudi Arabia has enough reserves to markedly raise output beyond previous peak levels if market conditions warrant it. Whether the Saudis choose to produce at full capacity is another matter, however, since they have served as the residual supplier within OPEC and have sometimes single-handedly supported OPEC's oil price through deep production cuts.

This range of future production possibilities also characterizes the situation in other oil-producing countries, although more appear to be like the United States than like Saudi Arabia. For example, production in Venezuela has fallen nearly 40 percent from its 1970 high of 3.7 million barrels per day. Other major producers experiencing more-recent declines include Algeria, Iran, Iraq, and Kuwait. With production of the major North Sea exporters, the United Kingdom and Norway, projected

to turn downward within a few years, substantial future output increases are expected in only a few countries, notably China and Mexico.[33]

Oil production declines in some countries, such as the Soviet Union, are due to a decline in the reserves-to-production ratio that makes it physically impossible to continue to boost production. Elsewhere, notably in some of the members of OPEC, production is being reduced to support the world price of oil at an agreed level. Political disruptions, particularly in the Middle East, are also influencing production levels. And some governments, such as Saudi Arabia and Norway, are influenced by a "depletion psychology," a desire to stretch out the income from oil exports over a longer period. This attempt to postpone the day when the wells go dry could steadily lower world oil production in the late eighties and nineties. The market impact of the basically healthy fear of using up an irreplaceable resource is hard to gauge. But just as the changing market psychology drove prices up in the seventies, the emergence of a strong depletion psychology could markedly reduce oil production below the levels commonly projected for the remainder of this century.

The combination of geological, economic, and psychological factors is likely to place end-of-century oil output well below the current level.

All these uncertainties are enough to humble even oil experts who attempt to predict tomorrow's production levels. Nevertheless, common sense suggests that to extend petroleum's lifetime, production in the near term should fall. The key question is whether the long-term decline in world output will be gradual and orderly or irregular and disruptive. The combination of geological, economic, and psychological factors is likely to place end-of-century oil output well below the current level. Although a continuation of the 5 percent annual decline from 1979 to 1982 is obviously unlikely, a further drop, perhaps a total of 15 percent, between now and the year 2000 seems entirely possible, given the output declines now under way in most producing countries. This would put end-of-century world oil production at 16.3 billion barrels per year, down from 22.9 billion barrels in 1979. If projected population increases also materialize, production will fall to 2.6 barrels per person. (See Figure 3-5.) In effect, each person will then be using only half as much oil as at the peak of the oil age.

On the demand side, the price of oil will be the dominant influence on consumption. In its 1983 world oil price projections, the U.S. Department of Energy's middle scenario projects a rise in the price of oil to $37 per barrel in real terms in 1990. This projected rise in prices still leaves the long-term price of petroleum well below the cost of oil produced from tar sands in Canada. A Canadian survey of eight projects that were originally scheduled to start production between 1980 and 1990 indicates an average production cost of $52 per barrel. U.S. oil shale and coal liquefaction projects designed to produce liquid fuel show production costs consistently above the projected world price for conventional oil at least through 1990.[34]

Beyond price, future oil consumption will be determined by changes in personal income. Given the slowdown in global economic growth since 1979, it is by no means certain that the affluence to support oil-consuming habits, whether in the form of automotive fuel, cooking fuel, or otherwise, will increase appreciably. Unless real incomes rise faster than the projected rise in real oil prices, the scope for expanding oil consumption will be limited.

At the national level, mounting external debts in a number of Third World and East European countries are making it more difficult to import oil on the same scale as in the past. In country after country where the International Monetary Fund has had to intervene with emergency loans and has mediated debt rescheduling with private banks, substantial increases in petroleum product prices have been required as a condition of the loans. This is especially true for gasoline in countries such as Brazil and Mexico. Yugoslavia, in order to avert an unmanageable increase in its international debt, introduced gasoline rationing. Poland, far in arrears in payments on its international debt, also rations gasoline.[35]

As the age of oil slowly recedes, governments everywhere will be faced with difficult choices in the use of dwindling supplies. In industrial societies the question may eventually become a choice between public and private transportation, with the more efficient rail system ex-

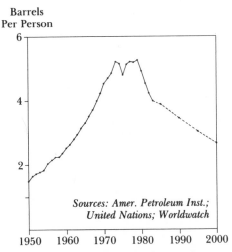

Barrels Per Person

Sources: Amer. Petroleum Inst.; United Nations; Worldwatch

Figure 3-5. World Oil Production Per Person, 1950-83, With Projections to 2000

panding at the expense of oil-dependent road transport. For many Third World countries still in the early stages of development, the adjustments will come in the form of conditions imposed by the International Monetary Fund and World Bank in exchange for continued financing of development. Increasingly, Third World governments will have to choose between fuel for private automobiles and fuel for cooking, or whether to use precious gasoline in cars or in irrigation pumps and tractors. Unless governments develop policies that channel scarce oil supplies to the most essential uses, affluent motorists could easily outbid farmers.

4

Conserving Soils

Lester R. Brown

Between 1950 and 1973 the world demand for grain doubled, spurred by both population growth and rising affluence. It will double again by the end of the century if the projected growth in population and income materializes. This unprecedented quadrupling in world food demand within 50 years is putting more pressure on many of the world's soils than they can sustain.

In the face of this continuously expanding world demand for grain and the associated relentless increase in pressures on land, soil erosion is accelerating. In effect, mounting economic pressures are degrading the resource base. In 1980 Anson R. Bertrand, a senior U.S. Department of Agriculture official, described the situation in the United States: "The economic pressure—to generate export earnings, to strengthen the balance of payments, and thus the dollar—has been transmitted more or less directly to our natural resource base. As a result, soil erosion today can be described as epidemic in proportion."[1] Bertrand's linkage between economic pressures and resource deterioration applies elsewhere as well; in most countries, however, the demand pressures come from indigenous rather than foreign sources.

Grave though the loss of topsoil may be, it is a quiet crisis, one that is not widely perceived. Unlike earthquakes, volcanic eruptions, or other natural disasters, this humanmade disaster is unfolding gradually. It is not always widely recognized because the intensification of cropping patterns and the plowing of marginal lands that leads to excessive erosion over the long run can lead to production gains in the short run, thus creating the illusion of progress and a false sense of food security.

Although soil erosion is a physical process, it has numerous economic consequences, affecting productivity, growth, income distribution, food sufficiency, and long-term external debt. Ultimately, it affects people. When soils are depleted and crops are poorly nourished, people are often undernourished as well.

THE CAUSES OF SOIL EROSION

The apparent increase in soil erosion over the past generation is not the result of a decline in the skills of farmers but rather of the pressures on farmers to produce more. In an integrated world food economy, the pressures on land resources are not confined to particular countries; they permeate the entire world. Many traditional agricultural systems that were ecologically stable as recently as mid-century, when there were only 2.5 billion people in the world, are breaking down as world population moves toward 5 billion.

Over the millennia, as the demand for food pressed against available supplies farmers devised ingenious techniques for extending agriculture onto land that was otherwise unproductive while still keeping erosion in check and maintaining land productivity. These techniques include terracing, crop rotations, and fallowing. Today, land farmed through these specialized techniques still feeds much of humanity. Although these practices have withstood the test of time, they are breaking down in some situations under the pressure of continuously rising demand.

In mountainous regions such as those in Japan, China, Nepal, Indonesia, and the Andean countries, construction of terraces historically permitted farmers to cultivate steeply sloping land that would otherwise quickly lose its topsoil. Centuries of laborious effort are embodied in the elaborate systems of terraces in older settled countries. Now the growing competition for cropland in many of these regions is forcing farmers up the slopes at a pace that does not permit the disciplined construction of terraces of the sort their ancestors built, when population growth was negligible by comparison. Hastily constructed terraces on the upper slopes often begin to give way. These in turn contribute to landslides that sometimes destroy entire villages, exacting a heavy human toll. For many residents of mountainous areas in the Himalayas and the Andes, fear of these landslides has become an integral part of daily life.[2]

Research in Nigeria has shown how much more serious erosion can be on sloping land that is unprotected by terraces. Cassava planted on land of a 1 percent slope lost an average of 3 metric tons per hectare each year, comfortably below the rate of soil loss tolerance. On a 5 percent slope, however, land planted to cassava eroded at a rate of 87 tons per hectare annually—a rate at which a topsoil layer of six inches would disappear entirely within a generation. Cassava planted on a 15 percent slope led to an annual erosion rate of 221 tons per hectare, which would remove all topsoil within a decade. Intercropping cassava and corn reduced soil losses somewhat, but the relationship of soil loss and slope remained the same.[3]

Much of the decline in inherent soil fertility that occurs under row crops is being masked by advances in technology.

Throughout the Third World increasing population pressure and the accelerating loss of topsoil seem to go hand in hand. Soil scientists S. A. El-Swaify and E. W. Dangler have observed that it is in precisely those regions with high population density that "farming of marginal hilly lands is a hazardous necessity. Ironically, it is also in those very regions where the greatest need exists to protect the rapidly diminishing or degrading soil resources." It is this vicious cycle, set in motion by the growing human demands for food, feed, fiber, and energy, that makes mounting an effective response particularly difficult.[4]

In other parts of the world farmers have been able to cultivate rolling land without losing excessive amounts of top-soil by using crop rotations. Typical of these regions is the midwestern United States, where farmers traditionally used long-term rotations of hay, pasture, and corn. Fields planted in row crops, such as corn, are most susceptible to erosion. By alternating row crops with cover crops like hay, the average annual rate of soil erosion was kept to a tolerable level. Not only do crop rotations provide more soil cover, but the amount of organic matter that binds soil particles together remains much higher than it would under continuous row cropping.

As world demand for U.S. feedstuffs soared after World War II and as cheap nitrogen fertilizer reduced the need for legumes, American farmers throughout the Midwest, the lower Mississippi Valley, and the Southeast abandoned crop rotations to grow corn or soybeans continuously. The risks associated with this shift in cropping patterns have long been known. Research undertaken in Missouri during the thirties showed an increase in soil erosion from 2.7 tons per acre (1 acre equals 0.4 hectares) annually when land was in a corn-wheat-clover rotation to 19.7 tons per acre when the same land was planted continuously to corn. (See Table 4-1.) The lower rate is within established erosion

Table 4-1. Cropping Systems and Soil Erosion

Cropping System	Average Annual Loss of Soil
	(tons/acre)
Corn, wheat, and clover rotation	2.7
Continuous wheat	10.1
Continuous corn	19.7

SOURCE: M. F. Miller, "Cropping Systems in Erosion Control," Missouri Experiment Station, Bulletin 366 (1936), reprinted in National Agricultural Lands Study, *Soil Degradation: Effects on Agricultural Productivity* (Washington, D.C.: 1980).

tolerance levels, whereas the higher rate would lead to the loss of one inch of topsoil in less than a decade. Much of the decline in inherent soil fertility that occurs under row crops is being masked by advances in technology, particularly by the increasing use of chemical fertilizer.

Fallowing has permitted farmers to work the land both in semiarid regions and in the tropics, where nutrients are scarce. In vast semiarid areas—such as Australia, the western Great Plains of North America, the Anatolian plateau of Turkey, and the drylands of the Soviet Union—where there is not enough moisture to support continuous cultivation, alternate-year cropping has evolved. Under this system land is left fallow without a cover crop every other year to accumulate moisture. The crop produced in the next season draws on two years of collected moisture.

In some situations this practice would lead to serious wind erosion if strip-cropping were not practiced simultaneously. Alternate strips planted to crops each year serve as windbreaks for the fallow strips. This combination of fallowing and strip-cropping permitted wheat production to continue in the western U.S. Great Plains after the Dust Bowl years.[5]

Rising demand for food has reduced the area fallowed in key dryland farming regions. As world wheat prices climbed sharply during the mid-seventies, U.S. summer fallow land dropped from 17 million hectares in 1969 to 13 million hectares in 1974.[6] This decline led Kenneth Grant, head of the U.S. Soil Conservation Service, to warn farmers that severe wind erosion and dust bowl conditions could result. He cautioned farmers against the lure of record wheat prices and short-term gains that would sacrifice the long-term productivity of their land. By 1977, the National Resources Inventory showed that wind erosion in wheat-growing states such as

Texas and Colorado far exceeded the tolerance levels.[7]

At the same time, the amount of fallowed land in the Soviet Union was also being reduced. During the late sixties and early seventies, the Soviets were consistently fallowing 17–18 million hectares each year in the dryland regions. But after the massive crop shortfall and heavy imports of 1972, the fallowed area was reduced by one-third. By the early eighties Soviet officials were returning more land to fallow in an effort to restore land productivity.[8]

In the tropics—such as parts of Africa south of the Sahara, Venezuela, the Amazon Basin, and the outer islands of Indonesia—fallowing is used to restore the fertility of the soil. In these areas more nutrients are stored in vegetation than in the soil. When cultivated and stripped of their dense vegetative cover, soils of the humid tropics quickly lose their fertility. In response to these conditions, farmers have evolved a system of shifting cultivation: They clear and crop land for two, three, or possibly four years and then systematically abandon it as crop yields decline. Natural vegetation soon takes over the abandoned field. Moving on to fresh terrain, farmers repeat the process. When these cultivators return to their starting point after 20–25 years, the soil has regained enough fertility to support crop production for a few years.

Mounting population pressures in the tropics are forcing shifting cultivators to shorten these rotation cycles. As this happens, land productivity falls. A 1974 World Bank study reported that in Nigeria "fallow periods under shifting cultivation have become too short to restore fertility in some areas."[9] In some locales the original cropping cycle of 10–15 years has already been reduced to 5. Since 1950, the cropped area in Nigeria has multiplied 2.5 times as new land, largely marginal, has been added and fallow cycles have been shortened. To-

gether, these two trends have offset the gains from the increased use of chemical fertilizer, the adoption of improved varieties, and the expansion of irrigation. Cereal yields are no higher than they were in the early sixties.

As population pressure has intensified in the river floodplains of northern Thailand over the last few decades, rice farmers have migrated to the nearby uplands where they practice rain-fed cropping. Early migrants adopted a "slash and burn" system with a cycle of eight to ten years, which seemed quite stable. As migration has continued, however, the forest fallow cycle has been shortened to between two to four years in many areas. In analyzing this situation, John M. Schiller concluded that "soil erosion problems are becoming clearly manifest in some areas and the effect of increased runoff is causing increased flooding in the lowlands and the siltation of dams. A potentially very unstable physical, economic, and social situation is developing in the affected areas."[10]

Similar pressures on land are evident in tropical Latin America. According to U.N. Food and Agriculture Organization researchers: "There is abundant evidence in certain regions of Venezuela that, with growing population pressure, the fallow period is becoming increasingly shorter so that soil fertility is not restored before recropping. This leads to a fall in the organic content and the water holding capacity of the soil. Soil structure deteriorates and compaction becomes more common . . . in other words, with the population of modern times, formerly stable, shifting cultivation systems are now in a state of breakdown."[11]

Another source of accelerated soil erosion in recent years has been the shift to larger farm equipment, particularly in the Soviet Union and United States. In the United States, for example, the shift to large-scale equipment has often led to the abandonment of field terraces constructed to reduce runoff on sloping lands. In dryland farming regions, tree shelter belts that interfere with the use of large-scale equipment have also been removed. The enlargement of fields to accommodate huge tractors and grain combines also reduces border areas that have traditionally served as checks on erosion.

This transformation of agricultural practices has been fueled by the growing worldwide demand for U.S. feed crops, particularly corn and soybeans, and by the availability of cheap chemical fertilizer. Demand growth, in turn, has been amplified by population growth that has hastened the deterioration of traditional agriculture in many countries. As a result, agricultural systems throughout the world are now experiencing unsustainable levels of soil loss.

DIMENSIONS OF THE PROBLEM

One of the first scientists to assess the dimensions of world soil erosion was geologist Sheldon Judson, who estimated in 1968 that the amount of river-borne soil sediment carried into the oceans had increased from 9 billion tons per year before the introduction of agriculture, grazing, and other activities to 24 billion tons per year. Judson observes: "There is no question that man's occupancy of the land increases the rate of erosion. Where that occupation is intense and is directed to the use of land for cultivated crops, the difference is one or more magnitudes greater than when the land is under a complete natural vegetative cover, such as grass or forest." His estimates indicate that humans have become an important geologic agent, accelerating the flow of soil to the oceans.[12]

Although detailed information on soil erosion at the local level is available for only a few countries, data on the sediment load of the world's major rivers and on the wind-borne movement of soil over the oceans do provide a broad-brush view of soil erosion at the continental level. The most recent figures on river sediment flow show the world's major rivers carrying heavy loads of soil to the oceans. Data compiled in 1980 by three Chinese scientists working for the Yellow River Conservancy Commission in Beijing indicated that river was carrying 1.6 billion tons of soil to the ocean each year. (See Table 4-2.) Hydrologists estimate that on average one-fourth of the soil lost through erosion in a river's watershed actually makes it to the ocean as sediment. The other three-fourths is deposited on footslopes in reservoirs, on river floodplains or other low-lying areas, or in the riverbed itself, which often causes channel shifts.[13]

Close behind the Yellow River, in terms of silt load, is the Ganges of India, which deposits 1.5 billion tons of soil into the Bay of Bengal each year. The Mississippi, the largest U.S. river, carries

Table 4-2. Sediment Load of Selected Major Rivers

River	Countries	Annual Sediment Load
		(million metric tons)
Yellow	China	1,600
Ganges	India	1,455
Amazon	several	363
Mississippi	United States	300
Irrawaddy	Burma	299
Kosi	India	172
Mekong	several	170
Nile	several	111

SOURCE: S.A. El-Swaify and E.W. Dangler, "Rainfall Erosion in the Tropics: A State of the Art," in American Society of Agronomy, *Soil Erosion and Conservation in the Tropics* (Madison, Wisc.: 1982).

300 million tons of soil into the Gulf of Mexico each year, far less than the Yellow or the Ganges. Yet it represents topsoil from the agricultural heartland and is thus a source of major concern for U.S. agronomists.[14]

Scientists have recently documented that vast amounts of wind-borne soil are also being deposited in the oceans as sediment. Island-based air sampling stations in the Atlantic, along with recent satellite photographs, indicate clearly that large quantities of soil dust are being carried out of North Africa over the Atlantic. Clearly visible from satellites, these huge plumes of fine soil particles from the arid and desert expanses of North Africa at times create a dense haze over the eastern Atlantic. Estimates of the amount of African soil being carried west in this way, reported in four studies between 1972 and 1981, range from 100–400 million tons annually, with the latest report being at the upper end of the range.[15]

A 1983 *Science* article reported a similar loss of soil from Asia, soil that is carried eastward over the Pacific. Air samples taken at the Mauna Loa Observatory in Hawaii from 1974 through 1982 indicate a continuous movement of soil particles from the Asian mainland, with a peak annual flow consistently occurring in March, April, and May, a time that coincides with a period of strong winds, low rainfall, and plowing in the semiarid regions of North Asia. Scientists at Mauna Loa can now tell when spring plowing starts in North China.[16]

Although soil erosion data are not available for most countries, a rough estimate of the excessive worldwide loss of topsoil from croplands is needed. Without such an estimate, assessments of the world food prospect are unrealistic. The estimate developed in the following pages is the best that we can construct from the information now available.

Other governments should follow the U.S. lead and take careful inventories of their soil resources so as to determine the rate of excessive erosion. Only then will they have the information needed to formulate intelligent agricultural and population policies.

The Soviet Union may be losing more topsoil than any other country.

In addition to broad-brush estimates of overall soil loss at the continental level, the other sources of more detailed information on soil erosion from croplands include governmental surveys, data on sedimentation of reservoirs and river sediment loads, reports from research plots, and the observations of agriculturalists.

The United States is one of the countries that has analyzed its soil losses in detail. In response to the Resource Conservation Act of 1977, the Soil Conservation Service undertook an exhaustive inventory of land use and soil loss. Based on some 200,000 data samplings, it yielded remarkably detailed information on local soil loss throughout the United States.

After the National Resources Inventory gathered data on soil erosion, subsequent analyses related the rate of soil loss to the tolerable level, a rate that would not impair long-term productivity. Calculated at from one to five tons per acre annually, depending on soil and climatic conditions, this figure represents the maximum level of soil erosion that will permit a high level of crop productivity to be sustained economically and indefinitely. The inventory showed that over one-third of U.S. cropland was losing more than five tons of topsoil per acre. In total, the loss of soil at this excessive rate from the U.S. cropland base of 413 million acres totaled 1.53 billion tons, with the bulk of it coming from less than one-tenth of the cropland.[17]

India is one of the few other countries to compile a national estimate of soil erosion loss. In 1975, Indian agricultural scientists collected data on local soil erosion from each of the research stations in the national network maintained by the Indian Council for Agricultural Research. Using these figures, they estimated that 6 billion tons of soil are eroded from India's croplands each year.[18] From this and from an estimate that 60 percent of the cropland is eroding excessively, the excessive topsoil loss can be calculated by subtracting from the total a tolerance level of five tons per acre. This yields an excessive topsoil loss from Indian cropland of 4.7 billion tons per year, more than twice the U.S. level. This estimate rests on far less data than does the figure for the United States but it is based on information from agricultural scientists familiar with local soils and it is corroborated by data on siltation of hydroelectric reservoirs, river sediment loads, and other indirect indicators.

The Soviet Union, which has the world's largest cropland area, may be losing more topsoil than any other country. Although detailed information on the extent of the loss is not available, numerous sources—including Soviet research reports, public statements by scientists and government officials, and the observations of visitors from abroad —indicate the severity of the problem. Papers published by the Soil Erosion Laboratory at the University of Moscow, for example, indicate a severe and worsening erosion situation.

During the early eighties the official Soviet press carried statements by soil scientists pleading with the agricultural bureaucracy to address the loss of topsoil. And in early 1981, Dr. Vladimir Borovsky, a prominent soil scientist and director of the Kazakh Institute of Soil Science, publicly charged the Academy of Agricultural Sciences with neglect of soil problems. In a broadcast on Moscow radio, Borovsky argued that Soviet agriculture will be retarded without effective soil management. His warnings have received some support at the highest levels of Soviet government, with Politboro member Mikhail S. Gorbachev urging planners to heed the advice of soil scientists.[19] But in the face of pressures to expand production and reduce the food import deficit—now the world's largest —soil scientists are often ignored and responsible soil management practices are cast aside.

As in the United States, erosion has been spurred by the shift to large, heavy equipment and the enlargement of fields, which eliminated many natural boundary constraints on erosion of soil by both wind and water. Each year an estimated half-million hectares of cropland are abandoned because they are so severely eroded by wind that they are no longer worth farming. One scholar of Soviet environmental policies and trends, Thane Gustafson, observes, "Fifty years of neglect have left a legacy of badly damaged soils."[20]

Although there are no official figures on soil erosion, an estimate of Soviet soil losses based on the local data that are available can be compared with the situation in the United States, where detailed erosion information has been collected. Two Soviet scientists, P. Poletayev and S. Yashukova, writing on environmental protection and agriculture in a Soviet economics journal in 1978, reported that "two-thirds of the plowed land in the Soviet Union has been subjected to the influence of various forms of erosion." Knowing the area affected by erosion, only the rate of erosion need be determined to estimate the total topsoil loss.[21]

Like the United States, the Soviet Union has an extensive dryland farming area and a substantial irrigated area. The European Soviet Union, which accounts for a large share of total farm output, has moisture levels similar to the U.S. Midwest. In terms of rainfall intensity, topography, and erodibility of prevailing soil types, nothing indicates that soil erosion in the Soviet Union would be markedly less than in the United States. Where cropping patterns are concerned, the Soviet Union relies much more heavily on small grains, whereas the United States relies relatively more on row crops, such as corn and soybeans.

The world is now losing an estimated 23 billion tons of soil from croplands in excess of new soil formation.

Much of the Soviet grain land, however, remains bare during the winter and early spring, when rainfall is heaviest in many regions of the country. In a paper presented in the United States in 1983, P.S. Tregubov of the Dokuchaev Soil Institute in Moscow reported that land left in bare fallow to be sown to winter crops sustained losses that far exceeded the rate of new soil formation. He observed that "spring was found to be the most dangerous period because soils are characterized by fluidity after snow thawing." To document this, Tregubov cited long-term experiments showing a mean annual soil loss on bare fallow of 59 tons per hectare annually in the Baltic Sea shore regions, 46 tons per hectare in the Rostov region, and 32 tons per hectare in the Transcaucasian region. By comparison, in the American states with the most severe erosion rates in 1977, Tennessee lost nearly 41 tons per hectare, Missouri lost 30 tons, and Iowa, just over 25 tons.[22]

These data and observations suggest it is not unreasonable to assume that Soviet soils are eroding at least as rapidly as those in the United States. If one-third of the land is affected by erosion at the same rate as in the United States, which may be a conservative assumption, the excessive loss of topsoil from Soviet croplands is nearly 2.3 billion tons per year.

In China, the fourth major food-producing country, river siltation is now a nationally recognized threat—one that has reached dimensions unmatched elsewhere. Dust storms in the north and the siltation of major rivers indicate the heavy soil loss. Observations by outsiders who have been called in to help assess soil conditions indicate that the erosion rate in China is at least as great as that in India, where more detailed data are available.

A comparison of the sediment load of the Yellow River in China with the Ganges in India indicates the relative magnitude of soil loss through erosion faced by these two population giants. The Ganges, with a drainage basin of 1.1 million square kilometers, carries an annual sediment load of 1.46 billion tons of soil, while the Yellow River, which has a drainage basin of 668,000 square kilometers, carries 1.6 billion tons of soil to the ocean each year. These numbers suggest that the rate of soil loss in China is substantially greater than in India. For the purposes of constructing a rough global estimate, however, it can be assumed that the erosion rate on China's cropland is the same as in India. Given China's smaller cropland area, this means that China's excessive loss of topsoil from its croplands totals 3.3 billion tons per year.

For most Third World countries information on soil erosion is largely indirect, such as data on sedimentation of reservoirs and river silt loads. Other indirect sources include information on cropland abandonment as a result of severe erosion and crop reports showing long-term declines in yields. Among the most graphic sources are reports by agricultural scientists, development technicians, and other observers. (See Table 4-3.)

Altogether, the excessive loss of topsoil from cropland in the four major food-producing countries, which have 52 percent of the world's cropland and account for over half of its food production, is estimated at 11.8 billion tons per year. To obtain a rough idea of excessive soil erosion for the world as a whole, an assumption must be made about other countries. If the rates of soil erosion for the rest of the world are similar to those of the "big four"—which is a conservative assumption given the pressures on land in the Third World—then the world is now losing an estimated 23 billion tons of soil from croplands in excess of

Table 4-3. Observations of Soil Erosion in the Third World

Country	Observation	Source
Nepal (Katmandu)	"Local inhabitants . . . all concur that the problem is more severe now than a generation ago."	*Mountain Research and Development* (Boulder, Col.), 1982
Peru	"Erosion is estimated to affect between 50 and 60 percent of the surface of the whole country."	*Mountain Research and Development* (Boulder, Col.), 1982
Indonesia (Java)	"Soil erosion is creating an ecological emergency in Java, a result of overpopulation, which has led to deforestation and misuse of hillside areas by land-hungry farmers. Erosion is laying waste to land at an alarming rate, much faster than present reclamation programs can restore it."	U.S. Embassy, Jakarta, 1976
Ethiopia	"There is an environmental nightmare unfolding before our eyes . . . over 1 billion tons of topsoil flow from Ethiopia's highlands each year."	U.S. AID Mission, Addis Ababa, 1978
South Africa	"The province of Natal, incorporating Kwazulu, is losing 200 million tons of topsoil annually."	John Hanks, Institute of Natural Resources, Natal, 1980
Bolivia	"Recent aerial photographs have shown the rapid extension of desert-like conditions caused by wind erosion."	Helene Riviere d'Arc, Institut des Hautes Études d'Amérique Latine, Paris, 1980
Iran	"The area of abandoned cultivated land has doubled in recent years."	Harold Dregne, Texas Tech University, 1971

new soil formation. (See Table 4-4.)

Because of the shortsighted way one-third to one-half of the world's croplands are being managed, the soils on these lands have been converted from a renewable to a nonrenewable resource. Assuming an average depth of remaining topsoil of seven inches, or 1,120 tons per acre, and a total of 3.1 billion acres of cropland, there are 3.5 trillion tons of topsoil with which to produce food, feed, and fiber. At the current rate of excessive erosion, this resource is being depleted at 0.7 percent per year—7 percent each decade. In effect, the world is mining much of its cropland, treating it as a depletable resource, not unlike oil.

When most of the topsoil is lost on land where the underlying formation consists of rock or where the productivity of the subsoil is too low to make cultivation economical, it is abandoned. More commonly, however, land continues to be plowed even though most of the topsoil has been lost and even though the plow layer contains a mixture of topsoil and subsoil, with the latter dominating. Other things being equal, the real cost of food production on such land is far higher than on land where the topsoil layer remains intact.

Table 4-4. Estimated Excessive Erosion of Topsoil From World Cropland

Country	Total Cropland	Excessive Soil Loss
	(million acres)	(million tons)
United States	413	1,500
Soviet Union	620	2,300
India	346	4,700
China	245	3,300
Total	1,624	11,800
Rest of World	1,499	10,900
Total	3,123	22,700

SOURCE: Worldwatch Institute estimates.

THE EROSION OF PRODUCTIVITY

Whenever erosion begins to exceed new soil formation, the layer of topsoil becomes thinner, eventually disappearing entirely. As the topsoil layer is lost, subsoil becomes part of the tillage layer, reducing the soil's organic matter, tilth, and aeration, and adversely affecting other structural characteristics that make it ideal for plant growth. This overall deterioration in soil structure is usually accompanied by a reduced nutrient retention capacity, which lowers productivity further. Additional chemical fertilizer can often compensate for the loss of nutrients, but the deterioration of soil structure is difficult to remedy.

The effects of erosion on productivity are not easily measured since they are usually gradual and cumulative. In an effort to understand the erosion/productivity relationship better, in 1980 the U.S. Secretary of Agriculture appointed a National Soil Erosion-Soil Productivity Research Planning Committee. Among other things, committee members began gathering data from past experiments to establish an empirical foundation for predicting the effect of continuing soil loss on crop yields and production costs. They reported that when corn was grown continuously on a plot in Iowa from which the topsoil had been removed, yields were only 20 percent of those on a control plot. In an experiment in Missouri, corn yields on a desurfaced plot were 47 percent of those on the control plot. In this case, the subsoil was a clay loam—a higher-quality subsoil than is commonly the case.[23]

In an experiment in East Texas, cotton yields on land with the topsoil removed averaged only 32 percent of the control plot's. And in Minnesota, yields on severely eroded soils were roughly two-thirds those on slightly eroded soils.[24] A 1979 experiment on piedmont soils in Georgia designed to measure the effects of erosion on corn yields showed that severely eroded, moderately eroded, and uneroded soils averaged 36, 75, and 92 bushels respectively. On these soils, researchers estimated that each centimeter of topsoil lost through water erosion reduced the average corn yield by 2.34 bushels per acre.[25]

Leon Lyles, an agricultural engineer with the U.S. Department of Agriculture, has provided probably the most comprehensive collection of research results on the effect of soil erosion on land productivity. Drawing on the work of U.S. soil scientists both within and outside government, Lyles compared 14 independent studies, mostly undertaken in the corn belt states, to summarize the effects of a loss of one inch of topsoil on corn yields. His survey found that such a loss reduced yields from a low of 3 bushels per acre to a high of 6.1 bushels per acre. (See Table 4-5.) In percentage terms, the loss of an inch of topsoil reduced corn yields at these 14 sites by an average of 6 percent. Results for wheat, drawing on 12 studies, showed a similar relationship between soil erosion and land productivity. The loss of an inch of topsoil reduced wheat yields 0.5–2.5 bushels per acre. In percentage terms, the loss of an inch reduced wheat yields an average of 6 percent, exactly the same as for corn. (See Table 4-6.)

All the studies on soil erosion and land productivity that Lyles cited showed that the excessive loss of topsoil lowered yields measurably, although the extent of yield reduction varied. And, as noted, his compilation of studies showed a remarkable similarity in the effect of soil erosion on the yield of wheat, a crop usually grown under lower rainfall conditions, and that of corn, usually grown in areas of higher rainfall. Recent, more detailed research on three soil types in Minnesota shows that the effect of erosion varies with soil type and depth. It specifically notes that on some deeper soils, such as the Kenyon soils that are 76 inches deep, the near-term effects of erosion are negligible.[26] For the world as a whole soils of this depth constitute a small share of the total, an exception to the more typical 6–8 inches of topsoil found on most cropland.

Perhaps the most detailed analysis to date of the long-term effects of soil erosion on land productivity and food production costs is one undertaken for the Southern Iowa Conservancy District.

Table 4-5. Effect of Topsoil Loss on Corn Yields

Location	Yield Reduction Per Inch of Topsoil Lost		Soil Description
	(bushels/acre)	(percent)	
East Central, Illinois	3.7	6.5	Swygert silt loam
Fowler, Indiana	4.0	4.3	Fowler, Brookston, and Parr Silt loams
Clarinda, Iowa	4.0	5.1	Marshall silt loam
Greenfield, Iowa	3.1	6.3	Shelby silt loam
Shenandoah, Iowa	6.1	5.1	Marshall silt loam
Bethany, Missouri	4.0	6.0	Shelby and Grundy silt loams
Columbus, Ohio	3.0	6.0	Celina silt loam
Wooster, Ohio	4.8	8.0	Canfield silt loam

SOURCES: Various reports cited in Leon Lyles, "Possible Effects of Wind Erosion on Soil Productivity," *Journal of Soil and Water Conservation,* November/December 1975.

Table 4-6. Effect of Topsoil Loss on Wheat Yields

Location	Yield Reduction Per Inch of Topsoil Lost		Soil Description
	(bushels/acre)	(percent)	
Akron, Colorado	0.5	2.0	Weld silt loam
Geary County, Kansas	1.3	6.2	(not available)
Manhattan, Kansas	1.1	4.3	Smolan silty clay loam
Columbus, Ohio	1.3	5.3	Cropped soil
Oregon	1.0	2.2	Deep soil
Oregon	2.5	5.8	Thin soil
Palouse Area, Washington	1.6	6.9	(not available)

SOURCES: Various reports cited in Leon Lyles, "Possible Effects of Wind Erosion on Soil Productivity," *Journal of Soil and Water Conservation,* November/December 1975.

Conducted by an interdisciplinary team of three scientists, this analysis assumed that soil erosion would continue at recent rates. The researchers classified the degree of erosion into three phases: soils that are slightly eroded, with no appreciable mixing of subsoil and topsoil in the plow layer; those that are moderately eroded, with some mixing of subsoil into the plow layer; and severely eroded soils, where the topsoil is largely gone and the plow layer is predominantly subsoil.

In 1974, the base year, 2.1 million of the district's 3.5 million acres of cropland fell into one of the three erosion phases, with the largest acreage being in the moderately eroded category. Assuming a continuation of the same rate of erosion, this would also be true for the year 2000. But by 2020, the researchers predicted, the largest share would be in the severely eroded category. As soils progress from the moderately to severely eroded category, the amount of nitrogen, phosphorus, and potash needed to grow corn increases by 38 pounds per acre. (See Table 4-7.) Closely paralleling this would be an increase in fuel requirements for tillage. As erosion proceeds, soils become more compact and difficult to till. The actual fuel increase varied widely by soil type,

but on the average the severely eroded soils required 38 percent more fuel for tillage than the slightly eroded soils.

Soil erosion would not only raise the costs of production by increasing the amount of fertilizer and fuel used, it would also reduce yields. For corn, a shift from slight to moderate erosion would reduce the average corn yield by 16 bushels per acre, while going from the moderate to severe category would lower yields another 7 bushels per acre. (See Table 4-8.) Although the soybean yield decline was much smaller, it was proportionate, since soybean yields are roughly one-third those of corn.

Although there are little reliable data on the effect of soil erosion on land pro-

Table 4-7. Increase in Fertilizer Needs for Corn as Soil Erodes, Southern Iowa

Change in Erosion Phase	Nitrogen	Phosphate	Potash
	(pounds per acre)		
Slight to Moderate	10	2	6
Moderate to Severe	30	1	7

SOURCE: Paul Rosenberry, Russell Knutson, and Lacy Harmon, "Predicting the Effects of Soil Depletion From Erosion," *Journal of Soil and Water Conservation,* May/June 1980.

Table 4-8. Reduction in Yields of Key Crops as Soil Erodes, Southern Iowa

Change in Erosion Phase	Reduction in Yield Per Acre		
	Corn	Soybeans	Oats
	(bushels)		
Slight to Moderate	16	5	9
Moderate to Severe	7	3	4

SOURCE: Paul Rosenberry, Russell Knutson, and Lacy Harmon, "Predicting the Effects of Soil Depletion From Erosion," *Journal of Soil and Water Conservation*, May/June 1980.

ductivity for most countries, some insights into the relationship can be derived from these U.S. studies. Given the consistency of the decline in productivity across a wide range of soil types and crops, it would not be unreasonable to assume that a similar relationship between soil erosion and land productivity exists in other countries, for the basic agronomic relationships are the same. Indeed, research on West African soils shows land productivity there to be even more sensitive to topsoil loss than in North America. The loss of 3.9 inches of topsoil in West Africa cut corn yields by 52 percent. Yields of cow peas, a leguminous crop, were reduced by 38 percent. This marked decline may attest to the fragility of tropical soils.[27]

EROSION'S INDIRECT COSTS

When farmers lose topsoil they pay for it in reduced soil fertility, but unfortunately the costs of erosion are not confined to the farm alone. As soil is carried from the farm by runoff, it may end up in local streams, rivers, canals, or irrigation and hydroelectric reservoirs. The loss of topsoil that reduces land productivity may also reduce irrigation, electrical generation, and the navigability of waterways.

The increase in the amount of irrigated land in the world went hand in hand with efforts to raise food supplies during the third quarter of this century. Often the centerpiece of national development strategies throughout the Third World, multipurpose dams represented enormous investments and an important part of the capital stock of new nations. Typical of these was the Mangla Reservoir in Pakistan. The designers of the reservoir projected a life expectancy for the dam of at least a century. What they did not reckon on was the effect of mounting population pressure on the watershed feeding the reservoir. A combination of the axe and the plow, as land-hungry peasants push up the hillsides, is leading to a rate of siltation that will probably fill the reservoir with silt at least 25 years earlier than projected. (See Table 4-9.) One recent estimate predicts it will be filled within half a century.[28]

In the Philippines, scores of hydroelectric and irrigation reservoirs have been constructed, many of them with assistance from international development agencies. Here, as in Pakistan, the combination of watershed deforestation and steep slopes being cleared for cultivation is yielding record siltation rates. A report of the Agency for International Development on the prospects for the Ambuklao Dam notes that "the cutting of timber and the subsequent loss of water retention capacity of land surrounding the reservoir has resulted in massive silting of the reservoir, reducing its useful life from 60 to 32 years."[29]

One reason for the excessively rapid siltation rates is that multipurpose dams are designed by engineers who sometimes fail to recognize the impoundments they build as part of a watershed, which often drains an area of several

Table 4-9. Siltation Rates in Selected Reservoirs

Country	Reservoir	Annual Siltation Rate	Time To Fill With Silt
		(metric tons)	(years)
Egypt	Aswan High Dam	139,000,000	100
Pakistan	Mangla	3,700,000	75
Philippines	Ambuklao	5,800	32
Tanzania	Matumbulu	19,800	30
Tanzania	Kisongo	3,400	15

SOURCE: S.A. El-Swaify and E.W. Dangler, "Rainfall Erosion in the Tropics: A State of the Art," in American Society of Agronomy, *Soil Erosion and Conservation in the Tropics* (Madison, Wisc.: 1982).

thousand square miles. The Anchicaya Dam in Colombia is a classic example. Engineers expressed little concern with the siltation problem, even though when the project began farmers were already invading the upper reaches of the watershed that feeds the dam. Within two years of its completion, the dam had already lost a quarter of its storage capacity because of siltation.[30]

In India, the indirect costs of water-eroded soil are summed up well by B. B. Vohra, Chairman of the National Committee on Environmental Planning. He observes that the "premature siltation of our 500,000 odd ponds and of the 487 reservoirs of our major and medium irrigation and multipurpose projects on which the community has invested over 100 billion rupees during the last three decades is a particularly serious matter." He notes that siltation rates are now commonly several times as high as the rate that was assumed when the projects were designed. (See Table 4-10.) Vohra observes that not only is the life expectancy of these projects being severely reduced, but "in most cases there will be no alternative sites for dams once the existing ones are rendered useless." A dam site is often unique. Once lost, it cannot be replaced. For India, what is at

Table 4-10. India: Siltation Rates in Selected Reservoirs

Reservoir	Assumed Rate	Observed Rate	Ratio of Observed to Assumed Erosion
	(in acre-feet)		
Bhakar	23,000	33,475	1.46
Maithon	684	5,980	8.74
Mavurakshi	538	2,000	3.72
Nizam Sugar	530	8,725	16.46
Panchet	1,982	9,533	4.81
Ramganga	1,089	4,366	4.01
Tungabhadra	9,796	41,058	4.19
Ukai	7,448	21,758	2.92

SOURCE: Adapted from S. A. El-Swaify and E. W. Dangler, "Rainfall Erosion in the Tropics: A State of the Art," in American Society of Agronomy, *Soil Erosion and Conservation in the Tropics* (Madison, Wisc.: 1982), and Centre for Science and Environment, *The State of India's Environment 1982* (New Delhi: 1982).

stake, according to Vohra, "is the loss of the irreplaceable potential—for irrigation, for electricity and for flood control —that these storages represent."[31]

The list of countries with soil-silting disasters goes on and on. The names change but the conditions are common. Whether in Nigeria, Indonesia, Pakistan, or Mexico, the same basic principles of soil physics are at work. When soil on sloping land is farmed improperly, it begins to move under the impact of rain and ends up in places where it usually does more harm than good.

Soil once used in the Midwest to grow corn now clogs the Mississippi waterways.

The third major indirect cost of soil erosion is the loss of navigability. Perhaps the most dramatic case occurs in the Panama Canal. The combination of deforestation and the plowing of steeply sloping land in the watershed area by landless campesinos is leading to an unprecedented siltation of the lakes that make up part of the Canal. If the trends of the late seventies and early eighties continue, the capacity of the Panama Canal to handle shipping will be greatly reduced by the end of the century, forcing many ocean-going freighters that have relied on its 10,000 mile shortcut to make the trip via Cape Horn.[32]

Within the United States, soil once used in the Midwest to grow corn now clogs the Mississippi waterways. One of the largest items in the budget of the Army Corps of Engineers is the dredging of inland waterways, particularly in the lower Mississippi River. Vast quantities of soil reach the Gulf of Mexico to become ocean sediment, but substantial amounts are deposited on the way, making large-scale dredging imperative, if

this major artery connecting U.S. farms with world markets is to continue to function.

THE ECONOMICS OF CONSERVING SOIL

Recent U.S. studies have rather consistently concluded that soil erosion control is often not economical for farmers, based on strictly dollars-and-cents criteria. The study of southern Iowa soils referred to earlier showed that the short-term cost to farmers of reducing soil erosion to a level that would not reduce inherent productivity would be three times as great as the benefits.

Narrow profit margins, such as those confronting U.S. farmers during the early eighties, might well mean that if farmers were to invest in appropriate conservation measures their profit margins would disappear entirely, forcing them to operate at a deficit. They would then face the prospect of bankruptcy in the near future. Alternatively, they could continue to follow existing agricultural practices and avoid near-term bankruptcy, but face the prospect of declining productivity over the long term and the eventual abandonment of land, if not by this generation then by the next. In the absence of a governmental cost-sharing program similar to those used so effectively in the past, a farmer's only choice is whether to go out of business sooner or later.

The economics of erosion control in the United States has recently become more attractive with the adoption of new minimum-tillage practices. In traditional tillage the moldboard plow, the principal farm implement, was used to turn over all the soil in seedbed preparation. With minimum tillage the land is not plowed in this traditional way. Crop residues are left on the surface and seeds are drilled directly into the unplowed land, with herbicides providing the weed control that mechanical cultivators previously did. The availability of herbicides enabled minimum tillage in the same way that the introduction of cheap chemical fertilizer permitted farmers to dispense with crop rotation containing legumes. More commonly, however, in minimum tillage narrow strips of land are tilled where the corn, soybeans, or other row crops are planted, leaving the space between the rows undisturbed.[33]

To conserve fuel, cost-conscious U.S. farmers were already experimenting with various reduced tillage practices in the early seventies. The oil price jump in 1973 reinforced this change. The fortuitous nature of this development lies in its effect on soil erosion. With land not being plowed and crop residues left on the surface, soil is protected from rain, and runoff is much less. The result is that farmers adopting minimum-till or no-till practices to conserve fuel have discovered that they are also conserving their soil. Individual farmers doing their own cost-benefit calculations could weigh the importance of both energy and soil savings in deciding whether to adopt the new practices.

Not all soils and not all situations lend themselves to minimum tillage, which increases soil moisture and slows soil temperature rise in the spring. In areas such as the northern corn belt, the short growing season could restrict the adoption of minimum tillage. Still, the growth in reduced tillage acreage in the United States has been remarkably steady, increasing every year since data collection began in 1972. In that year, nearly 30 million acres—roughly one-tenth of the cultivated area—was in reduced tillage. (See Table 4-11.) In 1983, it reached 126 million acres, one-third of all the land in crops.

Table 4-11. United States: Conservation Tillage, 1972–83

Year	Area in Conservation Tillage	Share of Harvested Cropland[1]
	(million acres)	(percent)
1972	29.7	10.0
1973	43.9	13.7
1974	46.7	14.2
1975	56.2	16.7
1976	59.6	17.6
1977	70.0	20.2
1978	74.8	22.2
1979	85.2	24.6
1980	88.5	25.1
1981	99.0	27.5
1982	111.9	31.2[2]
1983	125.8	34.5[2]

[1]Share of harvested cropland, calculated by Worldwatch, includes area harvested and that on which crops failed.   [2]Estimates; the Conservation Tillage Information Center puts the 1983 figure at 24 percent.
SOURCES: *No-Till Farmer*, March 1982 and March 1983; Worldwatch Institute.

Despite the encouraging increase in the use of minimum tillage, there is little information to date on its impact on severely eroding land. While noting the encouraging spread of reduced tillage farming practices, Robert Gray of the American Farmland Trust observes that even minimum-till and no-till practices should be forsworn on the most severely eroding land, which should not be in production at all.[34] Preliminary observations indicate that minimum tillage is being adopted by the more progressive, innovative farmers and that all too often these are not the ones on marginal lands, which are eroding most severely. Nonetheless, the overall effect of minimum tillage on soil conservation must be viewed as positive and hopeful.

Although roughly one-third of U.S. cropland was minimum-tilled as of 1983, the practice is not widely used in other parts of the world, though there are occasional references to it. For example, the two Soviet scientists cited earlier, who reported on environmental protection and agriculture, noted that "a method in which the soil layer is not turned in the treatment of the soil has been developed and has been widely introduced in production in Kazakhstan, the Altei, in the Urals, in the Lower Volga and other regions." They also indicated that the specialized farm equipment needed for minimum tillage is being manufactured in the Soviet Union.[35]

Some observers claim that erosion control is particularly uneconomical in the United States because of the untrammeled pursuit of profits. But all indications are that production quotas, as used in the Soviet Union for example, are at least as destructive of soils as the profit motive. Under the Soviet system, farm managers are judged not by how effectively they control soil erosion but by how successfully they fill quotas. In Western countries, landownership, particularly within a family, brings with it a certain sense of stewardship—although this obviously can be overridden by economic forces. Such a direct sense of stewardship does not exist in the Soviet Union.

Farmers adopting minimum-till or no-till practices to conserve fuel have discovered that they are also conserving their soil.

Others suggest that the economics of erosion control will become clear when cropland values decline as soil erosion reduces long-term land productivity. Unfortunately, the loss of topsoil does not alter the physical appearance of the land in the short run, nor does it show up as an immediately measurable loss of productivity. Given the other factors influencing land values, such as inflation and the speculative nature of investment, the effects of soil erosion on land values are simply not visible in the short run.

Interest rates also affect the economics of erosion control. The higher interest rates are, the less attractive become investments in the soil conservation techniques, such as terracing, that pay off over the long term. Indeed, interest rates have been so high in the United States in the early eighties that farmers have simply been unable to consider seriously most investments that have a long-term payback.

THE GOVERNMENTAL ROLE

Although the changes in agricultural practices needed to check excessive soil erosion can usually be implemented only by farmers themselves, there are several reasons why bringing erosion under control requires government involvement. To begin with, many farmers cannot easily determine whether their erosion is excessive. Measuring the gradual loss of soil requires scientific techniques and equipment; determining whether it is excessive requires information on tolerance levels for the particular cropland in question.

Another reason for government involvement is that individual farmers may be unable to afford the conservation practices that are needed. It may make sense for society to invest in soil conservation even if it is not profitable for the individual farmer. Only government can calculate the long-term aggregate cost of soil erosion for the nation as a whole, including off-farm costs such as the silt-reduced capacity of irrigation reservoirs, hydroelectric reservoirs, or water transport systems.

The first step for governments in countries where soil erosion is believed to be a serious threat is to assess carefully the extent of soil loss. Only when such an inventory has been done can all the needed national cost-benefit calculations be made and the appropriate conservation programs designed. In India, for example, which has a cropland base comparable in size to the United States and which has only broad estimates of soil loss, it is estimated that a comprehensive nationwide soil inventory would cost some $30 million—a small price indeed compared with the contribution it could make to more intelligent policy-making.

Most governments also need better information on the relationship between soil erosion and land productivity than they now have. The National Soil Erosion-Soil Productivity Research Planning Committee in the United States notes that "such experiments are costly and time consuming. Years of data are needed to evaluate the effects of the generally slow process."[36]

In some countries, the expenditures required simply to stabilize soils dwarf the total appropriations for agriculture.

The National Research Committee of the U.S. Soil Conservation Service calls work on the erosion/productivity relationship its top priority. A theoretical model called the Erosion-Productivity Impact Calculator, developed by the Department of Agriculture, is designed to evaluate both the physical process and the economic consequences of erosion. A Productivity Index that calculates the ratio between actual and potential crop yields at various levels of soil loss has been applied to soils in the major crop-producing regions of the United States and is being tested on soils in Nigeria, Mexico, and India. But the usefulness of such models will depend on the painstaking collection of years of data on many soil types, an effort that has just begun.[37]

Mobilizing public support for adequately funded soil conservation programs will require extensive public education on the dimensions of the problem and its many consequences. Scientific proof of the necessity of soil conservation is not sufficient. Although soil scientists can chart a national plan of action in detail, as they have in the United States, they cannot call forth the political support needed to fund and administer such a plan. At this point, national political leaders must become involved.

Perhaps one of the best examples of such involvement occurred in the United States during the thirties when Franklin D. Roosevelt was president and Henry Wallace was secretary of agriculture. Despite the fact that the country was in the midst of perhaps the worst economic crisis in its history, Roosevelt and Wallace convinced the U.S. Congress to fund within the Department of Agriculture a new agency—the Soil Conservation Service—that would have the responsibility for administering a comprehensive soil conservation program. Roosevelt proudly took credit for the planting of tree shelter belts in the Great Plains.[38]

The ingredient missing from unsuccessful responses to the growing menace of soil erosion is political will grounded in awareness. Over the past generation, scores of countries have become food-deficit but few have linked the shortages with the depletion of their soil by erosion. In many countries people know that food prices are rising, but most don't know quite why. An understanding that lost soil means lower inherent productivity, which in turn means costlier food, is needed to inculcate a national soil conservation ethic.

In many predominantly rural societies where most people are illiterate and live at the subsistence level, a lack of public interest in soil conservation has other roots. Farmers in many Third World villages can muster little concern about the future when their immediate survival is in question. In India, reports B. B. Vohra, "an informed public opinion cannot . . . be wished into existence over night. A great deal of painstaking and patient work will have to be done to wipe out the backlog of ignorance, inertia and complacency."[39]

In much of the world today, only the willingness of national governments to share the costs of the needed measures —terracing, contour farming, strip-cropping, cover cropping, rotating crops, fallowing, and planting shelter belts—will induce farmers to fight soil erosion. One World Bank official observes that if all the Bank's capital resources of $9 billion per year were devoted to soil conservation, it would cover only a small fraction of the land affected by erosion.[40] In some countries, the expenditures required simply to stabilize soils dwarf the total appropriations for agriculture.

Within the socialist economies, where land is publicly owned and governments are directly responsible for the quality of land management, there is a need for the ruling elites to be educated about basic agronomy. Unless national political leaders understand that a country's long-term security depends on protecting its cropland, it will be difficult to get the necessary commitment of leadership time and the budgetary resources to support an effective conservation program.

THE GLOBAL BALANCE SHEET

The long-term social threat posed by uncontrolled soil erosion raises profound questions of intergenerational equity. If our generation persists in mining the soils so that we may eat, many of our children and their children may go hungry as a result. Agricultural economist Lloyd K. Fischer of the University of Nebraska observes that the quality of our diet in the future will be "substantially lower and the costs dramatically higher if the management of our land and water resources is not improved." He notes further that "we must cease to behave as if there were no tomorrow, or tomorrow will be bleak indeed for those who must spend their lives there."[41]

Perhaps even more troubling than the current net loss of an estimated 23 billion tons of topsoil from the world's cropland each year is the likelihood that the process is accelerating as cultivation is extended into ever more marginal areas. In a world where 79 million people are being added each year and where the great majority of the earth's inhabitants want to upgrade their diets, the demand for food continues to climb, pushing farmers onto more steeply sloping lands.

Soil erosion is a physical process but it has numerous economic consequences for prices, productivity, income, and external debt. Labor productivity is affected in that as soils are depleted through erosion it becomes more difficult to raise the output of that substantial share of the world labor force that works on the eroding land. In largely agrarian societies this deterioration of the resource base makes it more difficult to raise income per person. Further, as growth in food output slows, so does overall economic output. In largely rural, low-income societies with rapid population growth this can translate into declining per capita income, as it already has for a dozen countries in Africa.

Over the longer term, world agricultural trade patterns and the international debt structure will also be altered. As soils are depleted, countries are forced to import food to satisfy even minimal food needs. Scores of countries in the Third World and Eastern Europe find their international indebtedness being aggravated further by their chronic dependence on imported food. And the loss of topsoil will force an energy-for-topsoil substitution as it increases the need for fertilizer and fuel for tillage. Other things being equal, the less topsoil there is, the more energy is needed to produce our food.

In efforts to conserve soil, the world is faring poorly. There are no national successes, no models that other countries can emulate. In this respect, soil conservation contrasts sharply with oil conservation, where scores of countries have compiled impressive records in recent years. Almost everywhere dependence on petroleum is declining as it is used more efficiently. But there is no parallel with soil conservation, even though soil is a far more essential resource.

The techniques for arresting soil erosion are well established, but halting excessive soil erosion is not a simple matter even for an agriculturally advanced society. U.S. farm programs over the years have demonstrated that land can be withheld from production for economic reasons. What is needed now is the integration of cropland set-aside policies with soil conservation needs. As policy analyst Kenneth Cook observes, the United States has "no policy to use the good land in preference to the worst. Indeed, with respect to matching export demand to the needs of U.S. farmers and their land and to the needs of people and resources in the developing world, we do not have responsible policy at all. We

have a simple-minded sales quota."[42]

The economic and political pressures to produce more food in the short run, with little regard for long-term consequences, have permeated the world food economy. For Third World countries, effective soil conservation initiatives are particularly difficult, complicated by fragmented landholdings. The lack of a technologically sophisticated farm population makes the implementation of conservation tillage a difficult undertaking.

Although there are no national success stories, there are occasional signs of hope. One is the trend toward reduced tillage in the United States, which was triggered by farmers' desire to reduce fuel consumption and operating costs. Although so far the farmers who are turning to reduced tillage are not usually the ones with the most rapidly eroding soils, reduced tillage may become an economically attractive first line of defense against erosion, particularly given the high cost of constructing terraces and adopting long-term rotations and other traditional approaches to soil conservation. Stabilizing soils that underpin the global economy will require widespread alterations in agricultural practices, including a reevaluation of the role of the plow. The changes in agricultural practices required to arrest soil erosion will not come easily.

Another encouraging development is that the international scientific community is beginning to respond to the erosion threat, as evidenced by several recent conferences and specially commissioned studies. The International Congress of Soil Science, which met in New Delhi in 1982, focused on the need for a world soils policy. In early 1983, the Soil Conservation Society of America convened an international conference on soil erosion and conservation; some 145 scientists from around the world presented papers. And the

American Society of Agronomy recently published proceedings of an international symposium on soil erosion in the tropics.[43]

Over the longer term, soil erosion will lead to higher food prices, hunger, and quite possibly persistent pockets of famine. Although the world economy has weathered a severalfold increase in the price of oil over the past decade, it is not well equipped to cope with even modest rises in the price of food.

In the absence of successful efforts to stem the loss of topsoil, the social effects of erosion will probably first be seen in Africa, in the form of acute food shortages and higher mortality rates, particularly for infants. Africa's record population growth and rampant soil erosion, and the absence of an effective response to either, combine to ensure that the continent will be at the forefront of this unfolding global crisis. What is at stake is not merely the degradation of soil, but the degradation of life itself.

Historically, soil erosion was a local problem. Individual civilizations whose food systems were undermined in earlier times declined in isolation. But in the integrated global economy of the late twentieth century, food—like oil—is a global commodity. The excessive loss of topsoil anywhere ultimately affects food prices everywhere.

5

Protecting Forests

Sandra Postel

Sustaining the world's forests presents a major global challenge. With ever greater demands for fuelwood and wood products and for land to feed growing populations, pressures on forests nearly everywhere are increasing. In the tropics, this pressure is most visible in the deforestation of at least 7.5 million hectares of closed forest and 3.8 million hectares of open woodland each year—an annual loss the size of Austria and Albania combined. At this rate, tropical forests will shrink by 10–15 percent by the year 2000.

In some temperate regions, where the forested area has been quite stable, air pollutants such as sulfur dioxide, nitrogen oxides, and heavy metals are threatening future forest growth and productivity. The ultimate extent and severity of this harm remains a large question. Yet existing circumstantial evidence of pollution-induced damage now renders continued levels of forest productivity highly questionable in important regions, particularly central Europe and eastern North America.

Deforestation appears to be affecting not only our natural systems but our economic and social systems as well. Fuelwood is becoming too expensive to

buy and too scarce to gather for many of that third of humanity who have no other source of cooking fuel. Floods and droughts that many believe are more severe because of deforestation have cost millions in lost crops, cattle, and human lives. As never before, unmitigated erosion of the natural resource base is having clearly visible economic and social costs.

THE FORCES BEHIND DEFORESTATION

Most numbers describing the world's forest resource base and its destruction are estimates at best. Many countries have not yet fully catalogued their forest resources and the quality of available data varies greatly. The most thorough study to date of tropical areas was completed in July 1981 by the Food and Agriculture Organization (FAO) of the United Nations.[1] Though comprehensive in scope, the report may be overly optimistic in light of FAO's obligation to accept official figures from national governments, figures that may not be wholly accurate. Nonetheless, the study, which included correspondence with 76 tropical countries and the selected use of satellite imagery, goes a long way toward documenting the current status of tropical forest resources.

Combining FAO estimates for tropical regions with U.S. Council for Environmental Quality figures for the rest of the world yields a rough picture of the world's forests. Wooded lands of all types cover about 4.89 billion hectares, an area more than triple that in crops. (See Table 5-1.) Over half this area is classified as closed forests, where the shade from tree crowns prevents substantial growth of grass. Nearly half these areas are in the tropics, with South and Central America accounting for one-quarter of the closed forests worldwide. About 25 percent of the total forested area is open woodland—areas of mixed forest and grassland typified by the Cerrado in Brazil and the wooded savannah of Africa. "Forest fallow" refers to areas cleared for agriculture and in various stages of regrowth; such areas may again support artificial or naturally

regenerated forest. Shrublands, which typically support vegetation no taller than seven meters, are so severely degraded, either because of a very short fallow period or very poor site conditions, that natural forest regrowth is virtually impossible.[2]

Though conversions of forestland are occurring everywhere, large-scale clearing of forests takes place primarily in the tropics. At least some of the continuing controversy over rates of tropical deforestation derives from confusion over a definition of terms. FAO's use of the word includes complete clearing of forest for some alternative use of the land. Not included in their estimates are other, less complete forms of alteration (from selective logging, for example) and the gradual degradation from practices such as repeated burning and overgrazing. According to FAO, 7.5 million hectares of closed forest and 3.8 million hectares of open woodlands are being cleared each year, for an annual tropical deforestation rate of 11.3 million hectares. Selective logging is thought to alter an additional 4.4 million hectares

Table 5-1. The Global Forest Resource Base

Region	Closed Forest	Open Woodland	Forest Fallow and Shrubland	Total
	(million hectares)			
Tropical America	679	217	316	1,212
Tropical Africa	217	486	609	1,312
Tropical Asia	305	31	109	445
North America	470	176	—	646
Europe	140	29	1	170
USSR	785	115	15	915
Pacific Area	80	105	5	190
Total	2,676	1,159	1,055	4,890

SOURCES: Estimates for tropical regions in 1980 from United Nations Food and Agriculture Organization, *Tropical Forest Resources,* Forestry Paper 30 (Rome: 1982); estimates for remaining regions are for early to mid-seventies from Council on Environmental Quality and U.S. Department of State, *The Global 2000 Report to the President,* Volume I (Washington, D.C.: U.S. Government Printing Office, 1980). Because of the different geographic groupings used in the two studies, the forest resources of several countries are omitted, though this should not greatly affect the regional totals.

per year. Dr. Norman Myers, a consultant on tropical forests and former resident of East Africa, estimates that conversion of all types—from deforestation to the lesser forms of degradation—is on the order of 20–24 million hectares per year. Myers's most recent estimate of deforestation of closed forests is 9.2 million hectares per year, slightly greater than FAO's figure.[3]

According to the FAO study, over half the 7.5 million hectares of closed forest cleared annually are in South and Central America. (See Table 5-2.) Forests are diminishing at an equal rate in all three tropical regions of the world at about 0.61 percent per year. Of the open woodlands cleared each year, 60 percent of the deforestation is occurring in Africa, with its large expanses of northern savannas; most of the rest takes place in tropical America. On average, 0.58 percent of all open woodlands are lost each year. If these deforestation rates continue, tropical forests and woodlands will shrink by an additional 10 percent by century's end.

Wherever it is occurring, deforestation is a direct manifestation of pressure placed on the natural resource base by the economic and social systems it supports. Fundamentally, these pressures are rooted in rising populations and rising incomes, the former driving the need for agricultural land and wood for energy and shelter, and the latter for forest products to meet consumer demands. With few exceptions, populations in tropical countries are growing between 2 and 3.5 percent per year. Conversion of forestland to cropland is by far the leading direct cause of tropical deforestation. Such conversion is often necessary: Agriculture is clearly the most beneficial use of land in some areas. The tragedy in the tropics is that increasingly the forest is cleared by landless peasants with no alternative for a sustainable lifestyle and it is happening either on land too infertile to sustain crop production over the long term or in a manner that prematurely depletes the land's productive capacity.

Shifting cultivation, which for centuries provided a sustainable agricultural system, has broken down with the population buildup of recent times. Traditionally, farmers would clear some forest, grow crops until the soil became too deficient of nutrients, and then clear a new area, returning to the original plot perhaps 20 years later. By then the land had lain fallow long enough to regain its fertility and could again support crops. But in many situations population densities no longer allow for the 10–20 hectares of land per person needed to sustain this farming system.[4] The land is overused, additional forests are cleared on soils that cannot sustain crops, and destruction spreads.

The new pattern of shifting cultivation is destroying forests and degrading soils in all tropical regions. The FAO study attributes 45 percent of all forest clearings to shifting agriculture, though the problem varies by region, being the principal cause of 70 percent of the closed forest clearings in Africa, nearly 50 percent in tropical Asia, and 35 percent in tropical America. Areas where deforestation is most pronounced are predict-

Table 5-2. Projected Annual Deforestation in Tropical Regions, 1981–85

Region	Closed Forest	Open Woodlands
	(million hectares)	
Tropical America	4.34	1.27
Tropical Africa	1.33	2.35
Tropical Asia	1.83	0.19
Total	7.50	3.81

SOURCE: United Nations Food and Agriculture Organization, *Tropical Forest Resources,* Forestry Paper 30 (Rome: 1982).

ably those where population densities are high. Nine countries of West Africa, where the population density is three times that of any other African region, account for half the forest losses in tropical Africa. Closed forests in the region are diminishing at an annual rate of between 4 and 6 percent, and the FAO report claims that the progressive disappearance of the coastal forest "is already a fact." In contrast, the Cameroon-Congolese forests in Central Africa, where the population density in forested areas is less than a tenth that in West Africa, are not yet critically threatened. Losses there average 0.2 percent per year.[5]

Conversion of forestland to cropland is by far the leading direct cause of tropical deforestation.

Examples abound of forests succumbing to shifting cultivation. A study by the Indian Institute of Science estimated that over half the forest losses in India between 1951 and 1976 were from conversions to agricultural land, where primarily the landless were "encroaching on good forests to bring the land under cultivation."[6] In Thailand, 30 years of effort by the Royal Forest Service failed to stop the encroachment of shifting cultivators into northern forests, where forest destruction has been on the order of 100,000 hectares per year.[7] Some 50,000 landless peasant families in Venezuela have been clearing 85,000 hectares of forest each year.[8] Perhaps the most striking site of shifting agriculture's effects is in the Peruvian Andes, as landless farmers push further toward the Amazon plains. In the Philippines, Nepal, northeastern India, and many other areas, increasing scarcity of land is forcing shifting cultivators up forested hillsides.[9]

To alleviate population stresses, some countries, most notably in Asia, are clearing forested land to encourage people to migrate to less populated territories. The Indonesian Government has been moving families from Bali and Java to the less populated islands of Kalimantan and Sumatra. Forests on these islands are rapidly being cleared and replaced with agriculture of relatively low productivity. Similarly, planned colonization in Malaysia is causing conversion of lowland forests to plantations of palm oil and rubber.[10]

No clearer connection between deforestation and the demands of affluent societies can be found than in the conversion of tropical forest to grazing land in Central America and Brazil, where cattle-raising offers export earnings that could help reduce external debt. Brazil has by far the greatest area of tropical moist forest in the world: 280–300 million hectares, triple the amount in either Zaire or Indonesia. Over 40 percent of that lies in the Amazon Basin, where population pressures are still minimal. The nation's staggeringly high foreign debt in recent years, now about $90 billion, explains why Brazilians now view the rich Amazon forests as an asset that can no longer be left "unused." Between 1966 and 1978, some eight million hectares of Amazon forest became cattle ranches.[11]

In Central America grazing land more than doubled between 1961 and 1978, while wooded land diminished by 39 percent. (See Table 5-3.) U.S. demand for beef has fostered considerable conversion of forest to pasture. A little over two decades ago, the United States imported only 2,000 tons of beef. By 1978 beef imports had risen to 100,000 tons and, although only a portion of these came from Central America, six out of the seven countries there were sending as much as 85 to 90 percent of their total beef exports to the United States.[12]

Table 5-3. Central America: Conversion of Forests to Grazing Land, 1961–78

Country	Grazing Land			Forests and Woodlands		
	1961	1978	Change	1961	1978	Change
	(thousand hectares)		(percent)	(thousand hectares)		(percent)
Costa Rica	969	1,764	+82	2,848	1,930	−32
El Salvador	606	690	+14	230	0	−100
Guatemala	1,039	1,976	+90	8,400	4,400	−48
Honduras	2,006	2,370	+18	7,100	3,900	−45
Nicaragua	1,710	2,820	+65	6,432	4,400	−32
Panama	899	1,430	+59	4,100	3,200	−22
Total	7,229	11,050	+53	29,110	17,830	−39

SOURCE: Norman Myers, "The Hamburger Connection: How Central America's Forests Become North America's Hamburgers," *Ambio*, Vol. X, No. 1, 1981.

Much of that beef feeds the growing demands of U.S. fast-food outlets, one of the few markets open to leaner beef from grass-fed cattle. Fast-food chains can offer low-priced hamburgers by using beef raised by low-cost labor on converted forestlands in Central America. Few people are aware of the full consequences of each bite into a fast-food burger, which Norman Myers has aptly called "the hamburger connection."[13]

Unlike forest conversions for agriculture and grazing land, fuelwood gathering by rural peasants rarely results in an immediate loss of a large block of closed forest. But the gradual degradation of open woodlands by fuelwood gatherers may eventually produce a virtual wasteland. With fuelwood gathering, as with shifting cultivation, it is primarily population pressure that has transformed a previously sustainable practice into one that is gradually destroying the resource base.[14]

For that one-third of humanity for whom firewood is the primary source of cooking fuel, demand will increase apace with population growth. Moreover, the fuelwood and charcoal needs of an emerging industrial sector are beginning to compete with those of fuelwood gatherers. In the southeast of Brazil, an estimated 38 million cubic meters of wood are converted annually to charcoal for the steel industry.[15] A growing commercial market for fuelwood also creates incentive for "entrepreneurial cutting." Near Nagpur, in central India, where people are permitted to collect dead wood in forest reserves for their domestic use, trees are apparently being cut illegally and taken to the city for sale.[16] Myers has estimated that some 150 million cubic meters of wood are cut for fuel from tropical closed forests each year. The extent of the resulting degradation of woodlands is not known. In fuelwood-short areas of Africa and Asia, however, people are having to turn to crop residues and cow dung for fuel.[17]

The role of timber harvesting in tropical deforestation is difficult to assess. FAO estimates that 210 million hectares of closed forest have been logged so far and that 4.4 million hectares of virgin forest are opened for logging each year. Because of the diversity of tree species in tropical forests, commercial loggers generally cut very selectively, taking only the most valuable species. Cutting in hardwood forests is particularly selective, with removals from a first cutting averaging 8–15 cubic meters per hectare. In Southeast Asian forests, where there is an unusually high density of commercially valuable species, hardwood removals average over 30 cubic meters per hectare.[18] But even though only 5 percent of the trees on a given hectare may be cut, the trees are so close together and connected by vines that logging can destroy 30–60 percent of the unwanted trees.[19] Moreover, three-quarters of logged forests are left unmanaged after the first cutting. Thus without economic incentives or regulations to encourage more-efficient use and better care for these forests, large numbers of trees are destroyed for a relatively small amount of wood actually sold.

ACID RAIN: AN EMERGING THREAT

Acid deposition, commonly called acid rain, is the term given to sulfur and nitrogen oxides that are chemically transformed in the atmosphere and fall to earth as acids in rain, snow or fog, or as dry, acid-forming particles. Scientists have amassed considerable evidence over the past decade that these air pollutants may adversely affect the ecosystems they enter. Although documentation of acidifying lakes in Scandinavia, eastern North America, and Canada is not new, evidence is mounting of acid deposition's severe threat to some of the world's most valued forests. Until recently, the link to the health and productivity of forests was largely speculative, and documentation of even potential effects was scarce. Studies of sick and dying trees in Europe and eastern North America, however, are leading researchers to put forth this link with greater confidence.

Over 560,000 hectares of forest in West Germany, nearly 8 percent of the nation's forests, showed damage in the fall of 1982. Just one year later, following an extensive nationwide survey, damage was estimated to cover one-third of West Germany's forests. Whereas 60 percent of the fir trees were affected in late 1982, three-quarters of them were suffering the following year. Damage was also visible on four of every ten spruce trees, which cover roughly 40 percent of West Germany's forestland.[20]

By 1990 as much as three million hectares of forests may be lost to acid rain if Poland proceeds with its present industrialization plans.

In Czechoslovakia, 500,000 hectares reportedly are damaged, with tree deaths widespread in a mountainous forested park near the East German border.[21] Another 500,000 hectares are affected in Poland. Forest researchers in Katowice, close to Krakow, say that fir trees are dead or dying on nearly 180,000 hectares and that spruce trees in areas around Rybnik and Czestochowa, also in the industrialized southern region, are completely gone. Environmental scientists warn that by 1990 as much as three million hectares of forests may be lost if Poland proceeds with its present industrialization plans.[22]

In the United States, detailed documentation of systematic forest destruction has come from research on Camels Hump, a peak forested with red spruce and balsam firs in the Green Mountains of Vermont. There, after nearly two decades of study and with the benefit of a complete inventory of the mountain's vegetation, researchers at the University of Vermont have found that half the spruce trees have died since 1965. Moreover, seedling production, tree density, and basal area have also been nearly halved.[23]

Reports on the current extent and severity of forest damage may belie the true magnitude of an impending problem. The process leading from slight to extensive damage appears to unfold rapidly. Widespread loss of silver fir trees had occurred in West Germany within a few years after the first signs of damage. And it is not always easy to recognize the symptoms. Without careful observation by a well-trained eye, early signs of damage may be overlooked. Moreover, the pattern of symptoms, such as discoloration and needle loss, may vary among species.[24]

Scientific evidence of acid deposition's link to this massive forest destruction is thus far inconclusive. Indeed, needle discoloring and a thinning of tree crowns can be caused by many things: frost, drought, wind, attacks by insects or fungi, and even poor forest management practices. But none of these causes alone seems to be sufficient to explain the patterns of forest destruction observed. As University of Vermont botanist Hubert Vogelmann writes regarding the massive spruce deaths on Camels Hump, "With many of the normal causes of tree mortality ruled out, suspicions have turned to one ingredient of our environment that has been introduced in the last thirty years—acid rain."[25]

In recent decades, the acidity of rain and snow has increased markedly in many locations. In widespread areas of eastern North America and northern and central Europe the annual average pH of precipitation is now between 4 and 4.5. For comparison, the pH of unpolluted rainfall is typically no lower than 5.6, slightly acidic from interactions with natural carbon dioxide in the atmosphere. Rain and snow in many industrial regions of the world are now 5–30 times more acidic than would be expected in an unpolluted atmosphere.[26]

This dramatic change is attributed in large part to the release of sulfur and nitrogen oxides into the atmosphere by the burning of fossil fuels and the smelting of ores. Since forest systems can usually benefit from additional quantities of nitrogen, sulfur compounds are generally considered to be the primary concern. The scientists studying West Germany's forests found that the needles of trees in severely damaged forest areas contained more sulfur than those in other areas. Also, damage was greater on west-facing mountain slopes, which are exposed to more pollutants and acid deposition.[27]

In portions of Europe, sulfur dioxide emissions from human activities have doubled since 1950. Excluding the Soviet Union (with estimated emissions of over 25 million metric tons per year), annual sulfur dioxide emissions in northern and central Europe now total nearly 27 million metric tons. Six countries account for 80 percent of this total: the United Kingdom, East Germany, West Germany, France, Czechoslovakia, and Poland. Sulfur dioxide emissions from North America are estimated at nearly 29 million metric tons per year, with over 80 percent from the United States.[28]

Before the advent of air pollution control strategies, most pollutants emitted to the atmosphere remained relatively close to their source. Between 1956 and 1976, however, the average height of the stacks at fossil-fueled power plants nearly tripled, as higher stacks were seen as better dispersers of emissions from source areas. Pollutants thus began to travel farther before returning to the earth's land and waters. Also, the longer the sulfur dioxide was in the atmosphere, the more likely it was to be oxidized to sulfuric acid.[29]

The precise mechanism by which acid deposition may be damaging trees so extensively is not known. Hydrogen ion concentration, the measure of acidity expressed as pH, affects interactions between the soil and living biomass of an ecosystem in complex and varying ways. Soil structure and composition, vegetation type, climate, and elevation are only some of the natural determining variables. Yet scientists have uncovered some common effects of increased acidity in soils. Among the most important is the leaching of vital life-supporting nutrients as the hydrogen ions react with soil materials and the buffering capacity of the soil is depleted. Both scientific theory and observation suggest that reduced quantities of nutrients such as calcium, magnesium, and potassium may be widespread in vulnerable soils after several decades or centuries of exposure to acid deposition. In addition, several studies have suggested that as soils become more acidic, aluminum, which is normally harmlessly bound in soil constituents, becomes soluble and toxic.[30]

Areas now witnessing the death of their lakes may soon be confronted with dying forests.

Dr. Bernhard Ulrich, a biochemist who has studied damaged beech and spruce forests in Solling, West Germany, for nearly two decades, has documented several phases in the acidification of forest systems. During the early stages, nutrients such as nitrogen added to the soil by acid deposition appear to increase tree productivity and growth. Between 1967 and 1969, the beech and spruce trees he studied showed double the expected growth rate. Yet during this period of increased growth, acids are building up in the soil, eventually triggering the leaching of vital nutrients and rendering aluminum soluble and toxic. When the toxic aluminum begins to attack the

root system, a tree becomes less able to take up moisture and to protect itself from insect attacks and droughts. The forests are also attacked from above by heavy metal and gaseous pollutants intercepted by tree crowns. From the patterns of tree damage he observed in Solling, Ulrich fears that every few years to every few decades a natural event will occur that, because of the accumulated air pollutants, will cause fatal tree damage.[31]

Laboratory research at the University of Vermont has shed additional light on these processes, providing evidence that acid deposition and heavy metals act synergistically in stunting the growth of trees, mosses, bacteria, algae, and fungi. This research also shows that loss due to acid rain of mycorrhizae, fungi essential to the health of a forest system, may play a role in overall forest destruction. Further, analysis of tree cores by these researchers lends credence to the link between acid rain and the mobilization of aluminum. The amount of aluminum in the wood was relatively constant throughout the first half of the century but began rising dramatically in some samples around 1950, about the time acid rain became more pronounced.[32]

Though fragmented and inconclusive, this evidence of acid deposition's effects on soils and forests can no longer be ignored. If Ulrich's description is accurate, areas now witnessing the death of their lakes may soon be confronted with dying forests. His findings offer a grave warning: Waiting for declines in forest growth as the sign of damage from acid rain may mean recognizing the problem in its advanced stages, perhaps when the damage is irreversible.

Although the amount of forest destruction that will be caused by acid deposition is a matter of speculation, both scientific researchers and political leaders are recognizing that the risks are great. Referring to the potential effects of acid rain on Canada's $20-billion forest industry, John A. Fraser, member of the Canadian Parliament, remarked in October 1982 that "the economic cost of doing nothing is staggering."[33] And in light of the large wood-volume declines on Vermont's Camels Hump since 1965 and the 57 percent drop in maple seedlings and saplings, Hubert Vogelmann echos this concern: "If such losses in only a few years are representative of a general decline in forest productivity, the economic consequences for the lumber industry will be staggering."[34]

One obvious remedy is to reduce emissions of sulfur and nitrogen oxides to the atmosphere. Without waiting for more solid proof of acid rain's link to forest destruction, the West German Bundestag passed legislation in early 1983 aimed at reducing sulfur emissions by a third within ten years. Yet even if West Germany succeeds in meeting these goals, the reduction of sulfur dioxide in its air will be much less, since about half the emissions originate outside the country. West Germany is also attempting to mitigate the existing damage by adding lime to soils in damaged areas to counteract the acidity.[35]

No doubt this link to the world's forests will heighten the international acid rain debate both within and between nations. It also implies that continued growth and productivity of some of the world's temperate forests can no longer be tacitly assumed. Developed countries with energy futures based on fossil fuels may need to reexamine the wisdom of their strategies and weigh the costs of pollution control against these new risks. Moreover, large portions of Brazil, southern Africa, India, Southeast Asia, and China have soils relatively susceptible to acidification.[36] As nations in these regions establish ambitious industrialization plans, in which fossil fuels typically figure strongly, they must consider that the means to their ends may undermine a more important and sustaining resource base.

ECONOMIC EFFECTS OF DEFORESTATION

Deforestation has thus far been fostered mainly by pressures to grow crops to feed increasing populations. Whether conversion is planned by governments to relieve food shortages or results from landless peasants seeking to survive, tropical forests typically have been viewed as an underused asset at best and an obstacle to development at worst. As forests dwindle, however, this view is bound to change. The growing scarcity of forest products will increase the comparative value of these forests and the products and services they provide. Signs of scarcity typically take two forms: shortages and rising real prices. Ultimately, scarcity fosters a shift in the way a resource is valued, used, and managed.

Firewood scarcity offers the most visible and dramatic example of deforestation's effects. In developing countries some three-fourths of the wood harvested is used for fuel. These countries both produce and consume 90 percent of the world's fuelwood; only one-tenth of 1 percent is exported.[37] Already, fuelwood scarcity is taking a heavy toll on the developing world's poor. With 90 percent of some national populations relying on firewood as their main fuel, numerous local and regional scarcities collectively bode a crisis of critical proportions.

In many West African and Central American cities a typical family may spend one-quarter of its earnings on fuelwood and charcoal, a proportion comparable to what a family in an affluent society might spend on housing.

Where wood is gathered rather than bought in a market, scarcities mean more time spent collecting wood for the family. In some parts of India, a woman or child may need to spend two full days gathering a family's weekly supply of wood.[38]

Fuelwood scarcity has fostered a dramatic rise in fuelwood prices in recent years. Whereas the real price of fuelwood—the price adjusted for inflation—showed no increase between 1963 and 1978, it went up by over 25 percent between 1978 and 1981. Since little of this commodity enters international markets, absolute prices and the trends in specific countries may vary considerably. In Dacca, Bangladesh, the retail price for fuelwood was in some years twice that of the average world export price.[39] In Indian towns, rising prices are fast making fuelwood purchases impossible for many residents. Between 1971 and 1980, the current-dollar retail price of fuelwood in Bombay more than tripled.[40] Price increases in Africa are equally telling. Fuelwood retailing for less than U.S. $8 per cubic meter in 1976 in the Central African nation of Cameroon sold for over $44 in 1981. Most extraordinary was the situation in the Ivory Coast in West Africa: Between 1976 and 1980 the retail price in the coastal commercial city

of Abidjan jumped from $26 to nearly $250 per cubic meter.[41]

These shortages are bound to worsen in the decades ahead. FAO projects that by the year 2000, the minimum fuelwood needs of some 2.7 billion people—over half the developing-world population projected for that year—either will not be met on a sustainable basis (a deficit situation) or will not be met at all (an acute scarcity). (See Table 5-4.) The situation is already a dire one. In 1980, an estimated 112 million people—half of them in tropical Africa—were experiencing acute scarcities of fuelwood. Nearly 1.2 billion people—70 percent of them in tropical Asia—were meeting their minimum fuelwood needs only by overcutting and depleting their forest resources. In all cases, rural people are the hardest hit.[42]

Wood shortages in some areas are reducing incomes and jobs. Basketweavers relying on the bamboo stocks of Tamil Nadu, at the southern tip of the Indian peninsula, reportedly now earn 25 percent less than in the early seventies and suffer periodic bouts of unemployment because of insufficient bamboo supplies. Stocks in the Western Ghats forests were once thought sufficient to keep local paper mills supplied indefinitely. Yet bamboo shortages have forced the in-

Table 5-4. Populations Whose Fuelwood Supplies Cannot Be Sustained, 1980, With Projections for 2000

| Region | 1980 | | 2000 |
	Acute Scarcity[1]	Deficit[2]	Acute Scarcity or Deficit
		(million)	
Tropical Africa	55	146	535
Tropical Asia	31	832	1,671
Latin America	26	201	512
Total	112	1,179	2,718

[1]Fuelwood consumption is below that required to meet minimum needs.

[2]Minimum fuelwood needs are met, but only by overcutting and depleting wood resources.

SOURCE: United Nations Food and Agriculture Organization, *Tropical Forest Resources,* Forestry Paper 30 (Rome: 1982).

dustry to operate at 70 percent capacity, compared with 90 percent in 1970, and some of the bamboo now comes from northeast India and the Himalayas. The plywood, match, and polyfiber industries in India are also facing shortages.[43]

The cost of repairing flood damages in India below the Himalayan watershed has recently averaged $250 million per year.

Though rarely valued monetarily, the loss of the ecosystem functions provided freely by a natural forest entails real economic and social costs. Flooding, droughts, and siltation in many parts of the world are more severe because of deforestation. A half billion people in India, Pakistan, and Bangladesh are affected by water runoff from the upper Himalayan watershed. Deforestation of Himalayan hillsides has greatly reduced infiltration and the land's ability to retain water. Rapid runoff during heavy rains and the resulting soil erosion and silting of rivers sets the stage for massive flooding downstream. The cost of repairing flood damages in India below the Himalayan watershed has recently averaged $250 million per year.[44]

In the Philippines, a government report blames deforestation for frequent flooding, erosion, the silting of rivers, and a loss of water supplies. Silting of the reservoir behind Ambuklao Dam has halved the hydropower plant's expected useful life.[45] Haiti's largest hydroelectric project may not survive past 1986 because of silting behind the Peligree Dam, and electricity rationing has already occurred in Colombia and Costa Rica because of lost reservoir capacity at hydroelectric facilities. Deforestation in Panama, besides causing siltation that

threatens the viability of the Panama Canal, has worsened both floods and droughts and rendered water supplies less reliable.[46]

The full effects of deforestation on national and international market economies are difficult to predict. With the exception of fuelwood, most forest products are part of complex international trade patterns. There is thus the potential both for shortages to echo resoundingly in faraway regions and for areas of continued forest abundance to fill in emerging supply gaps. Yet any changes in regional balances of supply and demand can shift and alter pressures on remaining tropical forests.

Demand for hardwood in the industrial countries for houses, furniture, panels, and other products has risen greatly since mid-century. Attention increasingly turned to the tropical forests, where hardwoods often comprised over 90 percent of the timber resource and labor costs were comparatively low. Consequently, annual production of sawlogs and veneer logs, the primary raw material for wood industries, more than doubled in the tropical regions between 1960 and 1980. (See Table 5-5.) Tropical Asia consistently dominated the production picture, accounting for half the average annual production in the early sixties and 58 percent in the seventies, over 95 percent of which was in hardwoods.[47]

Much of the increased production was shipped to Japan, North America, and Europe. These areas used 13 times more industrial hardwood logs in 1973 than in 1950, while consumption in the tropical regions themselves increased by only 2.5 times. Imports of tropical wood over this period increased ninefold in the United States and Europe and nineteenfold in Japan.[48] About three-fourths of Japan's supply was from Southeast Asia. Much of the tropical hardwood imported to the United States started in Southeast and

Table 5-5. Annual Production of Sawlogs and Veneer Logs in the Tropics, 1961–79[1]

	1961–65	1966–70	1971–75	1976–79
	(thousand cubic meters)			
Tropical America	22,360	26,420	32,260	42,390
Tropical Africa	10,320	13,660	15,760	16,710
Tropical Asia	32,050	47,020	65,320	80,020
Total	64,730	87,100	113,340	139,120

[1]FAO notes that these figures do not include illegal loggings, which in some countries may be 30 percent or more of recorded volumes.
SOURCE: United Nations Food and Agriculture Organization, *Tropical Forest Resources,* Forestry Paper 30 (Rome: 1982).

East Asia, often going through Japan for processing. Tropical hardwoods used in Western Europe largely originated in West and Central Africa, though in the late seventies imports from Southeast Asia increased significantly.[49]

The depletion of forests is reshaping trade patterns in tropical forest products as well as worsening some countries' balance of payments. Several long-time exporters have markedly reduced the amount of hardwood logs sent out of the country and now focus more on processing wood to meet their domestic needs. Some traditional suppliers in West Africa and Southeast Asia—areas where deforestation has reached critical proportions—have nearly eliminated their exports of sawlogs and veneer logs.[50] Ghana's 1981 raw log exports were only 7 percent what they were in 1964; Nigeria's were only 1 percent. Export declines began later elsewhere but were also dramatic: Thailand's log exports in 1981 were only 8 percent and those of the Philippines 15 percent of their peak amounts in recent years. While some countries have increased their exports of processed wood products and thereby sustained the total value of their forest exports, others have not. Nigeria's twentyfold decline in log exports between 1970 and 1980, for example, was matched by a sixteenfold decline in the export value of all its forest products.[51]

Between mid-century, when exports of tropical hardwoods began increasing rapidly, and the early seventies, a large portion of tropical logs left the producing countries in their unprocessed form. In 1973, the primary tropical wood producers exported nearly half their logs unprocessed; the notable exception was Latin America, which processed nearly all its logs and exported little of its forest products in raw form. Consequently, the unit value of forest product exports remained comparatively low. Value was added in those developing countries that processed wood into products such as plywood, particle board, and veneer sheets for domestic consumption or export. FAO economist S.L. Pringle noted in the mid-seventies that the tropical countries were failing to capture about $30–50 per cubic meter on logs used for sawnwood or veneer and $40–80 per cubic meter on logs used for plywood. If they had been able to process the 49 million cubic meters of unprocessed logs exported in 1973, tropical countries could have gained perhaps an additional $2 billion in revenue.[52]

Exports from Japan and the Philippines over the past decade are prime examples of this situation. About three-quarters of the main industrial wood exports from the Philippines in 1973 were unprocessed logs with a unit export value of $39 per cubic meter. Panels had a unit export value more than triple that of the logs but represented only 5 percent of exports. In contrast, Japan—historically a major importer of unprocessed logs from the Philippines—earned over $75 million in 1973 from exporting just 165,000 cubic meters of wood-based panels. Thus it took close to two million cubic meters of Philippine log exports to bring in as much revenue as the Japanese panels. In response to dwindling forests, rising domestic demands, and comparatively low unit export earnings for raw logs, the Philippines has decreased exports of all wood products, but especially of unprocessed logs. Higher-valued wood-based panels now account for 32 percent of forest-product export earnings, whereas in 1973 they represented just 13 percent.

These fiscally appropriate responses may prevent remaining tropical forests from following the route of other, now over-exploited areas. Indonesia, which still has 80–100 million hectares of tropical forest (roughly half of which is virgin forest), emerged as the leading exporter of tropical hardwoods in the mid-seventies and undoubtedly helped to fill the gap left by the Philippine cutbacks. (See Figure 5-1.) In 1980, over 80 percent of Indonesia's timber exports were still in the form of unprocessed logs.

Apparently realizing that it should get more financial mileage from its vast areas of remaining forest, the Indonesian Government is now strongly encouraging domestic processing of wood. With the aim of completely eliminating raw log exports by the mid-eighties, strict export quotas were imposed in 1980. George Ledec of the World Bank notes that this measure was instituted despite significant economic obstacles, including protective tariffs applied by importing countries such as Japan to processed wood products but not to raw logs. Ledec also notes that Indonesia's action has piqued multinational corpo-

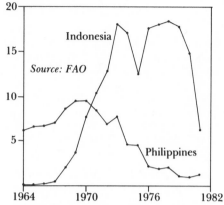

Million
Cubic Meters

Source: FAO

Figure 5-1. Sawlog and Veneer Log Exports, Philippines and Indonesia, 1964-81

rations' interest in Papua New Guinea, where deforestation and logging have not yet occurred on a large scale.[53]

The picture painted is thus one of shifting pressures within the tropical forest resource base and of more active attempts by tropical countries to derive greater value from remaining resources. Given that a raw wood supply of at least 15–30 years is needed to justify investment in local wood processing facilities, countries with substantial areas of tropical forests remaining—and desiring greater value from them—have an incentive to manage their forests on a more sustainable basis. Ironically, deforestation's implications may in this sense help reverse some of the forces that have perpetuated it.

LESSONS FROM RECENT INITIATIVES

Fuelwood shortages, uncontrolled clearing of trees for agriculture, mining of timber resources, and the increasing severity of deforestation's ecological consequences are fundamentally changing perceptions about the role of forests in tropical development. Initiatives spawned by these new perceptions have in common a new view of forests not only as complex systems in their own right but as natural systems inextricably linked to the human systems that revolve around them. Describing new forestry efforts in Honduras, Marco Antonio Flores Rodas, an FAO official and former Forestry Manager of the Honduran Corporation for Forestry Development, notes "it was intended that the distinction between forest, industry and peasant should be forgotten since they are one and the same thing."[54] Putting forestry on a sustainable footing in the developing countries requires attacking the common roots of deforestation's direct causes—population growth, poverty, landlessness, and the absence of viable options for people and governments. Both inspiring and sobering, recent initiatives are focusing attention on new responses to a rarely asked question: forestry for whom and for what?

India's western state of Gujarat is widely recognized as having that country's most innovative and initially successful social forestry program. At its core is a plantation effort under which state foresters encourage villages to establish plantations on a portion of their communal land. Recent features added to the program focus on individual forestry initiatives, supplementing the somewhat faltering progress made through community forestry.[55] One such change includes assigning to landless families 37.5 hectares of degraded forestland to be planted with seedlings at the rate of 2.5 hectares per year for 15 years. In return for a commitment of 40 days of work per month, each family is paid a fixed monthly sum of 250 rupees and offered free housing material, some

forest produce, and 20 percent of the net profit from the harvest in the fifteenth year. With a stake in the profits, families thus have both an incentive to care for the trees and a steady income until the year of harvest. Another component of Gujarat's program furnishes farmers with free seedlings to be grown on degraded and marginal farmland. Each year these farmers receive 250 rupees for each hectare they tend, provided that at least 70 percent of the trees survive.[56]

Despite its successes, social forestry in Gujarat and other areas of India has recently come under severe criticism. Particular concern has been raised about promoting the planting of eucalyptus trees. A study in the Kolar district of Karnataka State by the Indian Institute of Management found that social forestry was not achieving its goals and in fact in many ways was worsening the lot of the poor people it presumably was designed to benefit. Introduction of eucalyptus encouraged private landholders to grow trees for sale in the markets, thus supplanting traditional community dependencies and disrupting community development. Although increasing fuelwood supplies is a primary goal of social forestry, eucalyptus has thus far provided little fuel for the villagers. With the trees worth 250–300 rupees per ton, about 80 percent of the eucalyptus grown in Kolar was sold as raw material for the rayon industry in Harihar. The authors found that the plantations in Kolar did not help meet rural people's desperate need for fuel and warned that the firewood crisis may well worsen despite the "impressive" growth of eucalyptus plantations in the villages.[57]

Planting eucalyptus on cropland makes it more difficult for the poor to obtain food, income, and other basic necessities beyond fuel. Although tree planting programs are intended for marginal agricultural land, the area planted to ragi—a staple millet in rural areas—

declined by 66 percent in the Kolar district between 1977 and 1981, as much of the area was converted to eucalyptus plantations. Ragi prices in the state doubled in the course of two years, partly a result of a crop failure in 1980–81 but no doubt also a reflection of the reduced area in production. Although growing eucalyptus rather than food crops can double or even quadruple a farmer's annual income, it deprives landless laborers of employment. The Indian Institute authors estimate that each hectare shifted from food crops to eucalyptus results in a loss of 250 days of work per year. Eucalyptus is also replacing native trees that better met some of the rural people's basic needs: The loss of Honge trees, which traditionally provided oil for lighting, has made local people more dependent on expensive and unreliable supplies of kerosene.[58] Even those who dispute these criticisms of social forestry agree that the present form of these efforts threatens to widen the gap between the rural rich and poor.[59]

Social forestry as often practiced to date emerges from these assessments as very much a double-edged sword. Benefits clearly do accrue, but to whom and at what social, economic, and environmental costs? Are program objectives being met if, rather than meeting rural people's basic needs directly, success relies on benefits trickling down from those fortunate enough to derive income from supplying eucalyptus wood to the rayon industry? These complex questions demand serious attention not only in India, where forestry programs in some 100 districts are planned, but in other countries as well. One thing is clear: Measuring the success of social or community forestry efforts merely by the number of seedlings planted, without concern for what species is planted where, by whom, and for whose benefit, is insufficient and inappropriate.

Another approach to reforestation,

known as agroforestry, integrates wood and crop production. These schemes hold particular promise for areas in Central America and the semiarid African Sahel where traditional farming systems have begun to crumble under the pressure of rising populations. Attempts to squeeze more crops from marginal lands have resulted in shortened fallow periods, declining soil fertility, and reduced crop productivity; rising fuelwood demand has spread desertification.

Agroforestry projects in a number of countries are attempting to reverse these deteriorating conditions. In the Kordofan region of Sudan, where desertification and firewood shortages are extremely severe, efforts have focused on restoring the traditional practice of growing nitrogen-fixing acacia trees along with food crops. Turi Hammer, designer of the Sudan program, attributes the willing cooperation of villagers largely to this emphasis on rebuilding time-tested sustainable land-use practices, as well as to their perception that the program would supply food and water along with fuel. Overall, Hammer states, "the fact that close to 1,000 farmers have actually planted seedlings together with their agricultural crops and that many more are in line to join next year's activities shows that the farmers themselves—small and large, men and women—regard the restocking of the gum belt through agroforestry as one important measure to help secure a safe livelihood in the area."[60]

Alleviating pervasive fuelwood shortages in the tropical countries requires not only programs to increase wood supplies but also efforts to use existing supplies more efficiently. Open fires, which waste over 90 percent of the heat they generate, are still a primary means of cooking. In Kenya, where the fuel crisis is particularly acute, it takes nine million tons of wood to produce one million tons of charcoal. Yet without more-efficient stoves, this charcoal burns with only a 5–10 percent efficiency. Given that 70 percent of the charcoal is used in cities while 90 percent of Kenya's people live in rural areas, it is questionable whether Kenya can afford to use its wood in this way, even though it does ease the transport of fuel to urban areas.[61]

Although stoves are available that can cut fuel consumption in half, their introduction has met with limited success. Observers have found that rural people resist using these stoves because they often are not well suited to local social and cultural practices. Researchers at the Beijer Institute in Sweden, following extensive study of the fuel crisis in tropical Africa, concluded that "efforts to improve stove design are essentially misguided in that the criteria for design is physical efficiency rather than social efficiency."[62] As with social forestry programs in general, working with the local people in the planning and design of technologies to improve their cooking and heating methods is essential.

In several countries where logging has contributed to forest depletion, programs have been introduced to protect forests from wasteful and unsound timber practices. One apparently successful effort in the Philippines integrates local processing of pulpwood with an agroforestry program aimed at stabilizing the livelihoods of the shifting cultivators largely responsible for forest destruction. The Paper Industries Corporation of the Philippines (PICOP), a 30-year-old public corporation, was a pioneer among tropical countries in developing domestic wood processing facilities. By 1971, PICOP had established pulp and newsprint mills, a container board plant, a sawmill, two plywood mills, a veneer plant, and a blackboard plant. PICOP's integrated complex allows it to use nearly all the tree species and qualities of wood found on the 183,000 hectares of public land it manages under license from the Philippine Government.[63]

PICOP's innovative program encourages nearby small farmers to grow trees on their marginal farmland for sale as pulpwood for the industry's mills. This program, funded in part by the World Bank, offers loans to farmers through the Development Bank of the Philippines and helps participants to plant and care for the seedlings. The tree grown is albizia, a fast-growing legume especially suitable for manufacturing newsprint. Through PICOP's extension services, farmers have also been taught ways to improve their farming and livestock methods. By March 1978, a total of 3,400 farmers were growing roughly nine million seedlings on 16,600 hectares.[64] John Spears of the World Bank cautions that cash-tree programs such as this are suitable mainly when a processing plant is located within a reasonable distance. Transportation costs prevented small farmers outside a 100-kilometer radius of the PICOP mill from participating. Nevertheless, similar schemes hold promise for other countries, and tree-farming projects are being developed near other processing plants in the Philippines.[65]

China and South Korea have been widely lauded for their success in reforesting their countrysides to restore the environmental support functions of their degraded lands. More countries are now following suit. The World Bank is funding watershed protection efforts in India, Indonesia, Nepal, the Philippines, and Thailand. These projects involve not only soil conservation and reforestation projects but also measures to improve irrigation, flood control, and farming and grazing practices so as to create more-sustainable land use systems in these areas. An analysis of benefits accruing to farmers from a soil conservation and forestry program in Thailand showed that increased crop yields and fuelwood and fodder production would give the project a rate of return of 13 percent—evidence of the real economic value of ecologic restoration.[66]

THE PROSPECTS FOR SUSTAINABILITY

Sustaining the forest resource base involves defining the socially optimal magnitudes and mix of wooded lands—old-growth natural forest, natural or artificially regenerated forest, plantations, and woodlots—that will both allow demand for wood products to be met without depleting the forest capital and preserve the essential nonmarket values of the forest ecosystem. Changes now taking place in the structure and composition of tropical forest resources resemble those that occurred in the temperate zone in past decades. Increasing demands for wood and wood products have diminished old growth natural stocks, bringing demand and available supplies into closer range. This has fostered a gradual shift away from reliance on natural forests toward greater production and use of wood from higher-yielding plantations.[67]

The current rate of planting would have to be increased more than 13 times to reach the level needed to meet year 2000 needs.

In most regions of the tropics this transition has begun only recently. The FAO assessment of tropical forests projects a resource base in 1985 of about 2.9 billion hectares, of which 40 percent will be closed natural forest; 24 percent,

Table 5-6. Projected Tropical Forest Resource Base, 1985

Forest Type	Area
	(million hectares)
Closed Natural Forest	1,163
Open Woodlands	715
Forest Fallow	435
Shrubland	622
Total	2,935

SOURCE: United Nations Food and Agriculture Organization, *Tropical Forest Resources,* Forestry Paper 30 (Rome: 1982)

open woodlands; 15 percent, forest fallow; and 21 percent, degraded shrubland. (See Table 5-6.)

Plantations are expected to cover 17 million hectares by 1985, only 1 percent of all natural forest and open woodlands. Based on estimates of existing plantations and programs planned or under way, FAO projects that 59 percent of these plantations will grow trees for industrial wood uses—primarily sawlogs, veneer logs, and pulpwood—while the rest will be nonindustrial plantations growing trees to provide wood for fuel or charcoal, nonwood products such as fruits and gum arabic, or protection of soil and catchment areas. (See Table 5-7.) Industrial plantations are expected to increase at 580,000 hectares per year between 1981 and 1985, 15 percent more than during the preceding five years. Nonindustrial plantations are projected to grow by 519,000 hectares per year, a 24 percent rise over the preceding five years.[68]

At this rate of planting, the ratio of tropical areas being deforested to areas being planted with trees will be ten to one. Some of the deforested areas will support secondary growth; overall, however, planting will fall far short of compensating for deforestation. More important is the extent to which the projected mix and productivity of forest

**Table 5-7. Establishment of Plantations in the Tropics, 1976–80,
With Projections for 1981–85**

Plantation	Annual Area Planted		Total Area by 1985
	1976–80	1981–85	
	(thousand hectares)		
Industrial Plantations	503	580	9,968
Fast-growing hardwoods	149	214	3,185
Other hardwoods	127	100	2,734
Softwoods	227	266	4,049
Nonindustrial Plantations	418	519	7,039
Fast-growing hardwoods	286	385	5,211
Other hardwoods	90	87	1,310
Softwoods	42	47	518

SOURCE: United Nations Food and Agriculture Organization, *Tropical Forest Resources,* Forestry Paper 30 (Rome: 1982).

resources could meet future world needs on a sustainable basis. Here the picture is sobering, particularly for fuelwood in the developing world.

Given current planting rates, tropical nonindustrial plantations will cover 14.8 million hectares in the year 2000, slightly more than twice the area today. If the wood from all these plantations were used for fuel, and if each hectare annually yielded 20 cubic meters, 296 million cubic meters of fuelwood would be available from plantations in the year 2000. Extrapolating prevailing per capita consumption levels to the year 2000, when the developing world's population is projected to be 4.86 billion, yields a requirement of 2.19 billion cubic meters of fuelwood. Thus fuelwood plantations would meet only 14 percent of these needs. The current rate of planting would have to be increased more than 13 times to reach the level needed to meet year 2000 needs. Moreover, since 112 million people lacked sufficient fuelwood as of 1980, per capita consumption figures are below what they would be if fuel needs were being met adequately. Indeed, FAO projects that 3 billion cubic meters of fuelwood might be needed for the developing world in the year 2000. Meeting this target would require an eighteenfold increase in current planting.[69]

Although no cause for complacency, the global picture for industrial wood appears bright next to these foreboding figures for fuelwood. A team of experts assembled by FAO from industries, universities, and governments estimated that global resources in the year 2000 could supply over 2.5 billion cubic meters of wood on a sustainable basis and that demand under moderate growth assumptions should be about 2 billion cubic meters. However, the team's projections pointed to large imbalances in regional demand and supply. Western Europe and Japan are projected to have net trade deficits in the year 2000 of 75 and 118 million cubic meters, respectively, and collectively the industrial countries (excluding the Soviet Union and Eastern Europe) are expected to need imports totaling 130 million cubic meters. Moreover, higher rates of population and economic growth would increase demand worldwide. Under FAO's high-growth assumptions, demand in 2000 would be about 2.6 billion cubic meters, exceeding projected available supplies.[70]

The FAO team assumed that wood from developing countries could fill in two-thirds of the expected 130-million-cubic-meter gap in industrial countries through less-selective cutting of existing stocks, logging of less accessible areas, and plantations. Based just on estimates of forest area and productivity, the Soviet Union could comfortably supply the additional 50 million cubic meters needed to balance the global demand-supply equation. Of the Soviet Union's estimated 785 million hectares of forests, only about half are considered accessible for timber operations. Softwood taken from these exploitable forests is already thought to be outpacing the sustainable harvest, yet hardwood removals are only about one-fourth the estimated sustainable yield of 250 million cubic meters. Thus while balancing overall numbers, the study team foresees strains on supplies of tropical logs, softwood logs, and pulpwood.[71]

Clearly, the practical reality may not match the on-paper possibility of balancing world wood needs with supplies in this manner. Export decisions by the Soviet Union and developing countries undoubtedly will be shaped by domestic goals and policies that may not accord with the needs of wood-short regions. And per capita consumption of wood products in the developing world has risen dramatically in recent years. (See Table 5-8.) The combination of these trends and Third World population increases will intensify pressures for domestic use of tropical wood. China was assumed by the FAO team to be self-sufficient in both hardwoods and softwoods over the long term. Yet log exports to China from the United States jumped from 210,000 cubic meters in 1980 to 1.28 million cubic meters in 1982—a sixfold increase.[72] Chinese import needs in the future will depend on population growth, industrialization plans, and the success and scale of

Table 5-8. Per Capita Consumption of Wood Products in Developing Countries, 1970 and 1980

Product	1970	1980	Change
	(cubic meters)		(percent)
Fuelwood and Charcoal	.445	.452	+ 2
Industrial Wood[1]	.090	.118	+31
Paper and Paper Board	.005	.008	+60

[1]Industrial wood is the sum of industrial roundwood, sawnwood and sleepers, and wood-based panels.

SOURCE: United Nations Food and Agriculture Organization, *Regional Tables of Production, Trade and Consumption of Forest Products: World Economic Classes and Regions* (Rome: 1982).

afforestation efforts, all presently open to speculation. Indeed, the team concluded that if world demand reaches the projected high-growth level of 2.6 billion cubic meters, the additional needed wood might come "at a considerably increased cost, from the tropical forests of the Amazon Basin and the less accessible coniferous forests of Siberia and from lower quality North American hardwoods. Additional quick-growing plantations in the tropics would also be needed."[73]

Although laced with uncertainties, these trends clearly portend rising prices and greater pressure to log tropical forests. Competition for increasingly scarce tropical logs between importing countries and wood-processing industries within the producing countries will also raise prices. Use of more species and grades of wood from tropical forests, as well as of mill residuals for pulpwood, can counterbalance some of these pressures. Yet with an exacerbating fuelwood crisis in the developing world and the newly recognized possibility of declines in forest productivity in some key temperate regions from acid deposition, sustaining an adequate global timber supply will present some hard choices.

More plantations are clearly a key to meeting future demands. The story of plantations so far in tropical countries is one of unrealized potential. Eighty-five percent of the areas undergoing reforestation are planted with one of three types of trees: pines, eucalyptus, or teak. Many other species may prove more useful in meeting not only demands for wood but also the varied needs of local populations. Initial experiments with some little-known tropical legume species, for example, are showing great promise. The characteristics of many legumes make them ideally suited to the multiple purposes of reforestation efforts. They are natural pioneers in plant succession, and thus a logical choice for reforesting degraded lands and controlling erosion. Many species can be seeded directly, avoiding the expense and complications of distribution from nurseries; with their ability to fix nitrogen, they require little or no fertilizer. Their inherent hardiness suits them remarkably to degraded nutrient-poor soils and a variety of climates and environments. A recently published manual describing 90 different firewood species includes 35 belonging to the legume family.[74]

Although clearly optimistic about these species' potential, scientists who have introduced and studied them in various locations and conditions are cautious not to view them as a panacea. Monoculture plantations, especially of introduced species, are not without ecologic risks, and the hardiness of some of these species raises the possibility of their becoming uncontrolled weeds. An informed verdict on the real potential and consequences of these tropical tree legumes will not be in for perhaps five to ten years. Yet results to date are promising.

Leucaena, which has shown productivities of 30–50 cubic meters per hectare, is being planted on thousands of hectares in the Philippines, including large areas of degraded grasslands. Leucaena supplies fiber suited for papermaking and wood for pulping, as well as forage, fuel, and fertilizer. Acacia trees have taken hold on barren spoil dumps from tin mining in Malaysia and helped to stabilize eroding hillsides in Indonesia. Foresters have planted over 15,000 hectares of degraded land in Malaysia with another acacia variety that appears to grow on quite acidic soils. Its high-quality wood offers potential for sawed timber, furniture, veneer, firewood, and charcoal as well as pulp and paper. Fuelwood plantations of calliandra now cover some 200,000 hectares in Java, many planted by local villagers who often intercrop these small firewood trees with fruit trees and vegetables.[75]

Many other species look equally promising. Collectively, they not only hold potential for helping to meet fuel and industrial wood demands, but also may enhance the prospects for a sustainable way of life for rural populations. Their beauty lies in their apparent ability to battle not only deforestation's consequences—both economic and ecologic—but its causes as well. If even 10 percent of the land now in forest fallow were planted with species yielding an average of 10 cubic meters per hectare, an additional 870 million cubic meters could be available each year to help meet fuelwood and other needs.

Plantations clearly cannot be the sole savior of tropical forests. Odd as it may sound, further exploitation of natural forests themselves may be a key to their survival—not traditional exploitation for timber, but exploitation and sustainable use of the multitude of other products this rich resource offers. Citing a host of specialty materials valuable to industry —including latex, gum, camphor, resins, tannins, and dyes—Norman Myers pictures the possibility of industrial centers using as raw materials tropical forest products harvested on a sustainable basis with little disturbance of the natural forest.[76] Ways to exploit tropical forests' economic potential while preserving their essential ecologic functions are many, though as yet they are little recognized or explored.

In most developing countries, the institutions, financial capital, and social mechanisms needed to chart a sustainable course for forest resources are not yet available. International lending organizations have a vital role to play not only in helping define this course but in providing the technical and financial means by which developing countries can embark upon it. The World Bank and U.N. lending agencies are now placing increased emphasis on community forestry, on projects for ecologic restoration, and on forestry's integral role in rural development. Although none of the agricultural and rural development projects funded by the World Bank between 1969 and 1972 included a forestry component, 17 of those between 1973 and 1977 did. Over 60 percent of World Bank loans for 1978–80 forestry projects were geared toward environmental protection and fuelwood production. FAO's 1982–83 budget for forestry programs was 30 percent higher than the previous year, including a 67 percent increase in projects for rural development.[77]

No infusion of dollars, however large, can alter the present course of forest destruction without the institutions and social mechanisms to direct these dollars to the problem's core. Recent efforts show that forestry programs are bound to fail if they neglect the basic needs of the forest's human dependents. As M.A. Flores Rodas of FAO states, "Once we are all convinced that, in order for the forest to survive, its inhabitants must survive first, we shall reach the point where both can survive."[78]

Greater emphasis on social forestry, reforestation, and forest preservation engender optimism. Yet the deforestation dilemma still cries for more commitment, clarity, and vision. Reforestation efforts are less than a tenth of what they need to be to avert a worsening fuelwood crisis. Dollar commitments for creating and maintaining tropical forest reserves are woefully inadequate to ensure that species and gene pools are preserved for this and future generations. New institutional mechanisms are needed to generate and wisely channel the billions of dollars needed over the coming decades to sustain the products and nonmarket values of these forests. It is neither plausible nor equitable to expect the developing countries endowed with this resource to shoulder the burden of its preservation unaided. Tropical forests' intrinsic role in maintaining ecologic integrity and biological and genetic diversity make them global assets warranting a global commitment to their preservation.

6

Recycling Materials

William U. Chandler

Wood, iron, and aluminum, the principal materials used in a modern economy, will serve as basic building blocks of a sustainable future. But their availability is threatened by the uncertain prospects for energy, a resource with painfully obvious constraints.[1] Simply maintaining current levels of materials production will require prodigious quantities of energy. World steel production alone consumes as much energy annually as Saudi Arabia produces. To raise global per capita use of metals to U.S. levels would require the energy output of seven Saudi Arabias, or 40 percent of commercial energy consumption. Many people still lack basic material amenities—metal for water pipes, wood for housing—and the earth's population is still growing. Recycling, fortunately, can cut the energy required in materials production by 50 to 90 percent and thus help narrow the widening inequity between the world's rich and poor.

Throwing away an aluminum beverage container wastes as much energy as pouring out such a can half-filled with gasoline; failing to recycle a weekday edition of the *Washington Post* or *Los Angeles Times* wastes just about as much.[2] Because producing and consuming energy to manufacture wood, aluminum, and steel products create severe environmental problems, recycling promotes environmental protection. And solid waste disposal, at $30–100 per ton, represents a major budget item for many cities.[3] Residents often react strongly against having dumps located near their homes, creating political roadblocks to waste disposal. The prospect of achieving a 40 percent reduction in solid waste, as some cities have done, offers leaders a tangible political and economic opportunity.

Recycling thus saves energy and expensive raw materials, protects the environment, and cuts waste disposal costs. Despite these advantages, only about one-quarter of the world's paper, aluminum, or steel is recovered for reuse. Nevertheless, certain areas have made remarkable progress. These cities, states, and countries have developed markets for the waste products they collect and have facilitated collection in a variety of ways. Many countries have invested in recycling equipment even when locally available scrap has been insufficient; imports of waste paper, scrap iron, and aluminum scrap have thus contributed to recycling elsewhere. Their investments have saved capital and energy and have helped nations compete in international markets by reducing debt, improving trade balances, and lowering the cost of products manufactured for export. A large international trade in recyclable materials has developed, in fact, providing a powerful new tool that can transform a wasteful world materials industry into one that is sustainable.

Wood, aluminum, and iron take priority in recycling because their production requires large quantities of energy and causes major environmental problems. Also, their abundance should satisfy demand for base materials in the foreseeable future. Among resources, however, wood takes a special place: It is a fuel, a building material, the raw material for paper, and a substitute for oil as a feedstock for chemicals production. And it is renewable. Sustaining the world's forests, already being depleted faster than they are being renewed, is therefore a special necessity. Yet progress in recycling paper has been slower than that of aluminum, and the paper recycling industry is much smaller than that of iron and steel.

Each material requires different recycling technologies, policies, and markets. The constraints on recycling may differ from resource to resource, much as trade barriers for iron scrap differ from tax subsidies for timber harvesting. Removing such obstacles may require action on planes as different as local zoning boards and international trade commissions. Each resource, its potential for recycling, and its special technical and political circumstances must be considered in turn.

THE VIRTUE OF NECESSITY

Recycling has been an environmental goal for a decade now, but only a few areas of the world have registered gains. Voluntary recycling efforts have brought some success, but progress has come about mainly in response to necessity. Countries that have increased materials recycling have been motivated by three main factors: short supply of raw materials, high energy and capital costs for processing materials, and high environmental costs in materials production and disposal. Countries that have not progressed have generally masked necessity with price controls and trade barriers. Those that have succeeded, however, have turned their handicaps to advantage. They have cut both environmental and economic costs of materials use.

Recycling half the paper used in the world today would meet almost 75 percent of the demand for new paper and would free 8 million hectares of forest from paper production.

Metals recovery reduces pollution. Using coke in iron ore reduction produces copious quantities of airborne particulates, including carcinogenic substances such as benzopyrene.[4] Recycling iron and steel reduces these particulate emissions by 11 kilograms per metric ton of steel produced. It also cuts coal and iron ore mining wastes by 11,000 kilograms per metric ton recycled. These solid wastes, unless handled properly, can contaminate surface and groundwaters with acid and toxic metal drainage. Recycling aluminum reduces air emissions associated with its production by 95 percent. (See Table 6-1.) Doubling worldwide aluminum recovery rates would eliminate over a million tons of air pollutants, including toxic fluoride.[5]

Table 6-1. United States: Environmental Benefits of Recycling[1]

Environmental Benefit	Paper	Aluminum	Iron & Steel
		(percent)	
Reduction of Energy Use	30–55[2]	90–95	60–70
Reduction of Spoil & Solid Waste	130[3]	100	95
Reduction of Air Pollution	95	95	30

[1]Percent reduction in BTUs, tons of waste, tons of particulates, etc., per ton of material recycled.
[2]Refers to combustion of both commercial energy and wood residues. [3]More than a 100 percent reduction is possible because 1.3 pounds of waste paper is required to produce one pound of recycled paper. If all paper were recycled, the waste reduction, of course, would equal only 100 percent.
SOURCES: R.C. Ziegler et al., *Impacts of Virgin and Recycled Steel and Aluminum* (Washington, D.C.: U.S. Environmental Protection Agency, 1976); *Waste Paper Recovery* (Paris: Organisation for Economic Co-operation and Development, 1979).

Paper recycling helps preserve forests. Paper products use about 35 percent of the world's annual commercial wood harvest, a share that will probably grow to 50 percent by the year 2000.[6] Although a sanguine attitude regarding the state of the world's forests has a certain following, there is little reason for complacency. As documented in Chapter 5, the world's tropical hardwood forests are expected to decline 10 percent by the end of the century. The softwood forests of western Russia have long been harvested at unsustainable rates, while those of central Europe are dying from air pollution. The resulting decline in wood production will put additional pressure on other forests.[7] The United States, producer of one-third of the world's commercial forest products, would be expected to take up much of this slack. But the harvest of mature softwood forests in the United States has exceeded replacement for several decades. Industry-owned forests, in fact, have been cut so heavily that mature trees have been depleted at an annual rate of 1 to 2 percent, apparently since the early fifties.[8]

Forests in the United States may not be as ample as many imagine, however, and may require additional protection. U.S. officials define a forest as an area as small as one acre that is 20 percent covered by trees. Mature softwood trees are identified as those over nine inches in diameter, though this describes a very young forest. Intensively managed woodlands will not retain the species diversity of natural forests and will not be as resilient against disease and pollution. Advocates of more intensive harvesting in the United States point out that "growing stock" has been cut at rates far below replacement, but they ignore the fact that, as the *Wall Street Journal* put it, "these forests are neither deep, nor dark, nor lovely."[9] Much of what is called forest can neither satisfy human aesthetic needs nor produce commercial timber.

Paper recycling can help satisfy additional paper needs for years to come. Only 25 percent of the world's paper is now recycled, though no technical or economic reasons prevent a doubling of this figure by the end of the century. Recycling half the paper used in the world today would meet almost 75 percent of the demand for new paper and would free 8 million hectares (20 million acres) of forest from paper production, an area equal to about 5 percent of Europe's woodlands. But projections of the future use of the waste paper resource are far less optimistic. Franklin Associates, a consulting firm specializing in paper recycling, projects that recycled paper will supply only 28 percent of world paper production in the year 2000.[10]

Less well known are the economic benefits of materials recycling. Producing paper, aluminum, and iron and steel from secondary instead of virgin materials typically halves investment costs and, though varying with the product and the country, can cut total costs significantly. Because energy costs are also lower, recycled paper can compete favorably in many markets, depending on the cost of collecting the paper. The total production costs for producing aluminum and iron and steel from scrap instead of ore can be 10 to 30 percent lower. Debt-ridden developing countries and their lenders could benefit from investing in recycling rather than materials production from virgin ores and fibers.[11]

Unfortunately, many nations—industrial as well as developing—continue to mask the growing necessity of capturing recycling's benefits. They subsidize energy use with price controls, production tax incentives, and the uncontrolled environmental cost of producing and using energy in materials processing. The full cost of energy-intensive materials is not accurately represented in prices, and the incentive to reduce these costs is consequently diminished. The true cost of energy includes damage to forests from acid rain, to human health from pollution, to human and aquatic populations displaced by hydroelectric projects, and so on. Solid-waste disposal costs usually are paid in general taxes, not by individuals who create waste, leaving no incentive to reduce costs. And export barriers have been erected specifically to reduce the price of metal scrap, a measure that reduces the incentive to collect scrap and makes it less available as a substitute for primary materials. Countries that lead in recycling have removed most, if not all, of these masks.

Waste Paper

World waste paper consumption has increased 140 percent since 1965. Paper consumption has doubled over the same period, however, so the share of paper recycled has changed only slightly, from 20 percent in 1965 to 24 percent in 1982. Despite this poor record, certain countries have achieved much higher rates of paper recycling than others. (See Table 6-2.) Moreover, much of this progress has been made only in the last ten years. (See Table 6-3.)

Japan, the Netherlands, Mexico, South Korea, and Portugal lead in waste paper recovery or use. Japan in 1980 collected almost half the paper used in the country. The Netherlands, which has

Table 6-2. Paper Use and Waste Paper Recycling, Selected Countries, 1978–80

Country	Annual Paper Consumption Per Capita	Recovery Rate[1]
	(pounds)	(percent)
Mexico	n.a.	50
Japan	326	45
Netherlands	347	43
Spain	156	40
South Korea	87	38
Hungary	132	37
West Germany	346	35
Sweden	477	34
Italy	205	29
Brazil	64	29
Australia	295	28
United States	580	26
Canada	417	18
Philippines	22	16
Nigeria	7	2
World Estimate	80	24

[1]Waste paper collected as a percent of paper consumption, three-year average, 1978–80.
SOURCE: United Nations Food and Agriculture Organization, Advisory Committee on Pulp and Paper, "Waste Paper Data 1978–80," Rome, 1981.

Table 6-3. Waste Paper Recovery, Selected Countries, 1960–80[1]

Country	1960	1965	1970	1974[2]	1980
			(percent)		
Australia	n.a.	16	n.a.	23	28
Austria	22	25	30	30	33
Canada	16	15	19	18	19
Denmark	21	13	18	28	27
France	27	27	28	31	30
West Germany	27	27	30	32	35
Italy	15	17	21	28	30
Japan	n.a.	37	39	39	47
Netherlands	34	34	40	46	44
Norway	16	20	17	21	22
Spain	25	28	28	32	38
Sweden	26	21	22	28	33
Switzerland	33	33	31	40	35
United Kingdom	28	29	29	28	34
United States	n.a.	22	21	24[2]	27
World Estimate	n.a.	20	21	24	25

[1]Waste paper collected as a percent of paper consumption.   [2]Data for 1975 unavailable, except for the United States.
SOURCES: 1960–74 data from Organisation for Economic Co-operation and Development, *Waste Paper Recovery* (Paris: 1979); 1980 data from United Nations Food and Agriculture Organization, Advisory Committee on Pulp and Paper, "Waste Paper Data 1978–80," Rome, 1981.

been a leader in paper recycling for decades, recovered 44 percent of its paper in 1980.[12] South Korea, Portugal, and Mexico doubly contribute to waste paper recovery: They have high recovery rates and they import waste paper.

Why do some countries perform better than others? Their admirable performance has been predictably promoted by necessity. These "fiber-poor" countries, without substantial forests available for pulpwood harvesting, have been pressed by price and scarcity to conserve waste paper. This may be partly a matter of choice for the Japanese, since they have forests on their northern islands that they do not heavily exploit. South Korea has made great strides in reforestation, but still places heavy demand on its forests, especially for firewood.[13]

Success in Japan and the Netherlands

has been promoted by twin necessities. In addition to being "fiber poor," both are crowded, land-poor countries with populations strongly opposed to waste dumps. These factors together have driven up both the economic and the political costs of wasting paper. Importing finished paper was expensive, and the Japanese passionately opposed dumps being located near their homes, making it politically costly for leaders to override residents' protests. The Dutch similarly opposed landfill disposal of municipal waste. Since 20 to 40 percent of Japanese and Dutch municipal solid waste is paper, recycling ameliorates waste disposal problems.[14]

Japan's efforts in recycling have historical roots but began in earnest in the mid-sixties. Now about 10 percent of Japan's total municipal waste is recycled, and efforts to increase this proportion continue.[15] Collection of waste materials is done in surprisingly diverse ways, suggesting that systems can be made to work in any number of circumstances as long as collected waste can be sold for a reasonable price.

One of the first programs in Japan resulted from the efforts of a private entrepreneur who in 1966 persuaded the government of Ueda City to pay him a portion of the "avoided costs" of landfilling the materials that his firm recycled. The city has found it preferable to pay a small recycling incentive than to pay a larger amount for waste disposal. The plan requires residents to separate refuse into combustible and noncombustible material. Glass is separated by hand at the dump and ferrous metal removed by magnet.[16]

Elsewhere in Japan, Hiroshima has achieved stunning success: Disposal of raw refuse has been reduced by 40 percent since 1976. Student clubs, parent-teacher organizations, and other nonprofit groups that organize source separation programs and the delivery of waste materials are paid at or above market rates, with a subsidy made possible by savings from avoided landfill fees. In Fuchi City, a suburb of Tokyo, the local government purchased recycling equipment for the use of a private firm. The firm must turn over to the city much of the revenue earned from sales of recyclable materials, but is permitted to keep 20 percent of any revenues above the costs of collection and operation of the facility. In a variation of this approach, the Shiki district of Tokyo made the initial investment in equipment, but lets a company earn all its revenues from the sales of recyclables.[17]

"We have to change [wasteful] culture from the very roots," asserts Muneo Matsumoto, an official in Machida, "the garbage capital of Japan." Machida boasts that its new recycling program of source separation and computerized processing recycles 90 percent of the city's garbage.[18] Progress such as this flows from the legendary discipline of the Japanese, their proclivity for efficiency, and their willingness to cooperate and solve problems. The grass-roots information system provided by citizens works well, apparently as a result of the incentives provided to groups. The Japanese make it easy to participate and difficult not to participate in paper recycling.

The Dutch have taken a different, though equally successful, approach to waste paper collection. As in Japan, necessity motivated national and local governments to encourage recycling: Both fiber resources and land for waste disposal have been scarce. The Netherlands has historically achieved the best paper recycling record in the world, using a few key policies to make the marketplace work better. For example, the government established the world's first waste exchange, a free brokerage service to match buyers and sellers of waste. The government has also attempted to stabilize the typical boom-and-bust cycles in recyclables by establishing "buffer stocks."

The recycling industry is particularly vulnerable to wild cyclical swings in the market, and the recent recession has been the worst since the Great Depression. Buffer stocks enable collectors of waste paper in the Netherlands to sell to the government-established fund when prices drop below a predetermined level. The stock is sold when prices go up again, and the fund is thereby replenished.[19] Some economists say this is costly and sometimes counterproductive. It is difficult to match its operation with the needs of the market and thus to avoid undesired market distortions. Yet the approach has been used in both Japan and the Netherlands, the two leading nations in paper recycling, and may merit further consideration elsewhere.[20]

The Netherlands also strongly promotes source separation, though differently from Japan, which has relied more on awareness, information, incentives, and armies of nonprofit organizations. The Dutch simply enacted a law requiring source separation in all municipalities that have contracted for collection of waste paper. Their success reinforces the point that any number of policies may be applied to effect recycling once a society makes it a priority.

Mandatory source separation has recently been applied with success in the United States. Islip, New York, was sued by the state to halt landfilling, partly because its dump was contaminating underground water and releasing vinyl chloride into the air. A court settlement required the city to initiate recycling. Residents may now be fined up to $250 for noncompliance. No major enforcement actions have been needed yet, however, because the 50 percent compliance rate has exceeded the city's capability to handle recyclables. The collection program has succeeded without costly investments in sophisticated engineering devices. Residents simply place recyclables in containers, putting glass and cans on top and paper underneath. The city sorts ferrous material with magnets and the rest by hand, as in Ueda City, Japan.[21]

"Markets first, collections second" should be the philosophy of recyclers, according to Ronald Rosenson of the National Association of Recycling Industries in the United States. That is, the first priority in materials recycling policy should be to establish demand for recyclable products. If markets are established, collection will follow. To encourage market development, the Scandinavian countries have created a cooperative waste exchange; Sweden, in fact, helps industries with hazardous wastes find buyers who can put the material to productive use. These exchanges are based on the principle that one firm's

waste may be another's raw material. A West German waste exchange founded in 1974 has brokered over 20,000 offers and requests for recyclable materials and has expanded into Austria, Switzerland, northern Italy, and France. But as the experience in the most successful countries suggests, simultaneously establishing markets and encouraging collection with various strong measures is important.[22]

Machida (Japan) boasts that its new recycling program of source separation and computerized processing recycles 90 percent of the city's garbage.

Necessity is the mother of collection, and uneven distribution of the world's forest resources provides some nations with local abundance despite global scarcity, thereby lessening their pressure to recycle. But just as wasting gasoline in an oil-rich country carries an opportunity cost in lost export sales, so does waste of recyclable paper. If properly promoted, the new and growing international market for waste paper could provide a strong incentive to all countries. International waste paper trade has grown from almost nothing in the early seventies to about 10 percent of all waste paper collected, or 2–3 percent of all paper used in the world. The value of this trade totals some $600 million, depending upon volatile market prices.[23]

Mexico now produces half its paper from waste paper. In South Korea, imported waste provides 40 percent of the fiber used in paper production. Almost half of Italy's paper production also depends on waste, a significant portion of which is imported. Canada imports half the waste paper it uses.[24] This, unfortunately, is a consequence of the low collection rate within its own borders. Most other importers have high domestic rates of waste paper collection. The high percentages achieved in Japan, the Netherlands, South Korea, and Mexico are all the more remarkable considering that much of the paper they use is exported as packaging for manufactured goods.

The United States now dominates the international waste paper trade, accounting for 85 percent of net sales. The significant expansion of trade between this leader and Mexico, South Korea, and Japan during the seventies can serve as a model for development of waste paper trade elsewhere. China, India, the Philippines, and Thailand could all become large markets for recyclable paper.[25]

But obstacles to trade could effectively block such development. Though trade in waste paper has so far met with few serious constraints, several factors have kept it below its potential. South Korea, for example, imposes a 10 percent import fee on waste paper. Because the United States is the main source and shipping rates are extremely favorable on this route, the tariff has not deterred paper exporters. Under less favorable transportation terms, however, tariffs and constraints on licensing imports would hinder recycling. Transportation, in fact, has been a serious impediment. Waste paper trade between the United States and Venezuela has been crippled by high rates, and inadequate rail facilities have hampered trade between the United States and Mexico. Another significant impediment has been unstable currency exchange rates. High values for the U.S. dollar have reduced the country's exports of waste paper.[26]

In addition to encouraging the expansion of international trade in this resource, paper recycling can be promoted by creating or widening its cost advantages over paper made from virgin pulp. One advantage could be provided by increasing the price of virgin wood pulp to reflect its true economic value. In nations where mature softwood forests are harvested faster than they are replaced, reducing the rate of harvest would put the price of pulp closer to its long-term economic value. Forests would thus be afforded greater protection and waste paper recycling would be encouraged. Paper and wood prices need not increase as long as additional quantities of waste paper are recovered and recycled.

The U.S. Government could take a major step in this direction, since it owns half the softwood forests in the country. The U.S. Forest Service directly affects the price of pulp by leasing large areas of national forests each year regardless of market demand. The suspension or modification of this practice, coupled with a setting aside of more publicly owned forests for wilderness and parkland, would reduce the environmental subsidy of the use of virgin pulp and increase the relative attractiveness of waste paper. The United States may also find it particularly advantageous to acquire and protect forests in the Southeast, where wood harvesting is growing rapidly.

The price of waste paper can be stabilized by increasing demand for it and by expanding its collection. Higher, more stable prices would provide an incentive for commercial collection. Local zoning ordinances to reduce landfill disposal of paper wastes, along with broader regional or national laws requiring source separation and mandatory collection of waste paper, will increase supplies and thus serve to prevent drastic price increases. Indeed, the greater problem will be to maintain demand for waste paper. International markets will be essential for this purpose.

Waste paper will not be used unless there is the means to use it, and this implies that a marked change is needed in investment strategies in the papermaking process. Following World War II, most Canadian and U.S. papermakers built mills to exploit virgin pulp. A different type of mill is required to produce paper from waste. Private companies will be induced to build recycling mills mainly by policies that increase the price difference between virgin pulp and waste paper.

In developing countries, however, using cheap waste paper—domestic or imported—rather than imported pulp or finished paper products has already proved economically attractive. International development agencies and financial institutions have begun to recognize the cost-cutting potential of investment in waste paper recycling in the Third World. The World Bank contributed almost $1 million in 1982 to improve the efficiency with which Egypt's outcasts and garbage pickers, the Zebaleen, collect Cairo's wastes. The organization has also supported a multimillion-dollar project in Egypt that will recycle paper.[27] Such investments in developing countries can lead to higher rates of waste paper collection by creating a ready market.

Government procurement of recycled paper stimulates recycling. By law, the U.S. Government must purchase paper made from recycled fibers, but the Carter and Reagan administrations have ignored this requirement. The state government of Maryland, however, has effectively complied with a similar law: Twenty-five percent of the state's paper is now recycled stock.[28] The Organisation for Economic Co-operation and Development also encourages procurement of recycled paper for its own use as well as for that of its 24 member nations.

The use of waste paper as a fuel in the United States has unfortunately created an obstacle to increased recycling, which J. Rodney Edwards of the American Paper Institute calls "the worst threat to paper recycling." This threat is "flow control," or government monopoly of the flow of waste materials. The opposition to and cost of landfilling has drawn municipal governments to the use of re-

source recovery systems, which burn refuse to produce energy. But some cities have gone beyond using refuse and want to burn paper now being recycled. Akron, Ohio, for example, has built a resource recovery plant and has fought to control all waste products in the city. The plant's creditors successfully pressured the city to ensure that all burnable waste would flow to the facility in order to increase the revenues generated by its energy sales. This meant that would-be recyclers collecting old newspapers, cuttings from envelope manufacturers, or corrugated containers from supermarkets could be forced to deliver these materials to the city dump to be burned.[29] As a fuel, waste paper is worth about $20 per ton, while recyclable paper has a value of $40–60 per ton or more.

The Japanese, the Dutch, and others also widely use incineration and energy recovery, but only after recyclable waste paper has been collected. These facilities can be sized in advance to account for paper removed for recycling. If they are not, however, cities will have a powerful incentive to discourage recycling. Many U.S. facilities were planned in the energy crisis atmosphere of the seventies. But as David Brower, founder of Friends of the Earth, said in opposition to a resource recovery plant in his home town, they may be "a good idea whose time has passed."[30] Some U.S. advocates of recycling call for a federal law to protect recyclers from monopoly control of municipalities' wastes. Since the United States has 34 energy recovery facilities in operation, 20 nearing completion, and many others under consideration in communities facing shortages of landfill space, millions of tons of recyclable waste paper could soon be "wasted" in municipal incinerators.

Another government constraint on recycling stems from the control of energy prices. The United States, for example, controls the price of natural gas, which ranks second only to waste wood as a fuel for the U.S. paper industry. As a result, the industry uses more natural gas and less waste wood to produce paper. Paper prices do not reflect the true energy costs of production, and this in turn lowers the rate of paper recycling by decreasing the relative value of waste paper. Because the United States produces one-third of the world's paper, the government's policy on natural gas prices in effect reduces waste paper demand throughout the world.[31]

RECOVERING ALUMINUM

Substituting aluminum for heavy steel in automobiles saves gasoline. Substituting it for glass or for steel packaging saves energy in transportation and may allow easier, more efficient recycling. Yet primary production, from bauxite, requires 20 times as much electricity as using aluminum scrap as a metallic feedstock. Bauxite and coal must be strip-mined, and rivers are often dammed to generate hydroelectric power for smelting. Discarded aluminum containers spoil the environment. Because these problems are serious, and because aluminum will play an important role in any industrial society, aluminum recycling is essential.

The world is far from achieving the technical potential for aluminum recycling. Although some analysts estimate that 80 percent of aluminum can be recycled, less than 30 percent of that produced in 1981 came from scrap. Half the recycled aluminum came from industrial wastes—scrap produced in the smelting or cutting and fabrication of finished products.

The low worldwide rate of aluminum recycling is caused in part by rapid growth in the production of durable consumer items such as appliances.

These products last many years and so do not soon yield their metal to recycling. Purchases of washing machines, refrigerators, and automobiles in Brazil, for example, grew at an annual rate of 24 percent in the early seventies.[32] Such countries, moving from low to high per capita rates of aluminum consumption or experiencing high rates of population growth, can expect somewhat less aluminum to be available for recovery. But many countries—such as Australia, Canada, Norway, and the United States—have had high per capita rates of aluminum consumption for years yet recycle relatively small amounts. (See Table 6-4.) Low recycling rates in these countries

Table 6-4. Aluminum Use and Recycling, Selected Countries, 1981

Country	Aluminum Consumption Per Capita	Recovery Rate[1]
	(pounds)	(percent)
Netherlands	21	42
Italy	27	41
West Germany	45	33
United States	56	32
United Kingdom	20	28
France	26	27
Japan	42	25
Switzerland	34	21
Norway	42	20
Sweden	34	19
Australia	41	16
Canada	36	16
Austria	27	15
Brazil	5	13
Mexico	7	10
Soviet Union	n.a.	10
World Estimate	7	28

[1]Aluminum collected as a percent of consumption.

SOURCES: The Aluminum Association, Inc., *Aluminum Statistical Review for 1981* (Washington, D.C.: 1982); U.S. Bureau of Mines, *Minerals Yearbook 1981* (Washington, D.C.: 1982).

may be due to historically low energy prices.

Since energy accounts for 20 percent of the cost of producing aluminum from virgin ore, the progress made in recycling during the seventies can be explained in part by energy price increases. (See Figure 6-1.) Great strides were made in the United States, illustrating that modern society can adapt to increasing scarcity without sacrificing living standards. U.S. aluminum recycling has reduced both environmental pollution and the need to construct costly new power facilities, thus freeing scarce capital for use elsewhere in the economy.

Canada, Japan, the Soviet Union, the United States, and West Germany produce 60 percent of the world's aluminum. Australia, China, France, Italy, Norway, Spain, and the United Kingdom bring the total to over 75 percent. Italy produces half its aluminum from scrap, while West Germany and the United States produce one-third of theirs from recycled aluminum. Italy's performance is particularly impressive because its per capita consumption has long averaged less than half that in the United States and 60 percent that in West Germany.[33]

Norway is the world's sixth largest aluminum producer and the fourth highest per capita consumer. The country is often cited as an example of environ-mental sensitivity, yet it directly recycles only 4 percent of the aluminum it consumes and exports large quantities of scrap, which brings the total to 20 percent. Much of Norway's scrap finds its way either directly or indirectly to Italy, another sign of the importance of international trade in recyclables.

The Soviet Union, the world's second largest aluminum producer, altogether recycled and exported only 10 percent as much aluminum as it consumed in 1979 or 1980. This low level may be attributed to the complicated and highly centralized control of materials production and allocation and to energy price distortions similar to those caused by U.S. price controls during the seventies.

These aluminum recovery rates can only provide a relative index of how well a nation has performed. The figures include scrap from fabricating mills, which undoubtedly overstates progress in each major producing country. Nevertheless, the dramatic differences, especially between countries with high rates of production and consumption, can be instructive.

Just ten years ago the United States ranked low in recycling among the world's major aluminum producers. (See Table 6-5.) Subsidized hydroelectric power and cheap coal kept electricity prices low. But coal price increases and cost overruns at nuclear power plants in the aluminum-producing Tennessee Valley and Pacific Northwest greatly increased the cost of power and, thus, of primary aluminum.[34] These rising energy costs had a dramatic effect in this field: Recycling grew from 17 percent to 32 percent in ten years.[35] U.S. scrap consumption jumped 17.7 percent in 1981. The most dramatic change came in aluminum cans. Only 15 percent of aluminum cans were recycled in the United States in 1972; by 1981, over half were recycled.[36] The United States recycled as much aluminum-can scrap in 1981 as

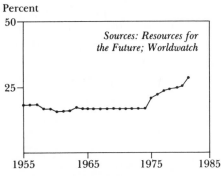

Percent

Sources: Resources for the Future; Worldwatch

Figure 6-1. World Aluminum Scrap Use, 1955-81

Table 6-5. Aluminum Recycling, Selected Countries, 1954–81[1]

Country	1954	1960	1965	1970	1975	1981
			(percent)			
France	21	19	17	20	23	27
West Germany	45	39	39	34	30	33
Italy	27	29	33	37	41	41
Japan	19	26	29	28	15	25
United Kingdom	30	32	36	35	30	28
United States	18	16	17	17	26	32
World Estimate	19	16	17	17	21	28

[1]These countries represent 50 percent of world aluminum production. Recycling rates represent secondary recovery, including scrap aluminum consumed in both primary and secondary production, and net scrap consumption.
SOURCES: Data through 1970 from Leonard L. Fischman, *World Mineral Trends and U.S. Supply Problems* (Washington, D.C.: Resources for the Future, 1980); 1975–81 data from *Aluminum Statistical Review for 1981* (Washington, D.C.: The Aluminum Association, Inc., 1982).

the entire continent of Africa produced in both primary and secondary smelters. This also means, of course, that the United States threw away more recyclable aluminum in the form of beverage cans than Africa produced.[37]

Norway's poor recycling record is probably due to its abundance of inexpensive hydroelectric power. Although the long-term migration of energy-intensive industries to energy-rich countries such as Norway may be a positive step toward a sustainable society, in the current era of unattained recycling potential it presents a hidden pitfall.[38] Subsidies for energy use—whether they come in the form of energy price regulations, government and development bank financing of hydroelectric facilities, or environmental degradation from flooding, species extinction, and fuel combustion—unnecessarily waste resources.

The largely untapped potential of aluminum recycling suggests that many energy projects planned around additional primary aluminum production are unnecessary. Ten years of environmental opposition to hydroelectric development in Norway has restricted expansion of primary aluminum production

there.[39] Similarly, opposition halted a dam designed to produce power for aluminum smelting in Tasmania.[40] These actions may increase the availability of affordable aluminum since they will force a more economical use of resources.

Only 15 percent of aluminum cans were recycled in the United States in 1972; by 1981, over half were recycled.

Despite high energy costs, Japan recycles only about 25 percent of the aluminum it consumes. But per capita aluminum consumption was low in Japan until the last decade, when rates climbed sharply. Much of Japan's "consumption," in fact, is shipped out of the country in manufactured products such as automobiles. The Japanese mainly use steel cans and glass bottles for beverages, and so less aluminum scrap is available than in the United States. Yet Japan's primary aluminum industry has seriously lost its ability to compete.

(Italy's industry is in a similar position. It has tottered on the brink of collapse for several years, and its secondary industry may be the only healthy segment that remains.[41]) Japan generates electricity with oil, so power there now costs more than in most countries. Japanese primary aluminum production, as a result, has dropped by about 25 percent over the last ten years, and the industry's losses in 1982 totaled over $500 million. Less than 20 percent of the industry's primary aluminum production capacity, in fact, is deemed competitive.[42]

In 1981, the Japanese actually produced more aluminum from secondary metal than from primary sources. One-quarter of the scrap processed was imported from the United States: bringing back parts of Toyotas and Datsuns, as it were. In the meantime, Japan has imposed tariffs on imported aluminum ingot and has pursued investment in primary aluminum production in seven countries. Japan's share in these investments assures Japanese companies as much primary aluminum as the country used in 1982 (872,000 tons).[43]

As with waste paper, international trade brings a new and dynamic force to the recovery of scrap aluminum. Scrap moving across national boundaries in 1980 totaled 820,000 tons, representing more than 5 percent of world aluminum production. At 36¢ per pound, the value of internationally traded aluminum scrap amounted to almost $600 million in 1980.[44]

Three leading consumers of recycled aluminum—Italy, Japan, and West Germany—each import large quantities of aluminum scrap. Japan imported as much in 1981 as it used ten years earlier. With primary production declining as a result of oil price increases, secondary production in Japan increased 138 percent over the last decade, with as much as 70 percent of the increase made possible by scrap imports. Twenty percent of

the total aluminum production of both West Germany and Italy in 1980 can be attributed to scrap imports.[45]

In 1981, the Japanese produced more aluminum from secondary metal than from primary sources.

Yet European scrap smelters pose a threat to the free trade of aluminum. Seeking lower scrap prices, their owners argue for increased trade barriers to restrict scrap exports from their countries. A trade publication of the secondary smelter industry reports that "EEC [European Economic Community] secondary smelters are . . . endeavoring to ensure that the export of high value and energy-rich raw material is restricted by the re-introduction of export quotas." These quotas were removed by EEC countries in 1981 and replaced with a less restrictive export licensing system, after which exports of aluminum doubled.[46] The importance of trade to the growth of recycling is clear. The "markets first, collections second" strategy will be defeated by efforts to suppress aluminum scrap prices. Similar efforts to suppress iron and steel scrap prices have historically plagued recycling.

The importance of recycling aluminum cans is also clear. Fully one-quarter of all U.S. aluminum production goes into packaging, half of which is beverage containers. Mexicans used about 6.5 pounds of aluminum per capita for all uses, while Americans used 6.7 pounds per capita for beverage containers alone.[47] Although packaging can be an important means of protecting food and other products, unless it is recycled such consumption would not seem to be sustainable.

The private sector has made commendable progress in collecting aluminum cans for recycling. One of the most exciting innovations in recycling is the "reverse vending machine," a machine that accepts aluminum cans (rejecting ferrous cans, glass, or other unwanted objects), weighs the aluminum deposited, and dispenses money or coupons in payment. One machine in North Dakota reclaimed 109 tons of cans in one year, and 20 reverse vending machines in Denver, Colorado, paid out over $1 million in an 18-month period. Sweden plans to build and install an estimated 10,000 reverse vending machines as part of an effort to recover 75 percent of the aluminum cans used in the country. This would save 10,000 tons of aluminum annually (500 million cans), as much as Sweden imports each year.[48]

In the United States, the Colorado-based Coors Brewery makes a special effort to recycle cans: It has a contract with its aluminum supplier that provides a discount in return for recovered aluminum. Coors opened eight recycling centers in Atlanta, Georgia, even before it sold products there. The company each year collects over 50,000 tons of aluminum cans in more than 20 states.[49]

Though it is encouraging that Americans now recycle 54 percent of the cans they use, countries and individual states with container deposit legislation have made much more dramatic gains. Deposits are now required on all beverage containers sold in Sweden, Denmark, Norway, the Netherlands, and several provinces in Canada. Nine states in the United States now require such deposits, and the recent addition of New York, the country's second most populous state, to this list represents major progress for recycling. (See Table 6-6.) Return rates of both bottles and cans exceed 90 percent in most states where the programs have been in effect long enough to be measured, almost twice the U.S. national rate.

In almost all states with container de-

Table 6-6. United States: States with Beverage Container Deposit Laws

State	Refillable Bottles	Cans
	(percent returned)	
Oregon (1972)	95	92
Vermont (1973)	93	90
Maine (1978)	93	93
Michigan (1979)	96	96
Iowa (1979)	96	90
Connecticut (1980)	—	—
Massachusetts (1983)	—	—
Delaware (1983)	—	—
New York (1983)	—	—

SOURCES: William K. Shireman, *Can and Bottle Bills* (Stanford, Calif.: California Public Interest Research Group and Stanford Environmental Law Society, 1981); U.S. General Accounting Office, "States Experience With Beverage Container Deposit Laws Shows Positive Benefits," Washington, D.C., December 11, 1980.

posit laws, total litter has been reduced by 35 to 40 percent by volume, and beverage container litter by 75 to 86 percent. No state with a bottle bill has lost jobs on a net basis. Though container recycling may reduce jobs in materials production and container manufacturing, it creates jobs in container collection, transportation, and reprocessing. In Oregon, the U.S. pioneer in this policy, a net total of 200 jobs were created. In Michigan, the first state to test container legislation in a densely populated urban setting, 4,600 jobs were created. A nationwide beverage container law in the United States would, according to the U.S. General Accounting Office, create a net total of 100,000 jobs. As an additional benefit, litter cleanup costs could be reduced; in Maine, they were halved. For all these reasons, almost three-quarters of the U.S. population favor container deposit legislation.[50]

Promoting the use of aluminum containers in preference to others might actually conserve resources. The steel can, when it is tin plated, is so difficult to recycle that even the recycling industry calls it "a can of worms."[51] "Tin" cans, which are mostly steel with a thin coating of tin to prevent corrosion, are not easily recyclable because the tin fuses with the steel. Most recycled tin cans, in fact, are used as a catalyst in copper production. The metal in them is actually consumed in the process and cannot be recovered. The aluminum can, which is readily recyclable, could beneficially replace steel-alloy or bimetal cans, and even glass. Both glass production and recycling broken glass are energy-intensive processes, and unless a returnable bottle is re-used at least ten times before being discarded or crushed, it offers no energy savings over recycled aluminum cans. Replacing the steel and glass now used for food containers with aluminum would thus save energy and materials.[52]

Twenty reverse vending machines in Denver, Colorado, paid out over $1 million in an 18-month period.

Continued growth in recycling will depend on both market development and scrap collection. International markets, especially in developing countries, could provide the impetus for increasing collection in countries with high consumption rates. Investments in secondary recovery can be encouraged by international lending agencies, by nations that want to improve their balance of trade, by entrepreneurs, and by environmentalists. International banks could exploit this opportunity to promote environmentally acceptable and economically sustainable growth with a technology that produces aluminum for half the capital of primary facilities with only 5 percent as much energy. The World Bank, unfortunately, has apparently all but ignored this potential in the late-1983

draft of its forthcoming "World Aluminum Industry Study," preferring instead to ask traditional questions about how much new electric capacity investment will be required to run primary facilities.[53]

National governments, moreover, still seem interested mainly in primary aluminum production. The response of the Ministry of International Trade and Industry in Japan to the high cost of primary production there has been to move the industry to developing countries with cheap hydroelectric power.

Secondary aluminum provides an alternative to environmentally troublesome additional primary aluminum production. But taking advantage of the alternative will require investing time and money in campaigns to enact container deposit legislation, an assurance of free trade in scrap, and the introduction of energy pricing policies that reflect the real economic cost of energy.

IRON AND STEEL

The world steel industry now uses scrap for 45 percent of its iron requirements, and many countries rate high marks for iron and steel recycling. (See Table 6-7.) Those with some of the best records—Belgium and Luxembourg, Czechoslovakia, Italy, Spain, the United States, and West Germany—use scrap for 60 to 75 percent of the metal used in steelmaking, if steel mill scrap is included.[54] But steel mill scrap basically just recirculates in the production process, meaning that these percentages would be only half as large if only purchased scrap—scrap from fabricators and consumers—were counted. Post-consumer scrap recovery represents only one-quarter of the iron and steel recycled, and if the United States is any indication, only 45

Table 6-7. Steel Consumption and Scrap Recycling, Selected Countries, 1980–82

Country	Annual Steel Consumption Per Capita	Recovery Rate[1]
	(pounds)	(percent)
Belgium-Lux.	714	40
United Kingdom	715	35
United States	1,120	35
Netherlands	723	35
Japan	1,387	31
Poland	1,162	31
Czechoslovakia	1,607	30
Spain	514	29
West Germany	1,210	27
Italy	1,010	24
Sweden	1,096	24
Brazil	291	21
India	40	21
Soviet Union	1,250	17
China	99	9
World Estimate	400	25

[1]Represents steel scrap collected (excluding steel mill scrap and including net exports) as a percent of steel consumed; three-year average.
SOURCES: Worldwatch estimates based on U.S. Bureau of Mines, *Minerals Yearbook, 1981, Vol III* (Washington, D.C.: 1982), *Statistical Abstracts, 1983* (Washington, D.C.: U.S. Government Printing Office, 1983), and unpublished data provided by the Bureau International de la Recuperation, Brussels.

percent of the iron and steel that becomes obsolete—ready for recycling following consumer use—is actually recycled each year.[55] (See Figure 6-2.) Moreover, this rate is only half as high as in 1955, when the high rates encouraged by World War II still lingered.

One measure of the lack of progress in iron and steel recycling, in fact, is the increase in the stock of obsolete scrap. In 1978, the backlog of recoverable ferrous scrap in the United States alone totaled over 600 million tons. Since then, it has grown to 680 million tons and is expected to grow further.[56]

Certain countries appear to have far worse recycling records than others in iron and steel. Among East European nations, Czechoslovakia, Poland, East Germany, and Hungary consume scrap at relatively high rates. The Soviet Union, however, ranks as one of the lowest users of scrap in the world, with a rate half that of Japan, the United States, or West Germany. Argentina, Brazil, China, and Yugoslavia consume very low levels of scrap. Necessity again appears to be at work, for countries with sufficient indigenous sources of iron ore do less recycling.

But using iron ore because it is available may be a false economy. Scrap costs little more than iron ore and can be converted to steel with much lower capital costs. The most vibrant sector of the U.S. steel industry, in fact, is the "mini-mill," which includes electric arc furnaces. These use virtually 100 percent scrap, compared with 45 percent in open hearth furnaces and 28 percent in basic oxygen furnaces. Use of electric arc furnaces has grown dramatically around the world, especially in the countries with the highest recycling rates. The NUCOR mill in South Carolina exemplifies the advantage of building a "minimill" with an arc furnace: The mill earned a profit

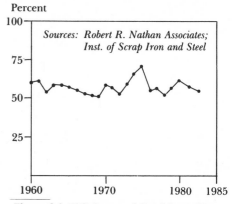

Figure 6-2. U.S. Iron and Steel Scrap Use (as a Percent of Scrap Generated), 1960-82

in 1982 during one of the worst years ever in the steel industry.[57]

A valuable new iron ore reduction technique, direct reduction of iron (DRI), eliminates coking and reduces energy costs. The pig iron produced by DRI is even called artificial scrap. Many countries, including Brazil and Nigeria, have adopted this technology. Total capital costs for direct reduction, however, run as high as for conventional steel production. Despite the advantage of scrap-based production, Brazil still has one of the world's lowest rates of scrap utilization.

Nigeria has recently moved to eliminate its dependence on imported steel by investing in DRI. At a new mill, directly reduced iron is mixed with scrap in four new electric arc furnaces, with scrap supplying 25 percent of the charge. The result has been unsatisfactory, however, since the total cost of Nigerian steel is $880 per ton compared with import prices of $315–450. Nigeria might instead have collected more of the cars now rusting in junkyards around the country and processed them in electric arc furnaces. The cost of scrap-based steel would probably have been even lower than the most favorable finished steel import price and only 25 percent of their current production costs.[58] Thus, developing countries with or without iron ore resources should find electric arc production the technology of choice, followed by direct reduction of iron ore.

Developing countries and all nations not well endowed with scrap may think that investing in electric arc furnaces is unduly risky. History has shown that scrap exports have been and could easily again be restricted. American steel-makers have consistently sought to keep scrap prices low by lobbying the government to restrict the export of scrap. Such policies seriously diminish the prospect for iron and steel recycling. They threaten the $11-billion world ferrous scrap industry, in which the United States has the largest stake. In 1980, before the worldwide recession devastated the scrap business, U.S. scrap dealers handled more than $5-billion worth of scrap, about 15 percent of which was exported. In 1980, the United States exported more than 11 million tons of scrap worth almost $1.3 billion, for 75 percent of the world's net international trade in iron and steel scrap.[59]

U.S. steel-makers may have legitimate complaints about unfair trade practices in some steel-producing nations. Western Europe, for example, provides extensive subsidies to steel-makers, many of which are owned in large part by governments. These subsidies are not reflected in steel prices and therefore not only permit unfair competition but also discourage more-cost-effective production, meaning greater use of scrap.[60] Just as the defense of free trade requires the maintenance of open borders, it also requires regulation of unfair trading practices.

Many metals are alloyed with iron to increase its strength, resistance to rusting, and ductility. Sorting, separating, and reprocessing these alloys has become a sophisticated business. Scrap processors now use shredders, flotation devices, melting furnaces, and other equipment to prepare complex mixtures of scrap metals for recycling. An automobile, for example, contains not only iron and steel but also copper wire and zinc handles. Scrap processors now are so proficient that virtually all the zinc in recycled automobiles is recovered. These skills will have to become even more highly developed, however, if recycling of iron and steel is not going to result in their contamination by other metals.[61]

Market development must be the first priority for recycling's promoters. Promotion would best be accomplished by stimulating investment in electric arc furnaces and removing trade barriers. The need to conserve energy has been the greatest impetus to the use of scrap because of the quantities of energy embodied in it. Eliminating subsidies for energy production and use should be a high priority for promoting iron and steel scrap recycling markets.

Norway imposed a $100 deposit on new cars, refundable with a $50 bonus for any car properly disposed of.

Promotion of iron and steel collection will be much more difficult. Beverage container deposits help recover steel as well as aluminum and glass. More importantly, as mentioned earlier, they virtually eliminate the use of the steel can. This saves resources overall. Flow control laws requiring that recyclables flow to publicly owned or backed resource recovery facilities can hurt steel recycling just as much as they hurt paper recycling. Monopolization of municipal markets for scrap collection diminishes the marketability of scrap by reducing economic incentives for its collection.

Norway and Sweden have been praised widely for what have been called model iron and steel scrap collection policies. In the early seventies, 400,000 abandoned car hulks littered the Swedish countryside. A 1976 law required the disposal of cars with authorized scrap dealers. In Norway, 50,000 autos had been abandoned, with 20,000 more each year being junked. Norway followed Sweden's example and introduced its own disposal law, but applied a tax rather than regulatory policy. Enacted in May 1978, the new law imposed a $100 deposit on new cars, refundable with a $50 bonus for any car properly disposed

of. In the first eight months of the program's operation, 33,000 car hulks were collected, compared with an average 20,000 per year before the law.[62]

Though Norway's car deposit and Sweden's disposal law have apparently been successful, they would have been unnecessary if there had not been artificial constraints on the scrap market. Sweden has essentially prohibited exports of iron and steel scrap since 1927, and Norway permits export of scrap only when the would-be exporter demonstrates that no market for it exists in Norway. The result is a greatly reduced market that permits price fixing and artificially suppressed prices.[63] Norway's iron and steel recycling rate remains substantially below the world average.

On the other hand, Norway produces iron ore, which in other countries has reduced scrap use.[64] The automobile deposit may have helped offset this factor. The refund system reduced the cost of abandoned automobile scrap collection and thus encouraged recycling. A similar policy could be applied to spur recycling in iron ore-rich countries such as Brazil.

STEPS TO A RECYCLING SOCIETY

As the age of cheap energy fades and as inflation, joblessness, and pollution intensify, sustaining material living standards in rich countries and satisfying basic material needs in poor ones becomes more difficult than ever. Recycling yields back much of the energy and capital invested in materials. In this way, recycling conserves energy, fights pollution and inflation, creates jobs, and helps put society on an economically and environmentally sustainable development path.

The seventies proved recycling's practicality and worth. Japan and the Netherlands collect half their waste paper. Successful programs in some Japanese cities have reduced the amount of land required for waste dumps by 40 percent, thus saving disposal costs and improving the environment. Beverage container deposit legislation in nine American states has pulled recycling rates for bottles and cans over 90 percent. In addition, Maine has cut its litter collection costs in half, and Michigan's economy has gained a net total of 4,600 jobs.

The development of a dynamic international trade in scrap paper, aluminum, and iron and steel has shown that huge markets can be created for collected waste. South Korea's ability to produce 40 percent of its paper from imported waste paper holds out the hope that paper use can be expanded in increasingly literate Third World societies without increasing pressure on forests. And because mills for recycling paper cost half as much to build as those using virgin pulp, recycling can reduce the debts of developing countries. Large imports of aluminum scrap by Italy and Japan have enabled them to sustain industries suffering from the high cost of oil-fired electricity. Spain and Italy have shown that they can compete successfully in steel markets by using purchased iron and steel scrap for half their production requirements. And the United States, with nearly $1.3 billion annual earnings from exported scrap iron and steel, has illustrated the tangible value of collecting waste.

Countries that have moved toward recycling paper, aluminum, and iron and steel have thus enhanced their competitive position in international markets. Recycling will become an even more important factor in international competitiveness as energy and capital costs increase the expense of producing goods.

Despite these gains, the world has fallen far short of achieving recycling's potential. The global recovery rates of paper, aluminum, and iron and steel could be doubled or tripled for each material. But three difficult steps must be taken to collect recyclable materials and to develop additional markets for them.

As a first step, consumers should pay the full costs of the materials they use. The world's forests have been cut faster than they have been replaced, a practice that makes wood cheaper now at the expense of future generations. Setting aside additional forest reserves would make virgin pulpwood more expensive compared with waste paper and would both assure the protection of some forests and encourage paper companies to buy waste. As owner of half the softwood timber in the United States, the U.S. Forest Service should consider reducing sales of trees for harvesting as long as waste paper is underutilized.

The global recovery rates of paper, aluminum, and iron and steel could be doubled or tripled for each material.

The first step also requires a special effort to reduce energy price subsidies. No single factor has increased recycling more in the last 30 years than the energy price increases of the seventies. Recycling saves energy, and industries adopt it to cut energy costs; but when the price of energy is distorted by subsidies, industries are less motivated to recycle. Thus when societies subsidize energy use by providing grants or loans for dams and power plants or by applying measures that hold the price of energy below replacement costs, they encourage environmental degradation. To subsidize energy consumption is to subsidize the "throwaway society."

The second step toward a recycling society involves building world markets for scrap paper, aluminum, and iron and steel. Wealthy countries restrain the export of scrap iron and steel and seriously inhibit the use of imported scrap in developing countries. The European Economic Community, for example, restricts scrap trade between its members and nonmembers. Austria, Denmark, and Sweden prohibit essentially all scrap exports, and the United States continually considers limiting scrap exports. Few countries needing new steel production capacity will risk reliance on imported scrap unless scrap-exporting countries remove the threat of scrap "embargoes."

The final step, one that will also reduce environmental subsidies, promote international scrap trade, and soften the impact of higher energy prices, demands the greater collection of wastes. Container deposit legislation can dramatically increase the return of beverage containers. Incentives, information, or the threat of fines and noncollection of garbage can induce higher returns of recyclable material. A wide variety of policies, in fact, will stimulate recycling and can be applied at national or local levels.

These steps will not be taken simply because they are logical or urgently needed, but because concerned citizens insist that they be taken. Conservationists, unfortunately, have shown too little interest in assuring market pricing for energy and free trade of scrap materials, though they have much at stake in these policies. National and local government leaders have shown little willingness to take the difficult step of requiring collection of recyclable materials, but the rising costs of litter cleanup and landfilling waste are bound to press them to do so. Industry leaders in individual countries will increasingly be forced by higher energy and raw materials prices to consider recycling or face a future in which they cannot compete in world markets.

The future of all society will be an uneasy one if a major portion of the world is forced to live with a low or declining materials standard. Materials recycling has become necessary if society is simply to maintain current living standards. But within this necessity lies the opportunity to improve the material well-being of all the world's people, and to do so without great cost to the environment. In this resides the great virtue of recycling.

7

Reassessing the Economics of Nuclear Power

Christopher Flavin

The eighties were supposed to be a decade of booming construction and copious electricity generation for the nuclear power industry around the world. The Organisation for Economic Co-operation and Development (OECD) projected in 1970 that its member nations in Western Europe, North America, and Japan would have 563,000 megawatts of nuclear generating capacity by 1985—approximately half the total generating capacity these countries now have.[1] Over 100 nuclear power plants a year were expected to be built during the eighties, many of them in the Third World.

Today, just a decade after some of the rosiest of these forecasts were made, the world is using less than half as much nuclear power as anticipated. Projections of future use have shrunk even more. Estimates for 1990 now show a nuclear sector only a third as large as once expected.[2]

The largest curtailments have occurred in the United States, where cancellations of plants have outrun new orders for nine years, but with only a few exceptions countries around the globe have cut back on their plans. The nuclear pipeline is now likely to run dry in most countries by the end of the decade. The *Financial Times Energy Economist,* a newsletter of the international energy establishment, reported in early 1983 that "the day when nuclear power will be the world's leading electricity source now seems to have been postponed indefinitely."[3]

Nuclear power is plagued by many se-

Many of the issues in this chapter are discussed in greater detail in Christopher Flavin, *Nuclear Power: The Market Test* (Washington, D.C.: Worldwatch Institute, December 1983).

rious issues that remain unresolved, including safety, waste disposal, and nuclear weapons proliferation. Something much simpler, however, is giving the industry most of its current problems. In most countries nuclear power is no longer economically attractive. Years of cost overruns have destroyed the economic underpinnings of many programs, and much slower growth in electricity use has called into question the need for many nuclear plants now being built. All indications are that nuclear power's economic competitiveness continues to deteriorate and could lead to further cutbacks. Indeed, the development of nuclear power may come to a complete standstill by the late eighties.

THE SELLING OF NUCLEAR POWER

Commercial nuclear power has a short history. Although the atom was first fissioned in Germany in 1938, a decade and a half later weapons of mass destruction, nuclear submarines, and some important medical uses of radiation were the only real "fruits" of the nuclear age. Yet enthusiasm ran high. To many people nuclear power seemed the key to the world's future. It would supply infinite amounts of energy indefinitely and would remove many of the constraints under which humanity had struggled for millennia.

In the early fifties, both the United States and the Soviet Union greatly accelerated their R&D programs to commercialize nuclear power. Many different reactor designs were tested and enormous technological strides were made. One result was the world's first electricity producing reactors: a small breeder plant built by the United States

in 1951 and a five-megawatt light-water plant built by the Soviet Union in 1954.[4]

The efforts of other countries to develop nuclear power in the fifties were hampered by the superpowers' early monopoly of nuclear technologies and fuel supplies. Among the governments that nevertheless launched substantial nuclear power programs were those of Canada, France, the United Kingdom, and West Germany, each pursuing its own approach to nuclear technology. Progress was slow due to the unexpectedly challenging engineering required and to the difficulty that all countries had going from tiny prototypes to commercial plants.

Private companies showed little interest in spearheading the commercialization of nuclear power, and so it was left to the U.S. Government to go where the Fortune 500 feared to tread. During the fifties, the United States spent hundreds of millions of dollars on a Power Reactor Demonstration Program in which large corporations built a half-dozen prototype plants. Then a major effort was mounted by the U.S. Atomic Energy Commission and nuclear equipment manufacturers to convince utilities that nuclear costs could be substantially lowered.

Still, utility companies demanded a guarantee that nuclear plants would be cheaper than the alternatives. In December 1963 General Electric and the Jersey Central Power & Light Company signed a contract for a "turnkey" nuclear plant that General Electric would build at a set price, competitive with the cost of a coal-fired plant. For the utility there was little financial risk, since it would simply pay the agreed bill and then "turn the key" to commence generation when construction was complete. This milestone agreement was followed by eight similar contracts, effectively launching commercial nuclear power in the United States.[5]

The next stage came quickly. In 1966

and 1967, the utilities ordered 51 additional nuclear plants, signing open-ended, cost-plus contracts that shifted the burden of potential cost overruns to the utilities and their customers. By the end of 1967 the United States had 28 times as much nuclear power capacity on order as it had in operation. Four U.S. nuclear reactor vendors competed aggressively for new orders, and utilities struggled to stay at the forefront of technology. Nuclear power was seen as the inevitable way to meet future electricity demand, which was growing at faster than 7 percent a year.[6]

This "bandwagon" psychology left little room for dispassionate analysis of the economics of nuclear power. Utilities had little understanding of these plants and the much more demanding engineering that would be required. Each new buyer was cited by the reactor manufacturers as proof of the economic soundness of their claims. The rush to nuclear power had become a self-sustaining process—self-sustaining, perhaps, but not sustainable indefinitely.[7]

Beginning in the mid-sixties, U.S. companies assisted by the government's "Atoms for Peace" program aggressively marketed nuclear technologies in Europe, Japan, and some developing nations. More than a dozen countries purchased U.S. plants or signed licensing agreements to obtain American nuclear technology. Today France, Japan, and West Germany, which along with the United States play a prominent role in the nuclear power industry, all build plants based on American designs. With the rapid growth of electricity demand and the relative scarcity of indigenous energy resources in Europe, there was little challenge to the notion that the commercialization of nuclear power deserved a high priority.

This period was also marked by a great expansion of programs in the Third World. Nuclear power was wel-

comed as an alternative to imported oil and as a way for developing countries to propel themselves into the twentieth century. Exports of the technology were vigorously promoted by the International Atomic Energy Agency of the United Nations and by government institutions such as the U.S. Export-Import Bank. Sixteen developing countries had nuclear power programs by the mid-seventies, some of them nations that still relied on fuelwood as their major domestic energy source.[8]

The development of nuclear power may come to a complete standstill by the late eighties.

By 1973, worldwide nuclear power capacity had risen to 43,000 megawatts, provided by 115 plants. The United States had half the total capacity and Britain one-eighth. France and the Soviet Union each had the equivalent of three 1,000-megawatt nuclear plants and Canada, Japan, and West Germany only two each. But nuclear construction programs were in full swing in a half-dozen countries, and a dozen more had plans to begin soon. In the peak growth years of 1971–74, over 200 plants were ordered worldwide, approximately doubling the number of planned reactors. Total capacity was expected to exceed 250,000 megawatts by the early eighties.[9]

The 1973–74 oil crisis was widely seen as the final guarantee that nuclear power would be the world's next preeminent energy source. Western political leaders in particular saw nuclear power as the necessary high-tech solution to the stranglehold the Organization of Petroleum Exporting Countries had on the oil market. The Nixon administration's Project Independence aimed for nuclear power to supply half of U.S. electricity by the year 2000. French Prime Minister Jacques Chirac undoubtedly spoke for many political leaders in the aftermath of the oil embargo when in early 1975 he said, "For the immediate future, I mean for the coming ten years, nuclear energy is one of the main answers to our energy needs."[10]

Today nuclear power supplies much less energy than was expected in the mid-seventies. But it has grown substantially nonetheless. As of late 1983, a total of 282 commercial plants in 25 countries provided over 173,000 megawatts of generating capacity—enough to supply approximately 9 percent of the world's electricity, or 3 percent of total energy. (See Table 7-1.) In industrial countries the share of electricity supplied by nuclear power varies widely, from approximately 40 percent in France to 17 percent in Japan, 13 percent in the United States, 6 percent in the Soviet Union, and zero in such nations as Australia and Denmark that have decided to forego

Table 7-1. Worldwide Nuclear Power Commitment, by End of 1983[1]

Country	Plants Operating		Plants Ordered and Under Construction		Total Commitment	
	(number)	(megawatts)	(number)	(megawatts)	(number)	(megawatts)
United States	77	60,026	64	70,376	141	130,402
France	31	21,778	31	34,520	62	56,298
West Germany	12	9,806	17	19,516	29	29,322
Soviet Union	34	18,915	11	9,880	45	28,795
Japan	25	16,652	15	12,649	40	29,301
Spain	6	3,820	7	6,801	13	10,621
Canada	12	6,622	12	8,710	24	15,332
United Kingdom	34	9,273	8	5,115	42	14,388
Sweden	10	7,300	2	2,110	12	9,410
South Korea	1	556	8	6,710	9	7,266
Switzerland	4	1,940	3	3,007	7	4,947
Czechoslovakia	2	880	8	3,520	10	4,400
Italy	3	1,285	3	2,004	6	3,289
India	4	804	6	1,320	10	2,124
Belgium	5	3,450	2	2,000	7	5,450
Taiwan	4	3,110	2	1,814	6	4,924
East Germany	5	1,830	2	880	7	2,710
Brazil	—	—	3	3,116	3	3,116
Argentina	1	335	2	1,292	3	1,627
Rest of World	12	5,205	21	14,044	33	19,249
World Total	282	173,587	227	209,384	509	382,971

[1]Preliminary estimate.
SOURCE: "The World List of Nuclear Power Plants," *Nuclear News*, August 1983; Atomic Industrial Forum, "Historical Profile of U.S. Nuclear Power Development," Washington, D.C., March 1983.

this power source altogether. In the next three years, about 100 nuclear plants are scheduled to commence operation, which would boost global nuclear capacity by 60 percent. Beyond the mid-eighties, however, the picture is much less clear.

COUNTING COSTS

Thirty years have passed since U.S. nuclear officials were quoted as saying that nuclear power would be "too cheap to meter." It was an unfortunate claim that the industry now wishes had never been made. These words will haunt them nonetheless, for they mark the beginning of a sad history of bold assertions and unsupported analysis that led to enormous uncertainty about the actual cost or economic merits of nuclear power. Even today it is difficult to find in any country a full and fair accounting of the economic status of nuclear power.

Cost estimates for nuclear plants in the United States have been rising ever since the first commercial plants were started in the early sixties. Most of the early evidence of economic troubles was ignored by experts who assumed that costs would begin to decline as the technology improved. Utility executives signaled their confidence by ordering 126 nuclear power plants between 1971 and the end of 1974—enough to increase U.S. generating capacity at that time by nearly half.[11]

But construction costs continued to rise throughout the seventies, and in 1981 economist Charles Komanoff published the first detailed assessment of the increases. Using the utilities' own data, but carefully separating out the effects of inflation and the cost of borrowed money, Komanoff concluded that real (inflation-adjusted) construction costs

for nuclear power plants had risen 142 percent between 1971 and 1978, or 13.5 percent annually. Based on these figures, Komanoff concluded that total generating costs for a nuclear plant would soon exceed those for a coal plant by a wide margin.[12]

The nuclear industry vigorously disputed these estimates, largely on the grounds that statistical analysis of the recent past was not a reliable predictor of future trends. Since the mid-seventies, however, cost estimates for individual nuclear plants have doubled every four years, rising faster than prices for gasoline, housing, or any other major expenditure. Reactors completed in the early eighties will cost on average almost $2,000 (1982 dollars) per kilowatt to build, over twice as much as coal plants. And because of the high costs and long construction times, the financing charges for a nuclear plant are now three times those for a coal plant and add approximately $500 million to the average construction bill.[13]

Since the mid-seventies cost estimates for individual nuclear plants have doubled every four years.

Some projects make these average figures look like bargains. The Limerick 1 plant in Pennsylvania is now budgeted at $3.4 billion and the Nine Mile Point 2 plant in New York at between $4.6 billion and $5.6 billion. Several recently canceled plants would have cost as much as $8 billion each had they been completed. Even the few economic "success stories" pointed to by the nuclear industry, such as the Palo Verde plants in Arizona, have suffered huge cost overruns that would be considered crippling in any other industry. Nuclear economics is not for the fainthearted. The annual cost overruns alone equal the government budgets of many nations.[14]

Operating costs for nuclear power plants, once expected to be negligible, have turned out to be another budget-buster. A 1982 study by economists with the Energy Systems Research Group found that operation and maintenance costs rose during the seventies at an average annual rate of 18 percent. By the early eighties, the average nuclear plant cost more than $30 million a year to operate, enough to add approximately 20 percent to the generating cost.[15]

The economics of U.S. nuclear power have also been hurt by plants operating on average at less than 60 percent of their rated capacity rather than the 75–80 percent of capacity originally expected. A range of technical problems that have required plants to be run at partial capacity and to shut down frequently for repairs are to blame. Since two-thirds of the cost of nuclear electricity comes from construction costs that must be paid regardless of whether the plant is operating, low capacity factors greatly increase the cost of power.[16]

U.S. industry and government studies have been slow to recognize the declining economic competitiveness of nuclear power. Cost estimates for individual plants continue to miss the mark by a wide margin and are commonly adjusted upward by several hundred million dollars each year. Industry-wide studies often make selective use of data or blithely assume that costs will be reduced and capacity factors improved. Many studies, failing to distinguish between real-cost trends and the effects of inflation, simply assume that all increases are caused by inflation and high interest rates.

Yet even government and industry officials are now much less bullish on the economics of nuclear power than they once were. In boardrooms and at regulatory hearings, cost overruns are frequently cited as a major problem. Careful analysis of the utilities' own data for the 30-odd U.S. plants scheduled for completion in the mid-eighties shows that the electricity they produce will cost on average from 10–12¢ per kilowatt-hour (1982 dollars).[17]

This cost is 65 percent more than coal-fired power and 25 percent more than oil-fired power, the high cost of which has often been cited as a major reason for building nuclear plants. (See Figure 7-1.) If all the electricity used by Americans were to cost as much as that generated by these new plants, the country's utility bills would rise approximately 130 percent.[18]

Enough information is now available to show conclusively that new nuclear power plants are no longer cost-effective in the United States. Even if all the unique safety and health risks of nuclear power were removed and cost escalation were halted, a U.S. utility planner choosing between a coal and a nuclear power plant based solely on economic considerations would have to select coal. In addition, nuclear power carries financial risks that frighten many utility execu-

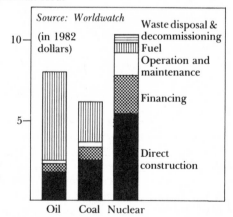

Figure 7-1. **Average Generating Costs for New U.S. Power Plants, 1983**

tives. S. David Freeman, a Director of the Tennessee Valley Authority, which once had the largest nuclear construction program in the United States, concluded in 1982: "The cost of nuclear power isn't just high, it's unpredictable. No sane capitalist is going to build something for which he can't derive a cost/benefit ratio because the cost is unknowable."[19]

Outside the United States, the economic status of nuclear power is more difficult to calculate. In most countries the data base is quite slim due to the small number of plants in operation, so statistical studies yield limited results. Further complicating the situation is the fact that most nations do not release the cost figures for individual nuclear plants that are essential for solid economic conclusions. As in the United States, companies and government agencies strongly committed to nuclear power selectively release data. The picture is somewhat murky but appears to show high and growing costs worldwide.

Fairly good data are available for the United Kingdom, where the government is in the midst of a major decision on the future of its nuclear program. The nationwide government-owned utility, the Central Electricity Generating Board (CEGB), has proposed that the country begin building a new generation of light-water nuclear plants based on the American Westinghouse design. Considerable controversy surrounds the economic soundness of the proposal. The CEGB now admits that the country's most recent gas-cooled nuclear plants cost twice as much to build as coal-fired plants, but it still argues that light-water plants can be produced at an attractive price.[20]

The CEGB's analytical techniques have come under attack in the course of lengthy hearings over the program. One of the most telling critiques comes from Gordon MacKerron of the University of Sussex, who concluded in a 1982 report that CEGB estimates for plants already built in the United Kingdom were biased in favor of nuclear power by failing to calculate the full value of past capital investments. The CEGB, MacKerron found, had not distinguished clearly between current and constant dollar costs or even between historical figures and projections.[21]

J.W. Jeffrey, a retired University of London professor, conducted a thorough economic assessment of British nuclear plants and concluded that nuclear power is considerably more expensive than coal-fired power. Although his figures were at first vigorously disputed, the CEGB was forced in 1983 to recant many of its earlier claims about the economic superiority of British nuclear plants. The case for light-water plants is still being made, but the tide seems to have turned against the proposal. Many observers agree with Jeffrey: "Nuclear power has not been economic, is not economic and is likely to get more uneconomic in the future."[22]

West Germany has a larger and more successful nuclear power program than the United Kingdom does, but it has suffered from major cost overruns nonetheless. Official figures compiled by the country's largest utility show direct nuclear construction costs rising sixfold between 1969 and 1982 while coal plant construction costs went up 3.5 times. Yet West German nuclear officials still maintain that nuclear power has a 30 to 50 percent economic advantage over coal power. This claim is now being used as justification for a government proposal to order as many as five additional plants in the mid-eighties—in a country that has only ordered one plant since 1975.[23]

The price of coal is quite high in West Germany, so there is some basis for the claim that nuclear power still has a generating cost advantage over coal-fired power, but it is unlikely that nuclear power can overcome a capital cost margin as large as the one that officials now admit to. Critics charge that German nuclear planners have consistently underestimated expenses and have used accounting methods that do not measure the full costs. A study by Jürgen Franke and Dieter Viefhues of the Freiburg Institute concluded in 1983 that due to the rapid escalation of construction expenses and interest rates, nuclear electricity now costs at least 60 percent more than coal-fired power.[24]

France is a key country in making international comparisons of nuclear economics, since the French nuclear construction program has an international reputation for efficiency and speed. Whereas U.S. nuclear plants take on average eight to ten years to build, French plants go up in less than six. Official French figures published in 1982 show real capital costs rising just 43 percent between 1974 and 1981. This works out to an annual rate of increase of 5 percent, one-third the rate in the American and West German nuclear industries. French planners maintain that nuclear power is 20–40 percent less expensive than coal-fired power.[25]

The scanty cost data released by French authorities make it difficult to draw conclusions, and there is no way to verify the official numbers. Most of the figures released are aggregate numbers compiled by planners with a vested interest in the economics of their program. And as no data are available for individual plants, it is impossible to confirm the figures or to correlate them with relevant variables. Also, Electricité de France (EDF) has run up a debt of $19 billion on its nuclear program. It is quite possible that hidden behind EDF's complex accounting practices are substantial subsidies for nuclear power.[26]

At least in relative terms, however, the French program has been an economic success. The margin may not be as large as official figures indicate, but nuclear power in France does appear to be less expensive than coal-fired power. One caveat to bear in mind, however, is that although capacity factors have generally been high and operating costs low, since 1982 many French plants performed poorly, which is likely to raise costs. Only more time and experience will tell how economical France's ambitious program really is.

The limited information available for other nations also shows substantial cost increases during the last decade. In Japan, average real construction costs have gone from $350 per kilowatt in the early seventies to $1,000 per kilowatt in the early eighties (in 1982 dollars) according to utility industry sources. The official Soviet figures released in the latest Five-Year Plan report that nuclear plants are 80–100 percent more expensive to build than coal plants. Data released by Ontario Hydro, the builder of Canada's CANDU nuclear plants, show that construction costs went from $400 per kilowatt in 1972 to $1,700 in the early eighties, a real rate of increase of 6 percent after accounting for inflation. And in India the government now admits that nuclear power is much more expensive than coal-fired electricity.[27]

Eighty-seven nuclear plants were canceled in the United States between 1975 and November 1983.

Comparing nuclear economics internationally in strictly quantitative terms is a hopeless endeavor. Not only are comprehensive and reliable data scarce, but constant variations in inflation, exchange rates, and fuel costs make it difficult to apply common standards across national boundaries. Enough figures are available, however, to show that cost overruns have been most severe in the United States, West Germany, and the United Kingdom. But substantial cost increases above inflation appear to have been near-universal—even in such "model" nuclear countries as France and Japan. This has badly hurt nuclear power's economic standing compared with its most direct competitor—coal-fired power. Perhaps most disturbing from a long-term viewpoint is that almost everywhere the situation seems to worsen over time. Many countries appear poised to repeat the disappointing economic experience of nuclear power in the United States.

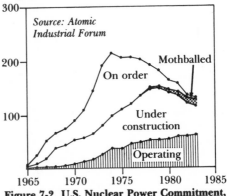

Thousand Megawatts

Figure 7-2. U.S. Nuclear Power Commitment, 1965-83

A U.S. FINANCIAL MELTDOWN

The first signs of trouble for the U.S. nuclear industry came just after its growth binge of the early seventies. Eleven projects were canceled in 1975 and another 32 from 1976 through 1979. During the same period only 13 nuclear plants were ordered. Many energy analysts argued at the time that this was a mid-course correction, a downward blip in nuclear power's healthy, growing future. They were wrong. The early eighties have witnessed a massive trimming of nuclear power programs by most of the country's utilities. Plans for 16 plants were scrapped in 1980; 6 in 1981; and a record 18 in 1982.[28]

For some utilities the cancellations constituted a major shift in their plans. The Tennessee Valley Authority reneged on 12 out of 17 nuclear plants it had planned to build and the Public Service Electric and Gas Company of New Jersey dropped plans for 5 out of 8. All told, 87 nuclear plants were canceled in the United States between 1975 and November 1983, with a net loss in future

nuclear generating capacity of 83,000 megawatts. (See Figure 7-2.) This is 30 percent more nuclear capacity than the United States currently has, enough to meet the electricity needs of any country except the Soviet Union or the United States. Meanwhile, U.S. commitments to coal-fired plants had a net increase of 58,000 megawatts.[29]

The depth of the nuclear recession in the United States is illustrated by the fact that only two plants ordered in the last nine years have not been subsequently canceled. And in the last several years a number of plants have been scrapped that were as much as 10 or 20 percent complete. In 1982 alone, reactors on which $5.7 billion had already been spent were abandoned, bringing the total bill for such plants to $10 billion. The only thing that will stop this wave of cancellations is the rapidly shrinking list of facilities that are not at least half-built and, therefore, very costly to give up.[30]

Behind the cancellations lie fundamental changes in the economic condition of the utility industry. High inflation and interest rates have made it more difficult to finance long-term, capital-intensive projects. Electricity demand growth has fallen from 7 percent per year a decade ago to between 1 percent and 3 percent today. The impact of this sudden shift has been exacerbated by the fact that most utilities failed to forecast it correctly and have altered their planning several years later than would have been prudent. The long lead times, large capital requirements, and soaring cost overruns of nuclear projects have wreaked particular havoc on utilities attempting to adapt to lower power demand and uncertain economic conditions.[31]

In recent years, nuclear projects have become a dominant and damaging part of utilities' capital budgets. Annual investment for nuclear construction has risen from $2 billion in 1970 to $19 billion in 1982, a fourfold increase even after discounting for inflation. (See Figure 7-3.) Whereas nuclear plants required only one-third of utilities' expenditures for new plants in 1970, by 1982 they soaked up two-thirds. And these increases have occurred despite the substantial drop in the total U.S. nuclear commitment since the mid-seventies. The amount now spent each year on nuclear construction is more than one-fourth the annual investment of the entire U.S. manufacturing sector and more than three times that of the automobile industry.[32]

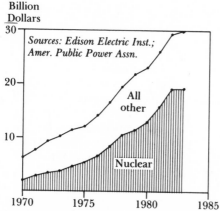

Figure 7-3. Expenditures by U.S. Utilities for New Generating Plants, 1970-83

As capital outlays soared and electricity demand stagnated the financial health of utilities deteriorated steadily. The proportion of expenditures that could be met using cash on hand fell, causing a rapid increase in borrowing and stock issuance during a period of high interest rates and low stock prices. The stock of many companies began selling at less than book value. Wall Street analysts have become worried about the draining nuclear construction programs of utilities and many recommend against buying stock in such companies. The Merrill Lynch Company has gone so far as to publish lists of plants that it believes are ripe for cancellation.[33]

Financial constraints have driven utilities with ongoing nuclear programs to great lengths to raise capital. Borrowing short-term funds at usurious interest rates and "creative financing" are common. The Consumers Power Company of Michigan, builder of the troubled Midland nuclear plant, has issued commercial paper against the utility's oil, gas, and coal inventories, sold and leased back the company's headquarters building, and borrowed heavily on the Eurodollar markets.[34] When massive emergency transfusions become commonplace, a patient is usually in deep trouble. The inability to finance many nuclear projects has been the key signal to cancel them. The fortunate utilities are those that have been able to cut their losses and get out early.

One company that investors are particularly concerned about is the Long Island Lighting Company (Lilco), builder of the 820-megawatt Shoreham nuclear plant in New York. That plant, ordered in 1967, is now scheduled to be completed in 1984 at a cost of $3.4–3.6 billion, approximately 15 times the original budget. The Shoreham plant will generate at most one-third of the utility's electricity but its cost exceeds the book value of Lilco's entire electricity system, including other generating plants, transmission lines, and maintenance facilities. Electricity rates on Long Island are expected to double in five years to pay for the plant. If the Shoreham reactor is ever permitted to operate, which is now in some doubt, it will yield the most expensive electricity ever produced by a large central generating station.[35]

Ribbon-cutting ceremonies for nuclear facilities now often serve to inaugurate a brave new world of higher electricity bills.

Nuclear cost overruns have put many state utility commissions in a difficult position. They are caught between the desire to keep electricity affordable for consumers and the need to provide utilities with enough revenue to preserve their financial health. U.S. electricity rates have more than tripled in the past ten years after being nearly stable during the previous decade. Much of the increase stems from higher fuel prices, but rising nuclear construction costs have become an increasingly important factor. Ribbon-cutting ceremonies for nuclear facilities now often serve to inaugurate a brave new world of 30 to 50 percent higher electricity bills, a phenomenon for which the term "rate shock" has been coined. In New England it is believed that the twin Seabrook plants could cause rates to more than double.[36]

There is no indication of an imminent revival of nuclear orders in the United States. The Atomic Industrial Forum, which represents the U.S. industry, opened a 1982 mid-year press release with the optimistic assertion that "the U.S. nuclear power program enters the home stretch of 1982 like a runner poised in mid-stride." But the positive indicators the industry pointed to are the number of plants entering service and the power they generate—each of which continue to lag earlier projections by wide margins. No longer is the industry offering firm predictions of when it would stop living off pre-1975 plants and start ordering new ones. Perhaps the most optimistic projection made recently is the Department of Energy's 1982 "mid-case" projection for the year 2000, which assumes that another 25 nuclear plants will be ordered in the eighties. This projection is probably little more than a fantasy however. It is hard to find any serious analyst at this point who expects to see additional nuclear orders before 1990.[37]

The industry's "preconditions" for the revival of nuclear power are usually dominated by regulatory reform, higher electricity rates to pay for the plants being built, and lower inflation and interest rates. These issues hardly scratch the surface of the industry's problems however. The kind of fundamental changes that would really be needed—a guaranteed reduction in nuclear construction costs and a major surge in electricity growth—are far less likely. The continuing financial crisis caused by the remaining nuclear projects hardly creates a climate conducive to major new investment programs.

THE OUTLOOK IN OTHER INDUSTRIAL COUNTRIES

It is not just in the United States that nuclear power faces a less secure future than was expected just five years ago. Although most governments with major nuclear programs—including France,

Japan, and the Soviet Union—remain strongly committed to nuclear power, there is a growing gap between rhetorical and monetary support and the actual achievements of the nuclear programs. Behind the lagging pace lie diminished growth in electricity demand and a long list of technical, economic, and political problems.

The total commitment to nuclear power in Europe has risen only 10 percent since 1978 and almost all the gain comes from France. The number of British and West German projects has risen slightly, while the numbers in Spain, Sweden, Switzerland, and Italy have fallen. The changed outlook is well illustrated by the Organisation for Economic Co-operation and Development's 1985 nuclear capacity projections, which have been lowered by nearly two-thirds since 1970. (See Table 7-2.)

West Germany had Europe's largest nuclear program until the late seventies, and it has enjoyed strong support from the country's leaders. In recent years, however, political opposition in West Germany has mushroomed. Major demonstrations have occurred at a number of plant sites, including one near Hamburg in 1981 that was described by the West German Interior Minister as the biggest police action in the history of the federal republic. Opponents have also been successful in raising issues of safety, environmental damage, and cost-effectiveness in licensing hearings and in the courts. Project delays and cost overruns have been common. Meanwhile, electricity growth rates have dropped substantially and the country has been under increasing economic pressure, which makes investment in major capital-intensive projects much less attractive.[38]

Only one nuclear power plant has been ordered in West Germany since 1975, and eight of those ordered prior to 1975 are not yet off the drawing boards, due largely to political opposition and ongoing court battles. Only eight plants are currently being built, four of which are at least 80 percent complete and another three half done. The West German nuclear industry suffers from considerable overcapacity as a consequence; component manufacturers in particular are reportedly losing a good deal of money, and many workers have been laid off.[39]

With only about 8,000-megawatts worth of nuclear plants now under construction, West Germany will have less than half the 45,000 megawatts of capacity that had been projected for 1990. Preliminary approval has been given for a "convoy" of largely standardized plants to be built in the next decade. But whether this proposal will survive critics' arguments that the plants are not

Table 7-2. Projections Made in 1970–83 of 1985 Nuclear Generating Capacity in OECD Countries

Area	1970	1974	1976	1977	1978	1983
	(thousand megawatts)					
Western Europe	202	175	167	125	84	73
United States	277	260	180	145	100	78
Japan	60	60	41	35	18	22
Other OECD	24	18	12	13	12	10
Total	563	513	400	318	214	183

SOURCES: International Energy Agency, *World Energy Outlook* (Paris: Organisation for Economic Co-operation and Development, 1982); Worldwatch Institute estimates for 1983.

needed and would be more expensive than available alternatives is doubtful. A growing number of utility officials are concerned about the rising costs of nuclear power. With a 50 percent reserve margin in most of the country's utility systems, they have little incentive to take major new risks.[40]

Unlike West Germany, France is keeping close to its ambitious nuclear plans of a decade ago. The country already has 30 nuclear plants in operation and 28 more under construction. France now derives 40 percent of its electricity from nuclear power and is on course to generate 75 percent by 1990. The French nuclear program is supported by a strong central government that allows little opposition. Both the utility industry and Framatome (the lead nuclear company) are adjuncts of the state. Moreover, the nuclear industry is an influential component of the French national economy, and the income and jobs it provides have become a strong political incentive to continue. The staying power of French nuclear power was demonstrated in 1981 when socialist President Mitterrand came to office calling the nuclear program "excessive, even dangerous" and then proceeded with business as usual, supporting nuclear power strongly.[41]

Economic realities have proved much more hazardous to the French nuclear program than political opposition. Electricity growth has been gradually slowing since the late seventies, and in 1982 the government reduced its forecast of growth in the eighties by 50 percent. This means France would have at least 13 percent too much generating capacity in 1990. Such projections led Electricité de France to introduce special subsidies for electric heating and to set up regional agencies that will encourage industries to use more power. The decommissioning of many relatively new coal-fired plants and the export of electricity are also planned. The upshot is

that even many of the strongest supporters of nuclear power in France now admit that from an electricity demand standpoint, no additional plant orders are needed for at least several years.[42]

Economic realities have proved much more hazardous to the French nuclear program than political opposition.

The French nuclear program is also becoming a burden on already strained capital markets. EDF has been forced to reschedule debts and borrow extensively on the Eurobond market to keep construction going. The director stated in 1982 that the utility was in its worst financial condition in 30 years. In 1983 a high-level government committee released a long-term study that concluded that France should not order any additional plants until 1987. Recognizing the consequences this would have for an industry geared to handle six new orders per year, the government decided instead to reduce nuclear plant ordering to just two units per year in 1984 and 1985; even this plan provoked warnings of massive layoffs of nuclear workers and the possibility that France's small nuclear supplier companies could be forced out of business.[43]

The French nuclear program, although a success politically and in narrow economic terms, has in a sense become the victim of its own achievements. Its low costs are mostly attributable to its large scale and to a dearth of political opposition, but these very factors have made it difficult to adjust to a period of rising costs and lower electricity demand. It will be increasingly difficult for the country's leaders to justify ordering even two plants per year. Although in the nineties it will almost certainly be the country that relies most on nuclear power, France's full-throttle nuclear expansion program may have slowed to a sputter by then.

The British nuclear program is in a much more anemic condition. Beyond the 8,500 megawatts of nuclear capacity that now supply 13 percent of the country's electricity, only another 5,500-megawatts worth are under construction, much of which is near completion. The high cost of the plants built so far and the forecasts that electricity demand will grow little, if at all, in the next decade provide ample economic hurdles to a revitalized nuclear construction program. The current Sizewell Inquiry on whether to build an American-style light-water plant will in effect provide a verdict on the future of nuclear power in Britain. That plan, which has been severely challenged on economic grounds, provides the only hope for additional nuclear orders in the near future. Without it, the nuclear industry in Britain would soon wither.[44]

Programs in other northern European countries are quite small and unlikely to grow rapidly in the near future. Belgium has five operating nuclear plants, Finland four, Switzerland four, and the Netherlands two; only Belgium, however, has additional plants being built. Sweden had a major program under way until 1980, when a national referendum on nuclear power was decided in favor of discontinuing the program and phasing out all the country's nuclear plants by the year 2010. Although Sweden has nine reactors in operation and gets over 30 percent of its electricity from nuclear power, only two plants remain under construction.[45]

The nuclear power programs of the Soviet Union and Eastern Europe are almost completely independent of those in the West, but they have followed a surprisingly parallel course. Construc-

tion of plants in the Soviet Union began in earnest in the early seventies, and the nation's nuclear capacity grew from 1,-600 megawatts in 1970 to 6,200 megawatts in 1975 and to 17,500 megawatts (at 29 plants) in 1983. Nuclear power is completely run and controlled by the government and the Communist party, which have a tradition of supporting electrification as a foundation of the modern economy. State-owned companies design and build the plants, and government officials determine in their Five-Year Plans how many reactors will be financed.[46]

The Soviet Union obtained half as much electricity from its nuclear plants in 1983 as was expected a decade ago, and the rest of Eastern Europe has missed its targets by similar margins. Nuclear power is nonetheless becoming an increasingly important energy source throughout the Eastern bloc, already supplying 6 percent of the Soviet Union's electricity, 12 percent of East Germany's, and 18 percent of Bulgaria's. Official projections call for reactors to supply close to a third of the region's electricity by 1990, which would require at least a tripling of nuclear capacity.[47]

In the past several years the Soviet nuclear program has concentrated on building the Atommash plant, designed to turn out as many as eight standardized nuclear reactors each year. This unprecedented effort at standardization should in theory help cut project lead times and reduce costs. It is also unique in that it is part of an internationally integrated nuclear program in which components made in various East European facilities will be used in each plant. The large Skoda facility in Czechoslovakia produces turbines, generators, pumps, and pipelines. Plants in Hungary, Bulgaria, East Germany, and Poland are also involved. It is a strategy that should be more efficient than having each nation build its own plants from the ground up.

As with much of the Soviet economy, the nuclear program is kept under tight wraps. Published information accentuates successes and downplays problems. Many examples have nonetheless emerged of technical and organizational difficulties that have slowed development, including labor-management problems and delays caused by builders and suppliers. The nuclear targets in the current Five-Year Plan are reportedly being missed by more than 6,000 megawatts. The Atommash facility itself is at least two to three years behind schedule and was the site of a major accident in mid-1983.[48]

Substantial cost overruns on the country's nuclear plants are conceded by Soviet authorities although there is no evidence that these have had a direct effect on the overall program, which continues to enjoy ample political support and proceeds as rapidly as various technical and management difficulties permit. The true test of Eastern Europe's nuclear power programs almost certainly lies ahead, since the scale of the efforts and the associated financial and technical risks are growing rapidly. Only time will tell whether the Soviet approach of massive centralization and the absence of political opposition and financial checks can lead to safe nuclear plants at a reasonable cost.

Japan has one of the largest nuclear development programs in the world today. Despite the painful legacy of the atomic bomb and considerable public fear of radiation, the government has made nuclear power the cornerstone of its energy policies in the last decade. With 117 million people squeezed into an area the size of California and with four-fifths of the country's energy supplies currently imported, nuclear power is viewed as the only means of rapidly enhancing the country's security. Japan has 25 nuclear plants in operation, supplying 16 percent of the country's electricity, and another 13 are under way. The government has ambitious plans to expand nuclear capacity sixfold by the end of the century, at which point it would provide approximately half the country's electricity.[49]

The first nuclear plants in Japan were essentially American-designed reactors licensed from overseas corporations. Major research efforts in recent years have tried to establish an indigenous nuclear technology and industry, a process that is now largely complete. In fact, Japan is now considered a leader in reactor technology and has taken the initiative in joint ventures with American and West German companies to design an advanced light-water reactor. As in other industries, Japanese companies appear to be positioning themselves to compete in the nuclear export market in case it revives in the years ahead.

Yet the continued development of nuclear power in Japan is not necessarily assured: Political opposition is growing as the number of communities affected by plants increases. Because it is a small country with one of the world's highest population densities, it is inevitable that nuclear plants are built in somebody's "backyard," often the site of a valuable fishery or beach resort. The accidental release of radiation from at least one nuclear plant has aroused enormous concern. Also at issue are the frequency of earthquakes, which could severely damage nuclear plants in virtually all parts of Japan, and nuclear waste disposal, a problem that will be particularly difficult to resolve in such a populous country.[50]

Japan, like other industrial countries, has failed to meet its early nuclear goals. The target for 1995 has already been reduced by 13,000 megawatts and there are indications that the recent recession will delay the nuclear program further.[51] Cost overruns have been a concern to Japan's nuclear managers but have not yet forced a wholesale reevaluation of the country's nuclear goals. Another concern is that many Japanese plants have shut down frequently for repairs. Yet the country's nuclear manufacturers, its privately owned utilities, and its energy officials are determined to forge ahead. The pace at which they do this will probably be determined largely by the operating and safety records of the plants and by their success in dealing with the waste disposal problem.

NUCLEAR POWER IN THE THIRD WORLD

During the sixties and seventies, developing countries had some of the brightest hopes for nuclear power, which Third World leaders viewed as a way to boost national prestige and reduce crippling oil import bills. Industrial country governments dispatched experts to promote the economic merits of nuclear power. In the early seventies, the International Atomic Energy Agency (IAEA) projected that developing countries would have 550,000 megawatts of nuclear capacity by the end of the century—40 percent more than worldwide operating and planned nuclear capacity in 1983.[52]

By mid-1983 six developing countries—Argentina, India, Pakistan, South Africa, South Korea, and Taiwan—had a total of 13 operating nuclear plants. Three other countries are building plants and several are considering programs. Still, the Third World represents just 6 percent of the total worldwide commitment to nuclear power. And since the mid-seventies the nuclear plans of these developing countries have been substantially reduced.[53]

A key obstacle to nuclear development is the small size of electricity grids in Third World countries. If a single power plant provides more than 15 percent of a grid's capacity, the whole system will "crash" if that facility is shut down. Using these figures, the IAEA estimates that only India, Pakistan, South Korea, and Taiwan have grids large enough to install a conventional 1,000-megawatt nuclear power plant. Nuclear manufacturers have responded by proposing "mini-reactors" in the range of 100–500 megawatts. But none is ready yet commercially. The estimated per-kilowatt construction cost for a plant of 200 megawatts is more than twice that of a 1,000-megawatt plant, making them even less attractive economically.[54]

A deteriorating world economy since 1980 has also led to a significant trimming of the Third World's most active nuclear power programs. The capital intensity of nuclear power plants makes them a burden to debt-strapped developing countries, particularly since much of the money must be spent abroad, draining scarce foreign exchange. Substituting nuclear import bills for oil import charges is not seen by most Third World leaders as much of a gain.

The "miracle economies" of the Far East have made the largest Third World commitments thus far. Rapid growth and sizable electricity grids in countries such as South Korea and Taiwan explain why they are likely to have over half of the Third World's nuclear capacity by 1990. Taiwan, clinging to an aggressive nuclear expansion program begun in the seventies, has four operating plants and two under construction. The pace slackened in 1982, however, when Taiwan deferred several reactors indefinitely because of economic constraints and a slowdown in electricity growth. South Korea has two operating plants and seven being built, but it too has decided against new orders in the early eighties. Leaders in these countries are strongly committed to nuclear power, but a major improvement in economic conditions is now a prerequisite to building additional plants.[55]

The Philippines once had ambitious plans for nuclear power, but the country's first plant, sited near an earthquake fault, suffered major delays and cost overruns while the seismic design was bolstered. Plans for additional ones have been scrapped. China has no nuclear plants, but some of the leaders in Beijing appear quite interested in this energy source. Capital requirements have made them cautious about making major commitments so far, however, and the country has only one small nuclear plant on order as of 1983.[56]

India has the broadest range of nuclear technology and expertise of any Third World country. Its program is largely homegrown and much more independent than those of other developing nations. Four small plants are operating and another six are under construction. India realistically expects to obtain 10 percent of its electricity from nuclear power by the nineties. The early hopes of the country's nuclear scientists for this source of energy have not materialized, however. The plants proved to be expensive and have poor operating records. Additional orders are not foreseen in the near future.[57]

Among the Middle Eastern countries that once had ambitious plans for nuclear power are Egypt, Iran, and Iraq. Each has seen a combination of economic and political problems seriously jeopardize its program. Iran's Islamic revolution in 1979 killed an ambitious and costly effort aimed at installing 23,000 megawatts of nuclear capacity by 1994. Even before the revolution, however, critics questioned the size and economic viability of the Iranian program. Iraq's nuclear program came to a halt in 1981 when Israeli warplanes destroyed the research reactor that was its centerpiece. Egypt also considered building

nuclear plants in the eighties, but its efforts are now on hold.[58]

Latin America was a booming market for nuclear power in the seventies, but it too has fallen on hard times. Argentina has had a small plant operating since the early seventies and two more are being built. Wrapped in the cloak of nationalism, Argentina's nuclear program has enjoyed strong government support, and the country hopes to have six operating plants by the end of the century. Crippling debt problems, however, have cast doubt on these goals, and anything beyond the two now being built is unlikely.[59]

Substituting nuclear import bills for oil import charges is not seen by most Third World leaders as much of a gain.

Brazil, the world's sixth most populous country, has one plant complete and two under construction. The country planned to have eight plants operating by the early nineties, largely relying on West German technology, but major technical problems and a lack of capital have rendered these goals meaningless. Brazil will be lucky to complete the two now being worked on. Mexico was a latecomer to nuclear power, but as oil revenues soared in 1979 and 1980, the country's leaders announced plans to build seven plants during this decade. Today that vision has been obliterated by the country's debt crisis.[60]

Current plans indicate that developing countries will have at most 20,000 megawatts of nuclear capacity by 1990, which is only one-seventh as much as the IAEA had projected in the early seventies.[61] Yet even these numbers overrate the economic viability of nuclear power in developing countries. All the nuclear sales in the Third World so far were subsidized by industrial country governments or manufacturers. The day when nuclear plants are sufficiently cost-effective that developing countries will buy them at the full price is far off indeed.

Beyond these problems lies the more fundamental question of whether nuclear power is a wise use of scarce resources for a developing country. Nuclear power creates fewer jobs and requires more dependence on foreign companies and governments than does almost any other investment a Third World nation can make. It is also likely to serve a small minority who use electricity while bypassing the majority, who rely on fuelwood and charcoal. Investing in rural electrification using small-scale renewable energy sources or improving the efficiency of wood cookstoves would provide far greater benefits.

Nuclear power was greatly oversold in the Third World. Humanitarian and profit-seeking motives became confused, and projects were pushed that had little hope of being economical. Most nations would in fact benefit if any projects not yet built were swiftly canceled. And beyond the economic issue is the growing realization that nuclear power plants are inviting targets for military and terrorist attacks in politically unstable regions.

NUCLEAR POWER'S FUTURE

Worldwide, nuclear power development hangs by a much thinner thread than most policymakers yet realize. The global commitment to building nuclear power plants has declined by 31,000 megawatts since 1978, as major cancellations in the United States were not offset by the more modest orders in some

other nations. Further declines in the next few years are virtually certain since few orders are expected, and many of the 20–30 plants not yet under construction or on which work has been stopped are candidates for cancellation. The usually optimistic Nuclear Energy Agency of the OECD concluded in 1982 that, "There is some risk that the nuclear industry will not remain commercially viable in a climate of uncertain and variable markets." Markets of any kind are becoming rare indeed for the nuclear industry.[62]

Hard, cold economics is now doing to nuclear power what thousands of hot-blooded demonstrators never could. It is slowly, painfully shutting down the world's nuclear industries. The only countries in which development is proceeding at close to the pace planned a decade ago are those where there is no semblance of a market test and where nuclear power is pushed single-mindedly by a strong central government. Private investors who have a choice and who must bear the financial responsibility for their decisions are steering clear of nuclear power.

Important additional costs may further tip the economic scales. The disposal of nuclear wastes and decommissioning of old plants are critical problems that have yet to be effectively resolved in any country. Each presents enormous health and safety concerns that could affect societies for generations. Providing remedies will inevitably add to the cost of nuclear power. So far waste disposal and decommissioning are "uncounted costs" and their potential size can only be guessed. Official figures generally show the disposal and decommissioning adding 5–10 percent to the cost of nuclear power though unofficial estimates range up to an additional 50 percent or more. The degree of concern over these issues is evident in California: The state legislature there has on economic grounds banned the building of nuclear plants until there is a national program for waste disposal.[63]

Some would argue that even if nuclear power is expensive it is still essential as a replacement for imported oil. Although it is true that nuclear power has helped lower oil imports in some nations —particularly France and Japan—in most countries its contribution has been negligible, dwarfed by increased use of coal and energy efficiency. In the United States oil imports have fallen 50 percent since 1978, but nuclear power generation has risen only 5 percent. Today a small and shrinking fraction of the world's oil is used to generate electricity, and the oil versus nuclear equation is largely moot.[64]

Cold economics is now doing to nuclear power what thousands of hot-blooded demonstrators never could.

The choice between coal and nuclear power, as usually posed, is not an attractive one. Coal-caused air pollution has steadily increased in many countries, producing new evidence of health and environmental damage. Air pollution is shortening the lives of millions of people, particularly in developing countries that cannot afford pollution controls. Recently, acid rain and the threat of climate change through the greenhouse effect were added to the list of coal-related ills and appear much less open to simple technical fixes.

The world's energy options, however, are not limited to a choice between nuclear power and coal. The biggest change in the utility industry in recent years has been the new role of "end-use" energy efficiency as an alternative to new

power plants of any kind. By increasing the amount of light delivered by a light bulb or the work performed by an industrial motor for every kilowatt-hour of electricity used, the same energy services are gained at less than it would cost with a new generating plant.[65]

Many of today's efficiency investments save energy at a cost of between 1¢ and 2¢ per kilowatt-hour, which is one-tenth to one-fifth the cost of electricity from a new coal or nuclear plant. Utilities are beginning to take advantage of such bargains, in part because regulators are allowing them to include in the rate base the funds invested, say, in home insulation or a more efficient air conditioner, just as they do investments in new power plants. A 1983 survey of 120 U.S. utilities by the Investor Responsibility Research Center found that 75 percent have formal energy efficiency programs. Collectively the utilities surveyed estimate that improved efficiency will reduce their need for new generating capacity by 30,000 megawatts over the next decade at a cost of $6.6 billion, or less than one-sixth the cost of equivalent power from a new nuclear plant.[66]

These fundamental changes in the economics of electricity are greatly expanding the list of utilities' options. This broader context is likely to determine nuclear power's future. Donald Jordan, president of the Edison Electric Institute, said in 1983: "The huge construction program we face has damaged our industry and our company. The best thing for us would be no growth." Energy conservation programs have caught on more slowly outside the United States, but many are now beginning. Throughout virtually the entire industrial world electricity growth rates have slipped from the 6–8 percent annual rates of the early seventies to between 1 and 4 percent today. In much of northern Europe, electricity use could actually decline.[67]

When new generating capacity is needed, utilities will have many more options than when they last ordered plants. Promising renewable sources of electricity include small-scale hydropower, geothermal energy, biomass energy, wind power, and photovoltaic solar energy. In addition, cogeneration—the combined production of heat and power —is a rapidly growing alternative to central power plants. The cost of these energy sources today ranges from just below to substantially higher than the cost of power from new coal or nuclear plants. But the cost of the new sources is declining while those of coal and nuclear are still rising. (See Table 7-3.) In addition, many alternative energy projects can be built on almost any scale and plans quickly modified if demand shifts, an important advantage given utility forecasters' poor record for projections.[68]

Nuclear power is going to find it hard to stay alive in the emerging competitive economic climate. In the United States most utilities now state openly that they do not even consider it in their plans for new generating capacity for the next decade. In other countries the strength of nuclear development appears to decline in direct proportion to the degree of responsibility and risk the private sector is required to assume.

If an overriding national goal is the expansion of nuclear power, a centrally planned energy program appears best. However, providing energy services at the least cost and ensuring adequate capital for non-energy investments make a centralized commitment to nuclear power much less attractive. Even relatively successful programs are encountering cost overruns that cannot be entirely short-circuited via central planning. Many will pay for their "success" with high electricity rates and scarce capital for years to come.

The broad range of alternatives available and the pace at which the utility industry is changing make a balanced approach more important than ever. Adequate power at the lowest feasible price is the most sensible overall goal, with an internal accounting of the environmental costs associated with each energy source. If nuclear power does not pass this market test, which it may not, it will be replaced by more-appropriate energy sources.

Nuclear power's economic problems are not about to disappear. Costs continue to increase everywhere and high interest rates and tight capital markets are likely to remain, even with a vigorous economic recovery. Arguments over the economics of nuclear power are bound to grow more heated as cost increases begin to affect electricity consumers directly and as nuclear industries, starved for new orders, pressure for more support.

The question now is not whether to make a few small adjustments to encourage a thriving industry, but whether to introduce fundamental institutional changes and new economic subsidies to prop up a dying business. Leaders in many countries will be tempted to mud-

Table 7-3. Estimated Cost of Electricity From New Plants, 1983, With Projections for 1990 (in 1982 dollars)

Energy Source	1983	1990
	(cents per kilowatt-hour)	
Nuclear	10–12	14–16
Coal	5–7	8–10
Small Hydropower	8–10	10–12
Cogeneration	4–6	4–6
Biomass	8–15	7–10
Wind Power	15–20	6–10
Photovoltaics	50–100	10–20
Energy Efficiency	1–2	3–5

SOURCE: Worldwatch Institute.

dle through, making one decision at a time and so wading gradually into a financial quagmire. This could be the most costly approach of all. Many utilities in the United States have clung to nuclear projects long after their economic rationales had turned to dust. In the end, the plants were canceled, but often several years and hundreds of millions of dollars later than would have been prudent.

National leaders continue to be mesmerized by the once-great hopes placed in nuclear power and fail to see clearly the economic burden it has become. A basic business principle holds that money-losing enterprises should not be continued in an attempt to recover early losses if more promising investment opportunities are available. The time is at hand to decide whether nuclear power programs have reached this point. Many nations would benefit by cutting their losses and moving on to more-productive endeavors.

8

Developing Renewable Energy

Christopher Flavin
Sandra Postel

Efforts to develop renewable energy sources have unfolded at an unprecedented scale and pace since the 1973 oil embargo. In the early seventies, renewable energy was in a much weaker position than synthetic fuels, nuclear breeder reactors, and fusion power, energy sources in which great hope had been placed and on which much government funding had been lavished. The many disappointments and delays plaguing these heavily funded technologies since the late seventies are sharply contrasted by rapid progress made in developing a wide range of renewable energy sources.

Renewable energy development was stimulated by major new government research and development (R&D) programs in the mid-seventies, which were

Many of the issues in this chapter are discussed in greater detail in Daniel Deudney and Christopher Flavin, *Renewable Energy: The Power to Choose* (New York: W.W. Norton & Co., 1983).

soon joined by research efforts in university and corporate laboratories. R&D programs covered everything from genetic research aimed at developing better fuel-producing crops to large solar demonstration projects built by private companies with government funding. Not all the projects met their objectives, but the successes far outweighed the failures and helped pave the way for future progress.

In the development of any new technology there is a natural evolution driven by economic and political developments as well as technical change. New inventions often languish in the laboratory for years before their commercial potential is recognized, capital raised, and markets developed. Several renewable energy sources are now crossing this critical threshold, entering a stage of explosive growth that will dwarf past progress. The momentum established in the past decade appears sufficient to overcome the negative effects of stagnant oil prices, high interest rates, and diminished government support.

Renewable energy sources provide approximately 18 percent of the world's energy, mainly in the form of hydropower and wood fuel.

Since 1980, private companies have decisively taken the lead from governments in the development of renewable energy. According to International Energy Agency data for 17 industrial countries, governments spent $1.2 billion on renewable energy R&D in 1981 and industry spent $1.4 billion; total annual private investment in the actual development of renewable energy in these countries probably approached $10 billion in 1983.[1] Surprisingly, investments rose consistently during the worldwide recession of the early eighties. With the government spending cutbacks, the private sector is now leading the way in renewable energy development.

Today, renewable energy sources provide approximately 18 percent of the world's energy, mainly in the form of hydropower and wood fuel. That figure has risen only slightly since 1973, but more rapid growth is likely in the years ahead. The list of important renewable energy sources will grow to a half-dozen or more. Although none of these will be a cheap panacea, eliminating the need for oil overnight, collectively they appear capable of meeting many of the modest additional energy needs that will arise during the next decade. The renewable energy sources discussed in this chapter—wind power, wood fuel, geothermal energy, and photovoltaic solar cells—are among the energy sources in which recent progress has been substan-

tial. Other major sources, such as hydropower, methane generators, solar water heaters, and energy crops, will be dealt with in this report in subsequent years.

FARMING THE WIND

Wind power has moved to the forefront of the renewable energy scene in some countries in the past few years.[2] Although simple wind pumps have been used for over a millennium to lift water for agricultural and household uses, wind power development in the early eighties has been dominated by a new form of wind power: centralized wind-electric systems operated by or for utilities. "Wind farms"—clusterings of turbines connected to the electric grid—are now generating power commercially in California and a few other areas.

Harnessing the wind to generate electricity dates back to 1890, and wind generators were widely used to electrify farms in the early part of the century. About 20,000 wind turbines are used today at fire lookouts and remote airfields and on isolated ranches and coastal buoys.[3] When energy prices began rising in the seventies, the wind power industry made only fitful progress at first. Gradually the technology improved with the help of government-funded research and development. Aerospace engineers worked to develop wind machines with blades as long as a jumbo jet's wings and with generating capacities as high as 5,000 kilowatts, enough to supply power to over 1,000 modern homes.

At least eight giant wind machines have been erected in the United States, and others have gone up in Canada, Denmark, the Netherlands, the Soviet Union, Sweden, the United Kingdom, and West Germany. Success in these efforts has been mixed. Some wind machines have blown over and some generators have burned out—the usual problems of a new technology—and efforts are being made to reduce the cost of the wind turbines and improve their reliability. Employing aerospace designs and computer controls, these giant machines require world-class engineering. It will be several years before they are a viable commercial technology.[4]

Meanwhile, business interest in wind power blossomed. A 1981 survey found that 110 U.S. utilities had wind energy research programs, and many have installed experimental machines. The world's first commercial wind farm began generating power in New Hampshire in 1981, and the first municipal wind farm was installed in Livingston, Montana, in 1982.[5]

Since 1982, however, all these efforts have been overshadowed by those in California. Blessed with mountain passes that are ideal wind farm sites, this state is far and away the world's wind farm pioneer. Beginning in the late seventies, the state government conducted thorough wind resource assessments, offered generous wind energy tax credits, and required utilities to buy power from wind farms at a competitive price. Rapidly rising electricity prices provide added incentive in a state where utilities still depend heavily on oil- and gas-fired power generation.

The result was a wind farm boom that some have likened to the California gold rush of 1849. Starting almost from scratch, developers installed 900 machines at 20 separate locations in 1982. Surveys indicate that 4,613 wind turbines with a total generating capacity of 300 megawatts will have been installed by the end of 1983, enough to meet the needs of over 30,000 households. (See Table 8-1.) Three-quarters of them were installed in 1983 alone. Wind farms now in the planning stage that should be

Table 8-1. California: Commercial Wind Farms Installed, by Location, by End of 1983[1]

Location	Machines	Generating Capacity
	(number)	(megawatts)
Altamont Pass	2,143	142
Tehachapi Mountains	1,637	102
San Gorgonio Pass	603	34
Mojave	150	18
Salinas Valley	80	4
Total	4,613	300

[1]Preliminary estimate.
SOURCES: California Energy Commission, "Large California Wind Projects Installed in 1981 and 1982," and "Large-Scale California Wind Projects Planned for 1983," Sacramento, Calif., unpublished, 1983.

complete by the late eighties include 8,-600 wind machines with a generating capacity of about 1,500 megawatts.[6] The California Energy Commission's goal is for the state to have 4,000 megawatts installed by the end of the century, enough to supply 8 percent of the state's electricity.

Much of the early work in developing wind farms in California is being carried out by small innovative firms formed specifically to tap this power source. The companies have contracts with utilities to supply wind-generated electricity at the same price it would cost the utility to get the power from another source. The U.S. Windpower Company, one of the most successful developers, is one-third of the way toward its goal of providing 60 megawatts of generating capacity for the Pacific Gas and Electric Company. The small wind energy entrepreneurs typically raise their own financing through limited partnerships and lease the land on which the machines are constructed. Aided by generous federal and state tax incentives, such firms can invest in new power sources that utilities will not develop on their own. For the utilities, the arrangement is an almost risk-free way of adding a new power source. For the investors, a healthy tax credit is available, along with revenues from the electricity sales. As the technologies improve and wind-generated electricity becomes cost-competitive with conventional sources, the tax credits will no longer be necessary.[7]

California's wind farms have developed so quickly that the wind machine industry is still catching up. Since the large machines are not commercially ready, developers have relied on medium-sized turbines with generating capacities of between 30 and 100 kilowatts. So rapid is the growth that more turbines were built in the United States in 1982 and 1983 than in the previous ten years combined. Imported machines, primarily from the Netherlands and Belgium, filled the gap and currently supply 10 percent of California's wind power market. The state is serving as a major stimulus to the wind turbine industry worldwide.[8]

Wind farms now in the planning stage include 8,600 wind machines with a generating capacity of about 1,500 megawatts.

Modern wind turbines include the latest in transmissions, computer controls, and synthetic materials. The wind farms have not been without technical problems, however. Many machines have had to be shut down temporarily for repairs, and important lessons continue to be learned.[9] The most basic one is that a simple, rugged wind machine is likely to hold up the best, and some of the sophisticated, efficient designs have been aban-

doned. Large-scale assembly-line production of wind machines should begin soon, putting wind power about where the automobile industry was when Henry Ford introduced the Model T. The resulting machines are likely to be more reliable and less expensive. Gradually developers are ordering larger wind machines and it may be only a few more years before multi-megawatt machines are used commercially. Preliminary contracts have been signed to set up such wind farms.

The economic verdict on wind farms is in. If well-designed machines are placed at windy sites, electricity can already be generated for as little as 10¢ per kilowatt-hour. In parts of California, the U.S. Midwest, northern Europe, and many developing countries where wind speeds average at least 12 miles per hour and where oil-generated electricity is common, wind farms are close to being economically viable now. Studies in Europe and the United States indicate that later generations of mass-produced machines will be able to produce electricity at 3–7¢ per kilowatt-hour, making them commercially viable without special tax credits. By the nineties wind farms are likely to have an economic advantage over coal and nuclear power plants in many parts of the world. In the meantime, work is needed to further improve turbine performance and reliability.[10]

The environmental effects of wind machines are a potential constraint on the future of this renewable energy source. The availability of inexpensive land far from housing developments is key to wind farm acceptability. A "farm" generating power equal to a 1,000-megawatt power plant would cover approximately 82 square kilometers of land. Meeting California's goal of providing 8 percent of the state's generating capacity with wind farms requires the placement of between 10,000 and 100,000 machines on approximately 615 square kilometers. Yet this area is just two-tenths of 1 percent of the state's land. Based on such calculations, countries with ample wind should be able to get 10–25 percent of their electricity from this resource without infringing on land needed for agriculture or housing.[11]

Noise and safety are additional environmental concerns. Annoying sounds and inaudible vibrations have caused problems with some experimental wind machines. Residents living near Altamont Pass in California, site of the world's largest projects, complained about the incessant "swooshing" sound, and their land finally had to be purchased by wind power developers. In 1983, environmentalists fought a proposed wind farm to be located near the scenic northern California coast. Proper land use planning could prevent these problems. Wind farms clearly should be sited discriminately, and there are plenty of good locations where conflicts should not arise.[12]

California's wind farms have already gained worldwide attention and are likely to stimulate similar projects in other countries that can benefit from the technical and institutional lessons of these pioneers. In the Netherlands, the national electricity association is developing a 10-megawatt experimental farm and plans to be generating 7 percent of the country's electricity with wind power in the year 2000. Experimental wind farms have also been started in Denmark and Sweden, and several other northern European countries have similar plans. One of the most innovative is a British plan to create offshore "farms" in the windy North Sea, supported by platforms anchored to the sea floor.[13]

Government support is a prerequisite for the successful early development of wind power. The advances made in California would not have been possible without tax credits. By reducing the investment risk, tax incentives stimulate the early stages of wind power development. So far, most government support has been funneled into R&D programs, which are necessary but not sufficient to create a viable wind farm industry. Wind resource surveys are also essential. Those done in California, for example, revealed an energy source larger than anticipated and were the catalyst for the state's wind farm boom.

Today economics and politics—more than resource or technical limits—are constraining wind power development. In California, the expected boom in 1983 was slightly restrained by delays in extending the state's renewable energy tax credit. Oil price declines and the resultant lowering of the "buy-back rate" that wind developers receive from utilities have also slowed the progress. Since mid-1983 wind farming efforts have accelerated, however, and several thousand machines should be installed in the next few years. Wind power is shaping up to be a major energy success story of the eighties.

THE RESURGENCE OF WOOD

India and the United States, far apart on the economic spectrum, have at least one thing in common: They now burn approximately equal amounts of fuelwood. Yet in the United States the 130 million tons of fuelwood used annually represents only 3 percent of energy consumption, whereas in India this same amount supplies one-fourth the country's energy.[14]

These two countries highlight a striking dichotomy in world fuelwood use: overuse in the developing world, where fuelwood is a necessity in ever shorter supply, and great underuse in the industrial world, where despite its abundance wood was largely supplanted by other energy sources in the early twentieth century. For most Third World residents, fuelwood is the only viable cooking fuel. Over 100 million of these people cannot get enough wood to cook their food and over a billion are meeting fuel needs only by overcutting and depleting their wood resources. (As discussed in Chapter 5, massive tree planting is the only hope of averting this growing Third World energy crisis over the coming decades.)

Yet in many industrial countries fuelwood use has only scratched the surface of its potential. Millions of tons of wood waste and low-quality timber go unused each year in the forest-rich countries of North America and Europe. Now, after a century-long decline when cheap, abundant fossil fuels dominated, wood is edging its way back into the energy budgets of industrial nations.

Sweden, with one of the highest oil imports per capita in the world, has given wood a prominent role in its plans for a more self-sufficient energy future. Aiming to halve oil consumption by 1990, Sweden plans to get 15 times as much energy from fuelwood, wood chips, and forest residues as it did in 1980. Adding energy from pulp-mill wastes should bring wood's projected 1990 contribution to 12 percent of total energy supplies, nearly half oil's share. If the government's plans to reap energy from tree plantations are even modestly successful, wood will replace oil as the leading energy source before the end of the century.[15] Finland, too, is investigating "energy forests"—the planting of willow and other fast-growing, noncommercial species mainly on marginal lands. Estimating that wood waste could replace up to 30 percent of its oil imports, Finland has resolved to strive for 40 percent energy self-sufficiency by 1990.[16]

Canada derives 3.5 percent of its primary energy from wood, nearly all of which is used in the forest products industry. Burning wood for space heating has been limited to about 3 percent of Canadian homes, although the residential wood market is much stronger in some eastern provinces where wood supplies are nearer to towns. On Prince Edward Island, Canada's smallest province and the one most heavily dependent on oil, about half the rural homes are now heated with wood. The government's Forest Industries Renewable Energy Program, begun in 1978 to encourage the wood products industry to replace fossil fuels with wood wastes, had such a successful first three years that it was extended through 1986 and its budget was tripled to $288 million. Canada's $30-million wood energy research program is focused on displacing 10 percent of fossil fuel use by the year 2000.[17]

India and the United States now burn approximately equal amounts of fuelwood.

In the United States, the decisions of millions of homeowners and scores of companies are sparking wood energy's revival. After falling from 75 percent in 1870 to 2 percent in 1973, wood's share of national energy use is now up to 3 percent and climbing. In 1982, industries accounted for 60 percent of wood energy consumption; homes and small businesses burned the rest. Although industrial wood energy consumption has been rising for decades, it is the use by homeowners that has changed dramatically. Since 1973 wood energy use in the residential sector has more than doubled.[18] Annual sales of residential wood stoves increased ninefold between 1972 and 1979 and two million stoves for home heating were purchased in 1981 alone.[19] Americans collectively burned over 48 million tons of wood in their homes in 1981—equal in end-use heating value to nearly 100 million barrels of oil.[20] (See Figure 8-1.)

Between 1973 and 1981, Vermont residents halved consumption of home heating oil and tripled their burning of wood.

Wood's reentry into the U.S. home heating market is strongest where the fuel is abundant and where other energy sources have risen greatly in price. No region better exemplifies this than New England, where 80 percent of the land is forested and where the price of fuel oil —the most widely used home heating fuel—has jumped 240 percent over the last decade. Between 1973 and 1981, Vermont residents halved their consumption of home heating oil and tripled their burning of wood.[21] (See Figure 8-2.) In 1980 alone, $48-million worth of petroleum was saved and, since wood is a local energy source, its use increased local employment and in-

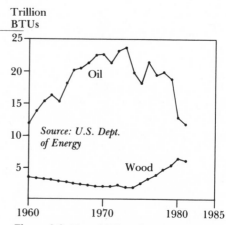

Figure 8-2. Use of Oil and Wood for Home Heating in Vermont, 1960-81

come. Although the pace of fuel switching no doubt will slacken over the coming years, if these general trends in oil consumption and wood use continue, wood may rival oil as the state's leading residential fuel within a decade.

Industrial use of fuelwood has long been dominated by the forest products industry. Recent progress toward greater self-sufficiency in this energy-intensive industry is impressive. Bark, pulping wastes, and wood chips now supply about half the U.S. pulp and paper industry's energy—equal to about 125 million barrels of oil annually— while the solid-wood products industry (making plywood, cabinets, pallets, and so forth) is now about 70 percent self-sufficient. Many of these companies are supplying power to nearby communities and industries. The Scott Paper Company cogenerates 30 megawatts at its Westbrook, Maine, plant and sells the surplus electricity to the local utility. Paper companies in Sweden are obtaining 60 percent of their energy from wood residues; those in Canada, 45 percent. These figures should keep rising as more firms find that extracting energy from their own waste matter makes economic sense.[22]

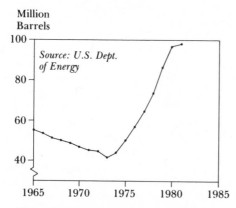

Figure 8-1. U.S. Residential Wood Use (in Equivalent Barrels of Oil), 1965-81

Wood fuel is now attracting other industries as well. By late 1985, at least 8 projects generating over 10 megawatts of electricity exclusively from wood will be on line in non-forest-products companies in the United States. (See Table 8-2.) By the end of the decade this number will easily exceed 25. Industrial boilers are being fired with scrap from furniture-makers, waste wood from pulp mills, residues from the forest, wood chips from land-clearing operations, as well as harvests from private forests. Proctor and Gamble spent $30 million to convert its large Staten Island, New York, plant from oil to wood in 1983 and expects energy savings of $3 million a year. Dow Corning Corporation, a leading manufacturer of silicon products, began cogenerating electricity and steam at its Midland, Michigan, plant in December 1982. Although the facility can burn wood, oil, natural gas, or coal (with modifications), wood is the economical choice for the eighties. Dow Corning is meeting all its own energy

needs and selling between 1 and 2 megawatts of electricity to Consumers Power, the area utility.[23]

Where conventional fuels are expensive and wood supplies abundant, electric utilities are also finding fuelwood an attractive alternative. A subsidiary of Washington Water Power Company is nearing completion of a 46-megawatt wood-fueled plant in Kettle Falls that annually will burn about 450,000 tons of wood waste from surrounding lumber mills. Vermont's Burlington Electric Department, which already has retrofitted two 10-megawatt coal units to burn wood, plans to have a 50-megawatt wood-fired boiler operating in early 1984. The half-million tons of wood chips consumed annually will come from privately owned forests within 50 miles of the city. Ultrasystems, Inc., of California is pioneering the development of small electric power plants to be run entirely on forest residues. Two plants that will tie into northern California's utility grid are slated for completion over the

Table 8-2. United States: Selected Plants Outside of Forest Products Industry Generating Electricity From Wood[1]

Project	Capacity	Wood Source	Start-up
	(megawatts)		
Burlington Electric Dept. Burlington, Vermont	50.0	private forestland harvests	Spring 1984
W.P. Energy Kettle Falls, Washington	46.0	mill residues	Fall 1983
Dow Corning Midland, Michigan	22.4	private forestland harvests	December 1982
Proctor and Gamble Long Beach, California	13.5	industrial waste wood	June 1983
Ultrapower, Inc. Burney, California	11.0	forest residues	September 1984
Ultrapower, Inc. Westwood, California	11.0	forest residues	September 1985
Proctor and Gamble Staten Island, New York	10.5	industrial waste wood; wood chips	June 1983

[1]Not included are utilities and industries blending wood with coal.
SOURCE: Personal communications with utility and industry officials.

next two years and the company plans to develop 20 of these plants nationwide over the next five years.[24]

Wood-fired electricity generation is also being pursued in developing countries. In the Philippines, the hearty legume tree leucaena (known there as the ipil-ipil) has been planted on some 15,000 hectares of shallow, infertile soils to supply wood to power plants throughout the island nation. Several of the 17 plants initially planned are nearing completion and at least two were expected to be operating by late 1983. About 1,200 hectares of leucaena are needed to supply each 3-megawatt power plant with fuel on a sustainable basis. The trees are planted and farmed by rural families, many of whom now have steady incomes for the first time. Each hectare annually produces wood equal in energy content to 20–25 barrels of oil—at one-fourth the price. With about six million hectares (20 percent) of the country's land area now denuded, there is ample room and reason to expand these plantations.[25]

Wood's resurgence as an energy source is owed in large part to new technologies of harvesting and processing it for fuel. Mechanized whole-tree harvesting, unlike traditional logging, removes not only the commercially valuable bole of the tree but its leaves and branches as well. Residues formerly left as slash in the forest are thus available for fuel. In just minutes, whole-tree chippers can convert virtually all parts of a tree into wood chips that can be easily transported to a waiting wood-fired boiler. As shown by Proctor and Gamble's plant in Staten Island, no longer must a company be surrounded by forests to fuel its boilers with wood.

Also, in the last few years wood pellets have increasingly moved from the research lab to the marketplace. The patented pelletizing process yields bite-sized bits of wood (or other biomass) that are denser, drier, and thus cheaper to transport than other wood fuels. Since converting boilers from coal to pellets is typically quite easy, pellet-producing companies see a large market ahead in fueling industries, schools, hospitals, and other institutions, as well as in heating homes. At least a dozen plants are now making pellets in North America. BioSolar Research and Development in Eugene, Oregon, and Shell-Canada are jointly building these plants in several Pacific Rim countries, expecting a sizable market where oil import bills are high.[26]

No longer must a company be surrounded by forests to fuel its boilers with wood.

Burning wood for fuel is not always environmentally benign. As demand for fuelwood continues to rise and emerging technologies make logging of small tracts and noncommercial wood more economical, the character and health of forests may change. In the United States, more than half the commercial forests are owned by nearly eight million private landowners. Many have never managed their forests for commercial purposes but may soon have an incentive to do so. The 50-megawatt power plant in Burlington, for example, may double the wood harvest of northern Vermont. Fuel for Dow Corning's Michigan plant will come from private forests within 50–75 miles.[27]

Foresters anticipate both benefits and problems in this situation. On the one hand, selective thinning and removal of old growth could increase the productivity of private forests, something that foresters have advocated for some time but that private landowners had little incentive to do. Yet whole-tree harvesting technologies will remove more biomass from the forest and will encourage more clear-cutting. Leaves and twigs have high concentrations of nutrients that, if left in the forest, revitalize the soil. Removing too much biomass could eventually cause declines in forest productivity. As the wood energy market grows, these potential effects must be monitored carefully and limits may need to be set on wood removal from some forests.

Like most energy sources, fuelwood is not without its pollution problems. Winter mornings in many wood-burning valley towns are now shrouded in a bluish-gray haze. Wood-stove emissions contain a high percentage of organic matter thought to be toxic and carcinogenic. Wood burning is now regulated in the state of Oregon and in some towns in Colorado and Montana. In other areas where such pollution is worsening, regulations undoubtedly will be forthcoming. Catalytic converters effectively control wood pollutants and recoup part of their $80–100 price tag by increasing efficiencies by 15–25 percent. Pollution controls for industrial wood boilers generally require a smaller capital investment than a comparable coal plant would, but costs are not insignificant. The electrostatic precipitator that removes virtually all particulates at Dow Corning's plant added 15–20 percent to construction costs.[28]

Although wood is unlikely to regain a place of dominance in the energy budgets of industrial countries, it is emerging as an important component of the renewable energy picture in many regions. Neither the forest management problems nor the pollution control challenges it poses are insurmountable. Before the century is out, wood's contribution to primary energy needs is likely to reach between 7 and 15 percent in several industrial countries, depending upon the success of energy plantations and the extent to which commercial forests come under more intensive management.

GEOTHERMAL ENERGY DEVELOPMENT

Whereas most renewable fuel sources draw upon the sun's energy, geothermal energy comes directly from the earth's vast subsurface storehouse of heat. Intense pressure and the decay of radioactive elements deep within the earth continuously generate heat that escapes through hot springs, geysers, and volcanoes. The world's geothermal riches include the area where the mid-Atlantic ridge bisects Iceland, areas around the Mediterranean, the Rift Valley in East Africa, and the "Ring of Fire" that extends around the Pacific Basin. Yet even outside these places, which constitute about 10 percent of the world's land mass, there are abundant lower-temperature geothermal deposits.[29]

For millennia people have flocked to hot springs, and by the ninth century Icelanders were using geothermal heat for cooking. In the Middle Ages several European towns distributed naturally hot water to heat homes. The 20 countries tapping this source today for chores other than bathing cull the energy equivalent of 91 million barrels of oil each year, about half in the form of direct heat and half as electricity. Although not yet a major component of the global energy budget, this is enough direct heat to meet the needs of over 2 million homes in a cold climate and sufficient electricity for over 1.5 million modern homes.[30]

Heating homes is the widest application of geothermal energy today. Since the turn of the century, the residents of Klamath Falls, Oregon, have drilled more than 400 wells to tap the 40–110° C water beneath their houses for space- and domestic water-heating. Household wells there have exchangers that transfer heat from the briny subterranean reservoir to the pure water circulating to the house. Using a heat exchanger conserves the resource, minimizes corrosion, and skirts the problem of wastewater disposal.[31]

Where human settlements sit astride geothermal resources, district heating is an unbeatable bargain. The most impressive example is Iceland, whose immense geothermal resources provide heat for 75 percent of the population. In Reykjavik, the capital, nearly all the 112,000 residents use heat from two geothermal fields under the city and from another field 15 kilometers away. Visitors to this frigid city in the thirties recall the pall of coal and wood smoke that engulfed it in winter. Today the air is clear, and heating homes costs one-fourth what it would if fuel oil were used.[32] France, Hungary, the Soviet Union, and the United States also have geothermal district heating systems in place.

Although geothermal technology has advanced far in recent decades, it is still the simplest uses that are the most popular. Japan's 1,500 hot-spring resorts are visited by 100 million people each year, for example, and require no drilling, little piping, and minimal capital. Yet it would take five large conventional power plants to heat these baths. In parts of Mexico, people wash clothes with naturally hot water; some Thais and Guatemalans use it to boil vegetables and make tea. The largest agricultural application is greenhouse heating: In Hungary, geothermal greenhouses cover 70 hectares, while Italy saves $600,000 worth of fuel oil a year by geothermally heating several greenhouses.[33]

This renewable resource is also used in industry. In northern Iceland a mineral-processing plant uses it to remove the moisture from siliceous earth. With 30 percent lower energy costs, the company now pockets an extra $1.3 million annually. At Brady's Hot Springs, Nevada, an onion dehydration plant using geothermal energy is saving $300,000 per year, enough to motivate the company's managers to expand the original plant and build an additional one.[34]

Converting geothermal heat to electricity allows the captured energy to be transported to cities and factories far from its source. Areas with the high-temperature geothermal water or steam needed for electricity generation are rarer than those suited for direct use. Even so, today over 130 geothermal power plants with capacities of 0.5–120 megawatts are operating in more than a dozen countries, and the number is growing rapidly. (See Table 8-3.) Collectively, these plants have a generating ca-

Table 8-3. Worldwide Geothermal Electrical Generating Capacity, June 1983

Country	Power Plants	Total Installed Capacity
	(number)	(megawatts)
United States	24	1,284
Philippines	14	594
Italy	41	457
Japan	8	228
Mexico	10	205
New Zealand	14	203
El Salvador	3	95
Iceland	5	41
Indonesia	3	32
Kenya	2	30
Soviet Union	1	11
China	10	8
Total	135	3,188

SOURCE: Ronald DiPippo, Southeastern Massachusetts University, private communication, September 1983.

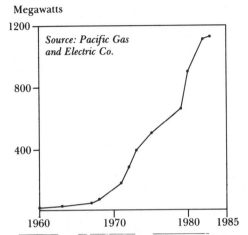

Megawatts

Source: Pacific Gas and Electric Co.

Figure 8-3. Electricity Generated at World's Largest Geothermal Project, The Geysers, California, 1960-83

pacity of over 3,000 megawatts.

The simplest technology for generating electricity is the dry steam system used at steam-only reservoirs. Four such systems are in operation: one commercial complex each in Italy and the United States and two smaller systems in Indonesia and Japan. Electricity generation at these rare, prime sites is mainly a matter of piping the steam to a standard turbine. The largest complex is one at The Geysers in northern California, which has been rapidly developed in the last decade. (See Figure 8-3.) In 1983, 17 power plants were providing 1,000 megawatts of generating capacity for the Pacific Gas and Electric Company (PG&E)—about 6 percent of the utility's generating capacity. Four other developers are active in The Geysers area, including the California Department of Water Resources, which uses the geothermal energy to pump water into its state water project aqueducts. Total generating capacity at The Geysers from the wells of all five developers may reach 2,500 megawatts before the century is out.[35]

More common are geothermal reser-voirs that contain both steam and water. Plants that tap this less ideal form of geothermal energy are found in at least ten countries, though many of the projects are still experimental. One of the most successful facilities, in Wairakei, New Zealand, has operated continuously since the mid-sixties. Electricity generation declined at this 190-megawatt plant at first, apparently because water was being extracted faster than it was being replaced. However, generation has stabilized since the mid-seventies.[36]

Over 130 geothermal power plants are operating in more than a dozen countries.

A major boost to geothermal development will occur when generating plants can use these more abundant geothermal resources. Conventional "separated steam" facilities use the naturally available steam alone to run the turbines. More-efficient "double flash" plants direct hot water brought to the surface to a vessel where pressure is reduced and additional steam generated. A recent innovation—the binary cycle plant—allows efficient electricity generation using lower-temperature water (between 150–200° C). Pilot plant tests in China, Japan, and the United States indicate that this promising design needs more research and operating experience, however. Geothermal cogeneration—using the same energy for both electricity generation and direct thermal use—can also increase efficiency.[37]

Improving the means of locating and drilling for geothermal resources would speed the pace of development of this energy source. Many industries and cities undoubtedly sit atop hidden geothermal resources that could provide them with relatively cheap energy. The drilling of wells often accounts for more than half the cost of some geothermal projects. Exploration and drilling relies on techniques similar to those used in natural gas development and improvements should reduce costs. The sophisticated remote-sensing techniques developed by petroleum geologists are being adapted to geothermal energy prospecting. This should lower costs, though by exactly how much is hard to predict.

Impurities such as salts and silicates, picked up from subterranean rock by the hot circulating water, typically cause scaling and corrosion at geothermal plants. Moreover, the materials that corrode or scale the inside of a geothermal system often become pollution outside it. Hydrogen sulfide, a noxious gas found at almost all geothermal sites, is occasionally concentrated enough to cause lung paralysis, nausea, and other health problems. Pollution control devices developed for use on coal plant emissions can remove approximately 90 percent of the hydrogen sulfide, but so far only The Geysers plant in California and a few others use them. As the cost of the devices would constitute less than 10 percent of the overall system, expense is no excuse for this lapse; geothermal plants need not become major polluters. Surface water supplies also must be protected from mercury, arsenic, and other substances often dissolved in geothermal water.[38]

Like all renewable energy sources, geothermal energy will not flourish without amenable institutions. Governments could help by conducting broad preliminary assessments to indicate where private industry should focus its efforts. Most countries with major development programs, including the Philippines and the United States, have begun such surveys, though few are as extensive as they might be.[39] Also, the uncertain legal status of geothermal resources inhibits development. In most market economies it makes sense to follow the petroleum model, giving the private sector primary responsibility for developing geothermal energy but standardizing leasing procedures and charging the industry royalty fees if the government owns the resource.[40] Governments may also need to set requirements on plant size and pollution levels to ensure that geothermal developments do not harm the environment and that they preserve other land values.

One approach to risk-sharing taken in France, Iceland, and the United States is for the government to reimburse some proportion of the cost of exploratory wells. In Iceland, an Energy Fund provides loans to cover 60 percent of exploration and drilling costs. If the well is successful, the loan is repaid at normal bank rates using the proceeds from the project. If it is dry, the loan becomes a cash grant and the project is dropped.[41]

Prospects for geothermal energy are bright. Its use has expanded more than 10 percent per year since the mid-seventies; in the two years leading up to June 1983, worldwide capacity rose by 26 percent. Reliance on this source is likely to increase five- to tenfold by the end of the century, with direct heating playing a greater role in the industrial countries and electricity generation being more important in the Third World.[42]

Estimates vary greatly on how quickly the direct use of geothermal heat will grow. France, which has low-temperature geothermal resources below two-thirds of its land area, aims to have a half-million geothermally heated homes by 1990. Canada, China, Japan, the Soviet Union, and the United States could also expand the direct use of geothermal heat dramatically. Through China's national exploratory program, approximately 2,300 hot spots have been identified, and geothermal experts expect the country to move rapidly in its development of direct geothermal heat. Much of the Soviet Union sits atop low-temperature geothermal deposits, and several district heating projects are under way.[43]

Geothermal electricity development could add up to 17,000 megawatts by the year 2000—five times the current level. The United States is likely to account for one-third of this total. Energy analysts in Hawaii estimate that geothermal sources could supply 1,000 megawatts of that state's electricity by century's end—one-third or more of Hawaii's total projected electricity supply. Some 20 potential sites throughout the islands have been identified, opening up the possibility of an interisland electric cable.[44]

The Philippines has nearly 600 megawatts of geothermal generating capacity today and plans to double this by 1989. Eventually geothermal energy will rival hydropower as that country's largest electricity source. Kenya, the only African nation now generating electricity with geothermal energy, has doubled its installed capacity in the last two years. El Salvador has generated one-third of its power from geothermal energy in some recent years, and Mexico plans to have 600 megawatts of geothermal capacity by the mid-eighties.[45]

By any sound reckoning, geothermal energy use will be substantial in the year 2000, though it will remain concentrated in a few areas. Countries such as Iceland and the Philippines will draw heavily on their rich geothermal endowment. And as the technology for tapping geothermal resources improves and some industries relocate to geothermally rich regions, many more countries will rely on this renewable resource. It will gradually become another strong link in a diverse global energy system.

ELECTRICITY FROM SUNLIGHT

Solar photovoltaic cells may become one of the most rapidly expanding energy sources—and one of the biggest growth industries—of the next 20 years. Production of these cells has nearly quadrupled since 1981, and worldwide sales totaled approximately $250 million in 1983. After a decade of being considered a futuristic solar energy prospect, photovoltaics are now entering the commercial marketplace with a full head of steam.[46]

Photovoltaic cells are a product of modern solid-state physics, and they directly convert sunlight, the world's most abundant and widespread renewable energy source, into electricity. Photovoltaic cells are virtually maintenance-free and are made from silicon, the second most abundant element in the earth's crust. The first silicon cells, developed in the United States in the fifties, were expensive—several hundred times the cost of conventional electricity sources. But the need for a lightweight and long-lasting power source for the space program helped rescue photovoltaics from obscurity. By the late sixties, U.S. companies were producing enough solar cells to power virtually all U.S. satellites, providing vital defense, scientific, and research services.

As fossil fuel prices rose in the seventies, solar cells became a much more attractive energy source; researchers in several European countries, Japan, the Soviet Union, and the United States began to develop solar cells for use on earth. Major advances in the efficiency and reliability of photovoltaic cells have been made in the last decade while costs have fallen to a small fraction of their earlier level.

Current uses for solar cells are quite diverse, though they have proved most popular in applications for which conventional energy sources are impractical or simply not available. A large share of photovoltaic systems are used at remote communications installations, for water pumping, and at isolated houses. Other solar cell applications range from portable modules that are popular on boats and train cabooses to larger systems for isolated mountain cabins and scientific research stations. Although most of these are still expensive, particularly since they normally require batteries, they are usually cheaper than the alternatives. Also growing in popularity since 1980 are solar-powered hand calculators and other portable electronic devices. About 60 million solar calculators were sold in 1983, using over 10 percent of the solar cells manufactured.[47]

Approximately 60 companies now manufacture solar cells in 20 different countries. The United States still holds 60 percent of the worldwide market, but other nations are gaining ground rapidly. Japan has the fastest-growing industry and now has a 20 percent market share. The rest of the industry is centered mainly in Europe, led by France, Italy, and West Germany. Countries with smaller photovoltaic industries include Australia, Belgium, Brazil, Canada, China, England, India, Mexico, the Netherlands, the Soviet Union, Spain, and Sweden.[48] Worldwide production of photovoltaics is generally measured by the kilowatts of peak capacity that the solar cells can generate. The manufacture of photovoltaics has grown 75 percent annually, from 500 kilowatts of peak-power capacity in 1977 to an estimated 18,000 kilowatts (18 megawatts) in 1983—over 100 times as much as when the space program was at its height. (See Figure 8-4.) The solar cell industry is currently one of the world's boom industries, and so far its growth rate shows no sign of slowing.[49]

Cost reduction is the key to solar elec-

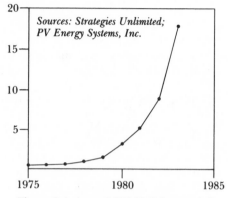

Figure 8-4. Annual World Shipments of Photovoltaic Cells, 1975-83

tricity's future role. Solar cells have followed a remarkable cost curve, with costs being at least halved every five years. Although actual average prices have not fallen quite as steeply as U.S. energy planners had hoped, they have declined from nearly $20 per peak watt in 1977 to $8 in late 1983. (See Figure 8-5.) Balance-of-system costs add $5–10 to the cost of a typical photovoltaic system. Commercial solar cells generate power for between 50¢ and $1 per kilowatt-hour, ten times the typical price of grid electricity in industrial countries.[50]

Solar cells are expensive for a number of reasons: energy-intensive processing, large labor requirements (including the meticulous hand-assembly of cells), and extensive supporting components. Costs will be reduced by half simply by developing less-expensive methods of manufacturing the single-crystal silicon cells that currently dominate the market. Similarly, the efficiency of these cells can be raised from 10 percent up to 15 percent. Another cost-reduction strategy is to develop any of several promising next-generation solar cells, such as amorphous silicon, that are likely to be cheaper to produce. The main challenge is to obtain efficiencies of at least 8–10

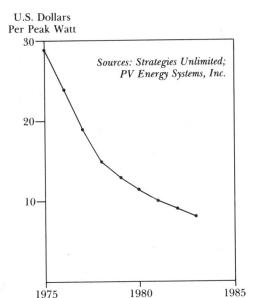

U.S. Dollars
Per Peak Watt

*Sources: Strategies Unlimited;
PV Energy Systems, Inc.*

1975   1980   1985

**Figure 8-5. Average Market Prices of
Photovoltaic Modules, 1975-83**

percent using materials that lack the inherently good photovoltaic properties of crystalline silicon. Commercial production of amorphous cells began in Japan in 1982 and in the United States in 1983. Some analysts think they will sweep the market by 1990.[51]

Larger manufacturing plants employing more-advanced and less-expensive processes are scheduled to come on-line in the next few years, and intense international competition for market shares is already helping to push prices down. By 1990, a total solar-electric system will cost between $4 and $8 per watt and generate electricity at a cost of between 15¢ and 30¢ per kilowatt-hour. This is getting close to the price consumers pay for electricity in many parts of the world, including Europe and Japan. Further reductions are likely after 1990. Since the costs of most electricity sources, including coal and nuclear power, will continue to rise, solar cells should be a competitive electricity source in all but a few areas of the world by the mid-nineties.[52]

Besides offering the prospect of inexpensive power, placing solar-electric systems on residential and industrial rooftops allows greater energy independence. In addition to the approximately 10,000 solar-electric residences currently in remote areas such as Alaska and the Australian outback, architects and engineers are designing photovoltaic homes connected to electricity grids in modern suburban communities. Excess electricity from residential photovoltaic systems is sold to the local utility, while the homeowner relies on the utility's power when the sun is not shining. Several photovoltaic homes have been built in the United States in the early eighties and have been successful, albeit quite expensive so far. Communities in all but the most overcast climates should eventually be able to obtain at least one-quarter of their electricity from rooftop solar systems.[53]

About 60 million solar calculators were sold in 1983, using over 10 percent of the solar cells manufactured.

The question of which use of solar electricity will prove most economical and popular in the future is still open to argument. Advocates of centralized solar power cite the economic advantages of large photovoltaic systems, since one set of power lines and control devices can serve a large installation. The U.S. Department of Energy financed a number of large photovoltaic projects in the late seventies, including a 225-kilowatt solar power project that provides electricity for the Sky Harbor Airport near Phoenix, Arizona. Soleras, the first major photovoltaic project in the Third World, was installed in Saudi Arabia in 1981. It generates 350 kilowatts of solar power for three villages, meeting the electricity needs of 3,600 people.[54] (See Table 8-4.)

In 1983 there was a blossoming of large solar-electric projects. The first privately funded photovoltaic power plant, built by ARCO Solar, Inc., was completed in southern California in February 1983. Made possible by the state's solar tax credits, the 1-megawatt project feeds power into the lines of the Southern California Edison Company. Edison's California rival in the alternative energy business, the Pacific Gas and Electric Company, now has a 16.5-megawatt photovoltaic project under way. The Sacramento Municipal Utility District (SMUD) has begun work on a 100-megawatt photovoltaic power plant —by far the world's largest—scheduled for completion by 1994 at a total cost of over $250 million. Early in 1983 ARCO Solar was awarded a contract to complete the initial 1-megawatt phase of the SMUD project for $5 a peak watt, a record low. By the late eighties, this project alone could install as many solar cells each year as were produced worldwide in 1983.[55]

Japan began operation of its first solar power plant, a 200-kilowatt facility, in late 1982. Solar panels are still being added to it, and when it is complete in 1986 it will have a total capacity of 1 megawatt. Japan's New Energy Development Organization, the principal funder of this plant, has several other projects in the works, including a 200-kilowatt experimental system for a Japanese university.[56]

The European Economic Community and individual European countries are developing 20 photovoltaic demonstration projects. The five largest will be completed in 1984. Italy's 1,150-kilowatt government-funded Delphos project was the world's largest operating plant in 1983. In West Germany, a 300-kilowatt plant is being installed on the island of Pellworm by AEG Telefunken, the country's leading photovoltaics company. The project will meet all the power needs of a recreation center, and excess electricity will feed into the utility grid. In 1983, 100-kilowatt photovoltaic plants were completed in Denmark, Greece, and Spain.[57]

Although much of the progress made

Table 8-4. The World's Twelve Largest Photovoltaic Projects, 1983

Project or Sponsor	Location	Size	Expected or Actual Completion Date
		(kilowatts)	
Sacramento Munic. Utility	California	100,000	1994
United Energy Corporation	California	20,000	1984
Pacific Gas & Elec. Co.	California	16,500	1985
United Energy Corporation	California	10,000	1984
Delphos	Italy	1,150	1983
ARCO Solar	California	1,000	1983
NEDO	Japan	1,000	1986
Soleras	Saudi Arabia	350	1981
AEG Telefunken	West Germany	300	1983
U.S. Department of Energy	Arkansas	245	1981
U.S. Department of Energy	Arizona	225	1982
Solarex	Maryland	200	1982

SOURCE: Worldwatch Institute, based on various sources.

in photovoltaics so far has been in industrial countries, the Third World may actually gain the most from solar electricity over the next few decades. Most villages and rural areas in developing countries still lack access to a steady supply of electricity, and in cities power is usually more expensive than it is in the industrial world. The dream of extending central grids into the "heart of darkness" has faded in the face of mounting debts and the rising cost of vast networks of power lines.

The most common electricity source in most villages today is a diesel generator. But these are unreliable and expensive—between 20¢ and $1 per kilowatt-hour—many times more than typical electricity prices in industrial countries. Photovoltaic systems are relatively maintenance-free, and if solar cell prices fall 50 percent or more in the next five years, as expected, solar power will become economical for most village electricity applications. In many villages, photovoltaics are already an economical way to run refrigerators, communications systems, television sets, lights, and mills. Water pumping is a particularly good use of solar electricity, since sunlight is usually available when water is most needed. In the Third World, just a few hundred watts of power—minuscule by industrial nation standards—can provide basic amenities for the first time.[58]

Currently over 90 percent of the world's solar cells are produced in industrial nations, but many developing countries will soon begin production. Most have entered the photovoltaics business through joint ventures with established companies and at first do only part of the manufacturing at home. As of mid-1983 there were at least eight commercial solar cell companies in the Third World; a half-dozen additional countries will soon have indigenous industries. Two Brazilian companies have joint ventures in Kenya and India, and the government of Pakistan is planning to introduce solar electricity in 14 villages by 1984.[59]

Two small U.S. companies, the Spire Corporation and the Chronar Corporation, are helping to create photovoltaic industries in the Third World by exporting manufacturing equipment. In early 1983 Chronar signed a contract with Morocco to build a photovoltaic factory. The plant, which will be completed in 1984 for $6 million, will manufacture 1-megawatt worth of solar cells per year initially and 20 megawatts of cells annually in a few years. A number of other countries—Egypt, Kuwait, and the Philippines—are understandably impressed and are negotiating with Chronar to purchase factories of their own.[60]

Some countries, including France, the United States, and West Germany, support photovoltaics through their foreign aid programs. Since the mid-seventies France has had major programs under way to install solar-powered pumps and television sets in West Africa. The television sets, modified to require as little as 20 watts of power, bring educational programs to people in remote areas at a reasonable cost. The U.S. Agency for International Development installed eight specially designed solar-powered vaccine refrigerators at rural health centers in 1982 and has another dozen small-scale projects under way.[61]

One of the more ambitious plans for photovoltaics is to provide electricity for whole villages. The first experimental village system was installed on the Papago Indian Reservation in Arizona in 1978. Since then its 3.5 kilowatts of cells have run water pumps, lights, refrigerators, and communal washing and sewing machines for the village's 96 residents, who previously had no electricity. A much larger, 25-kilowatt system installed in a Tunisian village in 1982 is pumping water, providing power for agricultural tasks, and meeting household needs. Thousands of village solar-electric systems could be in use by 1990. For this to occur, however, governments and international aid agencies must arrange innovative financing. One thing they can do is to use agricultural extension services and subsidized loans to encourage the use of solar pumps and mills.[62]

Although solar cells are still one of the most expensive renewable energy sources, they are also advancing the most rapidly. Based on recent industry trends, photovoltaics should begin replacing most diesel generators and become the largest new source of electricity for villages in developing countries within a few years. And with utilities taking the lead, centralized photovoltaic power stations could become a widespread electricity source in many industrial regions by the late eighties. By the early nineties, rooftop solar-electric systems should begin to catch on.

Worldwide annual production of photovoltaics is likely to exceed 200 megawatts of capacity by 1990 and pass 1,000 megawatts by the end of the century. This will make the photovoltaics business a $10-billion industry by the year 2000. Total installed solar-electric capacity will probably be between 5,000 and 10,000 megawatts by century's end. Although this will supply just a small fraction of the world's electricity, it will set the stage for widespread introduction of solar electricity. By the middle of the twenty-first century, photovoltaics may be providing 20–30 percent of the world's electricity and serving as a cornerstone of a sustainable global power system.[63]

ENCOURAGING DEVELOPMENTS

Diversity is a hallmark of the renewable energy developments of the past decade.

With more than a dozen renewable energy sources being explored in a variety of settings around the world, the occasional failed project or neglected opportunity does not jeopardize overall progress. In a time of scarce capital and high interest rates, spreading the risk inherent in developing new energy sources is clearly a benefit. Modern communications have permitted the rapid dissemination of information among researchers and entrepreneurs, accelerating renewable energy development far beyond the pace that would have been possible in a previous era.

This chapter only hints at the literally thousands of technologies and concepts being tested by individuals and companies around the world. Joining wind power, fuelwood, geothermal energy, and photovoltaic systems in the progress of the past decade are small hydropower, passive solar design, active solar heating, solar-thermal electricity generation, and liquid fuels from biomass. For renewable energy, the oil price rises of the seventies had a catalytic effect, stimulating a tremendous surge of innovation that has far from run its course.

Much of the progress in renewable energy is not apparent to those who confine their energy studies to the analysis of aggregate energy statistics, where many renewable sources do not yet appear at all. (Until recently, for example, the U.S. Department of Energy did not include residential fuelwood use in its statistical reports, although it ranks as the country's fourth largest heating fuel.) Yet the progress to date establishes a firm base for development. Even without further oil price increases, many renewable energy sources are economically competitive.

One sign that renewable energy has come of age is that conferences on the various technologies are now frequented by businesspeople and bankers talking about venture capital and "buy-back rates" as well as technical specifications. Newsletters are published for those interested in renewable energy investment; solar stock indices are available for those who want to keep track of their investments. Topflight scientists and engineers are involved in many of the research programs. Renewable energy is losing some of its counterculture image, though it is still strongly supported by many environmentalists, community leaders, and consumer groups who favor renewable energy for its environmental and social advantages.

In order to flourish, renewable energy development must be integrated with existing institutions. Only then will enough trained people and sufficient funding be available for long-term development. One of the encouraging trends of the early eighties is the creation of a variety of nongovernmental mechanisms to facilitate this. Most prominent are the "third party" developers in the United States who construct wind farms, wood-fueled power plants, and the like and sell the power to utilities. Aided by tax credits, these outfits are increasing the investment funds available for some renewable energy sources and are stimulating new industries to build and service the equipment.

Dozens of communities around the world have taken the initiative to develop their own renewable energy and conservation plans. This approach helps bypass the barriers posed by existing institutions that are reluctant to try something different—often the chief problem in getting a new energy source established. Energy programs in which individuals assume much of the responsibility for needed changes have generally proved more successful than those run by distant bureaucrats.

Most Third World countries already rely heavily on renewable energy but the difficulties they face in using it on a sustainable basis are considerable. Renew-able resources are eroding at a frightening rate in developing countries, and the technical expertise and financial resources needed to adapt or develop new energy technologies are often lacking. Mobilizing people and channeling available funds to productive use depends on a redirection of institutions. The community forestry program in South Korea and the biogas program in China are two examples of how properly harnessed efforts can accelerate the development of renewable energy while helping preserve a country's resource base.

No energy transition unfolds overnight. Switching from wood fuel to coal during the Industrial Revolution took most countries a century or more, and several decades were needed for oil and natural gas to take hold. The key to a viable renewable energy–based future is that the world manage the transition gradually—phasing in new fuels before the old ones run out and simultaneously reshaping economies and societies. The last decade's progress has cleared the way for gradual change. Energy conservation can continue to provide breathing room for development of new technologies and allow a smooth meshing of renewable and conventional energy sources during the transition. This historical transformation will provide opportunities for creativity and growth for generations to come.

Conservative projections compiled by Worldwatch Institute in early 1983 indicate that worldwide use of renewable energy will expand at least 75 percent by the end of the century.[64] This will be enough to meet half of the world's additional energy needs by that date and one-quarter of total energy needs. More rapid growth is likely after the turn of the century as oil supplies dwindle and prices rise—and as developers take advantage of the technological advances that will have occurred in the interim. By that time, there will be mature industries

producing wind generators, small hydroelectric turbines, and methanol distilleries for world markets.

With proper management, renewable
energy sources could easily supply as
much energy as the world uses today before running up against resource constraints. Assuming a substantially more
efficient world with twice the current
population and several times the current
wealth, renewable energy should be able
to meet our needs indefinitely. Reaching
that point will be difficult, but given the
failed promise of nuclear power and the
fact that fossil fuels are fading rapidly,
major reliance on renewable energy
after the year 2000 may be essential.

Fifty years from now historians will
look back at the world's heavy reliance
on one fuel as an unhealthy anomaly
born of decades of low oil prices. In the
future, differences in climate, natural resources, economic systems, and social
outlook will determine which energy
sources are used where. Some countries
will depend on five or six major sources
of energy—true energy security. As energy supply patterns change, so will
economies and societies. Industries will
tend to locate near large rivers, geothermal deposits, and other "lodes" of renewable energy since these fuels are less
portable than oil. New patterns of em-

ployment, new designs for cities, and a
revitalized rural sector could all emerge
with renewable energy development.

For individuals and for the environment the changes could be rejuvenating.
Because "renewables" are less polluting
than coal, people will breathe easier as
energy systems change, as will crops and
forests. And renewable energy offers
people striving for self-sufficiency the
chance to take more direct control of
their energy supply. For many people in
the Third World, renewable energy development will bring electric lights, running water, and television for the first
time.

Renewable energy is no panacea, however. As various forms of it are developed, land use pressures will intensify
and environmental conflicts arise—already foreshadowed by disputes over the
location of wind farms and the illegal
cutting of fuelwood. Each energy source
must be carefully developed and trade-
offs carefully weighed if renewable energy is to provide the maximum benefits
to society. The first step is recognizing
that renewable resources are a key to the
world's energy future. The record of the
past decade shows that they deserve a
much higher place on the energy agendas of nations.

9

Reconsidering the Automobile's Future

Lester R. Brown

In the rapidly changing resource and economic milieu of the late seventies and early eighties the future of the automobile has received too little attention. The only question seems to have been what the source of future fuel supplies would be. It has been assumed, perhaps too readily, that synthetic fuels could quickly replace gasoline and diesel fuel.

Within the auto industry, many believed it was only a matter of time until the automobile became the centerpiece of transportation systems everywhere. A 1978 study of the world automobile industry projected the world fleet would expand from just under 300 million vehicles at the time to some 700 million by the year 2000, reaching one car for every eight people.[1] Yet projections such as these are not materializing largely because they were based on a narrow information base and a correspondingly narrow set of considerations, failing to account for a long list of emerging resource, economic, and political constraints.

Competition for resources arises, for example, because automobiles require not only fuel but land as well. In densely populated China, where land is scarce, the private automobile is virtually unknown. International indebtedness on an unforeseen scale in the Third World and in Eastern Europe is restricting automotive fuel imports in scores of countries. At the individual level, the narrowing margin of global economic growth over that of population is preventing the rise in affluence needed if car ownership is to spread as projected.

THE AGE OF THE AUTOMOBILE

Although early automobile technology developed more or less apace in Western Europe and in North America, it was in the United States that the new technology first took root and flowered. Henry Ford's ingenious production approach, soon copied by other manufacturers, led to a rapid spread of automobiles throughout the United States. In 1900 there were 8,000 registered cars; by 1930 there were 23 million.[2]

The depression decade of the thirties and the war decade of the forties saw a slowing of growth. Nevertheless, the automotive society evolved much faster in the United States than in Europe. The country was still a relatively young one; its cities were young and, unlike those in Europe with their narrow streets, they made room for the automobile as they evolved. And the United States had another major advantage—its own oil fields.

Although the automobile became a commercially viable means of transportation shortly after the turn of the century, the great worldwide growth in its use did not occur until after World War II, when oil was priced at $2 a barrel and the world economy was embarking on a quarter-century of unprecedented growth. As recently as 1950 the world fleet numbered only 48 million. (See Table 9-1.) In its adolescence, during the early fifties, the world auto industry was producing just under 10 million vehicles per year. But in 1958 production began a steep climb that continued, with only an occasional interruption, until it reached 30 million per year in 1973. At this point some 100,000 automobiles rolled off the world's assembly lines each working day, underlining the economic importance of automobile manufacturing.[3]

In 1980 Japan produced 7 million autos, compared with 6.3 million American-made cars.

During the first half of the twentieth century, auto production and ownership was concentrated in the United States.

Table 9-1. World Automobile Fleet, 1950–82

Year	Passenger Cars[1]
	(millions)
1950	48
1955	67
1960	92
1965	130
1970	181
1971	194
1972	207
1973	220
1974	236
1975	249
1976	260
1977	270
1978	286
1979	297
1980	310
1981	321
1982	331

[1]Registrations as of January 1 of year listed.
SOURCE: Motor Vehicle Manufacturers Association, *World Motor Vehicle Data Book, 1982 Edition* (Detroit, Mich.: 1982).

Indeed, as recently as 1950 two-thirds of the world's automobiles were owned by Americans. (See Figure 9-1.) It was not until 1968 that the rest of the world finally caught up. Since then, two-thirds of the growth in the fleet has occurred outside the United States.[4]

A vigorous auto industry has emerged in Japan in recent decades. Although automobile manufacturing had scarcely begun in that country in 1960, the industry grew at a remarkable rate. In 1980 Japan produced 7 million autos, compared with 6.3 million American-made cars. For the first time since the automobile age began, the United States was no longer the world leader.[5] In contrast to the U.S. industry, Japanese automakers have been heavily export-oriented, pro-

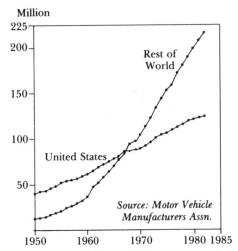

Figure 9-1. Passenger Car Registrations, United States and Rest of World, 1950-82

ward toward those businesses associated with car sales and maintenance, it is sometimes referred to as the "industry of industries."

THE DECLINE IN PRODUCTION

Given the near universality of oil as an automobile fuel, it is not surprising that the automobile's fate is so closely tied to the price of petroleum. The oil price hike of 1973 caused a drop in world auto production to 25 million in 1975. (See Figure 9-2.) As the price of oil stabilized in the mid-seventies and as the real price of gasoline again began to decline, the demand for automobiles resumed an upward climb. By 1978 production reached 31.8 million vehicles, the highest ever, and 1979 nearly matched that level. But after these two back-to-back records, production fell for three consecutive years. There was a slight upturn in 1983, though output that year was still some 15 percent below the peak years of 1978 and 1979.[6]

ducing cars that could be marketed throughout the world. Their success was reinforced by the oil price increases in 1973 and 1979, which greatly strengthened the market for the smaller, more fuel-efficient Japanese model. This combination of fuel efficiency, quality engineering, and low price has made Japanese cars formidable competitors in markets everywhere. So formidable, in fact, that by the early eighties the United States and several European countries were pressing the Japanese to voluntarily limit their exports.

As the seventies began, automobile ownership in the United States and in the industrial countries of northwestern Europe was nearing saturation, a situation where the market for new vehicles is dominated by replacement needs. The large, undeveloped markets appeared to be in Eastern Europe, the Soviet Union, and the Third World, where the private car was still a cherished status symbol. In the late twentieth century, automobile production has emerged as the world's leading manufacturing industry. With numerous linkages both backward toward the raw material suppliers and for-

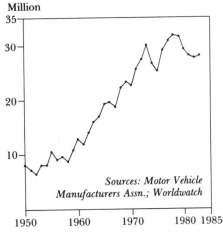

Figure 9-2. World Production of Passenger Cars, 1950-83

From 1950 to 1973, when oil cost $2 per barrel, oil production increased at 7.6 percent per year and automobile production at an almost equally phenomenal annual rate of 5.8 percent. (See Table 9-2.) The 1973 increase in the oil price to $12 markedly slowed the production of both petroleum and automobiles. Six years later, the second oil price hike actually triggered a decline in the production of both, with the annual drop in each case exceeding 5 percent over the next three years.

The decline in global automobile production since 1979 has not been distributed evenly among the world's principal manufacturers. In both the United States and Western Europe, the falloff was disproportionately great. The United Kingdom, with one of the least competitive industries, was hit hard. In this case a long-term decline resulting from gradual loss of competitiveness has been accelerated by the changing automobile market and rising fuel prices. In Japan, however, production actually increased in 1980 and then reached a plateau during the early eighties. In 1981 the automobile industry in North America was producing at 66 percent of capacity, Western Europe was at 79 percent of capacity, and Japan was at full capacity.[7]

Despite its historical lead and the advantage of the world's largest domestic market, American manufacturers were unable to fend off the challenge from the fuel-efficient, high-quality, lower priced Japanese vehicles. (See Figure 9-3.)

These advantages, which have given Japan the edge in the world auto market, are going to make it exceedingly difficult for the United States to regain the lead.

Within the Third World, growth of the dynamic Brazilian automobile industry was effectively checked by the 1979 price rise. Although somewhat protected by its increasing production of sugarcane-based alcohol fuel, Brazil was nonetheless affected by the overall downturn in global economic activity. Not only did automobile exports level off, but the severe internal economic stresses led to a sharp decline in domestic sales as well.[8]

Another of the world's most dynamic developing economies, South Korea, also found itself in difficulty in this sector. A latecomer to automobile assembly, the Korean industry, with the direct support and encouragement of the government, had been planning a severalfold increase in automobile output within a span of a few years. By 1980, however, it was using only 30 percent of its total production capacity of 235,000 vehicles per year.[9] Caught in the early phase of rapid expansion by the 1979 oil price increase, the country's export-oriented industry faced intensified competition and, in many cases, import restrictions in the major markets.

The fall in automobile production since 1979 is only partly due to soaring fuel prices and high interest rates. Also contributing has been the slowdown in global economic growth since 1979—a slowdown to the point where overall

Table 9-2. World Oil and Automobile Production, 1950–83

Period	Oil Price Per Barrel	Oil Production	Automobile Production
	(dollars)	(percent annual change)	
1950–73	2	7.6	5.8
1973–79	12	2.0	1.1
1979–83	31	− 5.2	− 3.0

SOURCES: American Petroleum Institute, *Basic Petroleum Data Book* (Washington D.C.; 1983); Motor Vehicle Manufacturers Association, *World Motor Vehicle Data Book, 1982 Edition* (Detroit: Mich.: 1982).

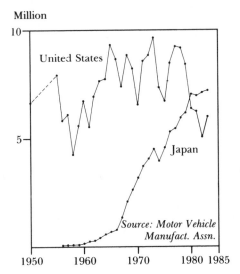

Figure 9-3. Production of Passenger Cars, United States and Japan, 1950-83

Million

United States

Japan

Source: Motor Vehicle Manufact. Assn.

1950   1960   1970   1980 1985

world economic growth barely matches that of population. The result is stagnating per capita income and purchasing power. Without income gains, the number of consumers who can afford automobiles will remain limited. In addition, governmental tax policies in many countries are discouraging automobile ownership. In many Third World countries that do not assemble their own automobiles, import duties are used to discourage vehicle ownership.[10] The combination of these economic trends dampening consumer demand and governmental policies discouraging car ownership may prevent a resumption in the growth in demand for automobiles that has characterized most of this century.

EFFECTS OF THE PRODUCTION DECLINE

The effects of the four-year, 15 percent decline in world auto production since

1978 are numerous and diverse. Coming on the heels of a tripling of world automobile output in less than two decades and at a time when rapid growth was projected in world auto sales, the downturn was traumatic, to say the least, especially in the United States. It drove some of the world's largest automobile manufacturers to the brink of bankruptcy; others survived only by merging.

The most immediate social impact was rising unemployment among automobile assembly-line workers. Among the major producers the rise in lost jobs was most pronounced in the United States. After peaking in 1978 at over one million, U.S. auto industry employment declined steadily in each of the next three years. By 1982 one-third of the work force was unemployed.[11] In some cases, a reduction in the number of shifts in a given plant caused the unemployment. In others, plants closed. From 1978 through 1981 some 20 U.S. automobile assembly plants shut down. Many, such as the Ford plants producing full-sized cars in Los Angeles and in Mahwah, New Jersey, closed permanently.[12]

Thousands of small firms supplying parts to the major auto manufacturers were also hit hard. In 1979, the U.S. Department of Transportation estimated that the American auto industry spent $73 billion on materials, parts, services, and equipment. Of this, some $55 billion was spent in the United States, providing an estimated 1.4 million jobs. As a result of the 1978–82 downturn, an estimated half-million jobs were lost in firms that supplied parts and components.[13]

The ripple effects also reach all the way to the manufacturers of basic automotive raw materials such as steel, rubber, and glass. Each of these industries has been affected both by the reduced vehicle output and by downsizing. With the auto industry accounting for close to one-quarter of U.S. consumption of iron and steel, and with the average weight of a new car dropping, the demand for steel fell sharply, further depressing an industry already in the doldrums. Not all the news is bad, however, because the downsizing in Detroit is generating a demand for lighter, stronger, more expensive steel. Although the volume of steel sales to the automobile industry may be down, unit profits are up.[14] The amount of rubber used by the automobile industry has also declined, both in new cars and as replacement tires on used cars. Projections indicate that by 1985 a majority of American vehicles will be rolling on 13-inch tires rather than the more traditional 15-inch ones.[15]

The stresses of the downturn have been no less severe on the industries at the consumer end of the marketing chain. The number of U.S. automobile dealerships has been gradually declining since 1950 as the larger, more efficient dealers acquire more of the market, but the rate of dealership closings accelerated in the early eighties. During 1978, for example, 144 new-car dealers closed their doors; by 1980, this had increased to 1,558—a near-record decline.[16]

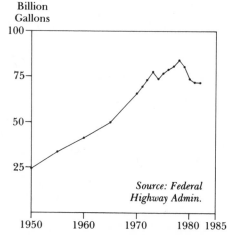

Billion
Gallons

*Source: Federal
Highway Admin.*

**Figure 9-4. Consumption of Gasoline by
U.S. Passenger Cars, 1950-82**

**Table 9-3. United States: Gasoline
Service Stations, 1970–83[1]**

Year	Service Stations
1970	220,000
1971	220,000
1972	226,500
1973	215,900
1974	196,100
1975	189,500
1976	186,800
1977	176,500
1978	172,300
1979	164,800
1980	158,500
1981	151,200
1982	144,700
1983[2]	139,200

[1]Does not include outlets at convenience stores, etc., where gasoline accounts for less than half of total sales.   [2]Preliminary.
SOURCE: *National Petroleum News Fact Book, 1983* (Chicago: Hunter Publishing Co., 1983).

Completing the circle of the far-ranging impact of rising oil prices, U.S. gasoline sales were hurt by falling auto sales, by the rising fuel efficiency of the cars of the road, and by a decline in miles driven. After increasing from 24.3 billion gallons in 1950 to an all-time high of 83.8 billion gallons in 1978, the amount of gasoline used in passenger cars dropped to 73.7 billion gallons by 1980. After this precipitous fall—12 percent within two years—the decline slowed markedly in 1982 and 1983.[17] (See Figure 9-4.)

The number of service stations, already affected by a movement toward larger outlets, fell even faster than gasoline sales. Between 1972, when the number of U.S. service stations peaked at 226,500, and 1983 over 87,000 stations closed. (See Table 9-3.) If the projected gains in U.S.-fleet fuel efficiency materialize, more service stations are likely to go out of business, reducing the total to perhaps half or less of the 1972 peak.

All in all, the second oil price increase had a far greater impact than the first one. The world auto industry could adjust with a modest effort to the 1973 increase, but the 1979 jump that pushed prices beyond $30 per barrel posed extraordinarily difficult problems. The first price rise could have been handled largely by downsizing automobiles and increasing fuel efficiency. The second one, however, has forced a general reevaluation of the wisdom of depending heavily on cars as a primary source of mobility.

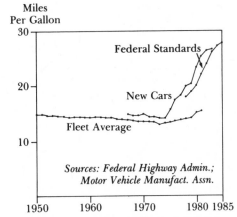

Miles Per Gallon

Federal Standards

New Cars

Fleet Average

Sources: Federal Highway Admin.; Motor Vehicle Manufact. Assn.

Figure 9-5. U.S. Automobile Fuel Efficiency, 1950-85

FUEL EFFICIENCY GAINS

A smooth transition to a sustainable society depends on the far more efficient use of liquid fuels. And since close to one-third of all oil is burned in automobiles, designing cars that are more fuel-efficient is the key. Worldwide, the adjustment has thus far been concentrated in the United States, which at the time of the 1976 Automotive Fuel Efficiency Act accounted for roughly half of world gasoline consumption.

Between 1950 and the 1973 oil price hike, the size and horsepower of the average U.S. automobile increased steadily, with the result that overall fuel efficiency gradually declined, reaching a low of 13.1 miles per gallon in 1973.[18] (See Figure 9-5.) The purpose of the 1976 legislation, which was to apply to each year's new models from 1978 through 1985, was roughly to double the fuel efficiency of American cars. Then shortly after Detroit had begun the massive redesign of automobiles required to achieve the federal standards, the 1979 oil price hike created market conditions that raised the average fuel efficiency of

new cars over the next three years even faster than required.

The combination of rising fuel prices and the federal efficiency standards led to a pronounced shift toward small cars. In 1970, some 37 percent of all new cars sold in the United States were subcompacts and compacts. Large cars—the luxury, standard, and intermediate sizes —accounted for 65 percent. By 1981 these proportions had been roughly reversed, with large cars representing about 35 percent of sales and small cars 65 percent. (See Table 9-4.) Marked declines in U.S. gasoline prices in 1982 and 1983, however, renewed buyer interest in larger cars, and the small-car share of sales dropped for the first time since the 1979 oil price hike.

To achieve the efficiency called for in the federal standards and demanded by the market, Detroit undertook a massive downsizing of new cars. The principal techniques used were weight reduction and a shift to smaller, less powerful engines. In 1975 the average new car produced in Detroit weighed 3,970 pounds, roughly two tons. But by 1982 the average weight had dropped to 3,001 pounds, a reduction of one-fourth in five years.[19]

Table 9-4. United States: Passenger Car Sales by Size, 1970–82[1]

Year	Small Cars	Large Cars	Total Sales[2]	Small-Car Share
	(million)			(percent)
1970	3.1	5.3	8.4	37
1971	3.9	6.3	10.2	38
1972	4.2	6.8	10.9	38
1973	4.9	6.5	11.4	43
1974	4.3	4.5	8.9	49
1975	4.6	4.0	8.6	53
1976	4.9	5.2	10.1	49
1977	5.4	5.8	11.2	48
1978	5.6	5.7	11.3	49
1979	5.9	4.7	10.7	56
1980	5.7	3.3	9.0	63
1981	5.5	3.0	8.6	65
1982	5.0	3.0	8.0	62

[1]"Small" category includes subcompacts, compacts and imports; "large" includes intermediate, standard, and luxury cars.   [2]May not add due to rounding.
SOURCE: Motor Vehicle Manufacturers Association, *Motor Vehicle Facts and Figures '83* (Detroit, Mich.: 1983).

The shift to less powerful, more fuel-efficient engines is equally impressive. As recently as 1977, 76 percent of all U.S.-manufactured automobiles had eight-cylinder engines. (See Table 9-5.) Since then, their share of the market has fallen precipitously, averaging 28 percent during the early eighties. Meanwhile, six-cylinder engines have picked up some of what was once the eight-cylinder market, increasing their market share from one-fifth to one-third. At the most efficient end of the spectrum, the number of four-cylinder engines jumped from less than 10 percent of the market during the mid-seventies to 41 percent in 1982. In addition to the pronounced shift toward four-cylinder engines, General Motors has a three-cylinder, two-passenger commuter vehicle in the wings that it may begin manufacturing if fuel costs rise enough to

assure a market for it.[20]

Other steps to improve fuel efficiency include adopting front-wheel drive and manual transmission and paying greater attention to aerodynamics. As recently as 1977 there were no front-wheel drive vehicles coming out of Detroit. By 1985, the overwhelming majority of American-made automobiles will have front-wheel drive. And manual transmissions should account for 17 percent of all American cars by then.[21]

Overall, the 1975–82 period witnessed a major transformation of the U.S. automobile industry, one far greater than any since its fledgling stage at the turn of the century. The transformation has been not only in the design, performance, and appearance of the automobile, but of the entire automotive industry and, because of its dominant role, of the U.S. economy itself.

Renault plans to have a vehicle on the market by 1985 that will get 80 miles per gallon on the highway.

Although the shift toward fuel efficiency was most dramatic in the United States, it was a worldwide phenomenon. West Germany, Japan, and the United Kingdom were also taking steps to increase the fuel efficiency of new automobiles. In West Germany, automakers agreed at the time of the 1979 oil price hike to raise the fuel efficiency of their new cars by 10–12 percent. In Japan, legislation was passed that same year setting a 32-mile-per-gallon average for new cars by 1982. (By comparison, the U.S. standard for 1985 is 27.5 miles per gallon.) Mexico belatedly responded to the need for greater fuel efficiency by banning the manufacture of eight-cylinder engines as of November 1984.[22]

Even as governments were raising fuel

Table 9-5. United States: The Changing New Car, 1975–82[1]

Model Year	Average Weight	Number of Cylinders Per Engine[2]				Average Fuel Economy
		8	6	4	Total	
	(pounds)	(percent)				(miles per gallon)
1975	4,058	72	19	9	100	14.7
1976	4,059	69	21	10	100	16.5
1977	3,944	76	18	6	100	17.1
1978	3,589	66	24	10	100	18.6
1979	3,485	57	24	19	100	19.0
1980	3,101	32	38	30	100	21.2
1981	3,099	24	35	41	100	23.5
1982	3,001	27	32	41	100	24.6

[1]Excludes imports.   [2]Total excludes diesel engines.
SOURCES: Motor Vehicle Manufacturers Association, *Motor Vehicle Facts and Figures '83* (Detroit, Mich.: 1983); Philip Patterson, U.S. Department of Energy, private communication, October 12, 1983.

efficiency standards, it became clear that cars could be far more fuel-efficient than they are now. In the United States, the Battelle Memorial Institute, one of the world's largest consulting firms, challenged its engineers to design a four-passenger car that could get 100 miles per gallon. Their response was a vehicle that would weigh just over 1,000 pounds; it would have a variable speed transmission with a microprocessor adjusting engine speed to achieve maximum fuel efficiency. Using only currently available technologies, the engineers showed that with a diesel engine this automobile could get 100–105 miles per gallon. Even with a conventional gasoline engine it could get 80–86 miles per gallon.[23]

Individual manufacturers were also moving forward. In France, Renault plans to have a vehicle on the market by 1985 that will get 80 miles per gallon on the highway. Across the channel, BL Ltd. (formerly British Leyland) began marketing a "mini-metro" in late 1980. At a steady 30 miles per hour, it can get 83 miles per gallon; in variable-speed urban driving, it can average 41 miles per gallon. BL plans to market this vehicle only in the United Kingdom and Europe.[24]

In the United States, the General Motors three-cylinder vehicle mentioned earlier can get 86 miles per gallon at a steady 25 miles per hour, and 60 miles per gallon on the highway. Although the engineering of this vehicle is largely completed, plans to move the demonstration model into production are uncertain.

In Japan, six of nine automobile manufacturers are marketing mini-cars, with engines of less than 550 cubic centimeters. This is less than half the size of the engine in yesteryear's small cars, such as the internationally marketed Volkswagen Rabbit, or the Japanese cars now marketed in the United States and Europe, which have engine displacements of roughly 1,200 cubic centimeters.

The Japanese mini-metros average more than 50 miles per gallon, or roughly double the federal requirements for U.S. vehicles in 1985. Weighing an average of 1,200 pounds, these vehicles were selling for $2,000–3,000 in Japan in 1983. Sales of mini-cars and their mini-truck equivalents there totaled 1.3 million in 1982.[25] With these small, highly efficient vehicles already in production, the Japanese are well positioned to take advantage of the next surge in world oil prices. The combination of economic conditions and future fuel price projections indicates a growing worldwide market for these smaller cars that provide adequate transportation at much lower purchase and operational prices.

ALTERNATIVE FUEL PROSPECTS

Governments, automobile manufacturers, and car owners are all keenly interested in the development of alternative automotive fuels in light of the inevitable depletion of oil reserves. Although there are many potential sources of automotive fuel beyond the conventional reserves of oil, progress in developing them has been limited to a few countries.

Prominent among the new fossil fuel sources of liquid fuel are coal, tar sands, and oil shale. The technology for liquefying coal was developed by the Germans in the twenties and thirties and used extensively during World War II to substitute for imported oil as supplies were cut off. After the war, however, West Germany quickly returned to refining imported oil, a much cheaper fuel.

As of 1984, only one country, South Africa, is producing liquid fuel from coal on a meaningful scale. For political reasons, South Africa has always felt particularly vulnerable to embargoes by various fuel suppliers and has accordingly made a strong effort to develop liquid fuels from its extensive coal reserves. The first commercial plant began operation in 1959, supplying some 10 percent of the country's automotive fuel. Since then output has expanded to the point where close to half of South Africa's automotive fuel now comes from liquefied coal.[26] Other national governments and

major oil companies developed plans to invest heavily in coal liquefaction during the late seventies, but unfortunately nearly all these were abandoned because they were not economical.

Reserves of a second source of liquid fuel—tar sands—in Canada, the United States, Colombia, and Venezuela contain as much petroleum as the oil fields of the Middle East, but the economic and environmental costs of extracting it are high. Leadership in this field has come from a Canadian consortium that includes the government and major oil companies. A $2-billion commercial facility located in the Athabasca River Basin of western Canada was designed to produce 100,000 barrels of oil per day, but thus far has managed to produce only half that amount.[27]

Extracting oil from shale deposits is even more difficult and costly than obtaining it from tar sands. Some of the world's richest oil shale deposits are found in the western United States, in Colorado, Utah, and Wyoming, where the oil is tightly locked into rock formations just beneath the surface. Although several companies, mostly in the oil business, are interested in exploiting this potential, the possibility for doing so seems always to recede as the cost of extraction continuously rises beyond the current world price of oil. As of mid-1983 the U.S. Synthetic Fuels Corporation, launched in 1979, has had trouble finding commercially viable synfuel projects to fund.[28] Projects to develop oil shale, to liquefy and gasify coal, or to convert peat into liquid fuel have rarely proved worthy of the corporation's support.

Another potentially important commercial automotive fuel is electricity. Here the constraint is the difficulty of designing an economically feasible electric car. One of the drawbacks of existing electric autos is limited range, which suggests they are better suited for commuting and short, fixed-route commercial applications than for long-distance road trips. The basic technology is appropriate for various specialized purposes, such as forklifts in warehouses, where the fumes from internal combustion engines are unhealthy, or golf carts, which are quite light, travel only short distances, and require little power. The cost of periodically replacing the batteries in electric cars is often prohibitive. Even though these can be recharged daily from conventional electricity outlets, they wear out within a year or two. Nevertheless, the technology does seem well suited to countries that have an abundance of cheap hydroelectricity.

The most successful biologically based synthetic fuel venture to date is the development of sugarcane-derived alcohol fuels in Brazil. At a stage of rapid industrialization and dependent on imports for 85 percent of its oil, Brazil has felt vulnerable to soaring oil prices and to supply disruptions. It has attempted to compensate for this by developing indigenous liquid fuel sources. With a poor endowment of fossil fuels but a relative abundance of land, the government decided in 1975 to launch a massive alcohol fuels project intended to achieve liquid-fuel self-sufficiency by the end of the century, if not before.

By 1983, Brazil was producing 4.5 billion liters (nearly 1.2 billion gallons) of alcohol motor fuel in some 280 distilleries that dot the countryside. (See Table 9-6.) Supplying close to one-quarter of the automotive fuel consumed, these distilleries are supplanting the oil refineries on which Brazilians traditionally depended.[29] Cars run on alcohol both in combination with gasoline and by itself. Initially Brazil exploited the ability of conventional engines to burn a gasoline-alcohol mix containing up to 20 percent alcohol without adjustment. At the same time the government required automakers to begin producing automobiles with

Table 9-6. Brazil: Estimated Production of Alcohol Fuel From Sugarcane, 1970–83, With Projections to 1985[1]

Year	Alcohol Fuel	Cropland Required[2]
	(million liters)	(thousand hectares)
1970	175	47
1971	238	64
1972	413	112
1973	286	77
1974	175	47
1975	175	47
1976	175	47
1977	636	172
1978	1,510	408
1979	2,210	597
1980	2,591	700
1981	3,036	820
1982	4,165	1,126
1983	4,546	1,229
1985	9,173	2,479

[1]Worldwatch Institute estimates derived from published figures and official projections. [2]Cropland area based on 1980 cane yields and an alcohol conversion rate of 3,700 liters per hectare.
SOURCES: World Energy Industry, *The Energy Decade 1970–80* (Cambridge, Mass.: Ballinger Publishing Co., 1982); *Journal of Commerce*, April 5, 1983; Worldwatch Institute estimates.

engines designed specifically to run on alcohol. By early 1983, a majority of new cars purchased in Brazil had alcohol fuel engines and well over a million hectares (1 hectare equals 2.47 acres) were planted to sugarcane for the production of alcohol.

The United States is the second largest alcohol-fuel producer. Although the U.S. Government has abandoned the 1985 production goal of 2 billion gallons that was established in 1979, some 375 million gallons of alcohol fuel were produced in 1983, accounting for 0.5 percent of national auto fuel consumption. Most of this came from corn and is used as an octane enhancer, mixed in small quantities with conventional gasoline. In agricultural terms, this required 135 million bushels of corn (nearly 2 percent of a typical U.S. harvest) and 1.3 million acres, which is 0.4 percent of U.S. cropland. (See Table 9-7.) The United States produced about one-fifth as much alcohol fuel as Brazil.[30]

In China, which has only one-tenth of a hectare of cropland per person, there simply is no room for cars.

Eventually the relative contributions of increased fuel efficiency and alternative fuels will gradually shift toward the latter as the potential efficiency gains are wrung out of the automotive system. Thus far, however, the adjustment between the potential excess of worldwide demand for automotive fuel over the available supply has been achieved largely through reducing demand rather than through producing new fuels. And for some time to come fuel efficiency gains will remain far cheaper than developing alternative fuels. Indeed, with the gains in efficiency that have yet to be

realized, this approach is likely to continue to dwarf the contribution of alternative fuels between now and the end of the century.

A TIME OF REASSESSMENT

As indicated, most projections of the world automobile fleet have assumed there would be dramatic growth over the remainder of this century. Typical of these is an Organisation for Economic Co-operation and Development study completed in 1979 that projected world automobile ownership would expand at a steady 3 percent per year during the eighties and nineties, nearly doubling fleet size by the end of the century. David Bayliss, transport planner for the Greater London Council, has compiled the results of 18 studies, all but three of them done in the eighties, that project annual automobile sales to the year 2000. The highest projected for that year is 72 million, in a study completed in 1978. This would be more than double the peak figure of just under 32 million in 1978 and close to triple the 27 million sold in 1983. At the low end of the spectrum is a 1983 study that pro-

Table 9-7. United States: Production of Fuel Alcohol From Corn, 1980–84

Year[1]	Corn Used for Fuel Alcohol	Area in Corn for Fuel Alcohol[2]	Fuel Alcohol Production[3]
	(million bushels)	(million acres)	(million gallons)
1980	15	0.14	58
1981	35	0.33	83
1982	80	0.76	230
1983[4]	135	1.28	375
1984[5]	160	1.52	440

[1]Fiscal year ending October 1 of year shown. [2]Assumes yield of 105 bushels per acre. [3]All fuel alcohol is marketed as gasohol. [4]Preliminary estimate. [5]Projection.
SOURCES: Unpublished data from USDA Economic Research Service; Worldwatch Institute.

jected 46 million cars would be sold at the end of the century, an increase of 70 percent over 1983 sales.[31]

Even studies done after the 1979 oil price increase show continuing substantial growth in the world automobile fleet. The average of the set of projections summarized by Bayliss anticipates 550 million cars by the end of the century, an increase of nearly four-fifths over 1980. Associated with this would be growth in annual sales from about 30 million in 1980 to 42 million in 1990 and 56 million in the year 2000.[32]

Unfortunately, most projections are based on a narrow set of conventional assumptions that exclude the many new factors shaping the automobile's future. Few, for example, appear to have accounted fully for the cost of developing alternative fuels. Nor have any given serious consideration to the equity issues arising as the changing economic outlook permanently limits automobile ownership to a small elite in most countries in Eastern Europe and the Third World.

Although initially questions about the future of the automobile arose from the sharp increase in fuel costs in 1973, during the following decade numerous other factors led governments and individuals to reexamine the role of the automobile. These other influences on the auto's future include land availability, the cost of vehicle ownership and maintenance, the saturation of some markets, the slowdown in economic growth both globally and in particular nations that would otherwise develop an auto manufacturing sector, the extent of international indebtedness, urban traffic congestion and air pollution, and a decline in the status traditionally accorded auto ownership.

Fuel costs influence the way national policymakers as well as potential owners think about the automobile. At the national level governments are concerned

with how fuel costs boost foreign exchange outlays if the country is among the overwhelming majority that import oil. At the individual level, fuel costs are an important expense and when they rise faster than real income they discourage auto use and ownership. And that's just what they are expected to do. The cost in real terms has risen markedly over the past decade and it is projected to continue to rise throughout the rest of this century. Although there may be short-term declines in world oil prices, as in 1983, the long-term trend is clearly upward.

An automobile-centered transportation system is land-intensive. Parking a subcompact requires a 10-by-20-foot plot of land, so a parking lot to accommodate 200 vehicles requires an acre. In addition to needing several parking spots per automobile, land is required for streets, roads, and highways. In some densely populated countries there is simply not enough land to support a fleet of automobiles. In China, for example, which has only one-tenth of a hectare of cropland per person, there simply is no room for cars. This is one reason why China, which exports a million barrels of oil a day, has virtually no private automobiles.[33] Other areas unable to develop a full-fledged auto-centered transportation system because of land shortages include Bangladesh, Egypt, and the island of Java, where most Indonesians live.

Only relatively affluent individuals can afford to purchase and operate an automobile. Without an income well above the world average, such a costly transportation vehicle is just far beyond the range of consumers. Until recently, it was widely assumed that income levels throughout the world would continue to rise rapidly for the indefinite future, thus bringing cars within the range of more and more people. With the slowdown in global economic growth, however, particularly since 1979, gains in per capita income have been modest, creating few new automobile owners.

At the affluent end of the economic spectrum, some national markets are becoming saturated with automobiles. The United States, for example, is approaching market saturation, with more than half as many cars as people, So, too, are other affluent industrial societies, such as West Germany, France, and Italy, with an average of one car for every three people. (See Table 9-8.) The United Kingdom and Japan are also probably nearing the saturation point, partly for space reasons. Most Third World countries, on the other hand, are far from saturation. Mexico, an oil exporter, has one car for every 21 people while Brazil, an oil importer, has one for every 16. For the world as a whole the average is 14 people per car, a figure that is a far cry from either 2 people per car in the United States or 18,000 per car in China.

As economic growth slows, so does the growth in public revenues—the very monies needed to create the infrastructure of streets, roads, highways, and bridges needed to support automobiles. With national budgetary deficits on the rise almost everywhere, public outlays for such things will be harder to come by. Likewise, slower growth will make it

Table 9-8. Prevalence of Passenger Cars in the Twenty Most Populous Countries, 1981

Country	Population	Passenger Car Registrations	People Per Car
	(million)	(thousand)	(number)
United States	232	121,724	2
West Germany	62	23,236	3
France	54	19,150	3
Italy	57	17,696	3
United Kingdom	56	15,438	4
Japan	119	23,660	5
Brazil	128	8,213	16
Mexico	71	3,360	21
Soviet Union	270	8,255	33
Iran	39	1,028	38
Turkey	48	711	68
Philippines	52	550	95
Egypt	45	428	105
Thailand	50	435	115
Nigeria	82	500	164
Indonesia	152	637	239
Pakistan	93	264	352
India	714	930	768
Bangladesh	93	22	4,227
China	997	55	18,137
World	4,585	320,513	14

SOURCES: Motor Vehicle Manufacturers Association, *World Motor Vehicle Data Book, 1982 Edition* (Detroit, Mich.: 1982); Population Reference Bureau, *1983 World Population Data Sheet* (Washington, D.C.: 1983).

more difficult for the private sector to amass capital for investment in new manufacturing capacity, especially on the scale needed if sales are to double by 2000. In countries where fleet expansion is projected, additional capital will be required for investment in dealerships, service stations, and repair garages.

The growth in international indebtedness during the late seventies and the early eighties, which reached an astronomical $750 billion during 1983, is concentrated in Eastern Europe and the Third World, in precisely those countries where the growth in autos is projected to be greatest.[34] Heavily burdened with debt, many of these nations can no longer afford to import oil for an ever-expanding automobile fleet. Indeed, among the conditions often imposed by the International Monetary Fund to assist governments with foreign exchange deficits is a higher price or tax on gasoline. In short, for many countries the existing international debt situation, which is likely to dominate national economic policies and priorities well into the nineties, is not conducive to the continuing evolution of an automobile-centered transportation system.

Countries that export petroleum as well as those that import it are reassessing the automobile's future. Under prodding from the International Monetary Fund to boost federal revenues and reduce domestic oil use, the Mexican Government raised gasoline prices sharply in 1983. Although the new price of 70¢ per gallon for regular gasoline (at the official exchange rate) was still low by international standards, it represented a sixfold increase in peso terms from the price at the beginning of 1983. Politically unpopular though it was, this raising of gasoline prices closer to world levels helped reverse the trend in oil consumption, which had grown some 10 percent per year from 1976 through 1981. Brazil was also forced to raise the price of gasoline in mid-1983, by 40 percent, before the Fund would agree to provide assistance.[35]

Heavily burdened with debt, many nations can no longer afford to import oil for an ever-expanding automobile fleet.

In an effort to reduce oil imports and maintain its international credit-worthiness, Yugoslavia adopted a rationing system in 1982 that limited motorists to 13 gallons per month. Poland, which is in arrears in interest payments on its international debt and which imports oil, has adopted stringent controls on gasoline use. In late 1983, gasoline purchases were rationed to 9 gallons per month, not nearly enough to permit regular use.[36]

Questions of equity also arise in considering the future of the automobile. Although owning a car is essential to the existing life-styles of ruling elites in the Third World, it will become more and more difficult to justify the use of a large share of a country's foreign exchange to import fuel, parts, or even new vehicles themselves. Earlier, when it could be assumed that rapid economic growth would continue exponentially, it was reasonable to think that most people who wanted a car would eventually own one, regardless of where they lived. As it becomes clear that this is not a reasonable prospect, then the use of the technology itself, which is elitist in nature, will be increasingly questioned.

Yet another constraint on autos is growing urban traffic congestion. Long a problem in the countries that first turned to the automobile, it is now a cause for concern in many Third World cities as well. Monumental traffic jams that can last for hours occur regularly in Mexico City, Lagos, and Bangkok. Air pollution, too, is a serious problem, particularly in the Third World. Seoul and Mexico City now reportedly have some of the worst air pollution found anywhere, largely because of auto emissions. The combination of traffic congestion, traffic noise, and air pollution has led many cities to impose restrictions on the use of automobiles. These range from increased bridge tolls, as in Manhattan, to restrictions on cars carrying only one person, as in Singapore.

Even some industrial societies, particularly those that import oil, are beginning to have second thoughts about the future of the automobile. Prominent among the affluent societies that are reexamining their attitudes are Denmark and Sweden. For Danes, who pay for their imported oil largely with farm products, the shift in the terms of trade between oil and agricultural commodities, described in Chapter 1, has been economically devastating. If the Danish auto fleet continues to grow, further increasing the demand for imported oil, it could so weaken the economy that a decline in living standards might be inevitable. To avoid this unhappy possibility, Denmark has adopted a number of policies to discourage private automobile ownership, including a high tax on gasoline and stiff parking fees for motorists. In addition, the Danish Government has launched a campaign to educate people on the national economic dangers of continuing to rely heavily on private cars. As public understanding rises, auto ownership has become socially less desirable, leading to a decline in the automobile fleet, the first national decline on record. Since 1979, when the Danish automobile fleet totaled 1.42 million automobiles, it has fallen to 1.36 million, a drop of some 3 percent.[37] (See Figure 9-6.)

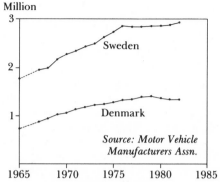

Figure 9-6. Automobile Registrations, Sweden and Denmark, 1965-82

At the same time that it is discouraging automobile ownership, the Danish Government has stepped up investment in public transport, with bus registrations increasing by over one-third between 1973 and 1981.[38] The goal has been to provide speedy, convenient transportation that is cheaper than that provided by automobiles, thus reducing new car purchases below the number of old cars retired.

Sweden has also acted vigorously to discourage the growth in automobile ownership. After increasing steadily from mid-century until 1976, growth in the Swedish auto fleet has stopped, remaining essentially static through 1981.[39] It seems likely that over time the forces that halted the growth of the automobile fleet will intensify and lead to a gradual decline.

At the other end of the income spectrum, Peru demonstrates rather graphically the changes that can occur in the outlook for the automobile in the Third World. Over a decade ago, Peru signed a pact with other Andean countries to produce automobiles, with each country producing certain of the basic components and with final assembly being done domestically. In Peru, which had been manufacturing an average of 17,-000 cars per year in the late sixties, this led to an increase to over 34,000 by 1976.[40] (See Figure 9-7.)

At this point, several economic problems brought the growth in production to a halt. Among other things, the collapse of the country's anchovy fishery sharply reduced the foreign exchange available to import oil. Shortly thereafter the International Monetary Fund required a severe restriction in consumer credit as a condition for additional loans. In 1979 the gasoline price was doubled. Real incomes in Peru were not increasing during this period. Indeed, in some years economic growth was failing to keep pace with population growth. Between 1976 and 1978, automobile production fell to just over 11,-000 vehicles. By 1981 it had recovered somewhat, to over 20,000 vehicles, but the future of the industry is nonetheless in question.[41]

There are many reasons to question whether automobile production in Peru will ever be significant. Indeed, does it make sense for Peru to continue to develop an automobile industry? It might fare better if it abandoned the automobile-centered industrial development model and shifted its resources into such

sectors as agriculture, renewable energy industries, and education—activities that would benefit more of the population.

It is quite possible that at the end of the century a number of countries will have even fewer automobiles than they do today. Others may join China and ban the private automobile except in special situations. Although some countries, principally oil exporters, may seek to expand their fleets rapidly, others may have second thoughts about investing heavily in a technology that depends on a nonrenewable resource. Accordingly, they may shift their emphasis toward the development of rail- and bus-centered transportation systems. Such a move would also facilitate more-efficient land use, itself an issue of widening concern.

Already, many forward-looking national governments are following the lead of Denmark and Sweden in devising policies to discourage auto-centered transport systems. Some are using a gasoline tax very effectively for this purpose; in several European countries, the tax on gasoline exceeds the value of the fuel itself. In other countries, where the price of gasoline is set by government either because of a state oil monopoly or public sector dominance (such as Mexico or the Soviet Union), the price of gasoline has been raised to discourage car purchases. A number of Third World countries that import automobiles, such as Kenya, are resorting to a stiff import duty, one that sometimes exceeds the market value of the vehicle. The International Monetary Fund, in its attempt to promote international monetary stability, is also urging higher taxes on gasoline as a way to supplement market forces that promote reduced dependence on imported oil.[42]

Each country must decide what place the automobile will occupy in its transportation system in the post-petroleum

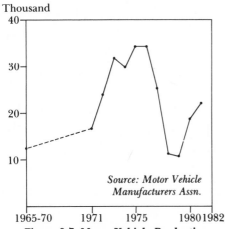

Thousand

Source: Motor Vehicle Manufacturers Assn.

Figure 9-7. Motor Vehicle Production in Peru, 1965-81

age, since no two face exactly the same set of constraints. In some, the affluence needed to become a nation of auto owners may never materialize. Others may lack the foreign exchange earnings to import oil to fuel a fleet of cars. Still others may abandon private motor vehicles for reasons of equity. Collectively, these pressures suggest the time has come for governments everywhere to reassess the future of the automobile.

10

Securing Food Supplies

Lester R. Brown

Measured just in terms of output, the past generation has been one of unprecedented progress in world agriculture. In 1950 the world's farmers produced 623 million tons of grain. In 1983 they produced nearly 1.5 billion tons. This increase of nearly 900 million tons was all the more remarkable because it occurred when there was little new cropland to bring under the plow.[1]

On closer examination this 33-year span breaks into two distinct eras—before and after the 1973 oil price increase. Modern agriculture thrives on cheap energy, and the age of cheap energy came to an end in 1973. For 23 years world food output expanded at over 3 percent per year and, although there was concern about rapid population growth, there was a comfortable margin in the growth of food production over that of population. Since 1973, however, annual growth has been less than 2 percent and the world's farmers have been struggling to keep pace with population.

The global increase in world food output also obscures wide variations in individual geographic regions. In North America, production has steadily outstripped demand, generating ever-larger export surpluses. In the Soviet Union, output has fallen behind demand over the past decade, making the country the largest grain importer in history. And in Africa, which has a population of 512 million and which has to feed 14 million additional people each year, food production per person has fallen steadily since 1970. Despite a tripling of grain imports since then, hunger has become chronic, an enduring part of the African landscape.

The 1983 drought in North America and Africa must be considered against this backdrop. The principal effect of the precipitous decline in the North American harvest was a reduction in stocks and a rise in food and feedstuff prices. In Africa, where national food reserves are virtually nonexistent, the drought translated into widespread hunger and, in a score of countries, the threat of famine.[2]

THE GLOBAL LOSS OF MOMENTUM

As the world recovered from World War II, hopes for improvement in world agriculture were high. An accumulating backlog of agricultural technologies such as hybrid corn and chemical fertilizers were waiting to be applied on a massive scale. Between 1950 and 1973 world grain production more than doubled, to nearly 1.3 billion tons. Although output expanded more rapidly in some regions than in others, all regions shared in the growth. This rising tide of food production improved nutrition throughout the world, helping to boost life expectancy in the Third World from less than 43 years in the early fifties to over 53 years in the early seventies.[3]

This period of broad-based gains in nutritional improvement came to an end in 1973. After the oil price hike that year the growth in world grain output slowed. Since 1973 world grain production has expanded at less than 2 percent yearly, barely keeping pace with population. (See Table 10-1.) Although the period since the 1979 oil price hike is too short to establish a trend, $30-a-barrel oil may well slow growth further.

In per capita terms world grain output climbed from 248 kilograms in 1950 to 326 kilograms in 1973, an impressive gain of 31 percent. (See Table 10-2.) Since then, however, annual grain output per person has remained around 325

kilograms. A global average, this figure embraces countries where yearly grain availability per person averages only 150 kilograms, requiring that it all be consumed directly, as well as countries where it exceeds 700 kilograms and is largely converted into meat, milk, and eggs.[4]

Since 1973 attention has focused on the impact of petroleum prices on food supply, but demand has also been affected. On the supply side, rising oil prices have increased the costs of basic agricultural inputs—fertilizer, pesticides, and fuel for tillage and irrigation —thus acting as a drag on output. On the demand side of the equation, escalating oil prices combined with ill-conceived national economic policies have contributed to a global economic slowdown so severe since 1979 that it has brought world growth in per capita income to a virtual halt. Had incomes continued to rise at the same rate after 1973 as they did before, prices of food commodities would have been stronger, thus supporting a more vigorous growth in farm investment and output. Agricultural underinvestment in Third World countries has also contributed to the loss of momentum, but the central point is

Table 10-1. World Oil Price and Grain Production Trends, Total and Per Capita, 1950–83

		Annual Growth		
Period	Oil Price Per Barrel	Grain Production	Population	Grain Production Per Person
	(dollars)		(percent)	
1950–73	2	3.1	1.9	1.2
1973–79	12	1.9	1.8	0.1
1979–83	31	1.0[1]	1.7	−0.7

[1]Severe drought in the United States and Africa and record idling of cropland under U.S. farm programs reduced the 1983 world harvest well below trend, thus the slowdown in grain production is overstated.

SOURCES: International Monetary Fund, *Monthly Financial Statistics,* various issues; U.S. Department of Agriculture, *World Indices of Agricultural and Food Production, 1950–82* (unpublished printout) (Washington, D.C.: 1983); United Nations, *Monthly Bulletin of Statistics,* various issues.

Table 10-2. World Grain Production, Total and Per Capita, 1950–83

Year	Population	Grain Production	Grain Production Per Person
	(billion)	(million metric tons)	(kilograms)
1950	2.51	623	248
1955	2.74	751	274
1960	3.03	845	279
1965	3.34	920	275
1970	3.68	1,101	299
1971	3.75	1,194	318
1972	3.82	1,161	304
1973	3.88	1,268	326
1974	3.96	1,222	309
1975	4.03	1,248	310
1976	4.11	1,360	331
1977	4.18	1,334	319
1978	4.26	1,461	343
1979	4.34	1,419	327
1980	4.42	1,440	326
1981	4.50	1,491	331
1982	4.58	1,540	336
1983	4.66	1,447	310

SOURCES: U.S. Department of Agriculture, *World Indices of Agricultural and Food Production, 1950–82* (unpublished printout) (Washington, D.C.: 1983); United Nations, *Monthly Bulletin of Statistics*, New York, various issues.

that the rise in oil prices, affecting both food supply and demand, has brought the era of robust growth in world food output to an end.

Oil is not the only resource whose questionable supply is checking the growth in food output. As discussed in Chapter 4, the loss of topsoil through erosion is now acting as a drag on efforts to produce more food. And the scarcity of water is also beginning to affect food production prospects. Since World War II, the world irrigated area has more than doubled, but the flurry of dam

building of the past generation has now subsided. With occasional exceptions, most of the remaining potential projects are more difficult, costly, and capital-intensive.[5]

In some situations, irrigated agriculture is threatened by falling water tables. The southern Great Plains, where much of the U.S. growth in irrigated area over the last two decades has occurred, provides a disturbing example. Irrigation there depends almost entirely on water from the Ogallala Aquifer, an essentially nonreplenishable fossil water reserve. As the water table in this vast agricultural area begins to fall with the depletion of the aquifer, the cost of irrigation rises. Already some farmers in eastern Colorado and northern Texas are converting to dryland farming. For the 32 counties in the Texas Panhandle, the U.S. Department of Agriculture projects that irrigation will be largely phased out by 1995.[6]

A somewhat analogous situation exists in the Soviet southwest, where the excessive diversion of river water for irrigation is reducing the water level of the Aral and Caspian seas. This has many long-term negative consequences, including a diminished fish catch and the gradual retreat of the water line from coastal cities that depend on it for transportation.[7] Given the strong internal pressures within the Soviet Union to produce more food, however, the diversion is continuing.

A second major threat to irrigated agriculture is the often intense competition for water between farming, industry, and cities. In the U.S. Southwest, the irrigated area is actually declining in states such as Arizona, where Sunbelt migration is swelling cities that are bidding water away from farmers. In agriculturally important Maricopa County, which had some 550,000 acres under irrigation in the fifties, the irrigated area has shrunk by more than one-fifth.[8] Nationally the net area under irrigation is projected to continue growing over the rest of the century, but at a more modest rate.

New research indicates water scarcities are also emerging in Africa. South Africa, adding 720,000 people each year, is fast running out of new irrigation sites. A 1983 report of the President's Council in South Africa identified the scarcity of fresh water as a constraint on that country's demographic carrying capacity.[9]

The worldwide loss of momentum outlined above will not be easily restored. Although agricultural mismanagement abounds, particularly in the Third World and Eastern Europe, it has not worsened appreciably over the years. Nor can the situation be explained by any farmers' loss of skills. The explanation lies in the more difficult circumstances facing farmers everywhere. In the mid-eighties it is far more difficult to raise world food output at a consistent 3 percent per year than it was during the fifties or sixties. The cheap energy that permitted farmers to override easily the constraints imposed by the scarcity of land, soil nutrients, or water is simply no longer available.

THE POPULATION/LAND/ FERTILIZER LINK

The changing relationship between world population size, cropland area, and energy supplies bears heavily on the human prospect over the remainder of this century and beyond. Increasingly, the energy used in agriculture will be in the form of chemical fertilizer. As population grows, cropland per person shrinks and fertilizer requirements climb. And erosion that has robbed soils of nutrients is forcing farmers to use

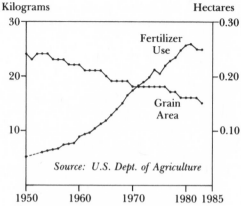

Figure 10-1. World Fertilizer Use and Grain Area Per Person, 1950-83

more fertilizers. Even urbanization is raising demand, since as people move to cities it is harder to recycle the nutrients in human and household waste. Yet the combination of rising energy costs and diminishing returns on the use of additional fertilizer raises doubts that adequate food supplies can be produced in the future at prices the world's poor can afford.

The central importance of the population/land/fertilizer relationship is a recent phenomenon. Before 1950 increases in food output came largely from expanding the cultivated area, but with the scarcity of fertile new land and the advent of cheap chemical fertilizer this changed. Between 1950 and 1983 world fertilizer use climbed from 15 million to 114 million tons, nearly an eightfold increase within a generation.[10] In effect, as fertile land became harder to find, farmers learned to substitute energy in the form of chemical fertilizer for land. Fertilizer factories replaced new land as the principal source of growth in food production.

This substitution of energy for land is graphically evident: In 1950, when world population totaled 2.51 billion, the harvested area of cereals per person was 0.24 hectares. (See Figure 10-1.) As growth in population greatly out-stripped that of cultivated area, the area per person fell steadily, declining to 0.15 hectares by 1983. While the amount of cropland per person declined by one-third, the fertilizer consumption per person quintupled, climbing from just over 5 kilograms in 1950 to 25 kilograms in 1983.

While the amount of cropland per person declined by one-third, the fertilizer consumption per person quintupled.

The hybridization of corn and the dwarfing of the wheat and rice varieties that have been at the heart of Third World agricultural advances over the last two decades figured prominently, of course, in the growth in world food out-put. So, too, did the doubling of irri-gated area. But the effectiveness of all these practices depends heavily on the use of chemical fertilizer. Without an ad-equate supply of plant nutrients, high-yielding cereal varieties hold little ad-vantage over traditional ones. Likewise,

an increase in irrigation is of little conse-quence if the nutrients to support the higher yields are lacking.

The response of crops to the use of additional fertilizer is now diminishing, particularly in agriculturally advanced countries. During the fifties, the applica-tion of another ton of fertilizer on aver-age yielded 11.5 more tons of grain. (See Table 10-3.) During the sixties, the fer-tilizer/grain response ratio was 8.3 to 1. By the seventies it had fallen to 5.8. Some countries, such as Argentina and India, still apply relatively little fertilizer and so have quite high response ratios. But worldwide the return on the use of additional fertilizer is on the way down. Although the biological constraints on fertilizer responsiveness can be pushed back with continued plant breeding, fur-ther declines seem inevitable.

Fertilizer manufacturing is one of the world's major industries. In an advanced agricultural country such as the United States, expenditures on fertilizer total some $10 billion per year.[11] Three basic nutrients—nitrogen, which is obtained from the air, and phosphate and potash, both mined from underground deposits —account for the great bulk of world chemical fertilizer production. The in-

Table 10-3. World Grain Production and Fertilizer Use, 1934–38 to 1979–81

Period	World Grain Production[1]	Increment	World Fertilizer Use[1]	Increment	Incremental Grain/Fertilizer Response Ratio
	(million metric tons)				(ratio)
1934–38	651		10		
1948–52	710	59	14	4	14.8
1959–61	848	138	26	12	11.5
1969–71	1,165	317	64	38	8.3
1979–81	1,451	286	113	49	5.8

[1]Annual average for period.
SOURCES: 1934–38 data from United Nations Food and Agriculture Organization (FAO), *Production Yearbook* (Rome: various years); U.S. Department of Agriculture (USDA), *World Indices of Agricultural and Food Production, 1950–82* (unpublished printout) (Washington, D.C.: 1983); FAO, *FAO 1977 Annual Fertilizer Review* (Rome: 1978); 1979–81 data from Paul Andrilenas, USDA, private communica-tion, December 1982.

dustrial fixing of atmospheric nitrogen in the form of ammonium nitrate, ammonium sulphate, urea, or other forms of nitrogen fertilizer is an energy-intensive process. Although natural gas is the preferred fuel and feedstock in the nitrogen fertilizer industry, oil figures prominently in the mining, processing, and transportation of phosphate and potash.

High energy prices have begun to shift nitrogen fertilizer production from the traditional industrial country producers, such as the United States and some in Western Europe, to countries with energy surpluses. Investment in this industry has been particularly attractive to oil-exporting countries that are flaring excess gas produced in conjunction with oil. To the extent that fertilizers are manufactured in countries such as Saudia Arabia, Iran, or Kuwait with gas that would otherwise be wasted, future price increases may be curbed. The Soviet Union, in a situation similar to the gas-surplus countries in the Middle East, is also investing heavily in nitrogen fertilizer production capacity.[12]

The distribution of phosphate rock, the principal source of phosphate fertilizer, poses a particular problem since reserves are concentrated in Florida and Morocco. With production concentrated around the Atlantic but with the world's population and future needs for phosphate mainly in Asia, high transportation costs—and thus high fertilizer prices in Asian villages—are inevitable.

With population growth projected to continue, the cropland available per person will continue to decline and the fertilizer needed to maintain consumption will continue to rise. At some point, biological constraints on crop yields will make the substitution of fertilizer for cropland increasingly difficult and costly. When this is combined with the projected long-term rise in real cost of the oil and natural gas used to manufacture, distribute, and apply chemical ferti-lizer, the difficulty in restoring the steady upward trend in per capita grain production of 1950–73 becomes clear.

REAL PRODUCTION TRENDS

When measuring growth, economists adjust current prices for the rate of inflation in order to distill out the real gains in production. Something similar is needed in agriculture, where growth in output is inflated by agricultural practices that are not sustainable. Such an adjustment would shed light on the longer-term outlook by distinguishing between gains that are real and those that are made at the expense of future output. For example, as farm commodity prices climbed in the mid-seventies U.S. farmers brought land under the plow that was not suited to cultivation. By 1977 the Soil Conservation Service had identified 17 million acres of land in crops that were losing topsoil so rapidly they would eventually be stripped of all productive value. The agency recommended that farmers convert this land to grass or forests to preserve its production capacities.[13] To reach a figure of real, not just current, U.S. agricultural output, the yield from these 17 million acres, roughly 4 percent of the U.S. cropland total, should be subtracted from overall output.

Similarly, adjustments should be made for the output from sloping land that was once in ecologically stable, long-term rotations of row crops with grass and hay but that is now in row crops continuously, for topsoil loss in these situations has become excessive. If American farmers were to take the steps needed to protect their topsoil, U.S. farm output and exports would be substantially less in the short run, but they would be sustainable over the long term.

Elimination of this agronomic deficit through a national soil conservation program that reintroduced the traditional practices cited above might also eliminate the troublesome short-term commodity surpluses that depress farm prices and income.

In addition to agronomic deficits, many of the world's farmers are also incurring economic deficits. Nowhere is this more evident than in the United States, where net farm income has narrowed almost to the vanishing point. Between 1973, when the world oil price began its astronomical climb, and 1982, farmers were caught in a squeeze between depressed commodity prices and the soaring costs for fuel, fertilizer, and equipment combined with high interest rates.

In 1982, many American farmers sold their products for less than they cost to produce. The U.S. Department of Agriculture reported that the average price received by farmers for broilers in that year was below the cost of production. Many farmers also sold wheat and corn for less than the production cost. For many, profit margins had virtually disappeared by 1982. (See Figure 10-2.) Between 1950 and 1982, U.S. farm output more than doubled, but net farm income in real terms (1967 dollars) fell from $19 billion in 1950 to scarcely $6 billion in 1982.[14] This precipitous decline occurred while the incomes of other Americans were rising steadily.

Farmers were able to sustain the heavy losses of the late seventies and early eighties only by going deeply into debt, borrowing against soaring land values. But the boom in land speculation came to an end in 1981 and land prices fell the following two years. As a result, many farmers suddenly lost their equity and faced bankruptcy.

Economic conditions fostering speculation in land have driven land values to a lofty level that bears little relationship

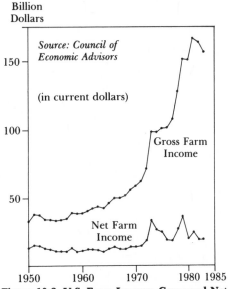

Figure 10-2. U.S. Farm Income, Gross and Net, 1950-83

to the land's productive capacity. Given the economics of the early eighties, buying U.S. farmland now with the hope of paying for it from the produce would be wishful thinking. Say, for example, someone had invested in prime midwestern farmland at $2,000 an acre in 1981 and planted it in corn that yielded 110 bushels per acre. With a mortgage at 15 percent, the annual interest payment would be $300 an acre. Yet at the 1981 price of $2.40 a bushel, the total income from each acre would have been $264, not enough to pay the interest, much less the principal or any of the production costs.

Nevertheless, it was these spiraling land values that until 1981 enabled many farmers to borrow and to stay in business. While net farm income has declined markedly, farm debt has soared. As recently as 1973, net farm income exceeded $30 billion compared with a farm debt of $65 billion, a ratio of roughly one to two. (See Figure 10-3.) By 1983, net farm income totaled $22 billion while the farm debt had climbed to $215

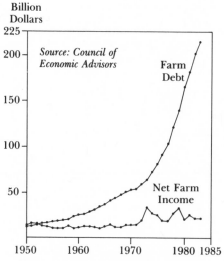

Figure 10-3. U.S. Farm Debt and Net Farm Income, 1950-83

billion—close to ten times income.[15]

As farmers have borrowed against the soaring prices of their land and other assets, not only have they supported themselves and their families, they have also subsidized food consumers everywhere. Borrowing against the inflated paper value of farmland has led to artificially low food prices in recent years. And just as productivity increases cannot go on forever when topsoil is being eroded, borrowing that is unrelated to the real value of the land cannot continue indefinitely—a lesson many rural banks and farmers are unfortunately learning. If farmers are to continue to produce, prices of farm products will need to rise. Without such an increase, the more vulnerable farmers and those who have attractive employment options or who are approaching retirement will stop producing, eventually reducing output and moving prices upward to a more realistic level.

Although U.S. data might allow the conversion of current farm output to real output by adjusting for soil erosion, similar information does not exist for most countries. And it is difficult to measure the extent to which farm output has been inflated in recent years by the growing indebtedness of farmers. If these adjustments could be made, however, it seems clear that the real world food output would be far below current consumption.

DEPENDENCE ON NORTH AMERICA

With grain, as with oil or any other basic resource, excessive world dependence on one geographic region for supplies is risky. As the North American share of world grain exports has increased it has surpassed the Middle Eastern share of oil exports and made the world more dependent on one region for its food than ever before.

This extraordinary dependence on one geographic region for grain supplies is a historically recent phenomenon and gives North America a politically and economically strategic role in the world food economy. Many of the world's cities, particularly those in the Third World, are fed largely with U.S. and Canadian wheat. Much of the world's milk, meat, and eggs are produced with U.S. feedgrains and soybeans.

As recently as the late thirties, Western Europe was the only grain-deficit region and Latin America was the world's leading grain supplier, exporting some nine million tons per year. North America and Eastern Europe (including the Soviet Union) each exported five million tons of grain annually. Even Asia and Africa had modest exportable surpluses.[16]

By 1950, the shift from regional grain surpluses to deficits was well under way and the outlines of a new world grain trade pattern were beginning to emerge. Today, with North America's unchallenged dominance as a grain supplier, international grain trade bears little resemblance to that of the thirties. (See Table 10-4.)

As North American agricultural growth gained momentum after World War II, U.S. and Canadian exports of grain climbed from 23 million tons in 1950 to 138 million tons in 1982, though they dropped back to 122 million tons in 1983 as a strong dollar and lethargic world economy weakened the buying powers of other countries. Feedgrains—principally corn, sorghum, and barley—have made up an ever larger share of the total. Today, North America is not only the world's breadbasket, but its feed bag as well.

While the United States was expanding its feedgrain exports, the shipments of soybeans grew even more rapidly. Although soybeans originated in China they have thrived in the United States, doing far better than in their country of origin. They have also found an economic niche in the world livestock economy, with soybean meal becoming the principal protein supplement in livestock and poultry feed. Today the United States produces over 60 percent of the world's soybean crop and accounts for two-thirds of soybean exports. (See Table 10-5.)

The reasons for North America's emergence as the world's dominant supplier of feedgrains and feedstuffs are many. On the supply side, the United States inherited a prime piece of agricultural real estate. In contrast to Latin America, where agricultural lands are concentrated in the hands of large hacienda owners, or Eastern Europe, where state farms and collectives dominate, U.S. and Canadian agriculture are centered on the family farm. Although large by international standards, they are nonetheless family farms and have all the attendant advantages of a strong link between effort expended by those working the land and the rewards of doing so.

North America is not only the world's breadbasket, but its feed bag as well.

The restructuring of world grain trade over the last generation has resulted in part from the soil erosion problems discussed earlier and in part from differential population growth rates, as a comparison of North America and Latin America shows. During the late thirties, Latin America had a larger grain export

Table 10-4. The Changing Pattern of World Grain Trade, 1950–83[1]

Region	1950[2]	1960	1970	1980	1983[3]
	(million metric tons)				
North America	+ 23	+ 39	+ 56	+ 131	+ 122
Latin America	+ 1	0	+ 4	− 10	− 3
Western Europe	− 22	− 25	− 30	− 16	+ 2
E. Europe and Soviet Union	0	0	0	− 46	− 39
Africa	0	− 2	− 5	− 15	− 20
Asia	− 6	− 17	− 37	− 63	− 71
Australia and New Zeal.	+ 3	+ 6	+ 12	+ 19	+ 9

[1]Plus sign indicates net exports; minus sign, net imports. [2]Average for 1948–52. [3]Preliminary.
SOURCES: United Nations Food and Agriculture Organization, *Production Yearbook* (Rome: various years); U.S. Department of Agriculture, *Foreign Agriculture Circular*, August 1983; author's estimates.

Table 10-5. Soybean Exports, Major Exporting Countries, 1960–83[1]

Year	United States	Brazil	Argentina
	(million metric tons)		
1960	4.6	-	-
1965	8.1	0.2	-
1970	16.4	1.1	-
1971	17.0	1.6	-
1972	15.7	3.1	-
1973	18.5	3.6	-
1974	21.1	6.0	-
1975	16.4	8.0	0.2
1976	21.0	8.6	0.4
1977	20.5	9.4	1.0
1978	26.1	7.6	2.3
1979	27.7	7.1	3.2
1980	32.8	8.4	2.9
1981	27.5	13.0	3.2
1982	33.2	11.3	3.0
1983	32.5	11.5	2.8

[1]Beans plus bean equivalent of meal.
SOURCE: U.S. Department of Agriculture, *Foreign Agriculture Circulars,* June 1981, August 1982, and August 1983.

surplus than North America, but the region's more rapid rate of population growth soon changed this. Indeed, if the regions had grown at the same rate since 1950, North America's population in 1983 would be so large that it would consume the entire grain harvest, leaving little or none for export. And North America, too, would now be struggling to maintain food self-sufficiency.

Today the countries with significant exportable surpluses of grain can be counted on the fingers of one hand—the United States, Canada, Australia, Argentina, and France. Of these, the United States accounts for over half and with Canada covers close to 70 percent of the total. The rest of the world's dependence on these supplies varies widely. A few countries, both industrial and devel-

oping, import more food than they produce; among these are Algeria, Belgium, Costa Rica, Japan, Lebanon, Libya, Portugal, Saudi Arabia, Switzerland, and Venezuela. Others that may shortly move into this category include Egypt, Senegal, and South Korea.[17]

This overwhelming dependence on one region, and on one country in particular, brings with it an assortment of risks. To begin with, both the United States and Canada are affected by the same climatic cycles. A poor harvest in one is often associated with a poor harvest in the other. When reserves are low, even a modest fluctuation in the region's exportable grain surplus can send price tremors through the world food economy.

An inadvertent agricultural policy miscalculation can also be costly. This was amply demonstrated in 1983 when miscalculations in the U.S. Department of Agriculture led to the idling of more cropland than had been projected, which was followed by a severe drought that further reduced harvests. Within a matter of weeks, concerned countries watched the world grain surplus change to a potential grain deficit. The U.S. corn crop was cut in half, effectively eliminating the world feedgrain surplus. A similar miscalculation in 1972, when record acreage of U.S. cropland was idled, contributed to the food shortages of the 1972–74 period.[18]

When food supplies are tight a North American grain export embargo, whether economically or politically inspired, can drive food prices upward everywhere outside the region. In 1973, for example, President Nixon embargoed soybean exports because of shortages at home. Although this helped curb food price rises within the United States, it worsened inflationary pressures elsewhere. During the same period, American millers and bakers were pressing for restrictions on grain exports, holding out the prospect of soaring bread prices if wheat exports were not restricted. Unfortunately, the world market conditions that would lead a principal exporter to restrict outgoing supplies are precisely the conditions that are most damaging to importing countries.

Some contend that the current generation of farmers has no right to engage in the agronomic equivalent of deficit financing.

In mid-July of 1975, the Canadian Wheat Board banned further exports of wheat until the size of the harvest could be ascertained. Similarly, the United States, yielding to political pressures generated by rising domestic food prices, limited grain exports to the Soviet Union and Poland in the late summer and early fall of 1975. Levied in 1972, in 1974, and again in 1975, such restrictions on exports became common when global grain supplies were tight. Perhaps more unsettling, these export controls were adopted despite the return to production of the previously idled U.S. cropland.

As with oil, exports of grain have been restricted for political purposes. In 1973, the Department of State compiled a "hit list" of Third World countries whose U.N. voting records were not compatible with U.S. interests so that they could be denied food assistance. More recently, President Carter imposed a partial embargo on exports of grain to the Soviet Union following its invasion of Afghanistan, and President Reagan delayed negotiating a new five-year grain agreement with the Soviet Union after the imposition of martial law in Poland.[19]

Countries that rely on North Ameri-can food should take heed of the philosophical debate emerging within the United States about the wisdom of mining the nation's soils to meet the ever-growing world demand. Both agricultural analysts and environmentalists argue that the country should make whatever adjustments in its agricultural practices are needed to protect the resource base, even though this would reduce the exportable surplus. Some argue that it makes little sense to sacrifice a resource that has been a source of economic strength since colonial days merely to buy a few billion barrels of oil. And some contend that the current generation of farmers has no right to engage in the agronomic equivalent of deficit financing, mortgaging the future of generations to come. The current trend is fraught with risks, both for those whose livelihoods depend on sustained land productivity and for those in countries dependent on food imports that eventually will dry up if the mining of soil continues. Even for the importers, reduced supplies in the short term and less pressure on North American soils would be better than losing the region's export capacity over the long term.

FOOD SECURITY INDICATORS

One of the most useful indicators of the world food situation is the food security index, which incorporates both grain carry-over stocks and the grain equivalent of idled cropland. This combines the world's two basic reserves of food and expresses them as days of consumption, a concept readily understood by policymakers everywhere. The two components of the index differ in important ways. Carry-over stocks, the grain in storage when the new crop begins to come in, are readily accessible and require only time for shipping arrangements to be made and for transport. Idled cropland, on the other hand, can take a year or more to be converted into food by farmers.

Carry-over stocks are held for the most part by exporting countries—the United States, Canada, Australia, Argentina, and France—largely as a service to importers. Other countries, particularly large ones such as India, maintain grain stocks as well, but these are usually designed specifically for their own use. India's grain stocks, typically ranging from 11–15 million tons, were drawn

Table 10-6. India: Grain Stocks, 1963–83

Year[1]	Beginning Stocks
	(million metric tons)
1963	11.7
1964	12.2
1965	13.0
1966	14.3
1967	12.9
1968	14.7
1969	15.5
1970	10.5
1971	12.5
1972	13.9
1973	10.4
1974	9.2
1975	5.3
1976	17.3
1977	21.2
1978	21.7
1979	21.3
1980	15.2
1981	12.2
1982	12.7
1983[2]	12.4

[1]Beginning April 1 of year shown.   [2]Preliminary.
SOURCES: U.S. Department of Agriculture (USDA), *Foreign Agriculture Circulars*, May 1976, July 1982, and June 1983; David Salmon and Tom Slayton, USDA, private communications, August 1983.

down to scarcely 5 million tons during 1973–75, a time of poor harvests. (See Table 10-6.) After this harrowing experience India adopted a target stock level of 21–24 million tons as part of a beefed-up food security system. Bumper harvests in the late seventies helped the government achieve its target, but after stocks were drawn down to 12–15 million tons during the 1979–80 drought, New Delhi has apparently decided for reasons of cost to maintain a more modest level of grain reserves.

Maintaining adequate grain stocks is expensive not only because of the cost of grain elevators but also because stored grain represents an investment. So when interest rates are high, the cost of carrying grain is also high. And even with the best of storage facilities there is always some loss involved, thus adding to the cost of maintaining the reserves.

Over time, for a reserve of grain to be adequate it should expand in tandem with world consumption. In 1960, for example, world reserves of 200 million tons were more than ample, representing nearly one-fourth of world consumption. In 1983, however, the same stocks would represent only one-eighth of world grain consumption. A level of grain reserves that was adequate in 1960 would be grossly inadequate in 1983.

The idled cropland component of the food security index consists of cropland set aside under farm programs just in the United States. Only occasionally have other countries intentionally idled cropland and the acreages have usually been negligible. During the sixties and early seventies U.S. idled cropland averaged close to 50 million acres, enough to produce an estimated 60 million tons of grain. (See Table 10-7.) As growth in world food output slowed after 1973, the United States returned cropland to production from 1974 through 1977 in an attempt to rebuild stocks. Then when grain reserves began to recover in the

Table 10-7. Index of World Food Security, 1960–83

Year	World Carry-Over Stocks of Grain	Grain Equiv. of Idled U.S. Cropland	Total	World Consumption
	(million metric tons)			(days)
1960	200	36	236	104
1965	142	70	212	81
1970	164	71	235	75
1971	183	46	229	71
1972	143	78	221	67
1973	148	25	173	50
1974	133	4	137	41
1975	141	3	144	43
1976	196	3	199	56
1977	194	1	195	53
1978	221	22	243	62
1979	197	16	213	54
1980	183	0	183	46
1981	221	0	221	56
1982[1]	260	13	273	66
1983[2]	191	92	283	68

[1]Preliminary.　[2]Projection.
SOURCES: Reserve stocks from U.S. Department of Agriculture (USDA), *Foreign Agriculture Circular*, October 1983; cropland idled in the United States data from Randy Weber, USDA, private communication, August 1983.

late seventies, some land was taken out of production in both 1978 and 1979. With reserves beginning to drop again in 1979, all land was released for production in 1980.

The Reagan administration, wishing to reduce government intervention in the marketplace, declined to idle any cropland in 1981 and only a modest acreage in 1982, even though world reserves had been rebuilt following two consecutive bumper harvests in the United States and a worldwide economic recession that dampened the growth in demand. In 1983, faced with the most severe rural depression since the thirties, the administration overreacted by devising two programs to encourage

farmers to divert land to nonproductive uses. The result was the largest diversion of acreage in U.S. history—over 70 million acres. Combined with a severe drought in the principal U.S. feedgrain and soybean producing areas, this led to a precipitous decline in the feedgrain harvest of over 40 percent. This in turn reduced the prospective carry-over stocks to one of the lowest levels in some years.[20]

Whenever grain stocks and the grain equivalent of idled U.S. cropland drop below 50 days of world consumption, grain prices customarily rise and become highly unstable. In 1973 and 1974, when the index dropped to 50 and 41 days, grain prices were nearly double traditional levels. The index again fell below 50 days of consumption in 1980, partly as a result of drought in the United States. This time, however, prices were not nearly as volatile as before, perhaps in part because interest rates were at record highs, making investors less inclined to speculate in commodities. By late 1983, prices, particularly of feedgrains, began to rise, largely because of the unprecedented reduction in the U.S. grain harvest—the product of government miscalculation and drought.

The food security index measures the adequacy of food supplies at the global level and thus the broad potential for responding to national shortages, but it says nothing about conditions within individual countries. Here the best indicator, of course, is the nutritional state of a country's population. At issue is whether a growing child gets enough food to develop his or her full physical and mental potential or whether a worker gets enough food to be fully productive. Per capita food availability for a country indicates what the national average is, but not whether an individual is adequately nourished. Assessing nutritional adequacy requires some knowledge of how the national food supply is distributed. But a lack of data on distribution makes it very difficult to estimate the extent of malnutrition, thus leaving the subject open to continuing debate.

The only time a decline in nutrition shows up officially is when it is severe enough to affect mortality. When this happens a country is facing famine, the most obvious and severe manifestation of food insecurity. Using this criterion, inadequate though it is, developments over the past decade have not been encouraging. From the postwar recovery years until the early seventies, famine virtually disappeared from the world. Except in China, which now admits to a massive famine in 1960–61, when it was largely isolated, the world enjoyed a re-

markable respite from famine for a quarter of a century. Whenever famine did threaten, the United States intervened with food aid, even when it required nearly one-fifth of the U.S. wheat crop two years in a row, as it did following monsoon failures in India in 1964 and 1965.[21]

By the early seventies, however, food deficits were widening and famine was unfolding in several African countries and in the Indian subcontinent. (See Table 10-8.) Several famines claimed hundreds of thousands of lives, providing a grim reminder of the fragility of food security even in an age of advanced technology. Most were the product of drought and a failure of international food relief mechanisms.

During the late seventies world reserves were rebuilt and, except for strife-torn Kampuchea, famines subsided— only to return in 1983, a year of widespread climatic anomalies. The capacity of poor countries with falling per capita food production and deteriorating soils to withstand drought and floods has lessened. As a result, more countries than ever before face the possibility of famine in early 1984. Among the threatened countries are Bolivia and Peru in

Table 10-8. Countries Experiencing Famine Since 1950

Year	Location	Estimated Deaths
1960–61	China	8,980,000
1968–69	Nigeria (Biafra)	1,000,000
1971–72	Bangladesh	430,000
1972	India	830,000
1973	Sahelian Countries	100,000
1972–74	Ethiopia	200,000
1974	Bangladesh	330,000
1979	Kampuchea	450,000
1983	Ethiopia	30,000

SOURCE: Worldwatch Institute estimates derived from various official and unofficial sources.

Latin America, and over a score of countries in Africa. An FAO team of agronomists assessing the food situation in Africa in late 1983 identified 22 countries where crisis seemed imminent—Angola, Benin, Botswana, Cape Verde, Central African Republic, Chad, Ethiopia, Gambia, Ghana, Guinea, Lesotho, Mali, Mauritania, Mozambique, Sao Tome and Principe, Senegal, Somalia, Swaziland, Tanzania, Togo, Zambia, and Zimbabwe. The team of experts concluded that four million tons of emergency grain supplies would be needed to avoid starvation among the 145 million people living in these countries.[22]

Since all governments gather mortality data, though not equally well, it is possible to document these severe food shortages. But equally troubling is the number of people suffering from chronic malnutrition—that vast middle ground between those who are well nourished and those who are starving. Their numbers are difficult to measure and therefore easy to ignore. Indian economist Amartya Sen observes that his government "has been able to ignore this endemic hunger because that hunger has neither led to a run on the market, and chaos, nor grown into an acute famine with people dying of starvation. Persistent, orderly hunger does not upset the system."[23]

A CRISIS OF MANY DIMENSIONS

There is no simple explanation of why efforts to eradicate hunger have lost momentum or why food supplies for some segments of humanity are less secure than they were, say, 15 years ago. Declines in food security involve the continuous interaction of environmental,

economic, demographic, and political variables. Some analysts see the food problem almost exclusively as a population issue, noting that wherever population growth rates are low, food supplies are generally adequate. Others view it as a problem of resources—soil, water, and energy. Many economists see it almost exclusively as a result of underinvestment, while agronomists see it more as a failure to bring forth new technologies on the needed scale. Still others see it as a distribution problem. To some degree it is all of these.

More countries than ever before face the possibility of famine in early 1984.

In an important sense, the food problem of the mid-eighties is the result of resource depletion. The depletion of oil reserves, the loss of topsoil through erosion, and the growing competition for fresh water are central to understanding trends in the world food economy. As world population expands, the shrinking cropland area per person and the reduction in average soil depth by erosion combine to steadily reduce the per capita availability of topsoil for food production. If between 1980 and 2000 there is a 6 percent net increase in cultivated land area and a continuation of recent soil erosion rates, the amount of topsoil per person will fall from 792 tons to 489 tons by the end of the century, a decline of 38 percent. (See Table 10-9.) Because the energy that farmers substitute for soil lost to erosion is becoming increasingly costly, production costs everywhere are on the rise.

In a basic arithmetical sense the food problem is a population problem. If world population were now growing at 1 percent instead of nearly 2 percent there

Table 10-9. World Soil Resources and Excessive Soil Loss, 1980, With Projections to 2000[1]

Year	Population	Cropland	Excessive Soil Loss	Remaining Topsoil	Topsoil Per Person
	(billion)	(billion acres)	(billion tons)		(tons)
1980	4.42	3.12	22.6	3,500	792
1985	4.83	3.17	23.1	3,385	701
1990	5.28	3.22	23.5	3,270	619
1995	5.73	3.27	23.9	3,150	550
2000	6.20	3.32	24.2	3,030	489

[1]Assumes a net growth in world cropland area of 6 percent between 1980 and 2000, and an average depth of topsoil of 7 inches (or 1,120 tons per acre) in 1980.
SOURCE: Worldwatch Institute estimates.

would still be an ample margin for improving diets, as there was from 1950 to 1973. As noted, however, the annual growth in food production has unfortunately fallen from the rather comfortable 3 percent of that period to a rate that barely matches that of population.

Those who see the food problem primarily as a distribution problem argue that if all the world's food were equitably distributed among its people there would be no hunger and malnutrition. This argument is technically sound but it represents a degree of global abstraction that is not very helpful in formulating policies. It would mean, for example, that much of the world would be even more dependent on U.S. farmers than they are today, failing to realize that the only long-term solution to hunger in most Third World countries is more internal production. And improving distribution is not just a matter of a better transport system or subsidized food distribution programs. It requires dealing with fundamental sources of political conflict such as land reform and with economic policies that encourage employment.

Achieving a more satisfactory balance between the world demand and supply of food requires attention to both sides of the equation. On the demand side, the success of efforts to upgrade diets may depend on an emergency program to slow world population growth. Currently farmers must produce enough additional food each year to feed an annual increment of 79 million people—people who must be provided for in years of good weather or bad.

Meaningful improvements in diet over the rest of the century will depend, too, on gains in per capita income, particularly in the Third World. Unfortunately those gains are narrowing or disappearing. During the seventies, 18 countries in Africa experienced a decline in per capita income. In most instances these national declines appear to be continuing in this decade. Unfortunately, the list of countries where incomes have fallen thus far during the eighties is far longer than it was in the seventies.

Farmers must produce enough additional food each year to feed an annual increment of 79 million people.

Also on the demand side is the question of how available food supplies are distributed. The most vulnerable segments of society in times of food scarcity are the rural landless in Third World countries. Data collected on famine deaths in Bangladesh in 1975, for example, show death rates among the landless of 36 per thousand, three times that of their neighbors who owned three or more acres of land.[24] Reducing the size of this extremely vulnerable, rapidly growing landless population will require far more vigorous family planning and land reform programs than most countries have so far been able to mount.

On the supply side, the scarcity of new cropland, the continuing loss of topsoil, the scarcity of fresh water, the end of cheap energy, and diminishing returns on chemical fertilizer combine to make expanding food production progressively more difficult. In addition, food-deficit Third World countries are now struggling with a heavy external debt load that is continuing to mount. Foreign exchange scarcities are reducing imports both of agricultural inputs and of food. In 1983, for example, Brazil, staggering under the world's heaviest debt load, reduced its imports of fertilizer and other key farm inputs. Scores of other countries are similarly affected.[25]

At a time when concessional food aid is needed more than ever, U.S. programs are at the lowest level of nearly a generation. From their launch in 1954 through the late sixties, U.S. food programs expanded, reaching a high of 15.3 million tons of grain in 1966. Enough to feed 90 million people in its peak years, this aid was an important defense against hunger in many countries. (See Table 10-10.) Preliminary estimates for 1983, however, indicate food aid shipments had dwindled to some 4 million tons of grain. Other assistance programs, such as the World Food Programme, have been developed and expanded, but they are small by comparison and cannot begin to offset the U.S. decline. In a modest effort to enhance food security in low-income countries, the International Monetary Fund launched a new

Table 10-10. United States: Concessional Grain Exports Under Public Law 480, 1955–82

Year	Quantity
	(million tons)
1955	5.4
1960	12.5
1965	15.0
1970	7.8
1971	7.3
1972	7.8
1973	5.5
1974	2.7
1975	3.7
1976	4.0
1977	7.2
1978	5.9
1979	5.9
1980	4.5
1981	4.1
1982	3.8

SOURCE: Dewain Rahe, U.S. Department of Agriculture, private communication, August 1983.

facility in 1981 that would provide short-term supplementary financing to food-deficit Third World countries suffering from temporary rises in food import bills.[26]

In addition to the traditional problems, political conflicts are creating an instability in the Middle East, Africa, and Latin America that makes agricultural progress difficult. This new hindrance to progress is reflected in the World Food Programme's emergency relief efforts. The share of emergency food relief going to victims of human-caused disasters (refugees and displaced persons) has come to dominate the Programme in recent years, after starting at a relatively modest level. By 1982, less than one-third of the Programme's resources were devoted to helping the groups who were the principal recipients in the early years, those affected by drought or caught in sudden natural disasters, such as floods or earthquakes. (See Table 10-11.)

Other disruptions borne of desperation are cropping up in food-deficit areas. In late 1983, reports from northeastern Brazil described hordes of hungry rural people pouring into the towns demanding food, water, and jobs. After the town of Crato was invaded on three different occasions, merchants began voluntarily distributing rations of beans, sugar, and flour to forestall sacking and looting. Merchants in another town reportedly lost some 60 tons of food to looters.[27]

Although drought and recession-induced unemployment are leading to hunger, the long-term forces converging to create these conditions in the Brazilian northeast are essentially the same as those that have led to the food crises in

Table 10-11. Allocation of World Food Programme Emergency Relief, 1963–82

Year	Drought	Sudden Natural Disaster[1]	Human-Caused Disaster[2]
		(percent)	
1963–72	44	33	23
1973	83	17	0
1974	54	36	10
1975	21	44	35
1976	30	18	52
1977	50	31	19
1978	25	41	34
1979	33	10	57
1980	33	5	62
1981	22	4	74
1982	20	11	69

[1]Includes earthquakes, floods, etc.

[2]Includes refugees, displaced persons, and others affected by civil disturbances.

SOURCE: World Food Programme, *Annual Report of the Executive Director on the Development of the Programme: 1982* (Rome: 1983).

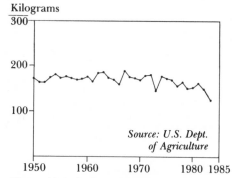

Figure 10-4. Grain Production Per Person in Africa, 1950-83

so many African countries: record population growth, underinvestment in agriculture, and physical deterioration in the countryside. Ecologists have for years warned that mounting population pressures in northeastern Brazil leading to deforestation and unsustainable agricultural practices would turn the area into a desert. That grim scenario is now unfolding.

Trends in Africa since 1970 are a harbinger of things to come elsewhere in the absence of some major changes in population policies and economic priorities. After rising from 1950 to 1970, per capita grain production in Africa has declined rather steadily.[28] (See Figure 10-4.) The forces that have led to this decline in Africa are also gaining strength in the Andean countries of Latin America, in Central America, and in the Indian subcontinent. Whether the declining food production now so painfully evident in Africa can be avoided elsewhere will be determined in the next few years.

The issue is not whether the world can produce more food. Indeed, it would be difficult to put any foreseeable limits on the amount the world's farmers can produce. The question is at what price they will be able to produce it and how this relates to the purchasing power of the poorer segments of humanity. The environmental, demographic, and economic trends of the seventies and early eighties indicate that widespread improvements in human nutrition will require major course corrections. Nothing less than a wholesale reexamination and reordering of social and economic priorities—giving agriculture and family planning the emphasis they deserve—will get the world back on an economic and demographic path that will reduce hunger rather than increase it.

11

Reshaping Economic Policies

Lester R. Brown

One need not be an economist to sense that we are living in difficult economic times. Economic growth over the last four years has been less than in any comparable period since the thirties and there have been no gains in per capita income for the world as a whole since 1979. In countries such as Argentina, Brazil, Mexico, and Poland, massive external debt is strangling economic progress.

A projection of Brazil's economic future by Data Resources indicates that the country should be able to pay off its debt, but that doing so means its depressed industrial output will not regain its 1980 level until 1990. By this time 37 million Brazilians will have been added to the 1980 population of 119 million, greatly reducing output per capita.[1] Unfortunately, this projected interaction between external debt, economic output, and population growth is not atypical. It confronts dozens of developing countries, large and small.

The budgetary deficits and external debts that confound policymakers today derive from more-fundamental shortcomings—outdated population policies, inappropriate economic policies, and misplaced priorities. In all-too-many countries, population policies belong to another age, a time when rapid population growth slowed but did not prevent improvements in living conditions. Economic policies, too, are a carry-over from a past when energy was cheap and resources were abundant. Existing priorities in the use of public resources were fashioned in an age when incomes were everywhere on the rise, when more guns did not preclude more butter.

The preceding chapters make clear the extent of resource deterioration, a deterioration that now undermines economic performance in many countries. Policymakers often lose sight of the relationship between the economic system, whose performance is monitored in great detail, and the resource base on which it depends. Glowing economic reports—with key indicators such as output, productivity, and exports continually setting new records in the short run

—are possible even as the economic policies that generate them are destroying the resource base. Indeed, one reason for the bullish indicators might be the consumption of the resource base itself, as the discussion of "Living Beyond Our Means" in Chapter 1 indicates.

The need for a new accounting system is now evident. Existing economic indicators need to be supplemented by others that distinguish between self-defeating and sustainable growth. Most fundamentally, the world needs a system of economic accounting that reflects more completely the effects of economic policies on the resource base and, conversely, the effect of changes in the resource base on the economy. This system must account for more than the short-run "bottom line"; it must incorporate values that maintain economic life.

A REVISED ACCOUNTING SYSTEM

The lack of a more complete economic accounting system has led many governments to adopt ill-conceived policies in the management and use of resources. It has permitted governments to focus on production, while largely ignoring the effects on the natural capital that makes production possible. In some instances the accounting gap has led to a more or less permanent loss of productive capacity. As this report documents, governments' shortsighted approach can be seen in one case after another: topsoil, water supplies, grasslands, forests.

Few annual accountings of soil formation and soil loss have been attempted, so national political leaders often do not know whether soils are being farmed or mined. Lacking data on soil erosion, governments cannot compute either the on-farm cost of soil loss or the off-farm costs of, for example, hydroelectric reservoir sedimentation. This in turn precludes complete cost/benefit analyses of soil conservation programs.

Glowing economic reports are possible even as the economic policies that generate them are destroying the resource base.

Resource accounting could help manage other resources intelligently as well. Water demands often exceed renewable supplies, leading to falling water tables, dwindling river flows, and shrinking lakes. Grasslands are being converted to desert in many areas of the world, but there is no effort to relate desertification to excessive livestock numbers and the loss of grazing capacity through overgrazing. And little accurate annual data on changes in forested areas exist, so in many situations trees are being felled faster than they are regenerating. Many countries simply do not know when they begin consuming the resource base itself. By the time it becomes physically obvious that they are doing so, it can be too late to act.

Changes in a few resource stocks are carefully monitored at the global level. For example, governments annually record the amount of oil produced and newly discovered, making it easy to determine changes in reserves. This information helps policymakers decide how rapidly the remaining oil reserves should be exploited. When aggregated at the global level, the sum of these national data provides information of great value to decision-makers everywhere, from individual consumers to political leaders.

At the national level, only Norway appears to have adopted a comprehensive resource accounting system. In 1974 the Norwegian Stortinget (Parliament) instructed the Ministry of Environment to prepare an annual review of natural resource stocks, their annual consumption, and any proposals for their future use. Work on the methodology for this assessment began in 1975 and a preliminary study was presented to the Stortinget in 1977. It included an accounting both of material resources and of basic biological life-support systems. Other countries, including Canada, France, Japan, and the Netherlands, have experimented with alternative accounting systems but none has progressed as far as Norway in developing a comprehensive accounting.[2]

Norway's goal in resource accounting is to maximize the "social profit" of resources and to prevent depletion or degradation wherever possible. In a United Nations Environment Programme review of the status of environmental accounting, Edward Weiller observes that "the concept of 'natural capital' is at the heart of the Norwegian resource accounting system."[3] Its early achitects decided, probably wisely, not to attempt to integrate it with the national economic accounts. In part this was because the latter are kept in monetary units, whereas resources are measured in physical units.

The Norwegian experience illustrates the value of a modest but realistic approach to accounting. It also demonstrates that each country needs to design its own system, one that is suited to its particular circumstances and needs. Japan, for example, a heavily industrialized and densely populated country, has focused on the costs of mitigating environmental damage, in particular the effects of air and water pollution on human health. South Korea, in a somewhat similar situation, has patterned its approach after that of Japan.[4]

In the Third World the primary need is to identify and measure the resource-degrading consequences of economic activity. Governments in these countries, where "natural capital" is so overwhelmingly important, need to know what is happening to soils, forests, grasslands, and water resources. If a desert is expanding, for example, policymakers in the area want to know how fast it is spreading and what can be done to reverse the process.

Occasionally a country will institute a detailed accounting system when a resource is of particular value or when its stock is known to be diminishing, which would have potentially serious long-term economic consequences. It was precisely these concerns that led the U.S. Congress to pass the Resource Conservation Act in 1977, which required the Department of Agriculture to conduct a national soils inventory, focusing particularly on the relationship between soil erosion and new soil formation. The first assessment, in 1977, drew upon some 200,000 samples from croplands across the country and provided the most detailed information ever on U.S. soils. The survey was repeated again in 1982, but with even greater detail. Relying on close to a million individual samples, it represented the most exhaustive inventory of soils ever undertaken by any country. The completion of the 1982 assessment provided U.S. soil scientists with two data points that can be compared to establish long-term trends.[5]

A resource accounting system provides a means of incorporating the costs of "externalities" such as acid rain or soil erosion into decision-making. The goal is more intelligent policymaking and a more enlightened public and private management of resources. Much more than a resource accounting system is needed, of course, for intelligent environmental and resource management, but this is a necessary yardstick for measuring a system's effectiveness.

NEW ECONOMIC INDICATORS

As the emphasis in economic policymaking and planning shifts toward sustainability, the inadequacy of many widely used economic indicators becomes obvious. As the goal of economic policy is redefined, new indicators are needed to measure progress. Central to this new definition is Kenneth Boulding's observation that "it is stocks of goods that contribute to human well-being while flows contribute to gross national product."[6] Under the existing national accounting system, the production of shoddy goods that have to be replaced or repaired frequently raises the GNP, whereas a modest additional investment in high-quality engineering that greatly extends the lifetime of products lowers the GNP.

A set of economic indicators designed to measure progress toward a sustainable society should include data, for example, on the recycling of major resources such as steel, aluminum, glass, and paper. The throwaway society evolved when energy was cheap, raw materials were abundant, and there were far fewer people competing for resources than there are today. Societies failing to realize that these days are over are likely to pay with a falling standard of living. The release of monthly data on materials recycling would help highlight the importance of this process for both the general public and key decision-makers. Such indicators are not particularly difficult to develop; recycled scrap steel, for instance, is processed through mills just as iron ore is and thus can readily be measured.

Changes in the relative values of the various factors of production also call for new economic indicators. From the beginning of this century until 1973, energy became progressively cheaper while labor became more expensive. That trend has since been reversed, with energy costs rising much more rapidly than those of labor. With extensive and growing unemployment in industrial as well as developing countries, these new relationships suggest a need to focus more on energy productivity, specifically on that of oil, the scarcest fossil fuel. The barrels of oil needed to produce $1,000 worth of GNP, a measure discussed in Chapter 3, is a useful way of determining how well a society is doing in weaning itself from this versatile but dwindling energy source. Similarly, since cropland area is essentially fixed, the value of land is increasing relative to that of labor, making land productivity relatively more important. This is not to imply that labor productivity is unimportant; rather it recognizes that raising the productivity of energy and of land increasingly holds the key to raising labor productivity.

In a world where the rate of population growth is often the principal determinant of efforts to improve living conditions, data on population growth become an important measure of progress. The need here is not for a new indicator but for the more systematic gathering and dissemination of data on birth rates. Reporting this data monthly, just as governments already do for employment and inflation, would remind people how much remains to be done in order to achieve population stability.

As pressures on the global resource base intensify, spurring the shift to development strategies focused on basic needs, indicators other than income may prove more useful in measuring living standards. Given the basic need for food, particularly in low-income countries, per capita grain consumption or caloric intake may be more telling measures of well-being. Indeed, Bangladesh has begun to define poverty not in terms of per capita income but in terms of caloric intake. In 1980 the government reported that 85 percent of the people were living below the poverty line, defined as 2,122 calories a day, and 54 percent below the extreme poverty level of 1,885 calories.[7]

A new set of economic indicators keyed directly to basic social needs could help guide the effort to create a sustainable society.

In a world where resource scarcities make rapid economic growth more difficult or less desirable, designing development strategies that focus more specifically on basic social indicators such as life expectancy or infant mortality may be useful. The Overseas Development Council has devised a Physical Quality of Life Index (PQLI) based on three social indicators—life expectancy, infant mortality, and literacy—as an alternative to per capita income. The profiles developed with this new index suggest that rather high levels of social well-being can be attained at rather modest levels of resource consumption, providing an appropriate development strategy is followed.[8]

Progress towards a sustainable society requires changes that will reduce the value of GNP as an indicator—underscoring the need for new economic indicators. For example, if the construction industry begins to incorporate the basic principles of climate-sensitive architecture, new buildings will require far less energy than existing structures. In effect, architectural design and engineering know-how will be substituted for energy, leading to much lower energy

use and a decline in gross national product, but also to an improvement in the standard of living.

Similarly, as planned obsolescence is abandoned in favor of high-quality goods emphasizing durability, this too could lead to a decline in apparent economic output. Stated otherwise, many of the practices that have led to such enormous increases in gross national product do not necessarily correlate with improvements in quality of life. In moving toward a sustainable society it is quite possible to have a short-term decline in GNP while living conditions are improving. A new set of economic indicators keyed directly to basic social needs could help guide the effort to create a sustainable society.

ECONOMIC POLICIES FOR FULL EMPLOYMENT

Economic analysts now put rising unemployment and international indebtedness at the top of the list of the world economic problems, both having at least temporarily superseded inflation as an issue of concern. Unemployment and underemployment have been growing steadily for more than a decade in the Third World as more and more young people reach working age. In some developing countries the unemployed and underemployed combined may constitute a third or more of the total labor force.

Even Western industrial societies are plagued with rising unemployment. In the United States, the United Kingdom, and several countries in Western Europe, unemployment reached double-digit levels in the early eighties. A ratchet effect can now be seen in the growth of unemployment in these socieites. During recessions unemployment increases, while during economic recovery the number of unemployed stabilizes or declines only modestly, leaving the total number of job-seekers little changed. Thus with each economic cycle unemployment moves higher.

Theoretically the factors of production—land, labor, and capital, which includes energy—should combine in the marketplace in optimum combinations. If a given factor is not fully used, its price should drop. But market rigidities such as minimum wages and fixed salaries for many categories of workers have over-priced labor relative to other productive factors, leaving many people without jobs. The result is a waste of labor and a less-than-optimum combination of the basic factors of production.

Neither national governments nor international development agencies have proved very proficient in devising economic policies that will take full advantage of a country's labor force. No government would consciously idle part of its energy flow or capital assets. Putting money in a mattress would be unthinkable because it would not contribute to productive capacity or earn interest. And yet labor is used as unproductively as money in a mattress as a result of poorly conceived economic policies. Governments can avoid this by systematically seeking opportunities to use unemployed labor to increase a country's energy output, to conserve energy, or to increase food production.

One of the more imaginative efforts of this kind is South Korea's reforestation campaign, which is described in some detail in Chapter 5. In the early seventies the government launched a national effort to replant the denuded hillsides of the country, land that was otherwise useless. By the end of the decade, seasonally unemployed villagers had planted an area in forest that was two-thirds as large as that in rice. This "greening of the countryside" was achieved by combining fast-growing pine seedlings from government-run nurseries, the organizational capacity represented by village-level cooperatives, and seasonally unemployed labor.

In effect South Korea has created a major energy resource, one that will provide fuelwood in perpetuity with a minimal expenditure of funds. Reforestation in this setting amounts to ecologic rehabilitation. By reducing runoff, forested lands reduce soil erosion and help recharge underground aquifers. South Korea's efforts, which have added to the country's resource stock and reduced its unemployment, are a model for other countries. Maintaining, culling, and harvesting the planted trees will provide employment to thousands of villagers for the indefinite future.

Another activity particularly important in rural areas is the construction of small dams that can be used for electrical generation and for water storage and irrigation. Small dams, which can be built almost exclusively with hand tools, can also reduce runoff and potential damage from flooding. China, which has some 89,000 small, locally constructed dams with a combined electrical generating capacity of nearly 3,000 megawatts, is the unquestioned leader in this resourceful use of labor.[9]

A closely related effort that can capitalize on rural seasonal employment is the construction of terraces on hillside cropland. As noted in Chapter 4, where population growth is rapid, farmers have moved up the hillsides so fast that time has not permitted construction of the terraces needed to stabilize and preserve agriculture on these sloping lands. Mobilizing seasonally unemployed workers for this task could ensure both that soil on this land is retained and that rainfall is captured and used to good effect.

In a world where water is becoming

increasingly scarce and a constraint on food production, reducing water loss from canals can yield a robust return. Even in advanced industrial societies such as the United States or the Soviet Union, irrigation canals are often dug in the bare earth without the benefit of any lining. Using stone, brick, or even a layer of plastic can sometimes virtually eliminate seepage, which can siphon off up to 40 percent of irrigation water supplies. In addition to reducing waterlogging, often a problem in irrigated areas with canal seepage, the investment of unemployed labor in this water conservation effort would also expand the irrigated area.[10]

One of the most promising areas for employment expansion is materials recycling.

The broad-based effort to develop renewable energy substitutes provides an abundance of job opportunities. The shift from gasoline to alcohol as an automotive fuel in Brazil illustrates this potential. The increase in cropped acreage needed to produce sugarcane for the distilleries is a source of direct employment in agriculture. At the same time the construction of alcohol distilleries in the countryside near the cane fields provides a form of industrial employment in the countryside. Although petroleum refineries need only a handful of workers, alcohol distilleries employ many.[11]

A similar advantage exists in the development of wind power, an energy resource that is widely available compared with coal or uranium. Turning to the wind rather than nuclear power in the Third World also creates manufacturing jobs locally since virtually all developing countries have the industrial capacity to produce wind-electric generators, while

they would have to import reactors.

Another energy source that can be exploited largely by indigenous labor is biomass, which can be converted into methane by using locally built methane generators. Every village in the Third World has a certain amount of organic material—human and animal wastes, household wastes, and crop residues—that can be converted into methane by an anaerobic digester. These methane generators extract the methane from organic material while leaving a nutrient-rich sludge that can be used as fertilizer. In effect, methane generators combine the production of energy and the recycling of nutrients, which is certain to become an appealing combination as fertilizer prices continue to rise.[12]

As electricity rates and oil and natural gas prices rise, a prime opportunity exists to substitute solar collectors for these conventional sources. A concerted worldwide effort to shift to this method of water heating, a move that makes more and more economic sense, would create millions of jobs in the fabrication, marketing, distribution, and installation of solar panels.

The manufacture and marketing of more-efficient stoves for cooking in the Third World is another industry ripe for development. Food cooked on an open fire uses several times as much firewood, cow dung, or crop residue as that cooked on more–efficiently designed closed stoves. One advantage of several new varieties of stoves is that they can be made entirely from local materials and produced by village-level industries. The social contribution of the reduced pressures on forests and of additional employment would be substantial.[13]

Within the United States, one of the most promising areas for employment expansion is materials recycling, which has the advantage of reducing energy requirements, consumer costs, pollution, and materials use. The use of virgin ores for the production of throwaway containers and other materials is capital- and energy-intensive but uses relatively little labor. Recycling, by contrast, is a labor-intensive activity that requires far less capital and energy.

One sector in which all societies can increase employment while reducing energy use is transportation. One of the attractions of the 55-mile-an-hour speed limit in the United States, in addition to the energy and lives it saves, is that it increases employment in both freight and passenger transportation. Another variation on this basic theme of exchanging energy for employment lies in the design of public passenger transport systems. In some developing countries, such as Indonesia, the Philippines, and Turkey, small vans that carry six to ten passengers are driven on established transportation routes, providing passenger transport that is easily competitive with buses in terms of cost but that uses less energy and more drivers.[14]

In some cases a combination of the initiatives cited above multiplies job opportunities. For example, the construction of a local water storage pond or reservoir in a rural community can permit double cropping. In many Third World countries an increase in water supplies during the dry season will make year-round cropping possible. In the Philippines, for example, a new rice-production system has developed in areas with continuous water supplies. A farmer with, say, four acres of land divides it into small plots that are in rice continuously except during the few days between harvest and replanting. Each week another plot is harvested and replanted. With such intensive rotation, the work load is distributed evenly throughout the year. Labor is used with maximum efficiency and the land yields three or four crops of rice annually.[15]

Mounting unemployment is not inevitable in either industrial or developing

countries provided national leaders understand what needs to be done and have the political will to carry it out. In most situations the limiting factor is imagination and the capacity to organize people at the local level to achieve common social goals, whether the objective is planting and maintaining a village firewood plantation or building a small dam to store water and generate electricity.

EQUITY AND STABILITY

As long as the world economy was expanding at 4–5 percent per year the question of how equitably wealth was distributed was largely defused. It was assumed that the rising economic tide would raise living standards everywhere, and in most countries it did. But now that economic growth has slowed it becomes more difficult to dodge the distribution issue.

As economic growth lost momentum during the early eighties it fell behind population growth in many countries. For hundreds of millions of people income levels in 1983 were less than in 1980. For this segment of global society the exhortations to be patient, that their lot would improve, are becoming less acceptable. As world population moved from 3 billion in 1960 to 4.6 billion in 1983 it outstripped the growth in many basic commodities on which humanity depends. When the per capita supply of a commodity is stagnant or falling for the world as a whole, if some people consume more, then others must consume less. Patterns of income distribution within and among societies must be considered against this shifting global economic and resource backdrop.

One common measure of the equity of income distribution within a society is the ratio of the income received by the wealthiest one-fifth of population to that of the poorest one-fifth. This provides a means for comparing income distribution regardless of the level of development. In the more socially progressive countries, such as those in Western Europe, the income ratio of the top one-fifth to the bottom one-fifth ranges from 4 to 1 to 6 to 1. (See Table 11-1.) Two other major industrial societies, Japan and Australia, are also within this in-

Table 11-1. Income Distribution, Selected Countries[1]

Country	Relationship of Income of Top One-Fifth to Bottom One-Fifth
	(ratio)
Finland	4/1
Denmark	5/1
Japan	5/1
Netherlands	5/1
Sweden	5/1
United Kingdon	5/1
Bangladesh	6/1
West Germany	6/1
Norway	6/1
Sri Lanka	6/1
Yugoslavia	6/1
India	7/1
Indonesia	7/1
Spain	7/1
South Korea	8/1
Tanzania	8/1
France	9/1
United States	10/1
Malaysia	16/1
Turkey	16/1
Venezuela	18/1
Mexico	20/1
Peru	32/1
Brazil	33/1

[1]Data are for latest year available
SOURCE: World Bank, *World Development Report 1983* (New York: Oxford University Press, 1983).

come distribution bracket. Within the Third World, India, Bangladesh, and Sri Lanka stand out, with income distribution ratios of 6 or 7. Other major industrial countries with somewhat less equitable income distribution patterns include France (9 to 1), the United States (10 to 1), and Canada (11 to 1).

At the other end of the spectrum are countries in Latin America and the Middle East. Brazil, which has by far the greatest concentration of wealth of any major country, is at the bottom of the scale, with a ratio of 33 to 1. This explains why Brazil is sometimes described as "a Belgium and an India" within the same boundaries. For the upper 10 percent, or roughly 13 million people, incomes are comparable to those in northwestern Europe; for many remaining Brazilians, incomes and living conditions are much closer to those in India. Mexico, the second largest country in Latin America, also has a highly skewed income distribution pattern. The wealthiest one-fifth of its population has an income 20 times as great as the poorest one-fifth. In Mexico, as in Brazil, this puts the poorest segments of society at a meager subsistence level of existence.

For governments wishing to achieve a more equitable distribution of income there are numerous public policy instruments that can be used. One of the most common, of course, is a progressive income tax, a principle of taxation that has been widely adopted throughout the world. Education, or more precisely access to education, can also play an essential role. To be an effective equalizer, the educational system must be accessible to all people regardless of their economic or social standing.

When policies to redistribute income do not adequately reduce inequalities, governments can turn to the redistribution of productive assets, relying on land redistribution or employee stock option plans. In largely agrarian societies, land redistribution is often the key to redistributing wealth. Prominent among those using this device are Japan, South Korea, and Taiwan, countries that implemented thorough land reform programs as part of the reconstruction following World War II. Other countries, such as the United States, have brought about land redistribution indirectly through initiatives such as the Homestead Act. Although land reform is often the key to both wealth redistribution and successful rural development, it is also a politically formidable undertaking.

It is a mistake to invest heavily in an extensive automobile infrastructure that will benefit only a small fraction of a country's population.

The selection of technologies often has an indirect impact on the distribution of wealth. For example, when Pakistan was granted a large loan by the World Bank to purchase four-wheel tractors of the sort used in Europe and the United States, the larger farmers, who were able to afford this equipment, acquired an advantage. With this tillage capability many began looking for additional land to add to their holdings, often absorbing smaller farms, whose owners lacked mechanical power. The net effect was a further concentration of land in the hands of wealthier landowners. A more equitable alternative would have been to use the resources to import or domestically manufacture smaller two-wheel power tillers of the Japanese variety, an approach that would have helped smaller farmers remain competitive.[16]

A similar situation exists with transportation planning. Given that there is not enough oil or other fuel to permit automobile fleets in the Third World to achieve the near-saturation levels of the United States or Western Europe, it is a mistake to invest heavily in an extensive automobile infrastructure that will benefit only a small fraction of a country's population. Social equity is better served by investing these same resources in an extensive public transportation system augmented by bicycles, mopeds, and motor scooters. Motorized three-wheel rickshas of the sort pioneered in India could be used as taxis.

Similarly, the selection of medical technologies influences the distribution of health care services. If a country invests in a large modern hospital in its capital city it will be able to serve a small elite rather well but will lack the resources to provide any medical services at all to the bulk of the population. In the Philippines, for example, a $50-million heart-surgery center has been constructed at a time when many Filipinos lack access to even rudimentary health care. The waste is even greater because those Filipinos who can afford open-heart surgery prefer to fly to the United States for the operation rather than entrust themselves to local surgeons.[17] Investing $50 million in village clinics and the training of paramedics could measurably reduce infant mortality and raise life expectancy in the Philippines.

In many Third World countries there is a particularly strong bias against rural areas that must be addressed. Urban areas invariably manage to command the lion's share of investment in public services. Development economist Michael Lipton points out that in India, for example, a youngster born in an urban setting is eight times more likely to gain admission to college than one born in a village.[18] Similar contrasts can be found throughout the world in investment in basic social services such as education and health care.

As it becomes clearer that the world

economy is not likely to resume the rapid growth of the last few decades, the emphasis in economic policymaking and development planning needs to shift toward efforts to satisfy basic needs if living conditions are to improve. The "basic needs" development strategy concentrates on nutrition, literacy, and health care. Social planners will need to acknowledge that for a person with a loaf of bread an additional crust is of little value, but for someone who has only a single crust of bread, a second crust can greatly improve the quality of life.

Countries with severely skewed income distribution patterns often lack social cohesiveness, making it difficult to mobilize for the achievement of specific goals. South Africa is facing this dilemma as it confronts a threatening population explosion. When commenting on a recent governmental commission report on projected population growth in South Africa, Professor David Welsh of the University of Capetown observed: "Reading the somber unemotive facts piled up by the science committee, one is made aware that we have a time bomb ticking away in our midst. If future populations are to control population growth the old order of racial supremacy and discrimination, of forced migrancy and poverty, of inadequate housing, and unequal education will all have to go." Without these social adjustments, the report concluded, it would be virtually impossible to bring fertility down fast enough to avoid a Malthusian catastrophe.[19]

Given the grossly inequitable income distribution patterns in many Third World countries, the potential for social unrest and political instability is high. This is painfully evident in Africa, where incomes are now falling in so many countries, and in Latin American countries with large external debts, where severe belt tightening measures are required to maintain credit-worthiness. At issue, as former U.S. Assistant Secretary of State C. William Maynes observes, is whether "the economic strains that Third World governments are experiencing are proving too great for existing political structures to sustain."[20] In a world experiencing economic stresses more severe than any since the thirties, political stability may depend on reducing income disparity to a range that is morally acceptable and politically tenable.

NOW GUNS OR BUTTER

The past generation has witnessed an unprecedented militarization of the world economy. Prior to World War II, military expenditures claimed less than 1 percent of gross world output. In 1983 they consumed 6 percent. In real terms, military expenditures increased some twentyfold between the early thirties and early eighties.

The militarization of the world economy, initially spurred by U.S.-Soviet rivalry, has spread to the developing world as well. Increasingly, countries are seeking security in military power. In 1983, this translated into global military expenditures of $663 billion, a sum that exceeds the combined income of the poorest half of mankind. (See Table 11-2.) This trend threatens society in two ways. As militarization and modernization have proceeded apace over the past generation, new weapons have evolved that possess an unprecedented destructive capacity. Much of this destructive potential is vested in some 50,000 nuclear weapons, 98 percent of them in the hands of the two superpowers.[21]

The second threat to society from militarization is less direct, stemming from the diversion of resources away from pressing social needs. Swedish Un-

Table 11-2. World Military Expenditures, 1973–83 (in 1980 dollars)

Year	Expenditures	Annual Increase
	(billion dollars)	(percent)
1973	474	—
1974	488	3.0
1975	503	3.0
1976	509	1.2
1977	519	2.0
1978	532	2.5
1979	554	4.1
1980	561	1.2
1981	579	3.2
1982	619	6.9
1983[1]	663	7.1

[1]Preliminary estimate by Worldwatch Institute.
SOURCE: Stockholm International Peace Research Institute, *World Armaments and Disarmament, SIPRI Yearbook 1983* (New York: Taylor & Francis, Inc., 1983).

der-Secretary of State Inga Thorsson, who chaired a U.N. group studying the relationship between disarmament and development, reports that the study "presents overwhelming evidence that contemporary military establishments significantly distort and undermine the very basis of sustained economic and social development in all countries."[22] Every dollar spent for military purposes reduces the public resources available for other purposes. The implications of this are most evident at the national level. Although the United States leads the world in military expenditures the military share of the Soviet economy is substantially larger, an estimated 9–10 percent compared with 6 percent for the United States. This drain of resources from agriculture and the consumer-goods sector of the Soviet economy is leading to a markedly slower rate of progress than was achieved as recently as a decade ago.[23]

Conditions within the Soviet Union suggest that its leaders will respond to a U.S. initiative that would lessen international tensions and permit the Soviets to focus on their internal economic problems. In his missile-freeze speech in early 1982, President Brezhnev said, "We have not spent, nor will we spend a single ruble more for these purposes than is absolutely necessary." As Soviet analyst Marshall Goldman notes, this departs from past statements since Soviet leaders normally omit cost considerations when discussing military matters, and it may well reflect a Soviet interest in reordering priorities.[24]

Although Brezhnev's successor, Yuri Andropov, has not publicly addressed this point, the Soviet economy is clearly suffering from the heavy diversion of investment capital to the military sector. One consequence of the heavy Soviet emphasis on military production is that the Soviet Union is militarily strong and agriculturally weak. Now the world's largest food importer, it depends heavily on grain imports from the United States, the very country its military buildup is aimed at.[25]

For the United States, the diversion of investment capital to the arms-producing sector is depriving the remainder of the economy of investment capital. One consequence is that old plant and equipment is not being replaced, leading to a decline in the U.S. competitive position in the world economy. The competitive advantage in basic industries such as steel and automobiles is shifting toward countries with more modern, more energy-efficient plants and equipment. Economist Robert Lekachman observes that "the huge deficit engendered by imprudent tax cuts and even more misguided enlargement of the Pentagon rakeoff from the economy have turned the Treasury into a potential competitor for relatively scarce investment resources and contributed heavily to the skittishness of the financial markets."[26]

At the global level, research expenditures devoted to the development of new weapon systems overshadow the strictly military share of the world economy. An estimated 23 percent of all investment in science and technology is designed to either improve existing weapon systems or develop new ones. (See Table 11-3.)

Some 500,000 of the world's finest scientists and engineers work in military research.[27] Given the skill levels required in developing new weapon systems, it is likely that the share of top talent engaged in this destructive field of endeavor is well above the 22 percent of scientists involved overall. Not only do military expenditures dominate the global research and development budget, but they far exceed the combined research funds to develop renewable energy technologies, expand food output, and improve contraceptives.

Costly though these diversions of financial and scientific resources are, they may be matched by the claims that militarization makes on the time of political leaders. More and more of the working day of these individuals appears to be absorbed in attempts to resolve international conflict in one part of the world or another. Not only does conflict divert the energies of political leaders from other tasks, but the confrontational climate that exists, particularly between the two superpowers, is not conducive to the cooperative address of problems.

The progressive militarization of the world economy is also beginning to affect the stability and integrity of the international economic system. Weapons purchases have contributed to the burdensome debt with which many Third World countries are now saddled. Within the United States, growth in military expenditures during the early eighties has contributed heavily to the record fiscal deficits. It is certain to keep interest rates high in world financial markets for years to come, pushing debt-burdened Third World countries toward default. As of the mid-eighties the greatest single threat to world financial security may be the enormous U.S. fiscal deficit, part of it incurred in the name of national security.

The economic backdrop to militarization is changing. During the third quarter of this century, the world was able to have both more guns *and* more butter. Since 1978, however, world military expenditures have expanded at more than 4 percent per year in real terms, compared with 1.7 percent for the world economy.[28] With per capita income for the world as a whole stagnating since 1979, increasing the military share of the gross world product has been possible only by reducing civilian consumption. It is this fundamental change in the eco-

Table 11-3. Estimated Diversion of World Resources to Military Use, 1980

Resource	Diversion to Military Use
Military expenditure	$561 billion
	6 percent of gross world product
Labor force	50 million workers
Land	1 percent of earth's land surface
Expenditure on military science and technology	23 percent of total expenditure on science and technology
Scientists and research workers engaged in military research	22 percent of world total

SOURCE: Worldwatch Institute estimates based on data in Inga Thorsson, "Guns and butter: Can the world have both?," *International Labour Review*, July/August 1983.

nomic backdrop against which resources are allocated between military and non-military sectors that may force political leaders back to the drawing board in allocating priorities.

That military expenditures could expand when the economy is stagnating is an indication that the roots of militarization are deep in the body politic. Ruth Leger Sivard, compiler of the annual *World Military and Social Expenditures,* notes that "even long established democracies, where civilian control of the military is a firm tradition, are not immune to the effects of the military power they have created in the name of defense."[29] Within national governments, departments or ministries of defense typically dominate the budgetary process.

Sivard notes that the arms-producing industry is "one of the most prosperous and powerful industries in the world today with unparalleled resources to influence political decisions. As sales agent for a burgeoning government sponsored trade in arms, it takes on important policy making functions which determine priorities both at home and in foreign countries."[30] Countering the military-industrial complex that President Eisenhower warned about as he was leaving office will not be easy. Only when people become aroused in large numbers is the militarization of the world economy likely to be reversed. Rising public awareness of where current world military expenditures and policies could lead has translated into some of the largest political demonstrations and mass rallies ever held in Western Europe or the United States. New organizations are springing up on both sides of the Atlantic to counter what is perceived to be a dangerous drift of events.

Another possible hope for reversing the trend toward militarization lies with the International Monetary Fund (IMF) and the World Bank. The IMF in particular is gaining leverage in many Third World countries as they are forced to turn to it for investment capital. If their economic viability and capacity to service debt hinges on reducing military expenditures and foreign exchange outlays for arms imports, the IMF may be able to turn national policies in a more rational direction.

Weapons purchases have contributed to the burdensome debt with which many Third World countries are now saddled.

Yet another possibility is the emergence of a strong national political leader or international figure who has the stature to turn the world away from militarization. An example of this process on a smaller scale is the way countries in Western Europe have successfully ended generations of enmity and conflict. In part this is due to postwar visionaries such as Jean Monnet who saw a European community as a solution.[31] Exactly how the current worldwide conflict between the military goals of governments and people's aspirations for a better life will be resolved remains to be seen. But it seems clear that if militarization of the world economy continues, the social costs will be high.

One glimmer of hope in this field resides in Argentina, where the newly elected government, the first nonmilitary government in almost eight years, is planning to reduce military expenditures sharply. Shortly after his election on October 30, 1983, President-elect Raúl Alfonsín announced plans to boost spending on education and welfare by cutting military spending. Should he succeed, he might be followed by other governments in similarly dire economic straits.[32]

PRIORITIES: BACK TO THE DRAWING BOARD

The mounting economic stresses of recent years make it clear that existing policies and priorities are not working well. In the absence of a massive reordering of priorities—one that shifts natural resources and political energies from the arms race to efforts to brake world population growth, to protect the agronomic and biological resource systems, and to spur the energy transition—economic conditions will almost certainly continue to deteriorate.

In many ways the human prospect is tied to two transitions—from primary dependence on fossil fuels to a reliance on renewable energy resources, and from an equilibrium of high birth and death rates to one of low birth and death rates. Completion of the former involves a restructuring of the global economy; the latter depends on basic changes in reproductive behavior.

As things are now going, the human prospect is being shaped by population growth, by the depletion of both renewable and nonrenewable resources, and by the arms race. Advances such as biotechnology, microcomputers, and the associated electronics revolution are sure to help shape the future, but the dominant influence will be the basic processes used to produce energy and food. German novelist Günter Grass eloquently made this point in a lecture: "To be sure, we can make great new discoveries with our technological skill and scientific ability—we can split the atoms, see to the end of the universe, and reach the moon. But these milestones of human progress occur in the midst of a society sunk in a statistically proven barbarism. All those atom-splitters, those conquerers of space, those who punctually feed their computers and gather, store and evaluate all their data; none is in a position to provide sufficient food for the children of this world."[33]

Faltering development strategies in the Third World can succeed only if they are reoriented. Auto-centered development models borrowed from the industrial countries and left over from the age of oil serve the needs of a small minority, an affluent elite. As Soedjatmoko, an Indonesian and rector of the United Nations University in Tokyo, has observed, industrial growth needs to be redirected toward meeting the needs of the majority.[34] Such an industrial strategy would focus less on large tractors and more on two-wheel power tillers, less on automobiles and more on motor scooters and bicycles, less on nuclear power plants and more on simple solar water heaters. To be successful, each country needs to forge its own industrial development strategy, one responsive to its particular needs and circumstances.

A successful transition from fossil fuels to renewable energy will require a far more energy-efficient economy than now exists. In the past, developing countries everywhere could simply emulate the oil-centered energy economies of the industrial countries. Now as they begin to move away from petroleum toward renewables, each country must tailor its energy plan to its indigenous endowment of replenishable energy resources. The transition to renewables can endow an economy with a permanence that oil-based societies lack. It could also lead the world away from the existing inequitable, inherently unstable international oil regime because renewable energy sources are locally available in all countries.

Completing the demographic transition—to low birth and death rates—is clearly possible, as a dozen countries have demonstrated. These societies have eliminated population growth as a source of ecological stress and resource scarcity. Not surprisingly, these 12 countries with zero population growth have highly equitable income distributions, all ranking near the top internationally. Their improvement in economic and social conditions has been so pervasive that no special effort was needed to bring population growth to a halt. Other major industrial countries outside Europe, such as the United States and the Soviet Union, however, have not reached zero population growth and do not yet have a policy for doing so. Within the Third World some countries are making steady progress in bringing down birth rates, but only a few have adequate programs. If these countries are to stop population growth within an acceptable time frame, vigorous national leadership and strong incentives for smaller families will be required. Governments that fail are likely to see their efforts to improve living conditions overrun by the growth in human numbers.

Given the obvious impact of rapid population growth on human welfare, it is inexcusable that an estimated two-thirds of all couples in the Third World, excluding China, still lack ready access to family planning services. An estimated fourfold increase in family planning expenditures—from $920 million to $3,700 million—is needed to make population stabilization a realistic goal. This increase of $2,800 million represents less than two days' worth of global military expenditures at the 1983 rate.[35]

In the simplest terms, we are in a race to see if we can slow, and eventually halt, population growth before local life-support systems collapse. And we are in a race to reverse the nuclear arms buildup before we self-destruct. For many, the threatened decline in living standards has become a reality. Some countries have tried to postpone such declines by going heavily into debt. But over the long term, only a basic reformulation of development strategies, including population policies, will save us. It is no longer a matter of tinkering with priorities. Only a thorough reordering will do.

The future is both discouraging and hopeful. With whole continents experiencing a decline in living standards there is ample ground for pessimism. The worldwide loss of momentum in improving living conditions is not encouraging. Yet the problems we face are of our own making, and thus within our control. On the optimistic side, every threat to sustainability has been successfully addressed by at least a few countries. Even without any further advances in technology every major problem can be solved, every major human need satisfied. The issue is not technology or resources, but awareness and political will. Whether the future is bright and promising or dark and bleak hinges on how quickly we can mobilize politically to bring about the changes in policies and priorities that circumstances call for.

Notes

Chapter 1. Overview

1. Implications of the phrase "nuclear winter," coined by research scientist Richard P. Turco of R & D Associates, Marina del Ray, Calif., were discussed by Carl Sagan at the Conference on the Long-Term World-wide Biological Consequences of Nuclear War, Washington, D.C., October 31–November 1, 1983. For the principal conference papers, see *Science,* December 23, 1983.

2. World oil consumption data are from American Petroleum Institute (API), *Basic Petroleum Data Book* (Washington, D.C.: 1983) with 1983 estimates by Worldwatch Institute based on "Midyear Review and Forecast," *Oil and Gas Journal,* July 25, 1983.

3. OECD projections of 1985 generating capacity are from International Energy Agency (IEA), *World Energy Outlook* (Paris: Organisation for Economic Co-operation and Development, 1982); reactor cancellations in the U.S. are from Atomic Industrial Forum, Washington, D.C., private communication, November 14, 1983.

4. This illustration compares the amount of nuclear electricity and firewood purchased by end users in 1982, expressed in equivalent energy units. Nuclear power data and conversion factors are from U.S. Department of Energy (DOE), Energy Information Administration (EIA), *1982 Annual Energy Review* (Washington, D.C.: 1983). Wood use estimate is from U.S. Department of Agriculture (USDA) and DOE, *A Biomass Energy Production and Use Plan for the United States, 1983–90,* Agricultural Economic Report No. 505 (Wash-

ington, D.C.: 1983). Increase in U.S. wood use is from DOE, *Estimates of U.S. Wood Energy Consumption from 1949 to 1981* (Washington, D.C.: U.S. Government Printing Office, 1982).

5. California Energy Commission, "Large California Wind Projects Installed in 1981 and 1982," and "Large-Scale California Wind Projects Planned for 1983," Sacramento, Calif., unpublished, 1983. Residential electrical needs estimated by Worldwatch Institute.

6. The current status of alcohol fuels in Brazil is reviewed by James Bruce, "Brazil's Alcohol Export Prospects Shrink But Domestic Mart Continues Growth," *Journal of Commerce,* April 5, 1983, and "Brazil's Alcohol Project Flourishing," *Journal of Commerce,* June 1, 1983; for a more critical review, see Peter T. Kilborn, "A Switch to Alcohol As Automobile Fuel is Gaining in Brazil," *New York Times,* November 12, 1983.

7. For waste paper recovery in the Netherlands and Japan, see United Nations Food and Agriculture Organization (FAO), Secretariat, Advisory Committee on Pulp and Paper, "Waste Paper Data 1978–80," prepared for 22nd session of Advisory Committee, Rome, May 25–27, 1981; U.S. container deposit legislation is reviewed in William K. Shireman et al., *Can and Bottle Bills: the CalPIRG-ELS Study Group Report* (Stanford, Calif.: California Public Interest Research Group and the Stanford Environmental Law Society, 1981); for worldwide recycling of aluminum, see Leonard L. Fischman, *World*

Mineral Trends and U.S. Supply Problems (Washington, D.C.: Resources for the Future, 1980) and The Aluminum Association, Inc., *Aluminum Statistical Review for 1981* (Washington, D.C.: 1982).

8. For a review of China's population policies, see H. Yuan Tien, "China: Demographic Billionaire," *Population Bulletin* (Washington, D.C.: Population Reference Bureau, April 1983).

9. Estimate of India's ultimate stationary population is from World Bank, *World Development Report 1983* (New York: Oxford University Press, 1983).

10. South Korea's reforestation program is discussed in Erik Eckholm, *Planting for the Future: Forestry for Human Needs* (Washington, D.C.: Worldwatch Institute, February 1979); Gujarat's program is described in Madhav Gadgil, S. Narenda Prasad, and Rauf Ali, *Forest Management in India: A Critical Review* (Bombay: Centre for Monitoring Indian Economy, 1982).

11. For topsoil loss, see calculations in Chapter 4, "Conserving Soils."

12. Based on grain production data for regions where grain is consumed directly rather than converted into livestock products, reported in USDA, Economic Research Service (ERS), *World Indices of Agricultural and Food Production 1950–1982* (unpublished printout) (Washington, D.C.: 1983).

13. Grain export data are from USDA, Foreign Agricultural Service (FAS), *Foreign Agriculture Circular* FG-13-82, Washington, D.C., April 1982; oil export data are from U.S. Central Intelligence Agency, *International Energy Statistical Review* (Washington, D.C.: 1982), and British Petroleum Company, *BP Statistical Review of World Energy* (London: 1982).

14. World military expenditures are from Stockholm International Peace Research Institute, *World Armaments and Disarmament, SIPRI Yearbook 1983* (New York: Taylor &

Francis, Inc., 1983). Per capita expenditure was calculated with world population from Population Reference Bureau, *1983 World Population Data Sheet* (Washington, D.C.: 1983).

15. Developing countries imported armaments in 1980 worth some $19.5 billion and wheat and coarse grains valued at $19.45 billion. Arms import data are from Ruth Leger Sivard, *World Military and Social Expenditures 1983* (Washington, D.C.: World Priorities, 1983); grain import data are from USDA, FAS, *Foreign Agriculture Circular* FG-28-83, Washington, D.C., September 1983.

16. Sivard, *World Military and Social Expenditures.*

17. For a discussion of the relation of advanced recovery techniques to future oil production levels, see IEA, *World Energy Outlook;* for a review of the range of estimates of ultimately recoverable reserves, see Richard Heede, *A World Geography of Recoverable Carbon Resources in the Context of Possible Climatic Change* (Boulder, Colo.: University of Colorado and National Center for Atmospheric Research, 1983).

18. Estimate of excessive soil erosion in the United States is based on total acreage affected by sheet and rill erosion from USDA, *Soil and Water Resources Conservation Act: 1980 Appraisal, Part II* (Washington, D.C.: 1980), and acreage in Great Plains states affected by wind erosion from USDA, Soil Conservation Service, and Iowa State University Statistical Laboratory, *Basic Statistics 1977 National Resources Inventory*, Statistical Bulletin No. 686 (Washington, D.C.: 1982).

19. FAO, Forest Resources Division, *Tropical Forest Resources*, Forestry Paper 30 (Rome: 1982).

20. George H. Tomlinson and C. Ross Silversides, *Acid Depostion and Forest Damage—the European Linkage* (Montreal, Que.: Domtar, Inc., 1982).

21. Council on Environmental Quality, *Environmental Quality 1982* (Washington,

D.C.: U.S. Government Printing Office, 1983).

22. FAO, *Production Yearbook* (Rome: annual, various years).

23. FAO, *Yearbook of Fishery Statistics* (Rome: annual, various years).

24. For a review of the value of genetic resources, see "Genes from the Wild," Earthscan Briefing Document No. 36, Earthscan, Washington, D.C., 1983.

25. Statistics on the world tanker fleet can be found in *Shipping Statistics and Economics* (London: H. P. Drewry, Ltd., monthly); for a discussion of shipbreaking, see Roger Vielvoye, "Scrapping Supertankers," *Oil and Gas Journal*, February 14, 1983.

26. Robert J. Enright, "World Oil Flow, Refining Capacity Down Sharply; Reserves Increase," *Oil and Gas Journal*, December 27, 1982.

27. Figure on unemployment in the auto industry is from U.S. Department of Transportation, *The U.S. Automobile Industry, 1980* (Washington, D.C.: 1981); U.S. and Japanese auto production data are from Motor Vehicle Manufacturers Association, *Motor Vehicle Facts and Figures '82* (Detroit, Mich.: 1982).

28. Data on auto dealers are from U.S. Bureau of the Census, *Census of Retail Trade* (Washington, D.C.: various years); data on gasoline service stations are from *National Petroleum News Fact Book* (Chicago, Ill.: Hunter Publishing Co., 1983).

29. Estimate of solar equipment sales in California is from Jerry Yudelson, Solar Initiative, Oakland, Calif., private communication, November 11, 1983; for alcohol fuels in Brazil, see Bruce, "Brazil's Alcohol Export Prospects Shrink," and "Brazil's Alcohol Project Flourishing"; the resurgence of the bicycle during the seventies is discussed in Lester R. Brown, Christopher Flavin, and Colin Norman, *Running on Empty: The Future of the Automobile in an Oil-Short World* (New York: W. W. Norton & Co., 1979).

30. Imports and recovery of scrap paper in South Korea and Mexico are discussed in William U. Chandler, *Materials Recycling: The Virtue of Necessity* (Washington, D.C.: Worldwatch Institute, October 1983); the electric arc furnace is discussed in U.S. Office of Technology Assessment, *Technology and Steel Industry Competitiveness* (Washington, D.C.: U.S. Government Printing Office, 1980).

31. For the role of Siberia in the Soviet aluminum industry, see Theodore Shabad, "The Soviet Aluminum Industry," *Raw Materials Report*, March 1983.

32. James Bruce, "Brazil May Join Top Aluminum Producers," *Journal of Commerce*, July 16, 1983.

33. The collapse of the Peruvian anchovy fishery is discussed in Erik Eckholm, *Losing Ground: Environmental Stress and World Food Prospects* (New York: W. W. Norton & Co., 1976); for statistics on the fish catch in Peru and other countries, see FAO, *Yearbook of Fishery Statistics*.

34. USDA, *Soil and Water Resources Conservation Act (RCA), Summary of Appraisal, Parts I and II, and Program Review Draft 1980* (Washington, D.C.: 1980).

35. *Economic Report of the President* (Washington, D.C.: U.S. Government Printing Office, 1983).

36. Ibid.

37. Developing country and Eastern bloc debt estimates by Worldwatch Institute based on various press reports.

38. Nigeria data are from FAO, *Country Tables of Production, Trade and Consumption of Forest Products, Africa 1970–1980* (Rome: 1982).

39. James L. Rowe, Jr., "Latin America Loans Taking Toll on Banks," *Washington Post*, November 6, 1983.

40. World Bank, *World Debt Tables* (Washington, D.C.: 1983).

41. International Monetary Fund, *Monthly Financial Statistics 1980* and *1983 Yearbooks* (Washington, D.C.: 1980 and 1983); General Agreement on Tariffs and Trade, *International Trade 1982/1983* (Geneva: 1983).

42. World oil consumption data are from API, *Basic Petroleum Data Book;* world oil trade data are from British Petroleum Company, *BP Statistical Review.*

Chapter 2. Stabilizing Population

1. Information on growth rates, referred to throughout this chapter, and other demographic parameters for international comparison can be found in Population Reference Bureau, *World Population Data Sheet* (Washington, D.C.: annual).

2. Population growth in recent years is reviewed in the United Nations, Department of International Economic and Social Affairs (DIESA), *World Population Trends and Policies—1981 Monitoring Report, Volume 1,* Population Studies, No. 79 (New York: 1982); 1983 estimates are from Population Reference Bureau, *World Population Data Sheet.*

3. Population. Reference Bureau, *World Population Data Sheet.*

4. Stephen Rapawy and Godfrey Baldwin, "Demographic Trends in the Soviet Union: 1950–2000," in Joint Economic Committee, U.S. Congress, *Soviet Economy in the 1980s: Problems and Prospects* (Washington, D.C.: U.S. Government Printing Office, 1983); Centre for Monitoring Indian Economy, *Basic Statistics Relating to the Indian Economy Vol. 2: States* (Bombay: 1982).

5. Population Reference Bureau, *World Population Data Sheet.*

6. Ibid.

7. H. Yuan Tien, "China: Demographic Billionaire," *Population Bulletin* (Washington, D.C.: Population Reference Bureau, April 1983); United Nations DIESA, *Demographic Yearbook Special Issue: Historical Supplement* (New York: 1979).

8. John Knodel, Nibhon Debavalya, and Peerasit Kamnuansilpa, "Thailand's Continuing Reproductive Revolution," *International Family Planning Perspectives,* September 1980; Peerasit Kamnuansilpa, Aphichat Chamratrithirong, and John Knodel, "Thailand's Reproductive Revolution: An Update," *International Family Planning Perspectives,* June 1982.

9. Henry P. David, "Mechai's Way," *People* (London), Vol. 9, No. 4, 1982.

10. Sergio Diaz-Briquets and Lisandro Perez, "Cuba: The Demography of Revolution," *Population Bulletin* (Washington, D.C.: Population Reference Bureau, April 1981); Henry P. David, "Cuba: Low Fertility, Relatively High Abortion," *Intercom,* Population Reference Bureau, Washington, D.C., July/August 1983.

11. Terence H. Hull, V.J. Hull, and M. Singarimbun, "Indonesia's Family Planning Story: Success and Challenge," *Population Bulletin* (Washington, D.C.: Population Reference Bureau, November 1977); Geoffrey McNicoll and Masri Singarimbun, "Fertility Decline in Indonesia I: Background and Proximate Determinants," and "Fertility Decline in Indonesia II: Analysis and Interpretation," Center for Policy Studies Working Papers, Nos. 92 and 93 (New York: Population Council, 1982).

12. John S. Nagel, "Mexico's Population Policy Turnaround," *Population Bulletin* (Washington, D.C.: Population Reference Bureau, December 1978); Jorge Martinez Manautou, ed., *The Demographic Revolution in Mexico 1970–1980* (Mexico City: Mexican Institute of Social Security, 1982).

13. Debbie C. Tennison, "Europe is Adjusting to a Long Recession That Some Economists See as Permanent," *Wall Street Journal,* December 2, 1982.

14. Economic Commission for Africa quote and World Bank assessment both from

World Bank, *Sub-Saharan Africa: Progress Report on Development Prospects and Programs* (Washington, D.C.: 1983)

15. Population Reference Bureau, *World Population Data Sheet.*

16. U.S. Department of Agriculture (USDA), Economic Research Service (ERS), *World Indices of Agricultural and Food Production, 1950–82* (unpublished printout) (Washington, D.C.: 1983).

17. World Bank, *Accelerated Development in Sub-Saharan Africa: An Agenda for Action* (Washington, D.C.: 1983).

18. Quoted in John Harte and Robert Socolow, eds., *The Patient Earth* (New York: Holt, Rinehart and Winston, 1971).

19. United Nations, *Prospects of Population: Methodology and Assumptions,* Population Studies No. 67 (New York: 1979).

20. Estimates of hypothetical stationary populations are from World Bank, *World Development Report 1983* (New York: Oxford University Press, 1983); current-year populations are from Population Reference Bureau, *World Population Data Sheet.*

21. See, for example, Lester R. Brown and Pamela Shaw, *Six Steps to a Sustainable Society* (Washington, D.C.: Worldwatch Institute, March 1982). For oil production trends, see Chapter 3 of this report; grain production trend is from USDA, ERS, *World Indices.*

22. Council on Environmental Quality and U.S. Department of State, *The Global 2000 Report to the President, Volume I* (Washington, D.C.: U.S. Government Printing Office, 1980).

23. Wassily Leontief et al., *The Future of the World Economy* (New York: Oxford University Press, 1977).

24. Gerald O. Barney and Associates, Arlington, Va., private communication, October 26, 1983.

25. Tien, "China: Demographic Billionaire."

26. Elizabeth J. Croll, "Production Versus Reproduction: A Threat to China's Development Strategy," *World Development,* June 1983.

27. See, for example, John Ratcliffe, "Kerala: Testbed for Transition Theory," *Populi,* U.N. Fund for Population Activities, New York, Vol. 5, No. 2, 1978, David Winder, "Literacy—the third world's beacon of hope," *Christian Science Monitor,* May 12, 1983, and W. Parker Maudlin, "The Determinants of Fertility Decline in Developing Countries: An Overview of the Available Evidence," *International Family Planning Perspectives,* September 1982.

28. Author's estimate, based on Bruce Stokes, *Filling the Family Planning Gap* (Washington, D.C.: Worldwatch Institute, May 1977) and subsequent progress in family planning programs in China and other countries.

29. Robert Lightbourne, Jr., and Susheela Singh, with Cynthia P. Green, "The World Fertility Survey: Charting Global Childbearing," *Population Bulletin* (Washington, D.C.: Population Reference Bureau, March 1982); Mary Mederios Kent and Ann Larson, "Family Size Preferences: Evidence From the World Fertility Surveys," *Reports on the World Fertility Survey 4* (Washington, D.C.: Population Reference Bureau, April 1982).

30. Nuray Fincancioglu, "Carrots and Sticks," *People* (London), Vol. 9, No. 4, 1982.

31. Ibid.

32. Pi-chao Chen, "11 M Chinese Opt for Only One Child Glory Certificate," *People* (London), Vol. 9, No. 4, 1982; Planned Parenthood Federation of Korea, *New Population Policy in Korea: Social and Legal Support for Small Families* (Seoul: 1982); Saw Swee-Hock, *Population Control for Zero Growth in Singapore* (Singapore: Oxford University Press, 1980).

33. Figures on current payments in India are from Pravin Visaria and Leela Visaria,

"India's Population: Second and Growing," *Population Bulletin* (Washington, D.C.: Population Reference Bureau, October 1981); Indian wage data are from Centre for Monitoring Indian Economy, *Basic Statistics;* Bangladesh information is from Michael Jordan, U.S. Department of State, Washington, D.C., private communication, January 5, 1983.

34. Judith Jacobsen, *Promoting Population Stabilization: Incentives for Small Families* (Washington, D.C.: Worldwatch Institute, June 1983).

35. For an early review of community incentives, see Lenni W. Kangas, "Integrated Incentives for Fertility Control," *Science,* September 25, 1970; efforts in Thailand are described in Henry P. David, "Incentives, Reproductive Behavior, and Integrated Community Development in Asia," *Studies in Family Planning,* May 1982; Indonesian efforts are described in Hull, Hull, and Singarimbun, "Indonesia's Family Planning Story."

Chapter 3. Reducing Dependence on Oil

1. World oil consumption data are estimates of demand for refined petroleum products from American Petroleum Institute (API), *Basic Petroleum Data Book* (Washington, D.C.: 1983). The 40 billion barrel estimate is based on a projection of 7 percent annual growth in consumption from the 1973 world oil consumption of 20.4 billion barrels.

2. The projection of hypothetical world oil consumption is based on the growth rate described in note 1; proven reserves of oil are from API, *Basic Petroleum Data Book;* estimate of ultimately recoverable reserves is from M. King Hubbert, "World Energy Resources," presented to the Tenth Commonwealth Mining and Metallurgical Congress, Ottawa, Canada, 1974.

3. Robert U. Ayres, for Oak Ridge National Laboratory, *Worldwide Transportation/Energy Demand Forecast: 1975–2000* (Spring-

field, Va.: National Technical Information Service, 1978).

4. Patricia Smith, U.S. Department of Energy (DOE), Washington, D.C., private communication, June 15, 1983.

5. DOE, Energy Information Administration (EIA), *1982 Annual Energy Review* (Washington, D.C.: 1983).

6. API, *Basic Petroleum Data Book;* DOE, EIA, *Monthly Energy Review,* Washington, D.C., August 1983; per capita consumption calculated with U.S. population data from U.S. Department of Commerce, Bureau of the Census, *Statistical Abstract of the United States, 1982–83* (Washington, D.C.: U.S. Government Printing Office, 1982).

7. DOE, EIA, *1982 Annual Energy Review.*

8. Philip F. Palmedo and Pamela Baldwin, *The Contribution of Renewable Resources and Energy Conservation As Alternatives to Imported Oil in Developing Countries* (Port Jefferson, N.Y.: Energy/Development International, 1980).

9. For example, coal delivered to power plants in 1980 at $28.76 per short ton (containing 21.3 million Btu) had an energy-content cost of $1.35 per million Btu. Residual fuel oil (#6) at 55.1¢ per gallon in 1980 and 5.8 million Btu per 42-gallon barrel carried an energy content cost of $3.97 per million Btu. From DOE, EIA, *1982 Annual Energy Review.*

10. DOE, EIA, *1982 Annual Energy Review.*

11. See Chapter 8, "Rivers of Energy," in Daniel Deudney and Christopher Flavin, *Renewable Energy: The Power to Choose* (New York: W.W. Norton & Co., 1983), and World Bank, Energy Department, "The Energy Transition in Developing Countries," Report No. 4442, Washington, D.C., April 15, 1983.

12. See Chapter 7, "Nuclear Power," in International Energy Agency (IEA), *World Energy Outlook* (Paris: Organisation for Economic Co-operation and Development, 1982).

13. Kenneth E. Skog and Irene A. Watterson, *Residential Fuelwood Use in the United States: 1980–81* (Madison, Wisc.: Forest Products Laboratory, U.S. Forest Service, U.S. Department of Agriculture, 1983).

14. Romanian oil production from DOE, EIA, *International Energy Annual 1981* (Washington, D.C., 1982); reviews of Soviet energy consumption patterns and fuel substitution strategies are found in Jonathan B. Stein, "Soviet Energy," *Energy Policy*, December 1981, and in Thane Gustafson, "Soviet Energy Policy," and Laurie Kurtzweg and Albina Tretyakova, "Soviet Energy Consumption: Structure and Future Prospects," both in Joint Economic Committee, U.S. Congress, *Soviet Economy in the 1980s: Problems and Prospects* (Washington, D.C.: U.S. Government Printing Office, 1983).

15. Estimates of alcohol production for automotive fuels in Brazil are from World Energy Industry, *The Energy Decade 1970–80* (Cambridge, Mass.: Ballinger Publishing Co., 1982), with estimates for 1980–82 by Worldwatch Institute based on data in "Brazil's Alcohol Export Prospects Shrink But Domestic Mart Continues Growth," *Journal of Commerce*, April 5, 1983, and "Brazil's Alcohol Project Flourishing," *Journal of Commerce*, June 1, 1983.

16. Emil Parente, Fluor Corporation, Anaheim, Calif., private communication, August 17, 1983.

17. DOE, EIA, *International Energy Annual 1981*.

18. "Towards a Minimum Oil Economy: Progress of Eight Countries," *OECD Observer*, July 1981.

19. B. H. S. Jayewardene, managing editor, *Ceylon Daily News*, private communication, August 27, 1979.

20. A blueprint for achieving the energy efficiency potential of buildings is outlined in Avraham Shama, "Energy Conservation in U.S. Buildings," *Energy Policy*, June 1983.

21. Lee Schipper and Andrea Ketoff, "Home Energy Use in Nine OECD Countries, 1960–80," *Energy Policy*, June 1983.

22. "Towards a Minimum Oil Economy," *OECD Observer;* Lester R. Brown, *Building a Sustainable Society* (New York: W.W. Norton & Co., 1981); Information Office, Embassy of France, Washington, D.C., private communication, June 2, 1981.

23. "Japan Advances in Diversifying Energy Sources," *Oil and Gas Journal*, January 18, 1982.

24. John Vinocur, "Germans Insist on Speed," *New York Times*, July 1, 1979.

25. "Towards a Minimum Oil Economy," *OECD Observer*.

26. Jose Goldemberg, "Energy Policies in Brazil," *Economic and Political Weekly*, February 26, 1983.

27. Gustafson, "Soviet Energy Policy."

28. Ibid.; Kurtzweg and Tretyakova, "Soviet Energy Consumption."

29. István Dobozi, "The 'Invisible' Source of 'Alternative' Energy," *Natural Resources Forum*, July 1983.

30. Vaclav Smil, "Energy Development in China," *Energy Policy*, June 1981.

31. DOE, EIA, *1982 Annual Energy Review;* "Midyear Review and Forecast," *Oil and Gas Journal*, July 25, 1983.

32. IEA, *World Energy Outlook.*

33. Ibid.

34. DOE, EIA, *1982 Annual Energy Outlook With Projections to 1990* (Washington, D.C.: 1983); Canadian survey from IEA, *World Energy Outlook;* "Slow Growth Seen for Synthetic Fuels," *Oil and Gas Journal*, May 2, 1983.

35. J.C. Barros, Petrobras, New York, N.Y., private communication, October 3, 1983; William Orme, Jr., "Mexico Raises Gasoline Prices," *Journal of Commerce*, April 8,

1983; "Yugoslavia Begins Gasoline Rationing to Counter Shortage," *Wall Street Journal*, October 11, 1982; "Poles Facing Further Cuts in Gasoline," *Journal of Commerce*, September 30, 1983.

Chapter 4. Conserving Soils

1. Anson R. Bertrand, "Overdrawing the Nation's Research Accounts," *Journal of Soil and Water Conservation*, May/June 1980.

2. The impact of land degradation on the patterns of daily life is made powerfully clear in "The Fragile Mountain," a documentary produced by Sandra Nichols and shown on the PBS series *Nova* on October 19, 1982.

3. P. O. Aina et al., quoted in R. Lal, "Effective Conservation Farming Systems for the Humid Tropics," in American Society of Agronomy, *Soil Erosion and Conservation in the Tropics*, ASA Special Publication No. 43 (Madison, Wisc.: 1982).

4. S. A. El-Swaify and E. W. Dangler, "Rainfall Erosion in the Tropics: A State-of-the-Art," in American Society of Agronomy, *Soil Erosion*.

5. These and other conservation practices introduced in the thirties are discussed in Donald Worster, *The Dust Bowl* (New York: Oxford University Press, 1979), especially in Chapter 14, "Making Two Blades of Grass Grow."

6. Figures on summer fallow are from U.S. Department of Agriculture (USDA), Economic Research Service (ERS), *Economic Indicators of the Farm Sector: Production and Efficiency Statistics, 1981* (Washington, D.C.: U.S. Government Printing Office, 1983).

7. Kenneth Grant, "Erosion in 1973–74: The Record and the Challenge," *Journal of Soil and Water Conservation*, January/February 1975; USDA, Soil Conservation Service, and Iowa State University Statistical Laboratory, *Basic Statistics 1977 National Resources Inventory*, Statistical Bulletin No. 686 (Washington, D.C.: 1982).

8. USDA, ERS, "World Agriculture Outlook and Situation," Washington, D.C., June 1983.

9. Wouter Tims, *Nigeria: Options for Long-Term Development* (Baltimore, Md.: Johns Hopkins University Press, for the World Bank, 1974).

10. John M. Schiller et al., "Development of Areas of Shifting Cultivation in North Thailand 'Thai-Australia Land Development Project,' " in American Society of Agronomy, *Soil Erosion*.

11. R. F. Watters, *Shifting Cultivation in Latin America* (Rome: United Nations Food and Agriculture Organization, 1971).

12. Sheldon Judson, "Erosion of the Land, or What's Happening to Our Continents," *American Scientist*, July/August 1968.

13. Jiang Degi et al., "Soil Erosion and Conservation in the Wuding River Valley" (Beijing, China: Yellow River Conservancy Commission, April 1980), cited in El-Swaify and Dangler, "Rainfall Erosion in the Tropics"; U.S. Water Resources Council, *The Nation's Water Resources 1975–2000, Volume 2: Water Quantity, Quality and Related Land Considerations* (Washington, D.C.: U.S. Government Printing Office, 1978).

14. Ganges data from American Society of Agronomy, *Soil Erosion*; Mississippi data from U.S. Water Resources Council, *The Nation's Water Resources 1975–2000*.

15. J. M. Prospero et al., "Atmospheric Transport of Soil Dust from Africa to South America," *Nature*, February 12, 1981.

16. Josef R. Parrington et al., "Asian Dust: Seasonal Transport to the Hawaiian Islands," *Science*, April 8, 1983.

17. Data on soil loss from water erosion are from USDA, *The Soil and Water Resources Conservation Act: 1980 Appraisal, Part II* (Washington, D.C.: 1980); data on wind erosion are from USDA, *National Resources Inventory*. The "excessive" loss of topsoil from wind erosion is probably understated when using the five-

ton-per-acre standard because of the slower rate of formation of Great Plains soils and the diminished opportunity to offset productivity losses with additional fertilization.

18. K. G. Tejwani, Land Use Consultants International, New Delhi, private communication, July 3, 1983; Centre for Science and Environment, *The State Of India's Environment 1982* (New Delhi: 1982).

19. Quoted in Vera Rich, "Soil First," *Nature*, February 12, 1982.

20. Abandoned cropland figure cited is from U.S. Central Intelligence Agency, *U.S.S.R. Agricultural Atlas* (Washington, D.C.: 1974); Thane Gustafson, "Transforming Soviet Agriculture: Brezhnev's Gamble on Land Improvement," *Public Policy*, Summer 1977.

21. P. Poletayev and S. Yashukova, "Environmental Protection and Agricultural Production," *Ekonomika Sel'skogo Khozyaystva* (Moscow), November 1978.

22. P. S. Tregubov, "Soil Rainstorm Erosion and Its Control in the U.S.S.R.," presented to the International Conference on Soil Erosion and Conservation, Honolulu, Hawaii, January 16–22, 1983; U.S. erosion rates are from USDA, *National Resources Inventory*.

23. National Soil Erosion-Soil Productivity Research Planning Committee, USDA, Science and Education Administration, "Soil Erosion Effects on Soil Productivity: A Research Perspective," *Journal of Soil and Water Conservation*, March/April 1981.

24. Ibid.

25. G. W. Langdale et al., "Corn Yield Reduction on Eroded Southern Piedmont Soils," *Journal of Soil and Water Conservation*, September/October 1979.

26. W. E. Larson, F. J. Pierce, and R. H. Dowdy, "The Threat of Soil Erosion to Long-Term Crop Production," *Science*, February 4, 1983.

27. Research by R. Lal of the International Institute of Tropical Agriculture, Ibadan, Nigeria, cited by El-Swaify and Dangler, "Rainfall Erosion in the Tropics." Even more pronounced yield reductions are investigated in J. S. C. Mbagwu, R. Lal, and T. W. Scott, "Effects of Desurfacing on Alfisols and Ultisols in Southern Nigeria I: Crop Performance," unpublished.

28. El-Swaify and Dangler, "Rainfall Erosion in the Tropics." The effects of environmental degradation on the life span of the Mangla Reservoir are discussed in Erik Eckholm, *Losing Ground: Environmental Stress and World Food Prospects* (New York: W.W. Norton & Co., 1976).

29. U.S. Agency for International Development, *Environmental and Natural Resource Management in Developing Countries: A Report to Congress* (Washington, D.C.: 1979).

30. Eckholm, *Losing Ground.*

31. B. B. Vohra, *Land and Water Management Problems in India*, Training Volume 8 (New Delhi: Ministry of Home Affairs, 1982).

32. Dr. Frank Wadsworth, "Deforestation —Death to the Panama Canal," in U.S. Department of State, Office of Environmental Affairs, *Proceedings of the U.S. Strategy Conference on Tropical Deforestation*, June 12–14, 1978 (Washington, D.C.: 1978).

33. A comprehensive introduction to the techniques and advantages of conservation tillage is provided in William A. Hayes, *Minimum Tillage Farming* and H. M. Young, *No-Tillage Farming* (bound in one volume) (Brookfield, Wisc.: No-Till Farmer, Inc., 1982).

34. Robert J. Gray, American Farmland Trust, statement before the Subcommittee on Conservation, Credit and Rural Development, Committee on Agriculture, U.S. House of Representatives, Washington, D.C., May 4, 1983.

35. Poletayev and Yashukova, "Environmental Protection."

36. National Soil Erosion-Soil Productivity Research Planning Committee, "Soil Erosion Effects on Soil Productivity."

37. The Erosion-Productivity Impact Calculator is described in USDA, Soil Conservation Service, National Bulletin No. 450-3-5, Washington, D.C., January 17, 1983. The Productivity Index (PI) is described in Larson, Pierce, and Dowdy, "The Threat of Soil Erosion to Long-Term Crop Production." International work on the PI is being coordinated by the International Federation of Institutes for Advanced Study (IFIAS) program, "Analyzing Biospheric Change," Delft, The Netherlands.

38. Roosevelt's personal commitment to soil conservation and particularly to the shelterbelt idea is recalled in Richard Strout, "Windbreaks: FDR Legacy," *Christian Science Monitor*, February 8, 1982.

39. B. B. Vohra, "Managing India's Land and Water Resources," Ministry of Petroleum, New Delhi, August 1978.

40. Alfredo Sfeir-Younis, Agriculture and Rural Development Department, World Bank, private communication, May 26, 1982.

41. Lloyd K. Fischer, discussion comments, in Harold G. Halcrow, Earl O. Heady, and Melvin L. Cotner, eds., *Soil Conservation Policies, Institutions and Incentives* (Ankeny, Iowa: Soil Conservation Society of America, 1982).

42. Ken Cook, "Surplus Madness," *Journal of Soil and Water Conservation*, January/February 1983.

43. Symposia papers of the 12th International Congress of Soil Science, February 8–16, 1982, were published as *Desertification and Soils Policy* (New Delhi: Indian Society of Soil Science, 1982). Proceedings of the International Conference on Soil Erosion and Conservation, January 16–22, 1983, should be available in 1984; abstracts of papers presented at the conference can be obtained from the Department of Agronomy and Soil Science, University of Hawaii at Manoa, Honolulu, Hawaii. Proceedings of the ASA symposium were published in American Society of Agronomy, *Soil Erosion.*

Chapter 5. Protecting Forests

1. United Nations Food and Agriculture Organization (FAO), Forest Resources Division, *Tropical Forest Resources*, Forestry Paper 30 (Rome: 1982).

2. FAO Forest Resources Division, *Tropical Forest Resources;* United Nations Environment Programme, "The Global Assessment of Tropical Forest Resources," Nairobi, Kenya, April 1982.

3. Norman Myers, Consultant in Environment and Development, "Comments on 'Global Forests' by Roger A. Sedjo and Marion Clawson," Oxford, England, June 1983.

4. Norman Myers, *Conversion of Tropical Moist Forests* (Washington, D.C.: National Academy of Sciences, 1980); Robert J. A. Goodland, "Environmental Ranking of Amazonian Development Projects in Brazil," *Environmental Conservation*, Spring 1980.

5. FAO Forest Resources Division, *Tropical Forest Resources.*

6. Madhav Gadgil, S. Narenda Prasad, and Rauf Ali, *Forest Management in India: A Critical Review* (Bombay: Centre for Monitoring Indian Economy, 1982).

7. John S. Spears, "Small Farmers—Or the Tropical Forest Ecosystem? A Brief Review of Sustainable Land Use Systems for Tropical Forest Areas," presented to International Tropical Forestry Symposium, Yale University, New Haven, Conn., April 15–16, 1980; Michael Arnold, "New Approaches to Tropical Forestry: A Habitat for More Than Just Trees," *Ceres*, September/October 1979; John I. Zerbe et al., for Forest Products Laboratory, U.S. Forest Service, U.S. Department of Agriculture (USDA), *Forestry Activities and Deforestation Problems in Developing Countries*

(Washington, D.C.: U.S. Government Printing Office, 1980).

8. Spears, "Small Farmers—Or the Tropical Forest Ecosystem?"

9. FAO Forest Resources Division, *Tropical Forest Resources;* Myers, *Conversion of Tropical Moist Forests.*

10. Zerbe et al., *Forestry Activities in Developing Countries.*

11. Myers, *Conversion of Tropical Moist Forests.*

12. U.S. Department of State, Interagency Task Force on Tropical Forests, *The World's Tropical Forests: A Policy, Strategy, and Program for the United States* (Washington, D.C.: U.S. Government Printing Office, 1980).

13. Myers, *Conversion of Tropical Moist Forests;* Norman Myers, "The Hamburger Connection: How Central America's Forests Become North America's Hamburgers," *Ambio,* Vol. X, No. 1, 1981.

14. Myers, *Conversion of Tropical Moist Forests.*

15. FAO Forest Resources Division, *Tropical Forest Resources.*

16. Erik Eckholm, *Planting for the Future: Forestry for Human Needs* (Washington, D.C.: Worldwatch Institute, February 1979).

17. Myers, *Conversion of Tropical Moist Forests.*

18. FAO Forest Resources Division, *Tropical Forest Resources.*

19. Myers, *Conversion of Tropical Moist Forests.*

20. The Federal Minister of Food, Agriculture, and Forestry, "Forest Damage Due to Air Pollution: The Situation in the Federal Republic of Germany," Bonn, West Germany, November 1982; results of 1983 forest survey are described in "One-Third of German Trees Hit By Acid Rain," *New Scientist,* October 27, 1983.

21. George H. Tomlinson and C. Ross Silversides, *Acid Deposition and Forest Damage—the European Linkage* (Montreal, Que.: Domtar, Inc., 1982).

22. Eugeniusz Pudlis, "Poland's Plight: Environment Damaged from Air Pollution and Acid Rain," *Ambio,* Vol. XII, No. 2, 1983.

23. Hubert W. Vogelmann, "Catastrophe on Camels Hump," *Natural History,* November 1982.

24. Federal Minister of Food, Agriculture, and Forestry, "Forest Damage Due to Air Pollution."

25. Vogelmann, "Catastrophe on Camels Hump."

26. Gene E. Likens et al., "Acid Rain," *Scientific American,* October 1979.

27. Federal Minister of Food, Agriculture, and Forestry, "Forest Damage Due to Air Pollution."

28. Gregory S. Wetstone and Armin Rosencranz, *Acid Rain in Europe and North America: National Responses to an International Problem* (Washington, D.C.: Environmental Law Institute, 1983).

29. National Research Council, Committee on the Atmosphere and the Biosphere, *Atmosphere-Biosphere Interactions: Toward A Better Understanding of the Ecological Consequences of Fossil Fuel Combustion* (Washington, D.C.: National Academy Press, 1981).

30. National Research Council, *Atmosphere-Biosphere Interactions.*

31. Bernhard Ulrich, "Dangers for the Forest Ecosystem Due to Acid Precipitation," translated for U.S. Environmental Protection Agency by Literature Research Company, Annandale, Va., undated.

32. Vogelmann, "Catastrophe on Camels Hump."

33. Debate between John Fraser, M.P., and John Madigan, U.S. Representative, Washington, D.C., October 25, 1982.

34. Vogelmann, "Catastrophe on Camels Hump."

35. John J. Metzler, "Germany Battles Acid-Rain Pollution," *Journal of Commerce*, April 13, 1983; Dr. Heinz D. Gregor, West German Federal Environmental Agency, discussion at Acid Rain Panel, Global Tomorrow Coalition Conference, Washington, D.C., June 2, 1983.

36. Swedish Ministry of Agriculture, Environment '82 Committee, *Acidification Today and Tomorrow* (Stockholm: 1982).

37. FAO, *Regional Tables of Production, Trade and Consumption of Forest Products—World, Economic Classes and Regions: 1970–1980* (Rome: 1982).

38. National Academy of Sciences, *Firewood Crops: Shrub and Tree Species for Energy Production* (Washington, D.C.: 1980); Eckholm, *Planting for the Future.*

39. FAO, Forest Resources Division, *Forest Products Prices, 1962–1981*, Forestry Paper 38 (Rome: 1982).

40. Ibid.; Vandana Shiva, H.C. Sharatchandra, and J. Bandyopadhyay, *Social, Economic and Ecological Impact of Social Forestry in Kolar* (Bangalore: Indian Institute of Management, 1981).

41. FAO Forest Resources Division, *Forest Products Prices, 1962–1981.*

42. FAO Forest Resources Division, *Tropical Forest Resources.*

43. Gadgil, Prasad, and Ali, *Forest Management in India.*

44. John Spears, "Preserving Watershed Environments," *Unasylva*, No. 137, 1982.

45. National Environmental Protection Council, *Philippine Environmental Quality 1977*, First Annual Report (Manila: 1977).

46. Earthscan Briefing Document No. 34A, Earthscan, Washington, D.C., May 1983; Catherine Caufield, *Tropical Moist Forests: The Resource, the People, the Threat* (London: Earthscan, 1982).

47. Myers, *Conversion of Tropical Moist Forests;* George Ledec, "The Political Economy of Tropical Deforestation," presented to the Second World Congress on Land Policy, Cambridge, Mass., June 20–24, 1983; FAO Forest Resources Division, *Tropical Forest Resources.*

48. S. L. Pringle, "Tropical Moist Forests in World Demand, Supply, and Trade," *Unasylva*, Nos. 112–113, 1976.

49. Myers, *Conversion of Tropical Moist Forests.*

50. Pringle, "Tropical Moist Forests"; Alan Grainger, "The State of the World's Tropical Forests," *The Ecologist*, January/February 1980.

51. FAO, *Yearbooks of Forest Products* (Rome: 1975 and 1981); FAO, *Country Tables of Production, Trade and Consumption of Forest Products* (Rome: 1982).

52. Pringle, "Tropical Moist Forests."

53. Ledec, "Political Economy of Tropical Deforestation"; Indonesian wood processing plans noted in *Unasylva*, No. 135, 1982.

54. Ricardo Ortiz, "An Interview with Marco Antonio Flores Rodas," Assistant Director-General, FAO Forestry Department, *Ceres*, July/August 1981.

55. Eckholm, *Planting for the Future;* Erik Eckholm, *UNICEF and the Household Fuels Crisis* (New York: UNICEF, 1983).

56. Gadgil, Prasad, and Ali, *Forest Management in India.*

57. Shiva, Sharatchandra, and Bandyopadhyay, *Social Forestry in Kolar;* Vandana Shiva, H. C. Sharatchandra, and J. Bandyopadhyay, "Social Forestry—No Solution within the Market," *Ecologist*, July/August 1982.

58. Shiva, Sharatchandra, and Bandyopadhyay, *Social Forestry in Kolar.*

59. Prem Shankar Jha, "Farm Forestry Under Attack: Equity Versus Growth," *Times of India*, August 2, 1983.

60. Turi Hammer, "Reforestation and Community Development in the Sudan," Energy in Developing Countries Series, Resources for the Future, Washington, D.C., September 1982, unpublished.

61. Calestous Juma, "Kenya: The Population Explodes and Fuelwood Disappears," *Unasylva*, No. 135, 1982.

62. R. Hosier et al., "Energy Planning in Developing Countries: Blunt Axe in a Forest of Problems?," *Ambio*, Vol. XI, No. 4, 1982; Bina Agarwal, "Diffusion of Rural Innovations: Some Analytical Issues and the Case of Wood-Burning Stoves," *World Development*, April 1983.

63. Michael Arnold, "New Approaches to Tropical Forestry: A Habitat for More than Just Trees," *Ceres*, September/October 1979.

64. Ibid.; Zerbe et al., *Forestry Activities in Developing Countries*.

65. Spears, "Small Farmers—Or the Tropical Forest Ecosystem?"

66. John Spears, "Preserving Watershed Environments," *Unasylva*, No. 137, 1982; Spears, "Small Farmers—Or the Tropical Forest Ecosystem?"

67. Roger A. Sedjo, "The Potential of U.S. Forestlands in the World Context," prepared for Conference on Coping with Pressures on U.S. Forestlands, Resources for the Future, Washington, D.C., March 30–31, 1981.

68. FAO Forest Resources Division, *Tropical Forest Resources*.

69. Data for these calculations are from Ibid. and FAO, *Regional Tables of Production, Trade and Consumption;* the population projection is from Population Reference Bureau, *1983 World Population Data Sheet* (Washington, D.C.: 1983).

70. FAO, Forest Resources Division, *World Forest Products: Demand and Supply 1990 and 2000*, Foresty Paper 29 (Rome: 1982).

71. Ibid.

72. "Big Log Sales to China Questionable in the Future," *Journal of Commerce*, June 24, 1983.

73. FAO Forest Resources Division, *World Forest Products: Demand and Supply 1990 and 2000*.

74. Noel D. Vietmeyer, "Tropical Tree Legumes: A Front Line Against Deforestation," *Ceres*, September/October 1979; National Research Council, *Mangium and Other Acacias of the Humid Tropics* (Washington, D.C.: National Academy Press, 1983); National Research Council, *Calliandra: A Versatile Small Tree for the Humid Tropics* (Washington, D.C.: National Academy Press, 1983); Elbert L. Little, Jr., *Common Fuelwood Crops: A Handbook for Their Identification* (Morgantown, W. Va.: Communi-Tech Associates, undated).

75. Vietmeyer, "Tropical Tree Legumes"; National Research Council, *Mangium and Other Acacias;* National Research Council, *Calliandra;* Little, *Common Fuelwood Crops*.

76. Norman Myers, "Stand and Deliver: Tropical Moist Forests," *IDRC Reports*, April 1981.

77. John Spears and Montague Yudelman, "Forests in Development," *Finance and Development*, December 1979; "The FAO Forestry Department's Programme of Work and Budget for 1982–83," *Unasylva*, No. 135, 1982; Spears, "Small Farmers—Or the Tropical Forest Ecosystem?"

78. Ortiz, "Interview with Marco Antonio Flores Rodas."

Chapter 6. Recycling Materials

1. See John H. Gibbons and William U. Chandler, *Energy: The Conservation Revolution* (New York: Plenum Publishing Company, 1981).

2. The analogy of the beverage container was first suggested by energy educator John

Yegge, formerly of Oak Ridge Associated Universities, Oak Ridge, Tennessee.

3. William E. Franklin, Marjorie Franklin, and Robert Hunt, *Waste Paper: The Future of a Resource* (New York: Franklin Associates and the American Paper Institute, 1982).

4. Some controversy exists regarding the carcinogenicity of benzopyrene.

5. Derived from R.C. Ziegler et al., "Environmental Impacts of Virgin and Recycled Steel and Aluminum," National Technical Information Service, Springfield, Va., 1976.

6. U.S. Office of Technology Assessment, *Wood Use: U.S. Competitiveness and Technology* (Washington, D.C.: U.S. Government Printing Office, 1983).

7. See "Wood and Plant Materials," *Science*, February 21, 1976, National Academy of Sciences, *Renewable Resources for Industrial Materials* (Washington, D.C.: 1976), Edgar Gaertner, "La Mort de la Foret," *Le Monde Diplomatique*, August 1983, and Chapter 5 of this report.

8. Marion Clawson, *The Economics of U.S. Nonindustrial Private Forests* (Washington, D.C.: Resources for the Future, 1979).

9. Thomas E. Ricks, "Timber Firms Moving to the South As Supplies in Northwest Diminish," *Wall Street Journal*, August 19, 1983.

10. Franklin, Franklin, and Hunt, *Waste Paper: The Future of a Resource.*

11. J. Rodney Edwards, American Paper Institute, New York, private communications, June 1983; Hershel Cutler, executive director, Institute of Scrap Iron and Steel, Washington, D.C., private communication, July 1983.

12. United Nations Food and Agriculture Organization (FAO), Secretariat, Advisory Committee on Pulp and Paper, "Waste Paper Data 1978–80," prepared for 22nd session of Advisory Committee, Rome, May 25–27, 1981.

13. Lester R. Brown, *Building A Sustainable Society* (New York: W.W. Norton & Co., 1981).

14. Organisation for Economic Co-operation and Development (OECD), *Economic Instruments in Solid Waste Management* (Paris: 1981).

15. The Clean Japan Center, *Saikuru No Chishiki* (Tokyo: 1983).

16. OECD, *Economic Instruments in Solid Waste Management.*

17. Clean Japan Center, *Saikuru No Chishiki.*

18. Geoffrey Murray, "Putting 220 tons of garbage a day where it belongs," *Christian Science Monitor*, March 10, 1983.

19. OECD, *Waste Paper Recovery* (Paris: 1979).

20. OECD, *Economic Instruments in Solid Waste Management.*

21. Janet Marinelli, "Recycling's Little Victories," *Environmental Action*, April 1982; Richard Hertzberg, "Islip, New York: Where Mandatory Recycling Works," *Resource Recycling* (Portland, Ore.), May/June, 1983; Elizabeth Gallagher, Assistant to the Commissioner of Environmental Control, Islip, New York, private communication, August 12, 1983.

22. Richard Hertzberg, "NARI's Look at State and Local Recycling Laws," *Resource Recycling* (Portland, Ore.), November/December 1982; OECD, *Economic Instruments in Solid Waste Management;* "W. Germany's waste exchange expands to nearby countries," *World Environment Report*, January 30, 1982.

23. Secretariat, FAO Advisory Committee, "Waste Paper Data"; Franklin, Franklin, and Hunt, *Waste Paper: The Future of a Resource.* The value of waste paper trade is estimated by using actual unpublished American Paper Institute data for U.S. exports and assuming that 40 percent of gross world trade in waste paper is American.

24. Franklin, Franklin, and Hunt, *Waste Paper: The Future of a Resource.*

25. See Ibid.

26. Franklin, Franklin, and Hunt, *Waste Paper: The Future of a Resource.*

27. John M. Bradley, "Cairo's Garbage Collectors Get Big World Bank Loan," *World Environment Report,* September 30, 1982; World Bank, press release, Washington, D.C., May 22, 1980.

28. Representative Ron Wyden (D-Oregon), "Use of Recovered Materials By Federal Agencies," fact sheet, Washington, D.C., May 10, 1983, describing H.R. 2867, amending the Resource Conservation and Recovery Act of 1976, 90 STAT. 2795; Daniel Saltzman, Legislative Assistant to Representative Wyden, Washington, D.C., private communication, August 12, 1983; Marinelli, "Recycling's Little Victories."

29. Edwards, private communications.

30. Mary Lou Van Deventer, "Whatever Happened To Recycling?," *Not Man Apart,* January 1983.

31. U.S. Office of Technology Assessment, *Industrial Energy Use* (Washington, D.C.: U.S. Government Printing Office, 1983).

32. Celso Furtado, "Dette exterieure: quel type de renegociation?," *Le Monde Diplomatique,* August 1983.

33. The Aluminum Association, Inc., *Aluminum Statistical Review for 1981* (Washington, D.C.: 1982).

34. See William U. Chandler, *The Myth of TVA: Conservation and Development in the Tennessee Valley, 1933–1983* (Cambridge, Mass.: Ballinger Publishing Co., 1984).

35. Aluminum Association, *Aluminum Statistical Review for 1981.*

36. Ibid.; Bureau of Mines, U.S. Department of Interior, *Minerals Yearbook, 1981, Volume I* (Washington, D.C.: U.S. Government Printing Office, 1982).

37. Aluminum Association, *Aluminum Statistical Review for 1981.*

38. Brown, *Building A Sustainable Society.*

39. Bureau of Mines, *Minerals Yearbook, 1981, Volume III.*

40. David Solomon, "Dam blocked in Australia's hottest environmental dispute," *Christian Science Monitor,* July 6, 1983.

41. Al Trumer, "Italy Set To Abandon Its Aluminum Industry," *Journal of Commerce,* July 21, 1982; "Italian Ministry Grants Aid to Aluminum Industry," *Journal of Commerce,* August 6, 1982.

42. Aluminum Association, *Aluminum Statistical Review for 1981;* Bureau of Mines, *Minerals Yearbook, 1981, Volume III.*

43. Bureau of Mines, *Minerals Yearbook, 1981, Volume III.*

44. Aluminum Association, *Aluminum Statistical Review for 1981;* Bureau of Mines, *Minerals Yearbook, 1981, Volume III.* The figure of 36¢ was the price of "old cast scrap" in April 1983. This price is down from 43¢ in June of 1979. Organisation of European Aluminum Smelters, *Aluminum Smelters: Europe, Japan, USA* (London: 1983).

45. Aluminum Association, *Aluminum Statistical Review for 1981.*

46. Organisation of European Aluminum Smelters, *Aluminum Smelters.*

47. Aluminum Association, *Aluminum Statistical Review for 1981.*

48. "Reverse Vending Machines," *Resource Recycling* (Portland, Ore.), November/December 1982; "Aluminum Recovery? Can Do!," *Sweden Now,* February 1982.

49. "Community Recycling Update," *Resource Recycling* (Portland, Ore.), November/December 1982.

50. William K. Shireman et al., *Can and Bottle Bills: The CalPIRG-ELS Study Group Report* (Stanford, Calif.: California Public Interest Research Group and the Stanford Envi-

ronmental Law Society, 1981); U.S. General Accounting Office, "States Experience with Beverage Container Deposit Laws Shows Positive Benefits," Washington, D.C., December 11, 1980.

51. "Is Recycling the Tin Can a Can of Worms?," *Phoenix Quarterly*, Spring 1977.

52. Suggested by Frank X. McCawley, physical scientist, Division of Nonferrous Metals, Bureau of Mines, U.S. Department of Interior, Washington, D.C., private communication, July 14, 1983.

53. This was the central purpose of the "World Aluminum Industry Study," according to Alfredo Dammert, a principal researcher on the project, World Bank, Washington, D.C., private communication, August 11, 1983.

54. Derived from Bureau of Mines, *Minerals Yearbook, 1981, Volume III*.

55. This figure represents automotive scrap as a percentage of all iron and steel products scrapped (that is, "becoming obsolescent") in the United States in the period of a year, according to an estimate for 1974 in U.S. Office of Technology Assessment, *Technical Options for Conservation of Metals: Case Studies of Selected Metals and Products* (Washington, D.C.: U.S. Government Printing Office, 1979).

56. "Near-Record 21 Million Tons of Ferrous Discards Added to Scrap Backlog in 1981," *Phoenix Quarterly*, Winter 1983; Denis Hayes, *Repairs, Reuse, Recycling—First Steps Toward a Sustainable Society* (Washington, D.C.: Worldwatch Institute, September 1978).

57. Leslie Wayne, "The Going Gets Tough at the Nucor Minimill," *New York Times*, August 7, 1983.

58. Donald Barnett, World Bank, private communication, July 14, 1983; Bureau of Mines, *Minerals Yearbook, 1981, Volume III*.

59. Bureau of Mines, *Minerals Yearbook, 1981, Volume I*.

60. U.S. Office of Technology Assessment, *Technology and Steel Industry Competitiveness* (Washington, D.C.: U.S. Government Printing Office, 1980).

61. "Zinc Die Cast—Autos Are Using Less, But Shredders Are Recovering More," *Phoenix Quarterly*, Winter 1983; Leslie R. Parkes, "Metals Face an Uncertain Future," *New Scientist*, July 14, 1983; Cutler, private communication, August 11, 1983.

62. C.L. Astedt, "The Recovery of Car Hulks in Sweden," in OECD, *Economic Instruments in Solid Waste Management;* J. Thompson, "The Recovery of Car Hulks in Norway," in OECD, *Economic Instruments in Solid Waste Management.*

63. Thompson, "Recovery of Car Hulks in Norway"; Astedt, "Recovery of Car Hulks in Sweden."

64. William T. Hogan, *World Steel in the 1980s: A Case of Survival* (Lexington, Mass.: Lexington Books, 1983).

Chapter 7. Reassessing the Economics of Nuclear Power

1. International Energy Agency, *World Energy Outlook* (Paris: Organisation for Economic Co-operation and Development, 1982).

2. International Atomic Energy Agency, *The Annual Report for 1982* (Vienna: 1983).

3. "Nuclear: World Status," *Financial Times Energy Economist*, January 1983.

4. Peter deLeon, *Development and Diffusion of the Nuclear Power Reactor: A Comparative Analysis* (Cambridge, Mass.: Ballinger Publishing Co., 1979); Arnold Kramish, *Atomic Energy in the Soviet Union* (Stanford, Calif.: Stanford University Press, 1959).

5. R. L. Perry et al., *Development and Commercialization of the Light Water Reactor, 1946–1976* (Santa Monica, Calif.: Rand Corporation, 1977).

6. Atomic Industrial Forum, "Historical Profile of U.S. Nuclear Power Development," Washington, D.C., March 1983.

7. Irvin C. Bupp and Jean-Claude Derian, *Light Water: How the Nuclear Dream Dissolved* (New York: Basic Books Inc., 1978).

8. James Everett Katz and Onkar S. Marwah, eds., *Nuclear Power in Developing Countries* (Lexington, Mass.: Lexington Books, 1982).

9. Atomic Industrial Forum, "International Survey—Annual," Washington, D.C., various years.

10. Quoted in Bupp and Derian, *Light Water*.

11. Atomic Industrial Forum, "Historical Profile."

12. Charles Komanoff, *Power Plant Cost Escalation: Nuclear and Coal Capital Costs, Regulation and Economics* (New York: Komanoff Energy Associates, 1981).

13. Ramesh N. Budwani, "Power Plant Scheduling, Construction and Costs: 10-Year Analysis," *Power Engineering*, August 1982; Charles Komanoff, private communication, New York, N.Y., September 19, 1983. These figures were confirmed by Richard Rosen using the data base of the Energy Systems Research Group, Boston, private communication, September 27, 1983.

14. Cost figures for individual plants were compiled from press reports and personal communications with utilities by Worldwatch Institute and are current as of late 1983. All cost figures are in current dollars unless otherwise indicated.

15. Richard A. Rosen, "Testimony Before the Indiana Public Service Commission," October 4, 1982, based on Energy Systems Research Group statistical data.

16. R. G. Easterling, *Statistical Analysis of Power Plant Capacity Factors Through 1979* (Washington, D.C.: U.S. Nuclear Regulatory Commission, 1981); Steve Thomas, *Worldwide Nuclear Plant Performance Revisited: An Analysis of 1978–1981* (Brighton, England: Science Policy Research Unit, University of Sussex, 1983).

17. These figures are Worldwatch Institute estimates based on the construction cost figures described earlier and on operation-and-maintenance and capacity-factor figures compiled by Energy Systems Research Group and Komanoff Energy Associates. Oil prices are assumed to rise at a 3.5 percent annual real rate beginning in 1986 and to hit $50 per barrel (1983 dollars) by the year 2000. Coal prices are assumed to rise at a 2 percent annual real rate. Generating cost figures are levelized costs over the lifetime of a power plant.

18. Figure based on a nuclear generating cost of 11¢ per kilowatt-hour that, with transmission and distribution costs and line losses, comes to a delivered price of 14.3¢ per kilowatt-hour. This compares with a U.S. average retail electricity price in 1983 of 6.1¢ per kilowatt-hour, according to U.S. Department of Energy (DOE), Energy Information Administration (EIA), *Monthly Energy Review*, Washington, D.C., September 1983.

19. S. David Freeman, "Nuclear Power Isn't Scary—These Reactors Are," *Washington Post*, November 28, 1982.

20. Central Electricity Generating Board, *The Case for the Sizewell B Nuclear Power Station* (London: 1982); "British PWR Can Cut Costs," *Nuclear Engineering International*, June 1982.

21. Gordon Mackerron, "Nuclear Power and the Economic Interests of Consumers," Electricity Consumers' Council, London, June 1982; Gordon Mackerron, "A Case Not Proven," *New Scientist*, January 13, 1983.

22. J.W. Jeffery, "The Real Cost of Nuclear Electricity in the U.K.," *Energy Policy*, June 1982; J.W. Jeffery, "An Economic Critique of the CEGB's Statement of Case for a PWR at Sizewell," University of London, unpublished, June 1983.

23. Gunter Marquis, "Experience with Nuclear Power Plant Investment Costs in the Federal Republic of Germany and Expected Future Electricity Production Costs," presented to the International Conference on Nuclear Power Experience, Vienna, September 13–17, 1982.

24. Jürgen Franke and Dieter Viefhues, *Das Ende Des Billigen Atomstroms* (Koln, West Germany: Institut Freiburg, 1983).

25. Leonard L. Bennett, Panos M. Karousakis, and Georges Moynet, "Review of Nuclear Power Costs," presented to the International Conference on Nuclear Power Experience, Vienna, September 13–17, 1982; Charles Komanoff, "Nuclear Power Costs: American Answers, French Questions," Komanoff Energy Associates, New York, N.Y., 1981; "Even with Increased Costs, EDF Finds Nuclear Far Cheaper than Coal," *Nucleonics Week*, January 27, 1983.

26. "Electricité de France Spent 9.76-Billion Francs in 1981," *Nucleonics Week*, February 25, 1982; "EDF Reschedules Debt," *European Energy Report*, January 21, 1983.

27. Japanese figures are unpublished estimates from Central Research Institute of Electric Power Industry, Tokyo, private communication, August 9, 1983, and an interview with the executive vice-president of Tokyo Electric Power Company, *Asiaweek*, August 12, 1983; Soviet figure is from "Comecon Presses Forward While the West Hesitates," *Financial Times Energy Economist*, August 1983; A. M. Yu and D. L. S. Bate, "Trends in the Capital Costs of CANDU Generating Stations," presented to the International Conference on Nuclear Power Experience, Vienna, September 13–17, 1982; Ontario Hydro, *Cost Comparison of CANDU Nuclear & Coal Fueled Generating Stations* (Toronto: 1982); Indian data are from Bennett, Karousakis, and Moynet, "Review of Nuclear Power Costs."

28. Atomic Industrial Forum, "Historical Profile."

29. Atomic Industrial Forum, Washington, D.C., private communication, November 14, 1983.

30. DOE, *Nuclear Plant Cancellations: Causes, Costs, and Consequences* (Washington, D.C.: 1983).

31. DOE, EIA, *Monthly Energy Review;* "33rd Annual Electrical Industry Forecast," *Electrical World*, September 1982.

32. "1983 Annual Statistical Report," *Electrical World*, March 1983; additional data are from unpublished documents of the Edison Electric Institute and the American Public Power Association; these numbers were compared with capital expenditure figures in U.S. Bureau of the Census, *Annual Survey of Manufacturers* (Washington, D.C.: 1983).

33. R.J. Nesse, "The Effect of Nuclear Ownership on Utility Bond Ratings and Yields," Battelle Pacific Northwest Laboratory, Richland, Wash., February 1982; Leonard Hyman, "Utility Industry: Congressional Hearings on Nuclear Energy," Merrill Lynch, Pierce, Fenner & Smith Inc., New York, October 26, 1981.

34. "Midland Deal Comes Unglued," *Energy Daily*, July 19, 1983.

35. Stuart Diamond, "Shoreham: What Went Wrong?," *Newsday*, December 6, 1981; Ron Winslow, "Lilco's Bid to Spread Nuclear Costs Riles Customers and State Officials," *Wall Street Journal*, September 1, 1983.

36. "Economic Factors Engulf Seabrook," *New York Times*, September 12, 1983.

37. Atomic Industrial Forum, "A.I.F.'s 1982 Midyear Outlook," press release, Washington, D.C., July 1982; DOE, *U.S. Commercial Nuclear Power: Historical Perspective, Current Status and Outlook* (Washington, D.C.: 1982).

38. William Drozdiak, "Greens' Power: West German Party Forces Nuclear Issue," *Washington Post*, February 19, 1983; John Tagliabue, "West Germans Clash At Site of A-Plant," *New York Times*, March 1, 1981.

39. William Walker and Mans Lonnroth, *Nuclear Power Struggles: Industrial Competition and Proliferation Control* (London: George Allen & Unwin, 1983).

40. "West Germany: Can a Nuclear 'Convoy' Run Over Its Opposition?," *Business Week*, August 9, 1982; information on concern within the West German utility industry is from Florentin Krause, Friends of the Earth, San Francisco, Calif., private communication, September 28, 1983.

41. "World List of Nuclear Power Plants," *Nuclear News*, biannual, various dates; International Atomic Energy Agency, *Annual Report*; Irvin C. Bupp, "The French Nuclear Harvest: Abundant Energy or Bitter Harvest?," *Technology Review*, November/December 1980; Mitterand quote from Judith Miller, "Paris Pushes Drive for Atomic Energy: Socialist Government Has Only Slightly Changed Program Undertaken by Giscard," *New York Times*, March 14, 1982.

42. "French Energy: Forecasts Fall," *Nature*, November 11, 1982; "Study Group's Call for French Nuclear Retrenchment Sends Shock Waves," *Nucleonics Week*, May 19, 1983; "Nuclear Power: Cooling Off," *The Economist*, July 30, 1983; "French Planners Accused of Cheating," *European Energy Report*, September 30, 1983; "EDF Seeking Maximum Flexibility in Operation of Its Nuclear Units," *Nucleonics Week*, February 17, 1983.

43. "EDF Reschedules Debt," *European Energy Report*, January 21, 1983; "Study Group's Call for French Nuclear Retrenchment Sends Shock Waves" *Nucleonics Week*; "France Eases Up on Pace of N-Power," *European Energy Report*, August 5, 1983; "Framatome is Bracing for Employment Problems Beginning in Mid-1984," *Nucleonics Week*, November 4, 1983.

44. Andrew Holmes, "Sizewell Inquiry Reveals U.K. Policy Vacuum," *Financial Times Energy Economist*, October 1983; Czech Conroy, "Why Britain Does Not Need a PWR," *New Scientist*, August 19, 1982.

45. "Nuclear: World Status," *Financial Times*.

46. "Comecon Nuclear Industry Set for Rapid Expansion," *European Energy Report*, July 8, 1983; Peter Holt, "Nuclear Power in Eastern Europe: Progress & Problems," *Energy in Countries with Planned Economies*, December 1981; Tom Sealy, "Comecon Presses Forward," *Financial Times Energy Economist*, August 1983.

47. Sealy, "Comecon Presses Forward."

48. "Problems Hit U.S.S.R. Nuclear Construction Industry," *European Energy Report*, August 5, 1983; Mark Wood, "Reactor Plant Mishap Hinted at by Soviets," *Washington Post*, July 21, 1983.

49. John W. Powell, "Nuclear Power in Japan," *Bulletin of the Atomic Scientists*, May 1983; "Nuclear Power: What Role in Asia?," *Asiaweek*, August 12, 1983.

50. "A Nuclear Power Plant in Japan Springs a Radioactive Leak," *World Business Weekly*, May 11, 1981; Henry Scott Stokes, "For Japan, Sudden Nuclear Misgivings," *New York Times*, May 17, 1981.

51. Powell, "Nuclear Power in Japan."

52. International Atomic Energy Agency, *Market Survey for Nuclear Power in Developing Countries: General Report* (Vienna: 1973).

53. "World List of Nuclear Power Plants," *Nuclear News*, August 1983; Jane House, "The Third World Goes Nuclear," *South*, December 1980.

54. Richard J. Barber Associates, *LDC Nuclear Power Prospects, 1975–1990: Commercial, Economic & Security Implications* (Washington, D.C.: U.S. Energy Research and Development Administration, 1975).

55. John J. Metzler, "Taiwan Extends Quest for Nuclear Power," *Journal of Commerce*, March 8, 1982; "KEPCO Shelving Construction of Nos. 11, 12 Nuclear Power Plants," *Korea Herald*, July 17, 1982.

56. S. Jacob Scherr, "Nuclear Power in the Philippines," in Katz and Marwah, *Nuclear Power in Developing Countries;* Christopher S. Wren, "China Is Building Atom Power Plant," *New York Times,* September 30, 1982.

57. R. R. Subramanian and C. Raja Mohan, "Nuclear Power in India," in Katz and Marwah, *Nuclear Power in Developing Countries;* Trevor Drieberg, "India's Nuclear Program Encountering Difficulties," *Journal of Commerce,* November 4, 1982.

58. Katz and Marwah, *Nuclear Power in Developing Countries;* House, "The Third World Goes Nuclear"; Eliot Marshall, "Iraqi Nuclear Program Halted by Bombing," *Science,* October 31, 1981; Muriel Allen, "Egypt Rethinking Plans for Reactors Due to Safety Fears," *Journal of Commerce,* May 5, 1981.

59. Jackson Diehl, "Ambitious Argentine Nuclear Development Program Hits Snags," *Washington Post,* August 31, 1982.

60. Victoria Johnson, "Nuclear Power in Brazil," in Katz and Marwah, *Nuclear Power in Developing Countries;* Richard House, "Brazil: Nuclear Road to the Future Takes a Turn for the Worse," *Financial Times Energy Economist,* May 1983; "Mexico Having Difficulty Completing Even One Nuclear Unit," *Nucleonics Week,* June 23, 1983.

61. Estimate based on nuclear plants under construction and operating in mid-1983, as listed in "World List," *Nuclear News.*

62. Atomic Industrial Forum, annual press releases on international outlook, Washington, D.C., various years; Nuclear Energy Agency, *Nuclear Energy and Its Fuel Cycle* (Paris: Organisation for Economic Co-operation and Development, 1982).

63. Ronnie D. Lipschutz, *Radioactive Waste: Politics, Technology and Risk* (Cambridge, Mass.: Ballinger Publishing Co., 1980); Sally Hindman, *Decommissioning Policies for Nuclear Power Plants: A Critical Examination* (Washington, D.C.: Critical Mass, forthcoming).

64. DOE, EIA, *Monthly Energy Review.*

65. Solar Energy Research Institute, *A New Prosperity: Building a Renewable Future* (Andover, Mass.: Brick House, 1981).

66. Douglas Cogan, *Generating Energy Alternatives At America's Electric Utilities* (Washington, D.C.: Investor Responsibility Research Center Inc., 1983).

67. Jordan quote is from Ibid.; electricity trends are from International Energy Agency, *World Energy Outlook,* and reports in various newsletters.

68. Renewable energy cost figures are Worldwatch Institute estimates based on various sources; see Daniel Deudney and Christopher Flavin, *Renewable Energy: The Power to Choose* (New York: W.W. Norton & Co., 1983).

Chapter 8. Developing Renewable Energy

1. International Energy Agency, *Energy Research, Development and Demonstration in the IEA Countries, 1981 Review of National Programmes* (Paris: Organisation for Economic Co-operation and Development, 1982).

2. For a detailed view of wind power developments in recent years, see Christopher Flavin, *Wind Power: A Turning Point* (Washington, D.C.: Worldwatch Institute, July 1981).

3. Carl Aspliden, U.S. Department of Energy (DOE), private communication, June 4, 1981.

4. Grant Miller, "Assessment of Large Scale Windmill Technology and Prospects for Commercial Application," working paper submitted to National Science Foundation, Washington, D.C., unpublished, September 8, 1980.

5. Elizabeth Baccelli and Karen Gordon, *Electric Utility Solar Energy Activities: 1981 Survey* (Palo Alto, Calif.: Electric Power Research Institute, 1982).

6. American Wind Energy Association, "AWEA Listing of Publicly Announced

Windfarm Projects," Arlington, Va., unpublished, August 1983.

7. Donald Marier, "Wind Farms Boom or Bust," *Alternative Sources of Energy*, May/June 1983; David Hoffman, "Windfarm Giant Planning Even Greater Expansion," *Renewable Energy News*, February 1983.

8. Vaughn Nelson, "State of the SWECS Industry in the United States," *Wind Power Digest*, forthcoming, 1984; David Hoffman, "Dutch and Danish Turbines Make Inroads in U.S.," *Renewable Energy News*, April 1983.

9. Interviews by Christopher Flavin with various California wind farm developers, private communications, September 1983.

10. Robert Lowe, "Expected Electricity Costs for the U.S. Mod-2 Windmill," *Energy Policy*, December 1980.

11. For the details of these calculations see Flavin, *Wind Power: A Turning Point*.

12. "Dreams Blow Away in the Breeze," *Washington Post*, August 13, 1983; Glen Price, Farallones Institute, Occidental, Calif., private communication, September 8, 1983.

13. "Dutch to Build 10MW Windfarm," *World Solar Markets*, March 1982; Bent Sorensen, "Turning to the Wind," *American Scientist*, September/October 1981; Judy Redfearn, "The Prospect for Ocean-Going Windmills," *Nature*, April 24, 1980.

14. K. Dharmarajan, "India—Energy Supply Policy Management," *Natural Resources Forum*, July 1983; DOE, *Estimates of U.S. Wood Energy Consumption from 1949 to 1981* (Washington, D.C.: U.S. Government Printing Office, 1982).

15. Thomas B. Johansson et al., "Sweden Beyond Oil: The Efficient Use of Energy," *Science*, January 28, 1983; "The Cold, Hard Facts," *Sweden Now*, No. 4, 1981; Steven Moore, "Sweden Readies Forests in Rapid Conversion to Bio-Energy," and "Pulp and Paper Lead Swedish Switch to Wood Fuel," *Renewable Energy News*, April 1982; "Energy

and Energy Policy in Sweden," The Swedish Institute, Stockholm, January 1980.

16. Vera Rich, "Finland Turns to Wood and Peat for Energy," *Nature*, April 5, 1979.

17. H. Swain, R. Overend, and T.A. Ledwell, "Canadian Renewable Energy Prospects," *Solar Energy*, Vol. 23, 1979, pp. 459–70; Chris Wood, "Canada's Fuelwood: Out of the Bush and Onto the Grate," *Wood 'n Energy*, January 1981; Brian Toller, "Ottawa's FIRE Program Expanded, Budget Near Tripled to $288 Million," and "ENFOR Research Moving Beyond Inventory Phase," *Canadian Renewable Energy News*, April 1981.

18. DOE, *Estimates of Wood Energy Consumption*.

19. Booz, Allen & Hamilton, Inc., "Assessment of Proposed Federal Tax Credits for Residential Wood Burning Equipment," Bethesda, Md., August 1979; Housing Industry Dynamics, Crofton, Md., private communication, August 8, 1983.

20. Based on 17.2 million Btus per dry ton of wood and 5.8 million Btus per barrel of fuel oil; assumes oil heating is 65 percent efficient and wood heating is 45 percent efficient. DOE, *Estimates of Wood Energy Consumption*.

21. Data on wood consumption are from DOE, *Estimates of Wood Energy Consumption*; data on oil use are from DOE, *State Energy Data Report 1960 through 1981* (Washington, D.C.: U.S. Government Printing Office, 1983); Mark R. Bailey and Paul R. Wheeling, *Wood and Energy in Vermont* (Washington, D.C.: U.S. Department of Agriculture, Economic Research Service, 1983).

22. Alberto Goetzl and Susan Tatum, "Wood Energy Use in the Lumber and Wood Products Industry," *Forest Products Journal*, March 1983, and private communication, September 1, 1983; Valerie Dow, "Wood Electrics—For U.S. Utilities, It's Wait and See," *Canadian Renewable Energy News*, April 1981; Swedish and Canadian data are from

Patricia Adams, "Wood Energy: Rekindling An Old Flame," Energy Probe, Toronto, Canada, March 1981.

23. R. Davidson, Employee Services Manager, Proctor and Gamble, Staten Island, N.Y., private communication, September 8, 1983; Phillip G. Sworden, Supervisor, Natural Resources Department, Dow Corning Corporation, Midland, Mich., private communication, August 19, 1983.

24. Bonneville Power Administration, *Bio-Energy Bulletin* (Portland, Ore.), December 1982; Tim Cronin, Director of Public Affairs, Burlington Electric Department, Burlington, Vt., private communication, August 19, 1983; Robert P. Kennel, Vice President for Development, Ultrasystems, Inc., Arlington, Va., private communication, September 7, 1983.

25. Ernesto Terrado, Biomass Specialist, World Bank, Washington, D.C., private communication, August 17, 1983; Frank H. Denton, Consultant, "The Twentieth Century Revolution? Energy from Tree Farms," Philippine National Electrification Administration, Manila, unpublished, 1982; Ministry of Energy, "Ten-Year Energy Program 1980–1989," Manila, Philippines, 1980.

26. Jourdan Houston, "Pelletized Fuels: The Emerging Industry," *Wood n' Energy*, January 1981; John I. Zerbe, "The Many Forms of Wood as Fuel," *American Forests*, October 1978.

27. U.S. Office of Technology Assessment, *Wood Use: U.S. Competitiveness and Technology* (Washington, D.C.: U.S. Government Printing Office, 1983); Colin High, "New England Returns to Wood," *Natural History*, February 1980; Sworden, private communication; U.S. Office of Technology Assessment, *Energy From Biological Processes, Vol. II, Technical and Environmental Analyses* (Washington, D.C.: U.S. Government Printing Office, 1980).

28. Eugene Carlson, "Smoke From Wood Becomes Big Polluter in Northern U.S.," *Wall Street Journal,* October 4, 1983; Charles E. Hewett and William T. Glidden, Jr., *Market Pressures to Use Wood as an Energy Source: Current Trends and a Financial Assessment* (Hanover, N.H.: Resource Policy Center, Dartmouth College, 1982); *Canadian Renewable Energy News,* December 1980; Office of Technology Assessment, *Wood Use;* Sworden, private communication.

29. Average thermal gradient is from Donald White, "Characteristics of Geothermal Resources," in Paul Kruger and Carel Otte, eds., *Geothermal Energy* (Stanford, Calif.: Stanford University Press, 1973); maximum temperature gradient is from Vasel Roberts, Electric Power Research Institute, Palo Alto, Calif., private communication, April 26, 1982; the world's geothermal zones are described in Erika Laszlo, "Geothermal Energy: An Old Ally," *Ambio*, Vol. X, No. 5, 1981.

30. Estimate of current geothermal energy use is derived from Ronald DiPippo, "Geothermal Power Plants: Worldwide Survey of July 1981," presented to the Geothermal Resources Council Fifth Annual Meeting, Houston, Tx., October 25–29, 1981, and Ronald DiPippo, Southeastern Massachusetts University, private communication, September 1983; "Report of the Technical Panel on Geothermal Energy," prepared for the United Nations Conference on New and Renewable Sources of Energy, Nairobi, Kenya, August 10–21, 1981; Jon Steinar Gudmundsson, Department of Petroleum Engineering, Stanford University, private communication, November 24, 1981; William W. Eaton, *Geothermal Energy* (Washington, D.C.: U.S. Energy Research and Development Administration, 1975).

31. Paul J. Leinau and John W. Lund, "Utilization and Economics of Geothermal Space Heating in Klamath Falls, Oregon," Geo-Heat Utilization Center, Oregon Institute of Technology, Klamath Falls, Ore., unpublished, undated; the life-cycle cost analysis is from John W. Lund, "Geothermal Energy Utilization for the Homeowner,"

Geo-Heat Utilization Center, Oregon Institute of Technology, Klamath Falls, Ore., unpublished, December 1978.

32. "Basic Statistics of Iceland," Ministry of Foreign Affairs, Iceland, April 1981; Jon Steinar Gudmundsson and Gudmondur Palmason, "World Survey of Low-Temperature Geothermal Energy Utilization," prepared for the United Nations Conference on New and Renewable Sources of Energy, Nairobi, Kenya, August 10–21, 1981; comparison with oil costs is from "Hitaveita Reykjavikur," a government pamphlet describing Iceland's district heat programs, Reykjavik, Iceland, undated.

33. Description of baths in Japan is from John W. Lund, "Direct Utilization—the International Scene," Geo-Heat Utilization Center, Oregon Institute of Technology, Klamath Falls, Ore., unpublished, undated; estimates of energy saved by Japanese baths and geothermal applications in Thailand and Mexico is from Gudmundsson and Palmason, "World Survey"; information on geothermal use in Guatemala is from Kathleen Courrier, Center for Renewable Resources, Washington, D.C., private communication, March 1983; greenhouse applications are described in Lund, "Direct Utilization," and in Gudmundsson and Palmason, "World Survey."

34. Industrial uses in Iceland and New Zealand are described in Paul J. Lineau, "Geothermal Resource Utilization," presented to American Association for the Advancement of Science Annual Meeting, Washington, D.C., January 3–8, 1980; the onion dehydration project is described in Joe Glorioso, "Geothermal Moves Off the Back Burner: Part II," *Energy Management*, October/November 1980.

35. For a thorough discussion of the different electricity-generating technologies and operating experience to date, see Ronald DiPippo, *Geothermal Energy as a Source of Electricity* (Washington, D.C.: U.S. Department of Energy, 1980); information about The Geysers is from the Pacific Gas & Electric Company, "The Geysers Power Plant Development," San Francisco, unpublished, March 26, 1982, and private communications, October 1983.

36. DiPippo, *Geothermal Energy as a Source of Electricity*.

37. Information on the prospects for double flash plants is from David Anderson, Geothermal Resources Council, Davis, Calif., private communication, June 18, 1982; the binary plant design is discussed in DiPippo, *Geothermal Energy as a Source of Electricity*, and in U.S. General Accounting Office, *Elimination of Federal Funds for the Heber Project Will Impede Full Development and Use of Hydrothermal Resources* (Washington, D.C.: 1982).

38. Hydrogen sulfide emissions and control information are described in DiPippo, *Geothermal Energy as a Source of Electricity*, and in J. Laszlo, "Application of the Stretford Process for H_2S Abatement at The Geysers," Pacific Gas & Electric Company, San Francisco, unpublished, 1976; contamination of surface water supplies is discussed in DiPippo, *Geothermal Energy as a Source of Electricity*.

39. For an example of a national resource assessment, see L. J. P. Muffler, *Assessment of Geothermal Resources of the United States—1978* (Washington, D.C.: U.S. Geological Survey, 1979).

40. The legal status of geothermal energy is discussed in "Report of the Technical Panel on Geothermal Energy," Nairobi Conference, and in Kenneth A. Wonstolen, "Geothermal Energy: Basic Legal Parameters," presented to the Geothermal Resources Council Fourth Annual Meeting, Salt Lake City, Utah, September 8–11, 1980.

41. A description of the French program is found in Ministere de l'Industrie du Commerce et de l'Artisanat, *La Geothermie en France* (Paris: 1978); the U.S. program is described in DOE, Division of Geothermal Energy, "Federal Cost-Sharing for Exploration of Hydrothermal Reservoirs for Direct Appli-

cations," Washington, D.C., unpublished, 1980; information on Iceland's program is from Gudmundsson, private communication, April 25, 1982.

42. The rate of growth of geothermal generating capacity since the mid-seventies is derived from Vasel Roberts, "Geothermal Energy," in *Advances in Energy Systems and Technology*, Vol. 1, 1978, from DiPippo, "Geothermal Power Plants," and from DiPippo, private communication; projections of future use are based on "Report of the Technical Panel on Geothermal Energy," Nairobi Conference, and on Roberts, "Geothermal Energy."

43. France's resource potential and utilization goals are from "France and geothermal power—a source with enormous potential," *Christian Science Monitor*, October 1, 1980; potentials in Canada, China, and the Soviet Union are from Gudmundsson, private communication, November 24, 1981; number of hot spots in China is from "China's Growing Geothermal Use," *Energy in Countries with Planned Economies*, November 2, 1979.

44. John W. Sharpe, "Energy Self-Sufficiency for Hawaii," *Science*, June 11, 1982.

45. National plans are from DiPippo, "Geothermal Power Plants," and DiPippo, private communication; Mexico's plans are described in "Report of the Technical Panel on Geothermal Energy," Nairobi Conference; El Salvador figure is from DiPippo, *Geothermal Energy as a Source of Electricity*.

46. Worldwatch Institute estimate based on shipments of 18,000 kilowatts of cells at a system cost of approximately $15,000 per kilowatt. For a more detailed discussion of recent developments in photovoltaics, see Christopher Flavin, *Electricity from Sunlight: The Future of Photovoltaics* (Washington, D.C.: Worldwatch Institute, December 1982).

47. Paul Maycock, Photovoltaic Energy Systems Inc., Alexandria, Va., private communication, November 9, 1983.

48. Robert R. Ferber, U.S. Jet Propulsion Laboratory, Pasadena, Calif., private communication, November 11, 1982, and Robert Johnson, Strategies Unlimited, Mountain View, Calif., private communication, November 12, 1982.

49. Historical figures are based on Strategies Unlimited, *1980–81 Market Review* (Mountain View, Calif.: 1981); the 1983 figure is from Maycock, private communication.

50. Strategies Unlimited, *1980–81 Market Review*; the 1983 estimate is from Maycock, private communication.

51. Efforts to reduce the cost of photovoltaics are discussed in Flavin, *Electricity from Sunlight*.

52. These figures are Flavin's estimates based on private communications with various industry analysts.

53. Steven J. Strong, "Pioneering PV Homes: A Trickle Down or Trickle Up Market?," *Photovoltaics: The Solar Electric Magazine*, June/July 1982; "Residential Retrofits Offer Enormous Existing Market, New Study Demonstrates," *Photovoltaic Insider's Report* (Dallas, Tex.), May 1982.

54. "Major Solar Projects Round the World," *World Solar Markets*, December 1981; "Fresnel Lens PV Systems Starting Up at Saudi Villages, Phoenix Airport," *Solar Energy Intelligence Report*, April 5, 1982.

55. Descriptions of various projects are from their developers, private communications, September 1983.

56. "Japan Earmarks Cash for PV Ventures," *World Solar Markets*, February 1983; "Japanese PV Plant Comes on Line," *World Solar Markets*, January 1983.

57. "Major Solar Projects," *World Solar Markets*; updates from various trade press reports, 1983.

58. Calestous Juma, "Photovoltaics and the Third World: Techno-Economic Expec-

tations and Policy Responses," Science Policy Research Unit, University of Sussex, Brighton, England, unpublished, July 1983.

59. Charles Thurston, "Heliodinamica Puts Brazil on Road to Photovoltaic Technology," *Renewable Energy News*, March 1983; "Pakistan Gets First of 14 PV Generators," *World Solar Markets*, October 1981.

60. Officials of Spire Corporation, Bedford, Mass., and Chronar Corporation, Princeton, N.J., private communications, 1983.

61. Description of the French effort is from Emile Gouriou, Bureau Yves Houssin, Paris, private communication, September 3, 1981; information on the U.S. effort is from Louis Rosenblum, Consultant, Ohio, private communication, November 4, 1983.

62. Bill D'Alessandro, "Villagers Light the Way: Solar Cell Power in Gunsight, Arizona," *Solar Age*, May 1979; "Ambitious 30 KW/P PV System to be Completed in Tunisian Village," *Photovoltaic Insider's Report* (Dallas, Tex.), September 1982.

63. These figures are Worldwatch Institute estimates; for further details see Flavin, *Electricity from Sunlight*.

64. Daniel Deudney and Christopher Flavin, *Renewable Energy: The Power to Choose* (New York: W. W. Norton & Co., 1983).

Chapter 9. Reconsidering the Automobile's Future

1. Robert U. Ayres, for Oak Ridge National Laboratory, *Worldwide Transportation/Energy Demand Forecast: 1975–2000* (Springfield, Va: National Technical Information Service, 1978).

2. Motor Vehicle Manufacturers Association (MVMA), *Motor Vehicle Facts and Figures '83* (Detroit, Mich.: 1983).

3. Worldwatch Institute estimates of automobile production are based on data from MVMA, *World Motor Vehicle Data Book, 1982 Edition* (Detroit, Mich.: 1982).

4. MVMA, *World Motor Vehicle Data Book.*

5. Ibid.

6. Ibid.; 1983 estimate by Worldwatch Institute.

7. U.S. Department of Transportation (DOT), *The U.S. Automobile Industry, 1981* (Washington, D.C.: U.S. Government Printing Office, 1982).

8. MVMA, *World Motor Vehicle Data Book.*

9. "South Korea: A radical redesign of the auto industry," *Business Week*, October 13, 1980.

10. See, for example, Richard R. Leger, "Oil-Price Surge Clobbers Less-Developed Nations Such as Kenya and Cuts Their Living Standards," *Wall Street Journal*, M'y 30, 1979, and DOT, *The U.S. Automobile Industry, 1980* (Washington, D.C.: 1981).

11. U.S. Department of Commerce, *The U.S. Automobile Industry, 1982* (Washington, D.C.: 1983).

12. DOT, *The U.S. Automobile Industry, 1980.*

13. DOT, *The U.S. Automobile Industry, 1980* and *The U.S. Automobile Industry, 1981.*

14. DOT, *The U.S. Automobile Industry, 1980;* Julius J. Harwood, "Automakers Lighten the Load," *Technology Review*, July 1981; U.S. Department of Commerce, *The U.S. Automobile Industry, 1982.*

15. Mark Potts and Warren Brown, "Auto Reduction Hits Suppliers," *Washington Post*, January 9, 1983.

16. DOT, *The U.S. Automobile Industry, 1981.*

17. Federal Highway Administration, *Highway Statistics* (Washington, D.C.: annual).

18. Federal Highway Administration, *Highway Statistics;* MVMA, *Motor Vehicle Facts and Figures '83.*

19. The vehicle weight used here—"inertial weight"—includes the weight of a driver and fuel for road testing purposes. Philip Patterson, Conservation Program, U.S. Department of Energy, private communication, October 12, 1983.

20. MVMA, *Motor Vehicle Facts and Figures;* Tony Grey, "U.S. two-seater cars may weigh as little as 1,200 pounds and get 80 miles per gallon," *Christian Science Monitor,* October 15, 1980.

21. DOT, *The U.S. Automobile Industry, 1980.*

22. John M. Geddes, "German Car Makers Set Fuel Cut," *New York Times,* May 1, 1979; Roger Gale, "Japan Gets New Conservation Law," *The Energy Daily,* September 27, 1979; Richard J. Meislin, "Mexico Set to Revamp Troubled Auto Industry," *New York Times,* September 15, 1983.

23. Sherwood L. Fawcett, "The 100 M.P.G. Car," *New York Times,* November 22, 1981; Representative Bob Shamansky, "To Join the Car Race," *New York Times,* February 2, 1982.

24. "France Launches Thrifty Car," *Financial Times European Energy Report,* June 26, 1981; Rushworth M. Kidder, "Will new, 83 m.p.g. car save Britain's king of the road?," *Christian Science Monitor,* September 16, 1980.

25. "The tiny cars that women are wild about," *Business Week,* February 28, 1983.

26. Emil Parente, Fluor Corporation, Anaheim, Calif., private communication, August 17, 1983.

27. Leonard Zehr, "Canadian Synthetic Fuel Project Provides Instructive, and Sobering Lesson for U.S.," *Wall Street Journal,* December 11, 1979.

28. "Slow growth seen for synthetic fuels," *Oil and Gas Journal,* May 2, 1983; "Synthetic fuels bubble set to burst," *New Scientist,* December 16, 1982.

29. James Bruce, "Brazil's Alcohol Export Prospects Shrink But Domestic Mart Continues Growth," *Journal of Commerce,* April 5, 1983.

30. 1983 estimate by Worldwatch Institute, based on data from Janet Livezey, Economic Research Service, U.S. Department of Agriculture, private communication, August 15, 1983.

31. Organisation for Economic Co-operation and Development, *Interfutures* (Paris: 1979); David Bayliss, Transportation and Development Department, Greater London Council, England, private communication, September 7, 1983.

32. For a discussion of the assumptions on which automobile demand projections are based, see David Bayliss, "Global Car Ownership in 1990 and 2000 A.D.," presented at the International Policy Forum, Hakone, Japan, May 16–20, 1982 (reprinted by the Future of the Automobile Program, Massachusetts Institute of Technology, Cambridge, Mass.).

33. Peng Feifei, Second Secretary, Embassy of the People's Republic of China, private communication, November 9, 1983.

34. Eliot Janeway, "The Prince of Pessimism says the system could topple," *Washington Post,* August 14, 1983.

35. William A. Orme, Jr., "Mexico Plans to Increase Domestic Fuel Prices," *Journal of Commerce,* October 27, 1983; information on Brazil is from J. C. Barros, Petrobras, New York, N.Y., private communication, October 3, 1983.

36. "Yugoslavia Begins Gasoline Rationing to Counter Shortage," *Wall Street Journal,* October 11, 1982; "Poles Facing Further Cuts In Gasoline," *Journal of Commerce,* September 30, 1983.

37. Tom Kennedy, "With so little native fuel, Danes stress conservation," *Christian Science Monitor,* October 6, 1979; MVMA, *World Motor Vehicle Data Book.*

38. MVMA, *World Motor Vehicle Data Book.*

39. Ibid.

40. Ibid.

41. Dennis R. Gordon, "The Andean Auto Program and Peruvian Development: A Preliminary Assessment," *Journal of Developing Areas,* January 1982.

42. Leger, "Oil-Price Surge Clobbers Less-Developed Nations"; "IMF Study Advocates Higher Gasoline Taxes," *New York Times,* February 24, 1980.

Chapter 10. Securing Food Supplies

1. Food production data in this chapter are drawn primarily from U.S. Department of Agriculture (USDA), Economic Research Service (ERS), *World Indices of Agricultural and Food Production, 1950–82* (unpublished printout) (Washington, D.C., 1983), and from USDA, Foreign Agricultural Service (FAS), *Foreign Agriculture Circulars,* various commodities, Washington, D.C., published monthly.

2. See, for example, Jay Ross, "Africa: The Politics of Hunger" (series), *Washington Post,* June 25–30, 1983.

3. Davidson R. Gwatkin, *Signs of Change in Developing-Country Mortality Trends: The End of an Era?,* Development Paper No. 30 (Washington, D.C.: Overseas Development Council, February 1981).

4. USDA, ERS, *World Indices.*

5. United Nations Food and Agriculture Organization (FAO), *Production Yearbook* (Rome: annual, various years).

6. Kenneth B. Young and Jerry M. Coomer, *Effects of Natural Gas Price Increases on Texas High Plains Irrigation, 1976–2025,* Agricultural Report. No. 448 (Washington, D.C.: USDA, Economics, Statistics, and Cooperatives Service, 1980).

7. Marshall I. Goldman, *The Spoils of Progress* (Cambridge, Mass: M.I.T. Press, 1972); Dr. John Gribben, "Climatic Impact of Soviet River Diversions," *New Scientist,* December 6, 1979; Grigorii Voropaev and Aleksei Kosarev, "The Fall and Rise of the Caspian Sea," *New Scientist,* April 8, 1982.

8. Arizona Water Commission, *Inventory of Resource and Uses* (Phoenix, Ariz.: 1975).

9. Republic of South Africa, *Report of the Science Committee of the President's Council on Demographic Trends in South Africa* (Capetown: The Government Printer, 1983).

10. FAO, *FAO 1977 Annual Fertilizer Review* (Rome: 1978); Paul Andrilenas, USDA, ERS, private communication, December 9, 1982.

11. USDA, *Agricultural Statistics 1982* (Washington, D.C.: U.S. Government Printing Office, 1982).

12. USDA, ERS, "Fertilizer Outlook and Situation," Washington, D.C., December 1982.

13. USDA, *Soil and Water Resources Conservation Act (RCA), Summary of Appraisal, Parts I and II, and Program Report Review Draft 1980* (Washington, D.C.: 1980).

14. *Economic Report of the President* (Washington, D.C.: U.S. Government Printing Office, 1983).

15. Ibid.

16. Lester R. Brown, *Man, Land and Food: Looking Ahead at World Food Needs,* Foreign Agriculture Economic Report No. 11 (Washington, D.C.: USDA, ERS, 1963).

17. USDA, FAS, "Reference Tables on Wheat, Corn and Total Coarse Grains Supply Distribution for Individual Countries," *Foreign Agriculture Circular* FG-19-83, Washington, D.C., July 1983.

18. Figures on cropland idled in the United States are from Randy Weber, USDA, Agricultural Stabilization and Conservation Service, private communication, August 23, 1983.

19. For a discussion of manipulation of grain exports for political purposes, see Dan Morgan, *Merchants of Grain* (New York: Penguin Books, 1980).

20. Weber, private communication. The grain equivalent of idled cropland is calculated assuming a marginal grain yield of 3.1 metric tons per hectare.

21. For a discussion of the demographic consequences of famine in China, see H. Yuan Tien, "China: Demographic Billionaire," *Population Bulletin* (Washington, D.C.: Population Reference Bureau, 1983); U.S. food aid shipments to India are unpublished data on P.L. 480 from Dewain Rahe, USDA, FAS, private communication, August 31, 1983.

22. Michael deCourcy Hinds, "U.S. Giving Peru and Bolivia Millions in Food Aid," *New York Times,* June 2, 1983; FAO and World Food Programme Special Task Force, "Exceptional International Assistance Required in Food Supplies, Agriculture and Animal Husbandry for African Countries in 1983/84," Rome, September 30, 1983.

23. Amartya Sen, "How is India Doing?," *New York Review of Books,* December 16, 1982.

24. Dr. Colin McCord, "The Companiganj Project," presented at the annual meeting of the American Public Health Association, Miami Beach, Florida, October 17–21, 1976.

25. USDA, ERS, *Latin America World Agriculture Regional Supplement Review of 1982 and Outlook for 1983* (Washington, D.C.: 1983).

26. U.S. food aid shipments under P.L. 480 are from Rahe, private communication; International Monetary Fund, Washington, D.C., press release, May 21, 1981.

27. Mac Margolis, "Brazil 'dust bowl' 5 times size of Italy," *Christian Science Monitor,* August 26, 1983.

28. USDA, ERS, *World Indices.*

Chapter 11. Reshaping Economic Policies

1. Data Resources Incorporated projection cited by Robert J. Samuelson, "Conviviality Mocked Global Debt Realities," *Washington Post,* October 4, 1983.

2. For a description of Norway's system of natural resource accounting, see Per Arild Garnasjordet and Petter Longva, *Outline of a System of Resource Accounts: The Norwegian Experience* (Paris: Organisation for Economic Cooperation and Development, 1980), and Petter Longva, *A System of Natural Resource Accounts* (Oslo: Central Bureau of Statistics, 1981); for a comparison of several countries' experiences with resource accounting, see Tony Friend, "Review of International Experience in Natural Resource Accounting," presented to the United Nations Environment Programme (UNEP), Ad Hoc Expert Consultative Meeting on Environmental Accounting and Its Use in Development Planning, Geneva, February 23–25, 1983 (referred to in following notes as UNEP Ad Hoc Expert Meeting).

3. Edward Weiller, "The Use of Environmental Accounting for Development Planning," presented to UNEP Ad Hoc Expert Meeting.

4. Japan's emphasis on pollution and other environmental consequences of industrialization is evident in Government of Japan, Environment Agency, *Quality of the Environment in Japan 1982* (Tokyo: 1983).

5. Results of the 1977 inventory are published in U.S. Department of Agriculture (USDA), Soil Conservation Service, and Iowa State University Statistical Laboratory, *Basic Statistics 1977 National Resources Inventory,* Statistical Bulletin No. 686 (Washington, D.C.: 1982). Analysis of the 1982 National Resources Inventory, conducted by the Soil Conservation Service and the Iowa State University Statistical Laboratory, should be available in 1984.

6. Kenneth Boulding, quoted in National Academy of Sciences, *Energy Choices in a Democratic Society* (Washington, D.C.: 1980).

7. "Critical Moment in Bangladesh," *People* (London), Vol. 7, No. 4, 1980.

8. The PQLI is discussed in Overseas Development Council, *The United States and World Development: 1977 Agenda* (New York: Praeger Publishers, 1977).

9. The development of small hydropower in China is discussed in Robert P. Taylor, *Rural Energy Development in China* (Washington, D.C.: Resources for the Future, 1981).

10. For an overview of the prospects for improving irrigation efficiency, see Mark Svendsen, Douglas Merry, and Worth Fitzgerald, "Meeting the Challenge for Better Irrigation Management," *Horizons* (Journal of the U.S. Agency for International Development), March 1983.

11. "Each additional million liters of alcohol distilled creates 45 new jobs." James Bruce, "Brazil's Alcohol Project Flourishing," *Journal of Commerce*, June 1, 1983.

12. For an introduction to anaerobic digestion technologies, see Andrew Barnett, Leo Pyle, and S. K. Subramanian, *Biogas Technology in the Third World: A Multidisciplinary Review* (Ottawa: International Development Research Center, 1978).

13. For efforts to develop appropriate and efficient stove designs, see Bina Agarwal, *The Wood Fuel Problem and the Diffusion of Rural Innovations* (preliminary draft) (Brighton, England: Science Policy Research Unit, University of Sussex, October 1980).

14. See Sigurd Grava, "Locally Generated Transport Modes of the Developing World," in National Academy of Sciences, Transportation Research Board, *Urban Transportation Economics* (Washington, D.C.: 1978).

15. Y. Morooka, R. W. Herdt, and L. D. Haws, *An Analysis of the Labor-Intensive Continuous Rice Production System at IRRI*, International Rice Research Institute Research Paper Series No. 29 (Manila: May 1979).

16. John P. McInerney et al., "The Consequences of Farm Tractors in Pakistan," World Bank, Washington, D.C., 1975.

17. Lewis M. Simons, "Social, Economic Inequities Fuel Philippine Insurgency," *Washington Post*, September 17, 1977.

18. Michael Lipton, "Urban Bias: Or Why Rural People Stay Poor," *People* (London), Vol. 3, No. 2, 1976.

19. David Welsh, Professor of South African Studies, University of Capetown, quoted in Mike Nicol, "Overpopulation Threatens South African Lifestyle," *World Environment Report*, April 30, 1983; Republic of South Africa, *Report of the Science Committee of the President's Council on Demographic Trends in South Africa* (Capetown: The Government Printer, 1983).

20. Charles William Maynes, "If the Poor Countries Go Under, We'll Sink With Them," *Washington Post*, September 18, 1983.

21. Ruth Leger Sivard, *World Military and Social Expenditures 1983* (Washington, D.C.: World Priorities, 1983).

22. Inga Thorsson, "Guns and butter: Can the world have both?," *International Labour Review*, July/August 1983.

23. Military shares of GNP are from Sivard, *World Military and Social Expenditures*. The effects of military spending on the Soviet economy are reviewed in Gregory G. Hildebrandt, "The Dynamic Burden of Soviet Defense Spending," in Joint Economic Committee, U.S. Congress, *Soviet Economy in the 1980's: Problems and Prospects* (Washington, D.C.: U.S. Government Printing Office, 1983).

24. Marshall Goldman, "Let's Exploit Moscow's Weakness," *New York Times*, April 4, 1982.

25. For a review of U.S.-Soviet food trade, see Lester R. Brown, *U.S. and Soviet Agricul-*

ture: The Shifting Balance of Power (Washington, D.C.: Worldwatch Institute, October 1982).

26. Robert Lekachman, "Remedies Available, Good Sense Lacking," *Challenge*, March/April 1983.

27. Thorsson, "Guns and butter."

28. Growth in military expenditures is calculated from data in Stockholm International Peace Research Institute, *World Armaments and Disarmament, SIPRI Yearbook 1983* (New York: Taylor & Francis, Inc., 1983); economic growth rate is derived from Herbert R. Block, *The Planetary Product in 1980: A Creative Pause?* (Washington, D.C.: U.S. Department of State, 1981), and Worldwatch Institute estimates.

29. Sivard, *World Military and Social Expenditures.*

30. Ibid.

31. For Jean Monnet's role in designing the European Community, see Mary and Serge Bromberger, *Jean Monnet and the United States of Europe* (New York: Coward-McCann, Inc., 1969).

32. Edward Schumacher, "Argentine Leader's First Crisis Will Be Cash," *New York Times,* November 6, 1983.

33. Gunter Grass, "Is a New Barbarism Overtaking Our World?," *Washington Star,* July 13, 1975.

34. Soedjatmoko, "Political Systems and Development in the Third World: New Directions for Social Science Research in Asia," *Alternatives,* Spring 1983.

35. Needed growth in population expenditures is from Dana Lewison, "Sources of Population and Family Planning Assistance," *Population Reports* (Baltimore, Md.), January/February 1983; the comparison with global military expenditures is based on data from Stockholm International Peace Research Institute, *SIPRI Yearbook 1983.*

Index